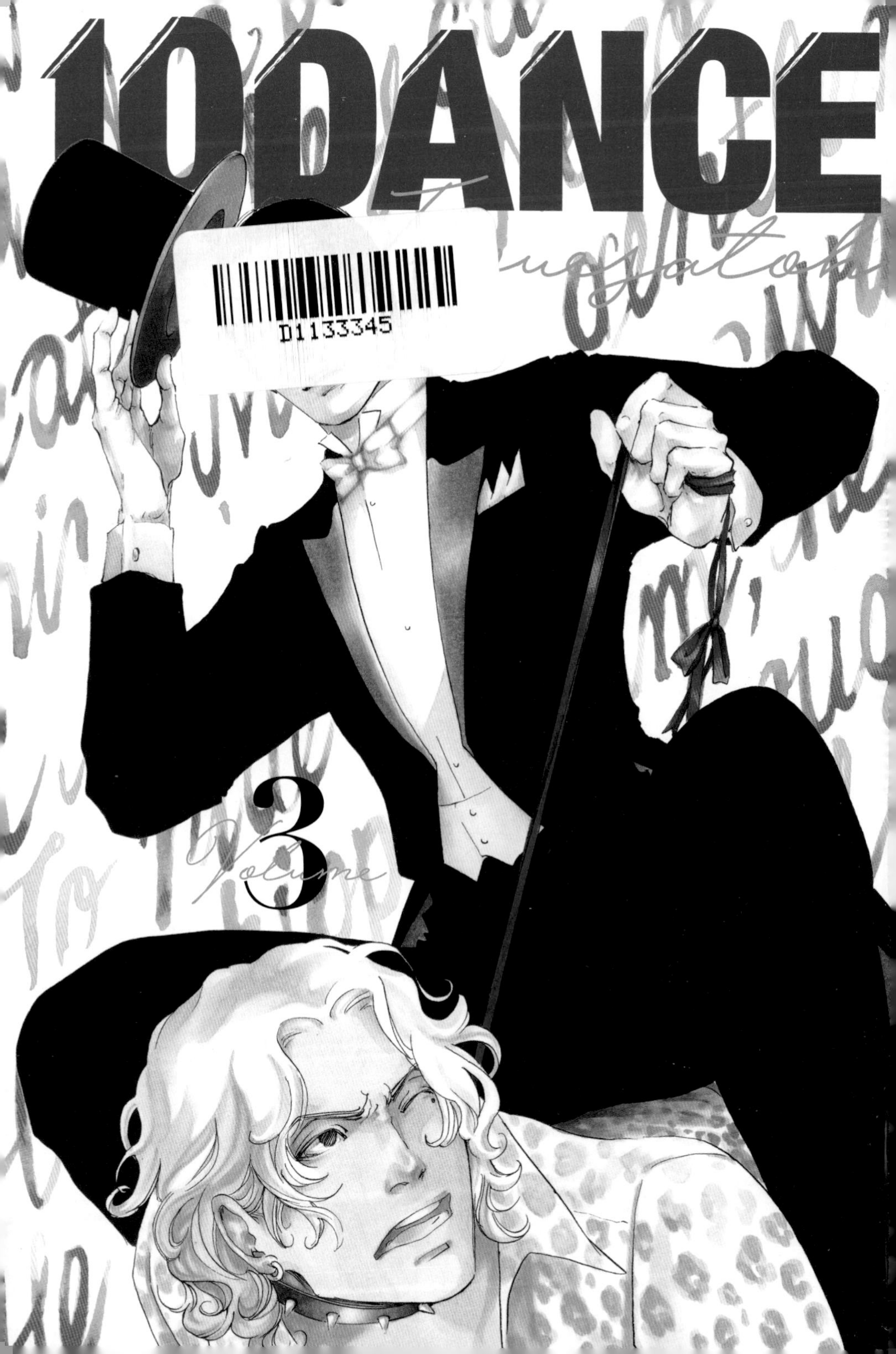
10DANCE
3
Volume

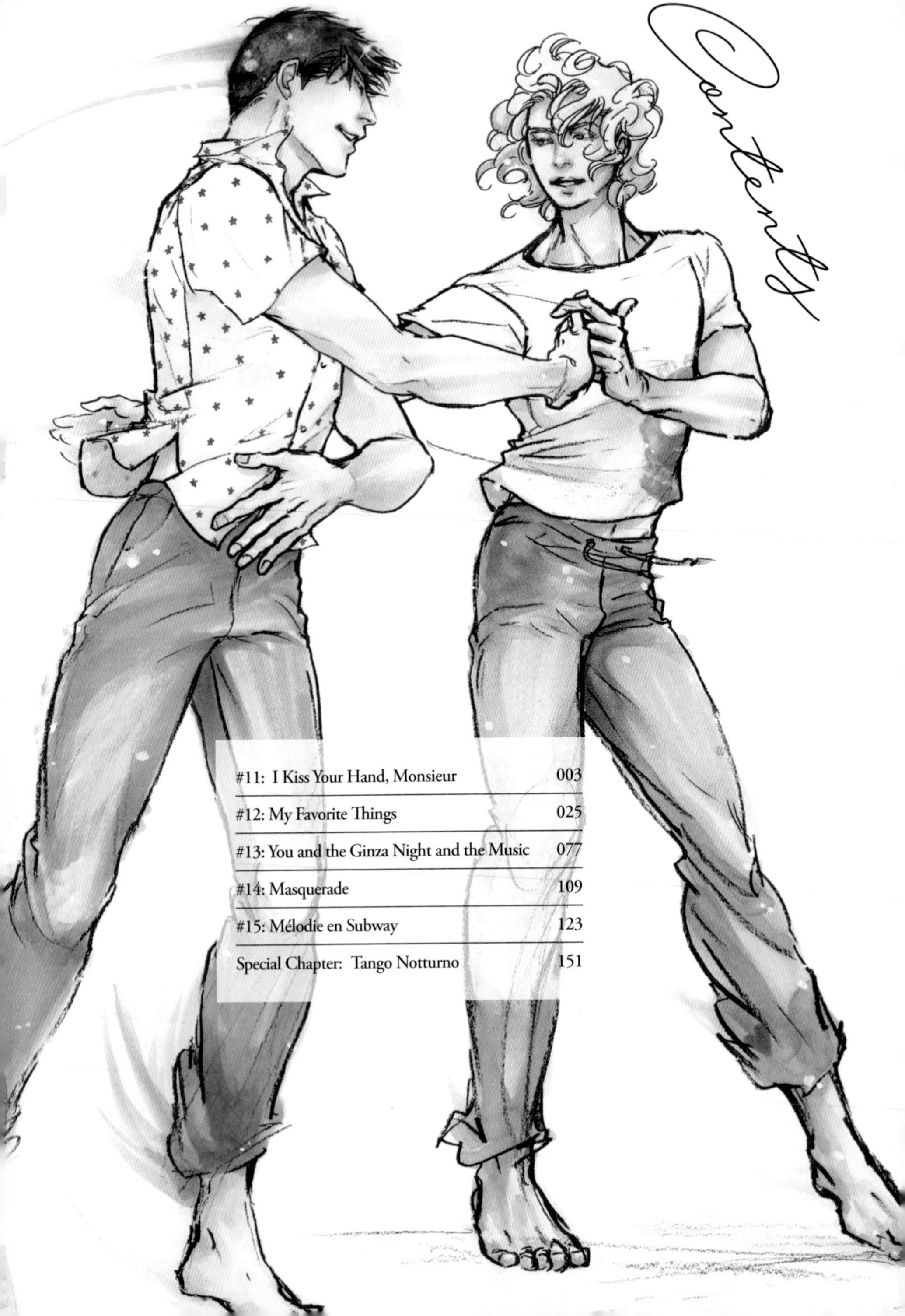

Contents

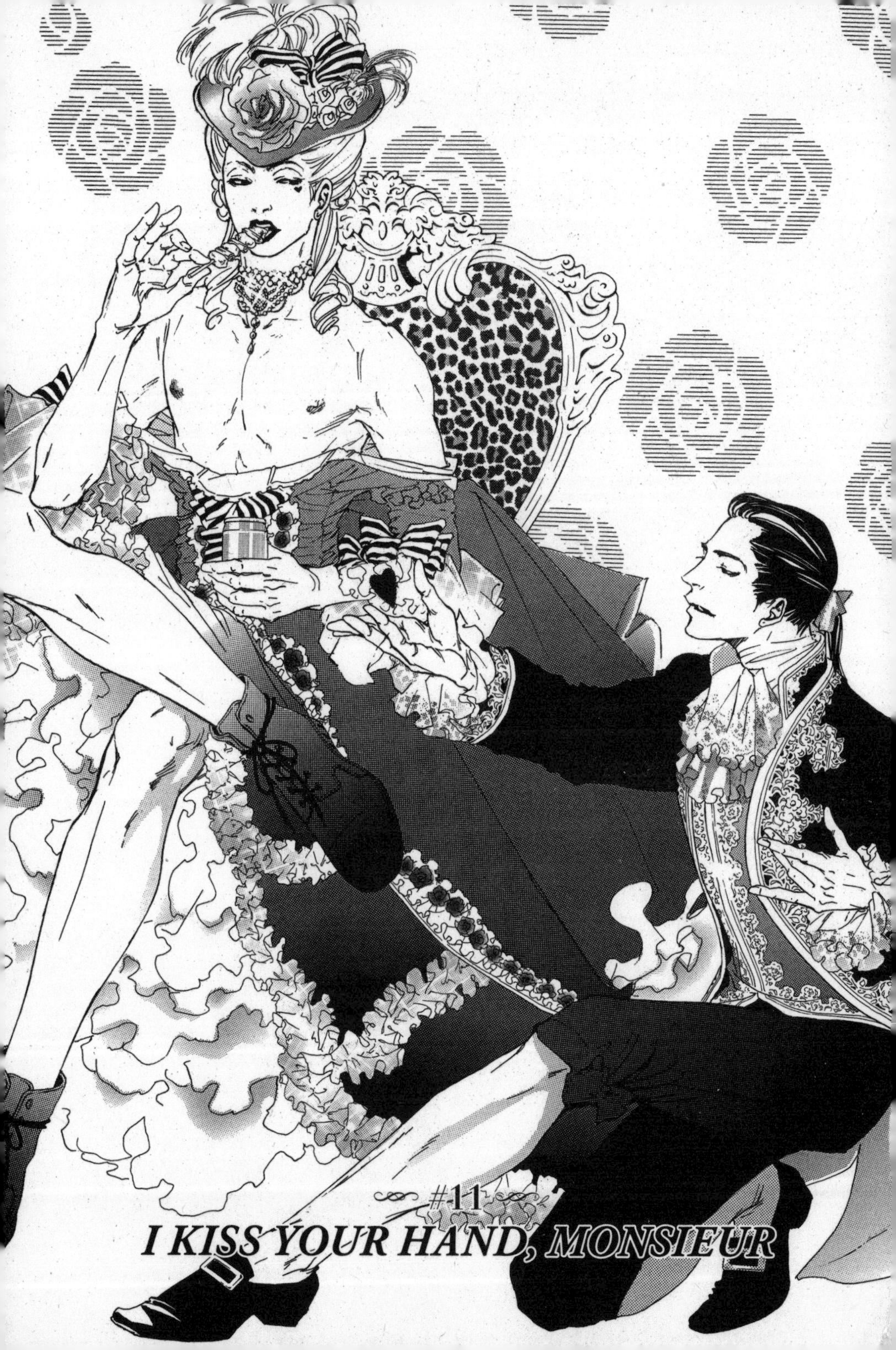
#11
I KISS YOUR HAND, MONSIEUR

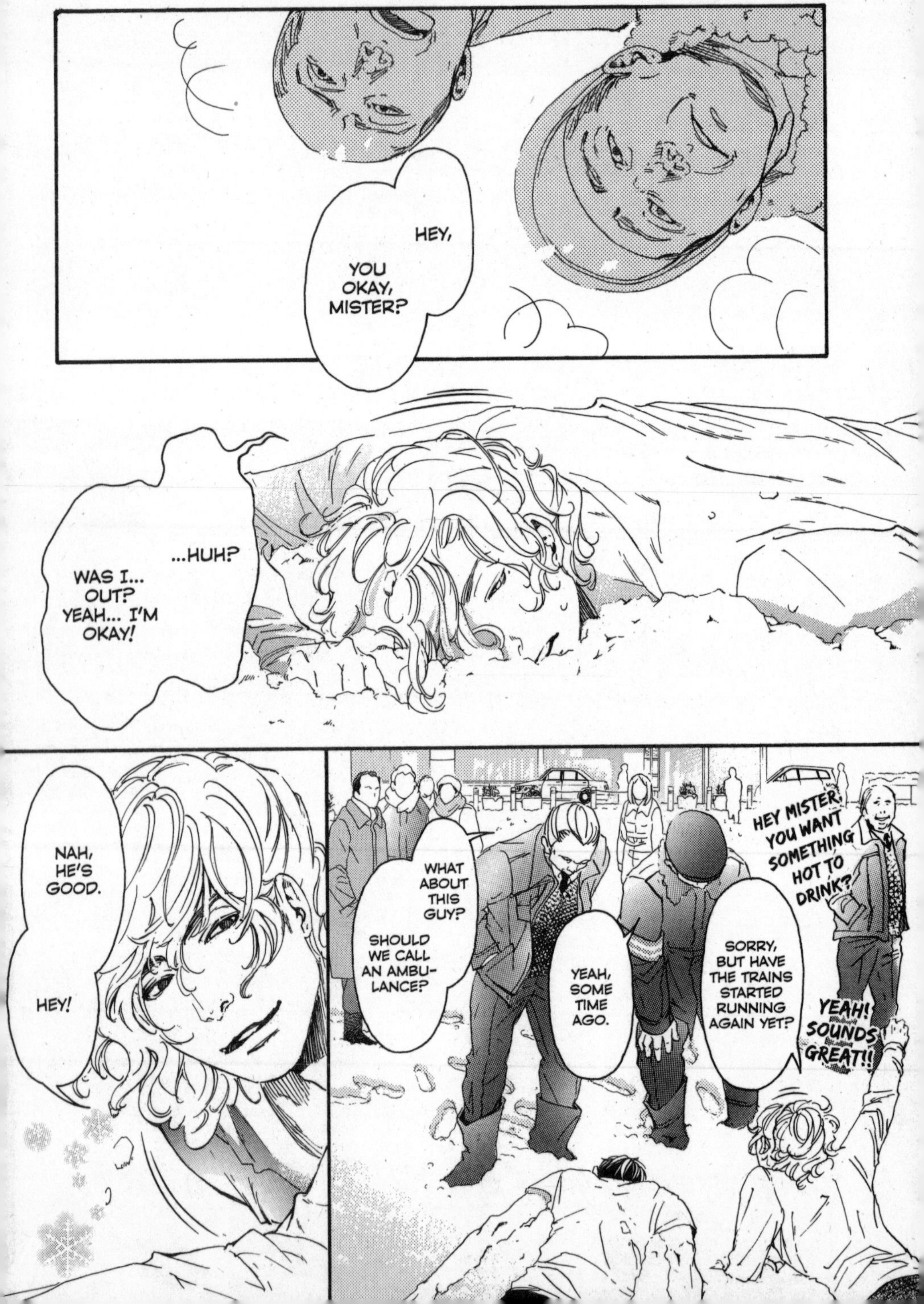
HEY, YOU OKAY, MISTER?
...HUH?
WAS I... OUT? YEAH... I'M OKAY!
HEY MISTER YOU WANT SOMETHING HOT TO DRINK?
YEAH! SOUNDS GREAT!!
SORRY, BUT HAVE THE TRAINS STARTED RUNNING AGAIN YET?
YEAH, SOME TIME AGO.
WHAT ABOUT THIS GUY?
SHOULD WE CALL AN AMBULANCE?
NAH, HE'S GOOD.
HEY!

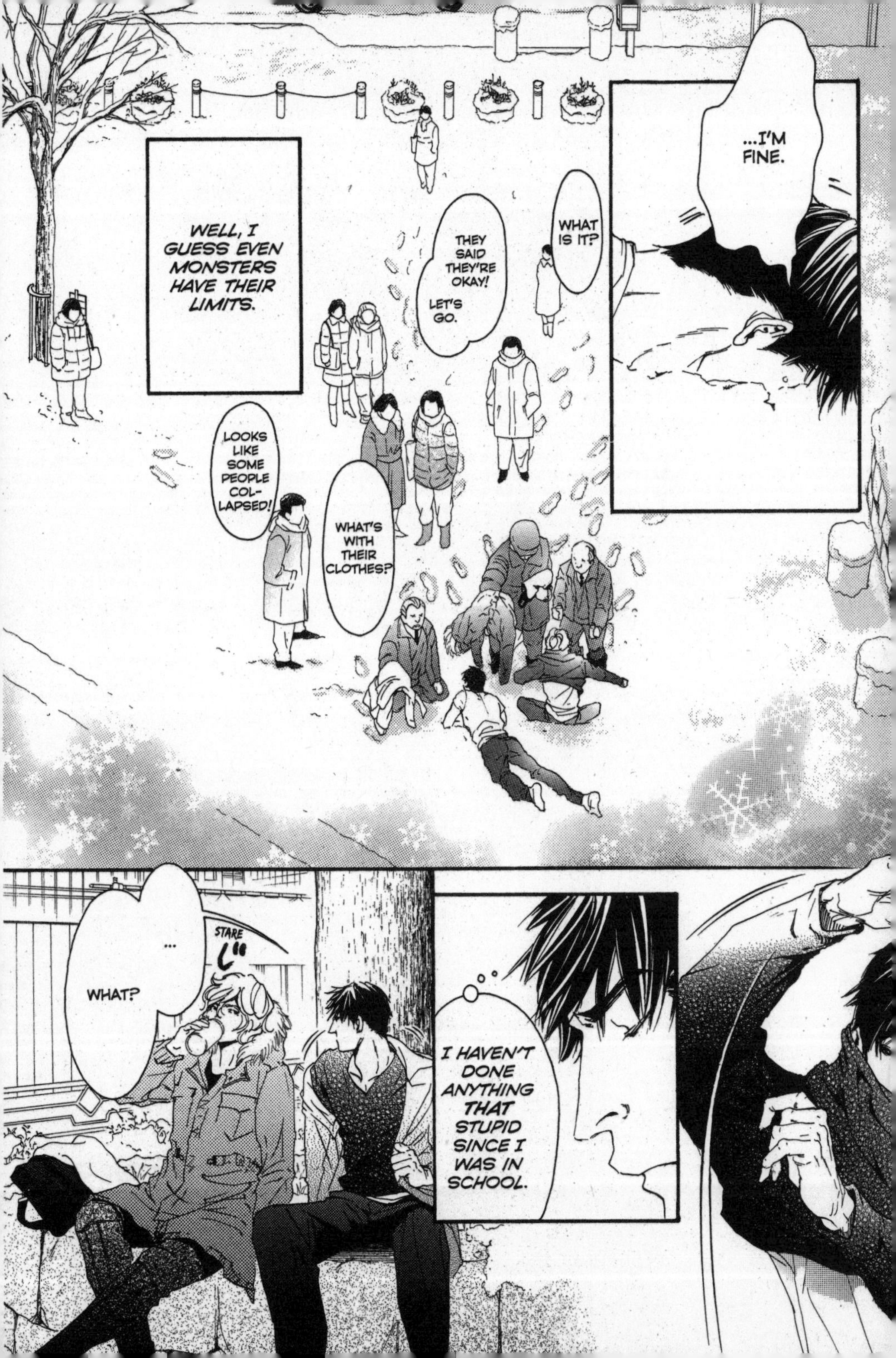
...I'M FINE.
WHAT IS IT?
THEY SAID THEY'RE OKAY! LET'S GO.
WELL, I GUESS EVEN MONSTERS HAVE THEIR LIMITS.
LOOKS LIKE SOME PEOPLE COL-LAPSED!
WHAT'S WITH THEIR CLOTHES?
I HAVEN'T DONE ANYTHING THAT STUPID SINCE I WAS IN SCHOOL.
STARE
...
WHAT?

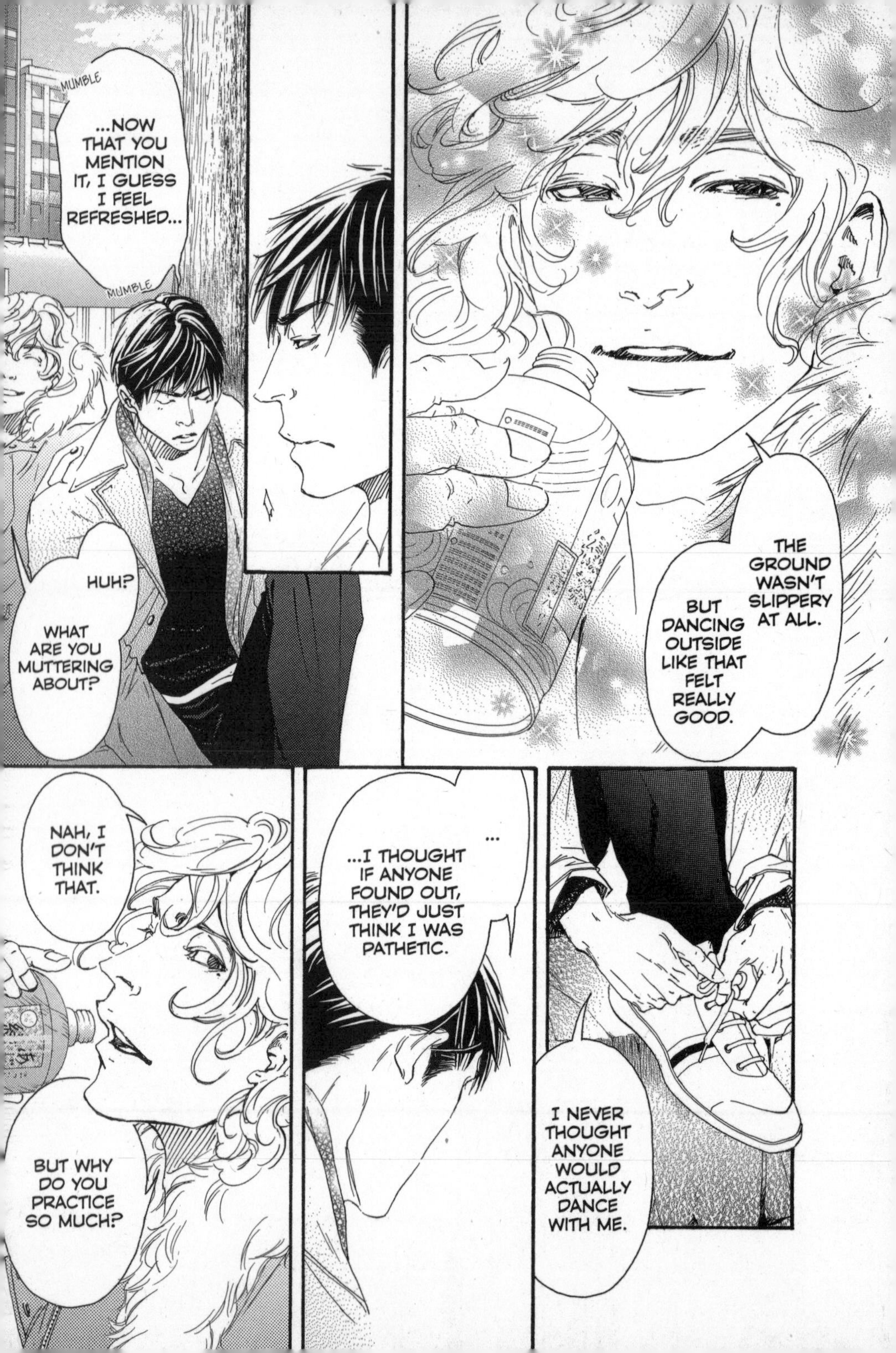
THE GROUND WASN'T SLIPPERY AT ALL.
BUT DANCING OUTSIDE LIKE THAT FELT REALLY GOOD.
MUMBLE
...NOW THAT YOU MENTION IT, I GUESS I FEEL REFRESHED...
MUMBLE
HUH?
WHAT ARE YOU MUTTERING ABOUT?
I NEVER THOUGHT ANYONE WOULD ACTUALLY DANCE WITH ME.
...
...I THOUGHT IF ANYONE FOUND OUT, THEY'D JUST THINK I WAS PATHETIC.
NAH, I DON'T THINK THAT.
BUT WHY DO YOU PRACTICE SO MUCH?

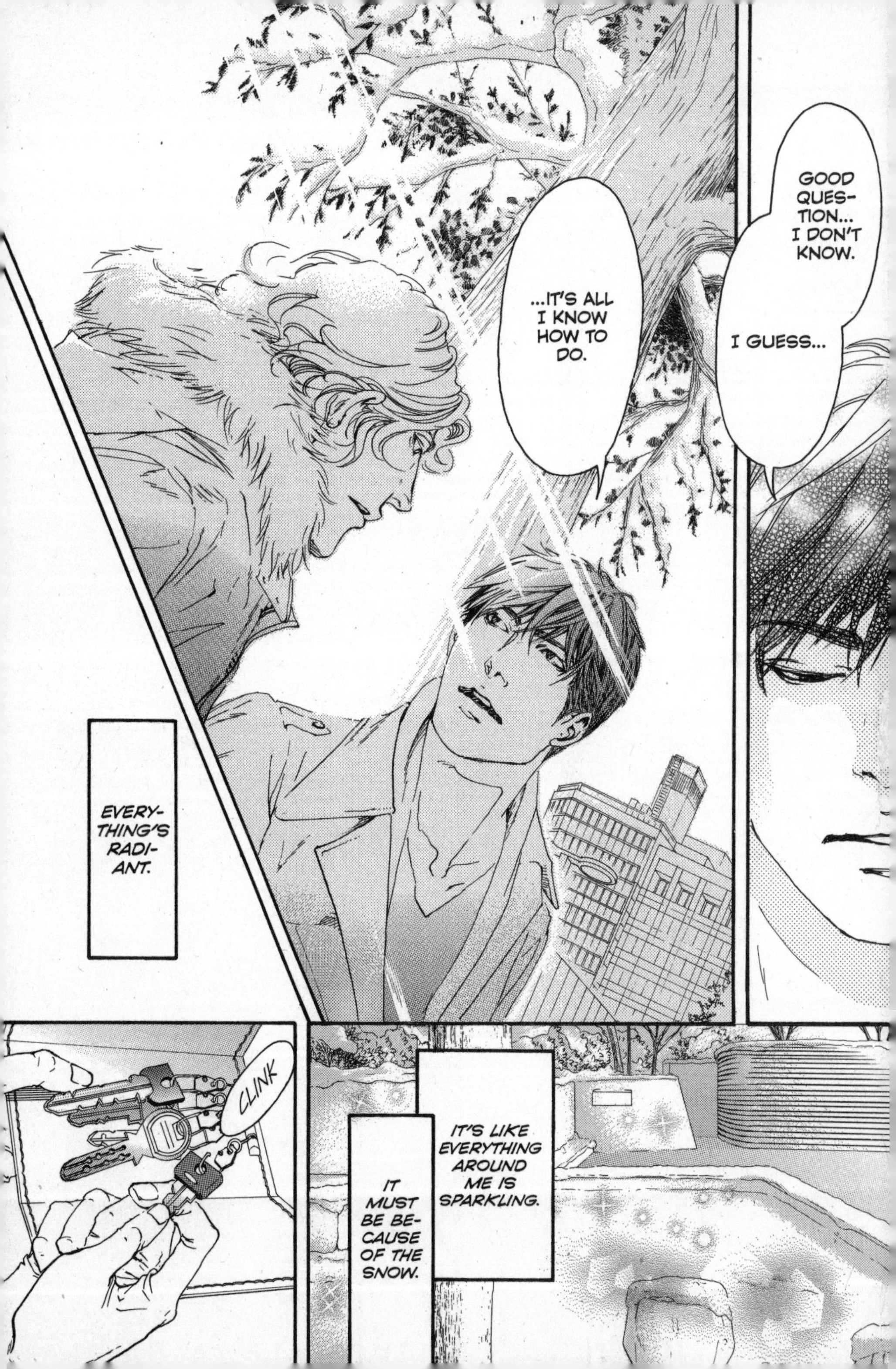
GOOD QUES-TION... I DON'T KNOW.
I GUESS...
...IT'S ALL I KNOW HOW TO DO.
EVERY-THING'S RADI-ANT.
IT'S LIKE EVERYTHING AROUND ME IS SPARKLING.
IT MUST BE BE-CAUSE OF THE SNOW.
CLINK

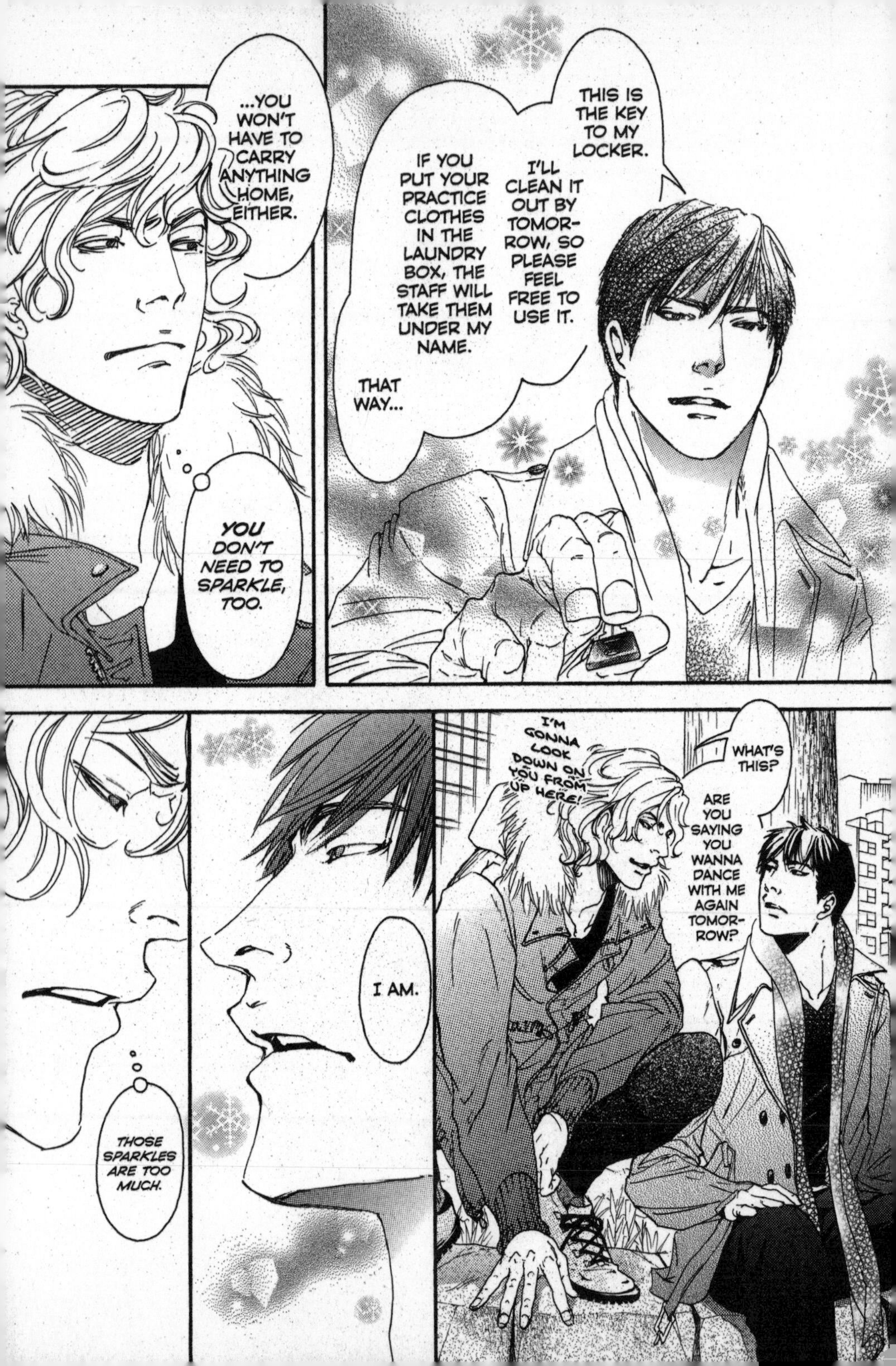
THIS IS THE KEY TO MY LOCKER.
I'LL CLEAN IT OUT BY TOMORROW, SO PLEASE FEEL FREE TO USE IT.
IF YOU PUT YOUR PRACTICE CLOTHES IN THE LAUNDRY BOX, THE STAFF WILL TAKE THEM UNDER MY NAME.
THAT WAY...
...YOU WON'T HAVE TO CARRY ANYTHING HOME, EITHER.
YOU DON'T NEED TO SPARKLE, TOO.
WHAT'S THIS?
ARE YOU SAYING YOU WANNA DANCE WITH ME AGAIN TOMORROW?
I'M GONNA LOOK DOWN ON YOU FROM UP HERE!
I AM.
THOSE SPARKLES ARE TOO MUCH.

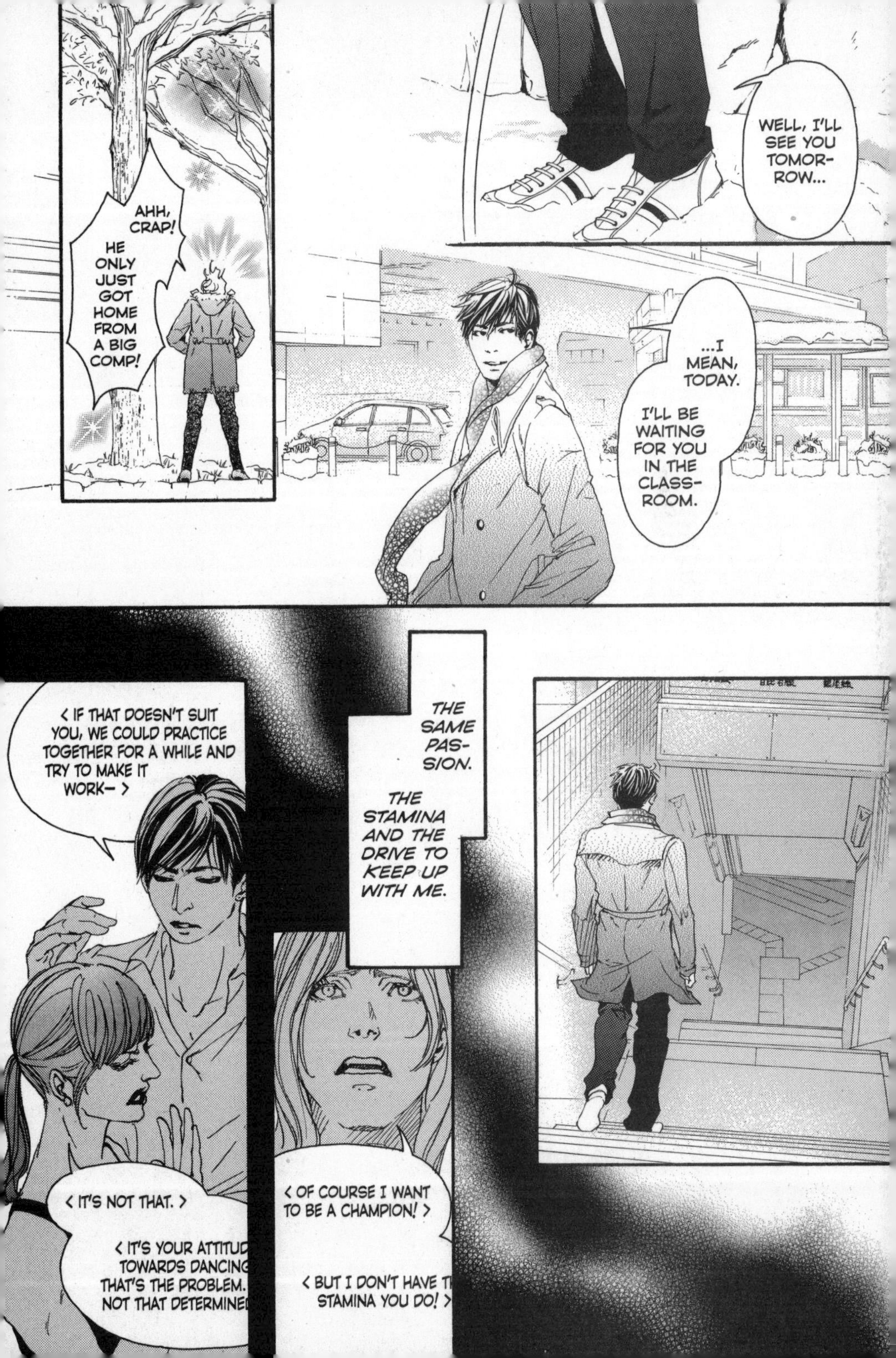
WELL, I'LL SEE YOU TOMORROW...
...I MEAN, TODAY.
I'LL BE WAITING FOR YOU IN THE CLASSROOM.
AHH, CRAP!
HE ONLY JUST GOT HOME FROM A BIG COMP!
THE SAME PASSION.
THE STAMINA AND THE DRIVE TO KEEP UP WITH ME.
< OF COURSE I WANT TO BE A CHAMPION! >
< BUT I DON'T HAVE T STAMINA YOU DO! >
< IF THAT DOESN'T SUIT YOU, WE COULD PRACTICE TOGETHER FOR A WHILE AND TRY TO MAKE IT WORK– >
< IT'S NOT THAT. >
< IT'S YOUR ATTITUD TOWARDS DANCING THAT'S THE PROBLEM. NOT THAT DETERMINE

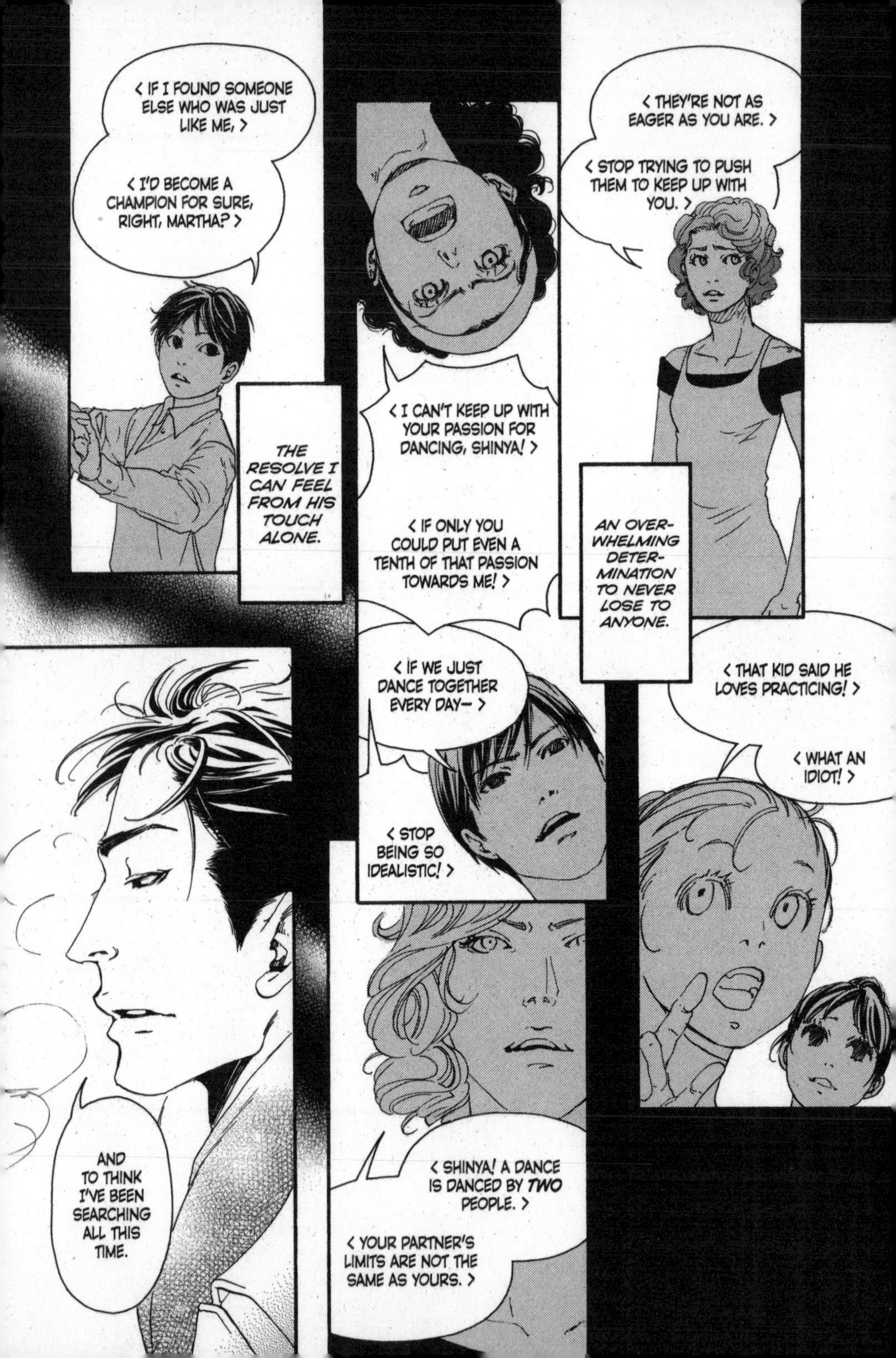
< THEY'RE NOT AS EAGER AS YOU ARE. >
< STOP TRYING TO PUSH THEM TO KEEP UP WITH YOU. >
AN OVER-WHELMING DETER-MINATION TO NEVER LOSE TO ANYONE.
< I CAN'T KEEP UP WITH YOUR PASSION FOR DANCING, SHINYA! >
< IF ONLY YOU COULD PUT EVEN A TENTH OF THAT PASSION TOWARDS ME! >
< IF I FOUND SOMEONE ELSE WHO WAS JUST LIKE ME, >
< I'D BECOME A CHAMPION FOR SURE, RIGHT, MARTHA? >
THE RESOLVE I CAN FEEL FROM HIS TOUCH ALONE.
< THAT KID SAID HE LOVES PRACTICING! >
< WHAT AN IDIOT! >
< IF WE JUST DANCE TOGETHER EVERY DAY— >
< STOP BEING SO IDEALISTIC! >
< SHINYA! A DANCE IS DANCED BY *TWO* PEOPLE. >
< YOUR PARTNER'S LIMITS ARE NOT THE SAME AS YOURS. >
AND TO THINK I'VE BEEN SEARCHING ALL THIS TIME.

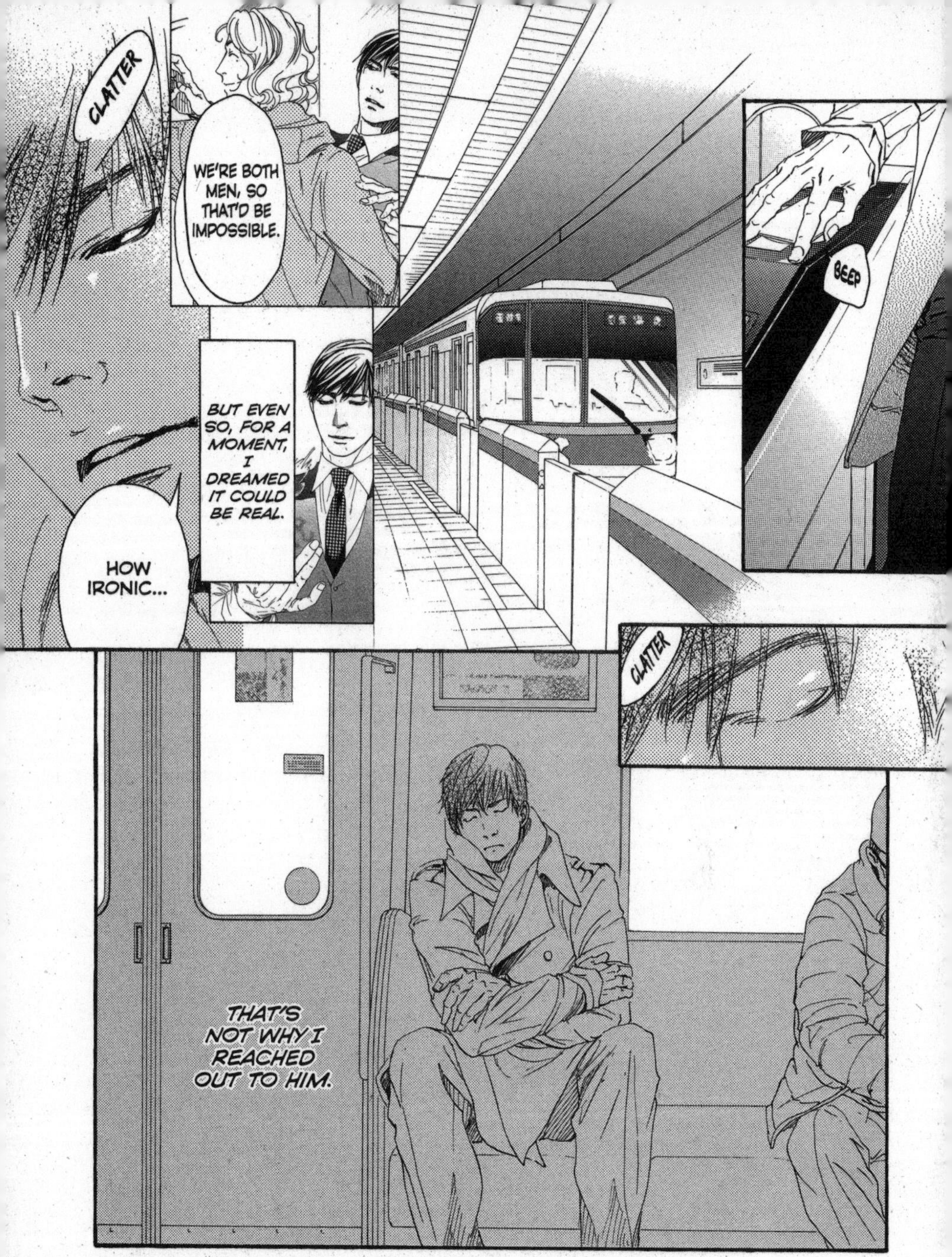
BEEP
WE'RE BOTH MEN, SO THAT'D BE IMPOSSIBLE.
BUT EVEN SO, FOR A MOMENT, I DREAMED IT COULD BE REAL.
CLATTER
HOW IRONIC...
CLATTER
THAT'S NOT WHY I REACHED OUT TO HIM.

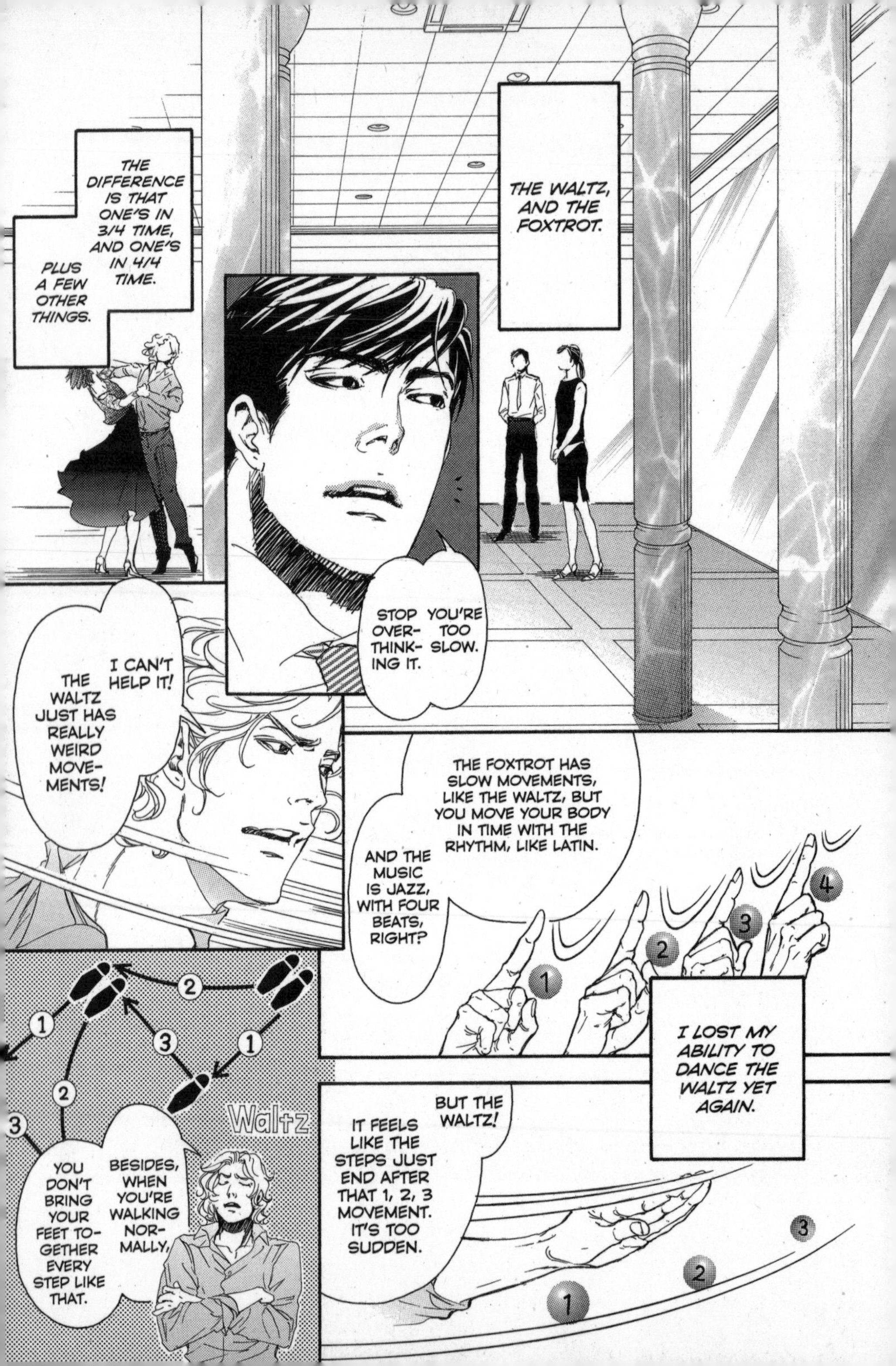
THE WALTZ, AND THE FOXTROT.
THE DIFFERENCE IS THAT ONE'S IN 3/4 TIME, AND ONE'S IN 4/4 TIME.
PLUS A FEW OTHER THINGS.
YOU'RE TOO SLOW.
STOP OVER-THINKING IT.
THE FOXTROT HAS SLOW MOVEMENTS, LIKE THE WALTZ, BUT YOU MOVE YOUR BODY IN TIME WITH THE RHYTHM, LIKE LATIN.
AND THE MUSIC IS JAZZ, WITH FOUR BEATS, RIGHT?
1 2 3 4
I CAN'T HELP IT!
THE WALTZ JUST HAS REALLY WEIRD MOVE-MENTS!
I LOST MY ABILITY TO DANCE THE WALTZ YET AGAIN.
BUT THE WALTZ!
IT FEELS LIKE THE STEPS JUST END AFTER THAT 1, 2, 3 MOVEMENT. IT'S TOO SUDDEN.
1 2 3
Waltz
1 2 3 1 2 3
BESIDES, WHEN YOU'RE WALKING NOR-MALLY,
YOU DON'T BRING YOUR FEET TO-GETHER EVERY STEP LIKE THAT.

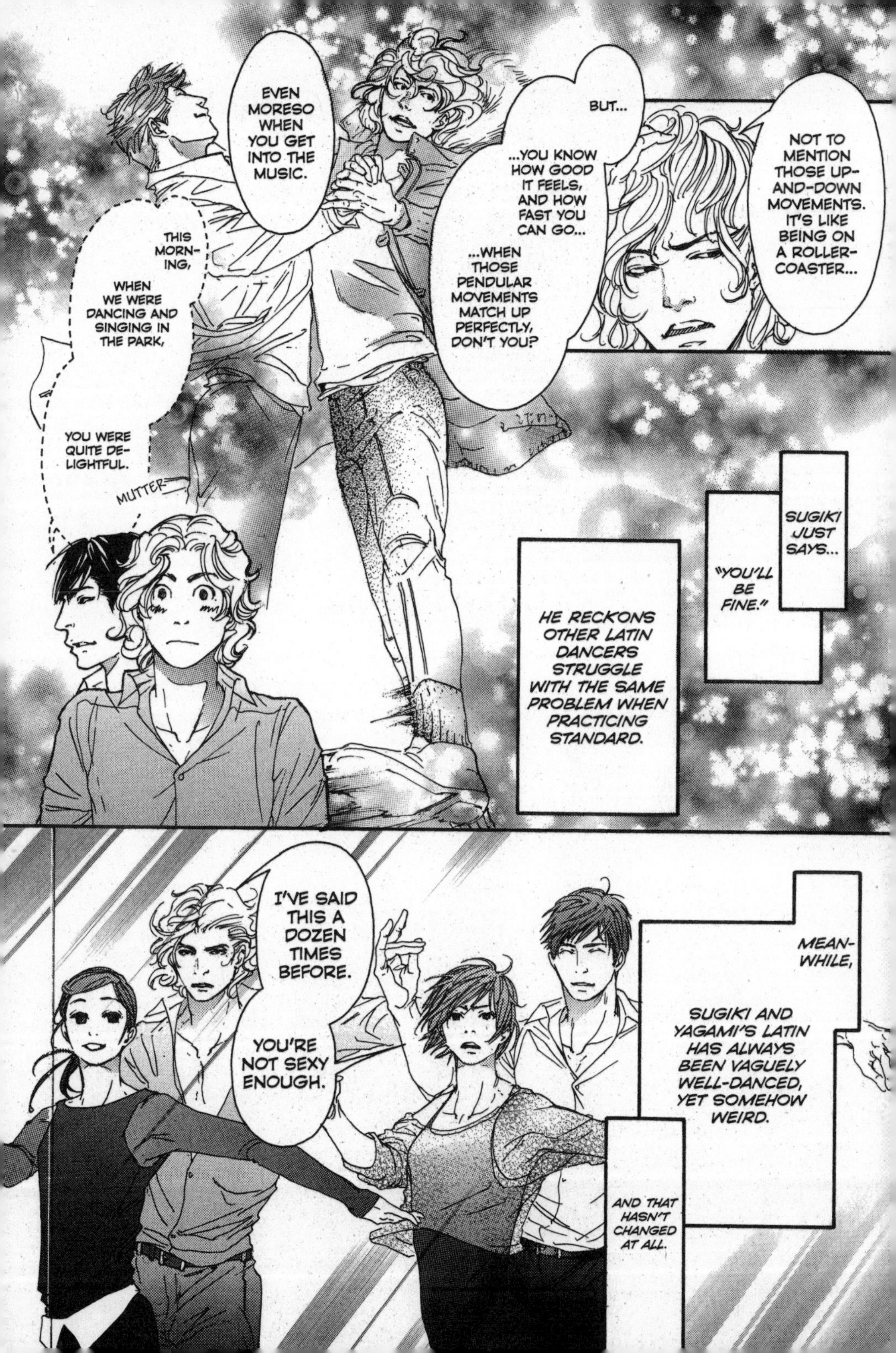
NOT TO MENTION THOSE UP-AND-DOWN MOVEMENTS. IT'S LIKE BEING ON A ROLLER-COASTER...
BUT...
...YOU KNOW HOW GOOD IT FEELS, AND HOW FAST YOU CAN GO...
...WHEN THOSE PENDULAR MOVEMENTS MATCH UP PERFECTLY, DON'T YOU?
EVEN MORESO WHEN YOU GET INTO THE MUSIC.
SUGIKI JUST SAYS...
"YOU'LL BE FINE."
HE RECKONS OTHER LATIN DANCERS STRUGGLE WITH THE SAME PROBLEM WHEN PRACTICING STANDARD.
THIS MORNING,
WHEN WE WERE DANCING AND SINGING IN THE PARK,
YOU WERE QUITE DE-LIGHTFUL.
MUTTER
MEAN-WHILE,
SUGIKI AND YAGAMI'S LATIN HAS ALWAYS BEEN VAGUELY WELL-DANCED, YET SOMEHOW WEIRD.
AND THAT HASN'T CHANGED AT ALL.
I'VE SAID THIS A DOZEN TIMES BEFORE.
YOU'RE NOT SEXY ENOUGH.

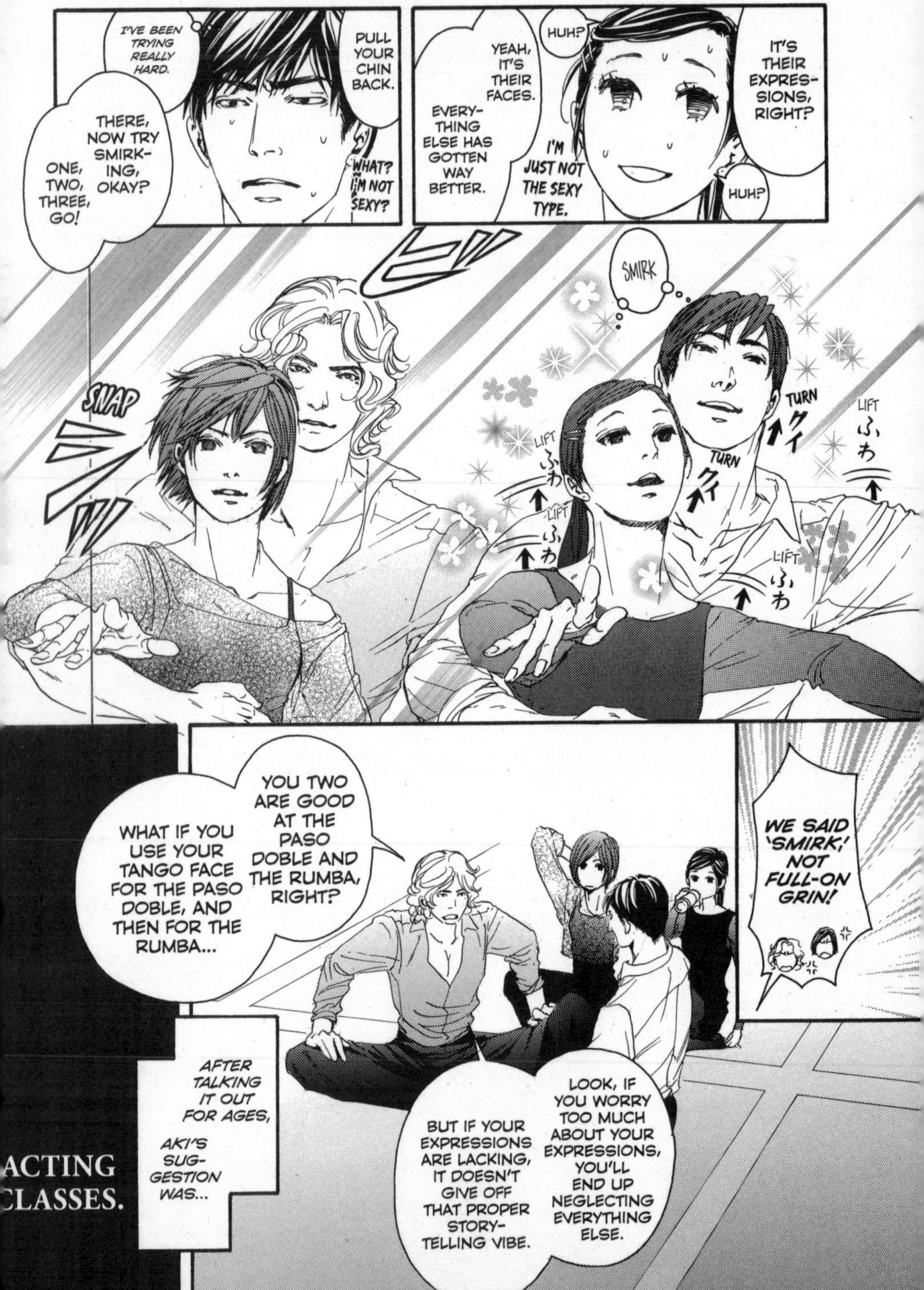
IT'S THEIR EXPRESSIONS, RIGHT?
HUH?
HUH?
YEAH, IT'S THEIR FACES.
EVERY-THING ELSE HAS GOTTEN WAY BETTER.
I'M JUST NOT THE SEXY TYPE.
PULL YOUR CHIN BACK.
I'VE BEEN TRYING REALLY HARD.
WHAT? I'M NOT SEXY?
THERE, NOW TRY SMIRK-ING, OKAY?
ONE, TWO, THREE, GO!
SMIRK
LIFT ふわ
TURN クイ
LIFT ふわ
TURN クイ
LIFT ふわ
LIFT ふわ
SNAP
WE SAID 'SMIRK,' NOT FULL-ON GRIN!
YOU TWO ARE GOOD AT THE PASO DOBLE AND THE RUMBA, RIGHT?
WHAT IF YOU USE YOUR TANGO FACE FOR THE PASO DOBLE, AND THEN FOR THE RUMBA...
LOOK, IF YOU WORRY TOO MUCH ABOUT YOUR EXPRESSIONS, YOU'LL END UP NEGLECTING EVERYTHING ELSE.
BUT IF YOUR EXPRESSIONS ARE LACKING, IT DOESN'T GIVE OFF THAT PROPER STORY-TELLING VIBE.
AFTER TALKING IT OUT FOR AGES,
AKI'S SUG-GESTION WAS...
ACTING CLASSES.

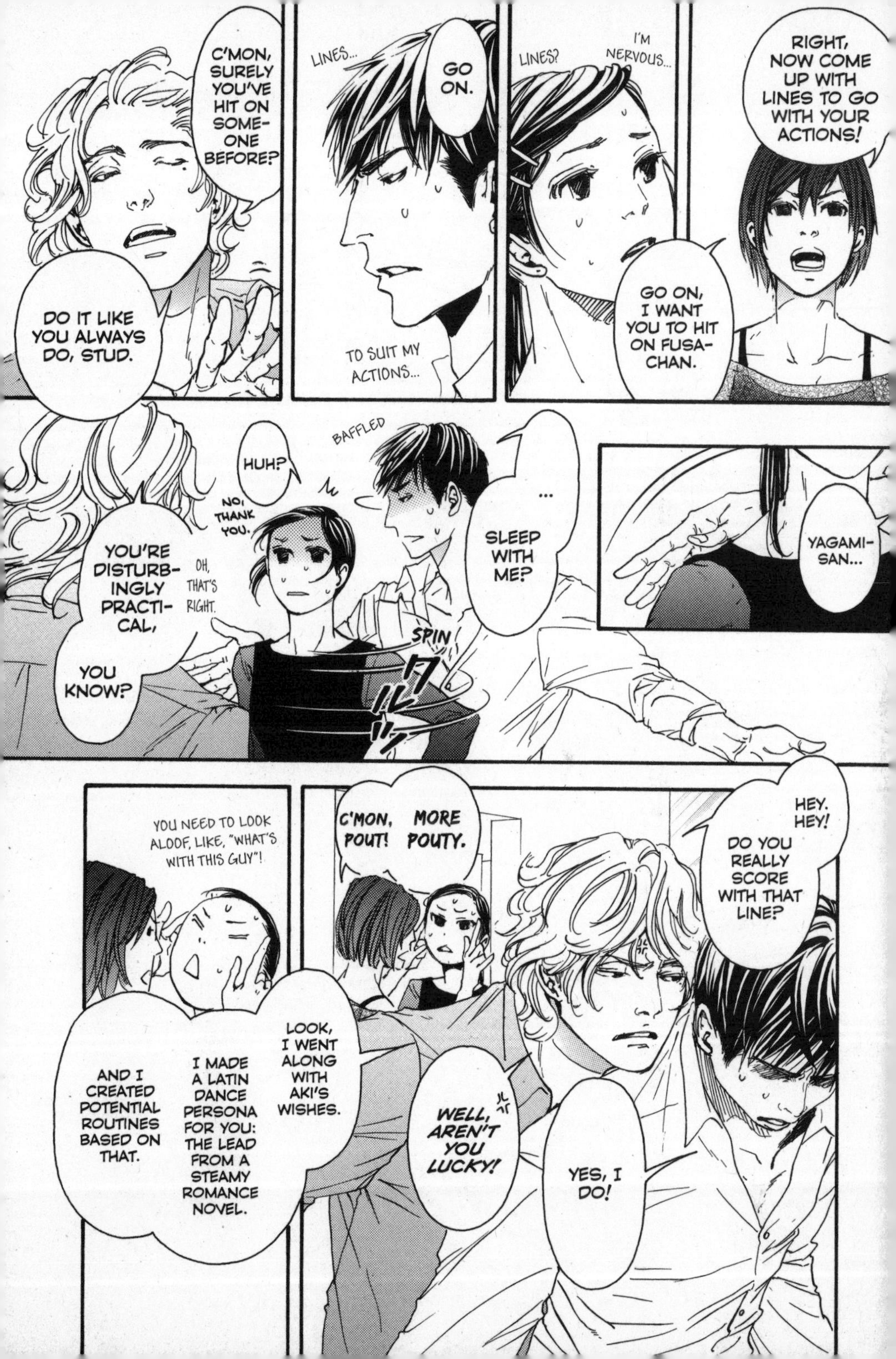
RIGHT, NOW COME UP WITH LINES TO GO WITH YOUR ACTIONS!
I'M NERVOUS...
LINES?
GO ON, I WANT YOU TO HIT ON FUSA-CHAN.
GO ON.
LINES...
TO SUIT MY ACTIONS...
C'MON, SURELY YOU'VE HIT ON SOMEONE BEFORE?
DO IT LIKE YOU ALWAYS DO, STUD.
YAGAMI-SAN...
...
SLEEP WITH ME?
BAFFLED
HUH?
NO, THANK YOU.
OH, THAT'S RIGHT.
YOU'RE DISTURBINGLY PRACTICAL,
YOU KNOW?
SPIN
HEY. HEY!
DO YOU REALLY SCORE WITH THAT LINE?
YES, I DO!
WELL, AREN'T YOU LUCKY!
C'MON, POUT! MORE POUTY.
YOU NEED TO LOOK ALOOF, LIKE, "WHAT'S WITH THIS GUY"!
LOOK, I WENT ALONG WITH AKI'S WISHES.
I MADE A LATIN DANCE PERSONA FOR YOU: THE LEAD FROM A STEAMY ROMANCE NOVEL.
AND I CREATED POTENTIAL ROUTINES BASED ON THAT.

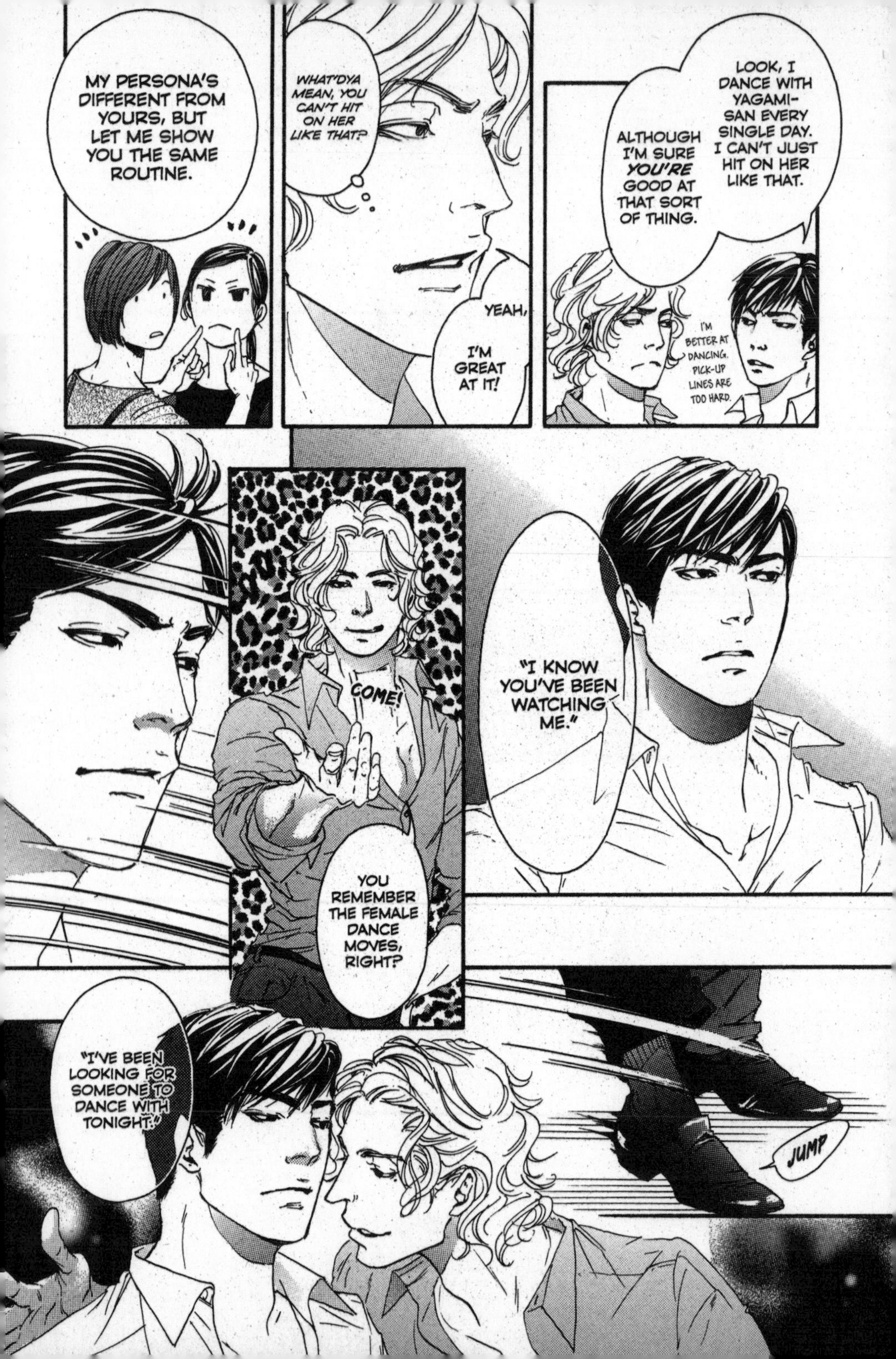
LOOK, I DANCE WITH YAGAMI-SAN EVERY SINGLE DAY. I CAN'T JUST HIT ON HER LIKE THAT.
ALTHOUGH I'M SURE YOU'RE GOOD AT THAT SORT OF THING.
I'M BETTER AT DANCING. PICK-UP LINES ARE TOO HARD.
WHAT'DYA MEAN, YOU CAN'T HIT ON HER LIKE THAT?
YEAH, I'M GREAT AT IT!
MY PERSONA'S DIFFERENT FROM YOURS, BUT LET ME SHOW YOU THE SAME ROUTINE.
"I KNOW YOU'VE BEEN WATCHING ME."
COME!
YOU REMEMBER THE FEMALE DANCE MOVES, RIGHT?
JUMP
"I'VE BEEN LOOKING FOR SOMEONE TO DANCE WITH TONIGHT."

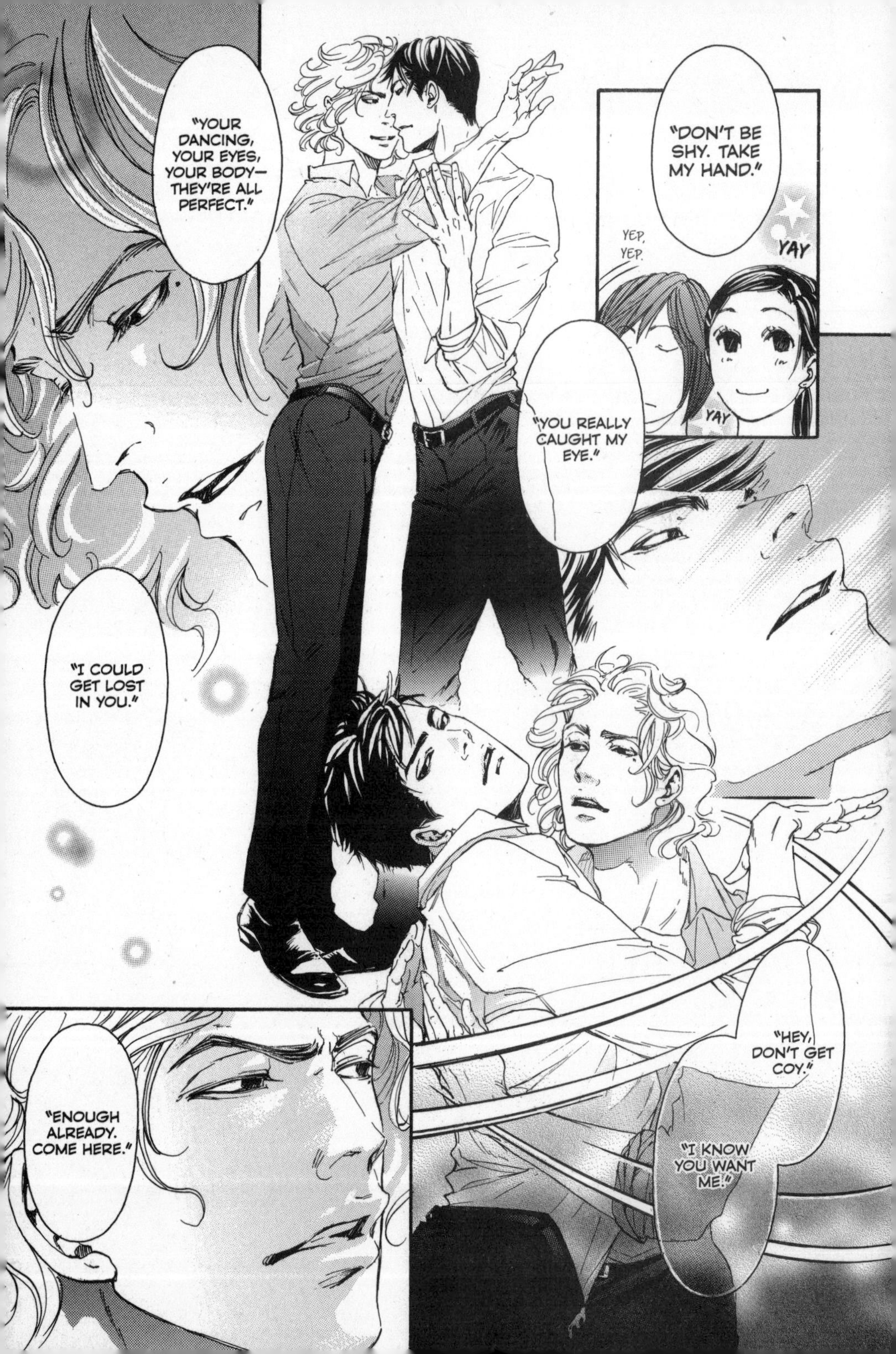
"DON'T BE SHY. TAKE MY HAND."
YAY
YEP, YEP.
YAY
"YOUR DANCING, YOUR EYES, YOUR BODY—THEY'RE ALL PERFECT."
"YOU REALLY CAUGHT MY EYE."
"I COULD GET LOST IN YOU."
"HEY, DON'T GET COY."
"I KNOW YOU WANT ME."
"ENOUGH ALREADY. COME HERE."

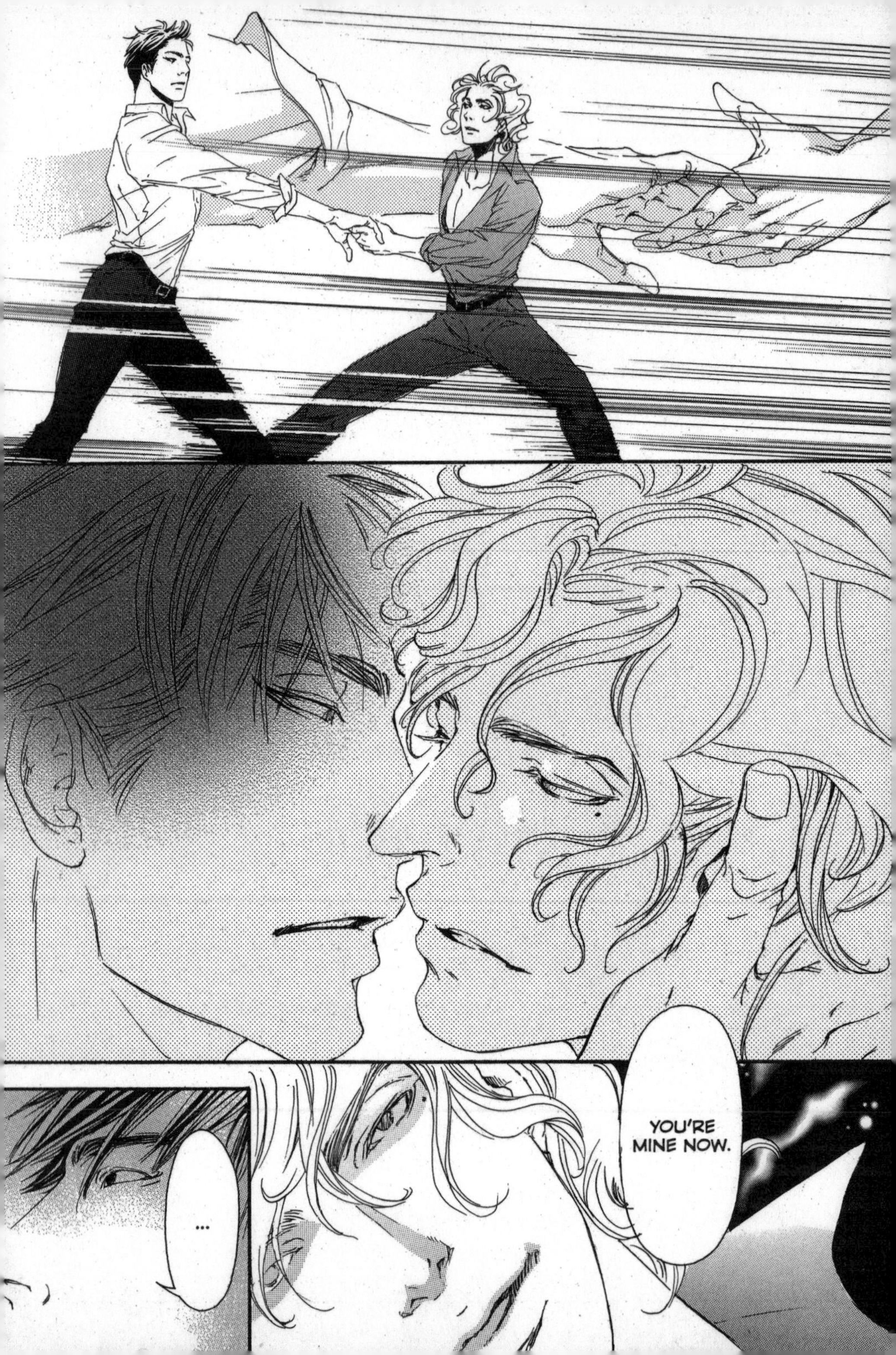
YOU'RE MINE NOW.
...

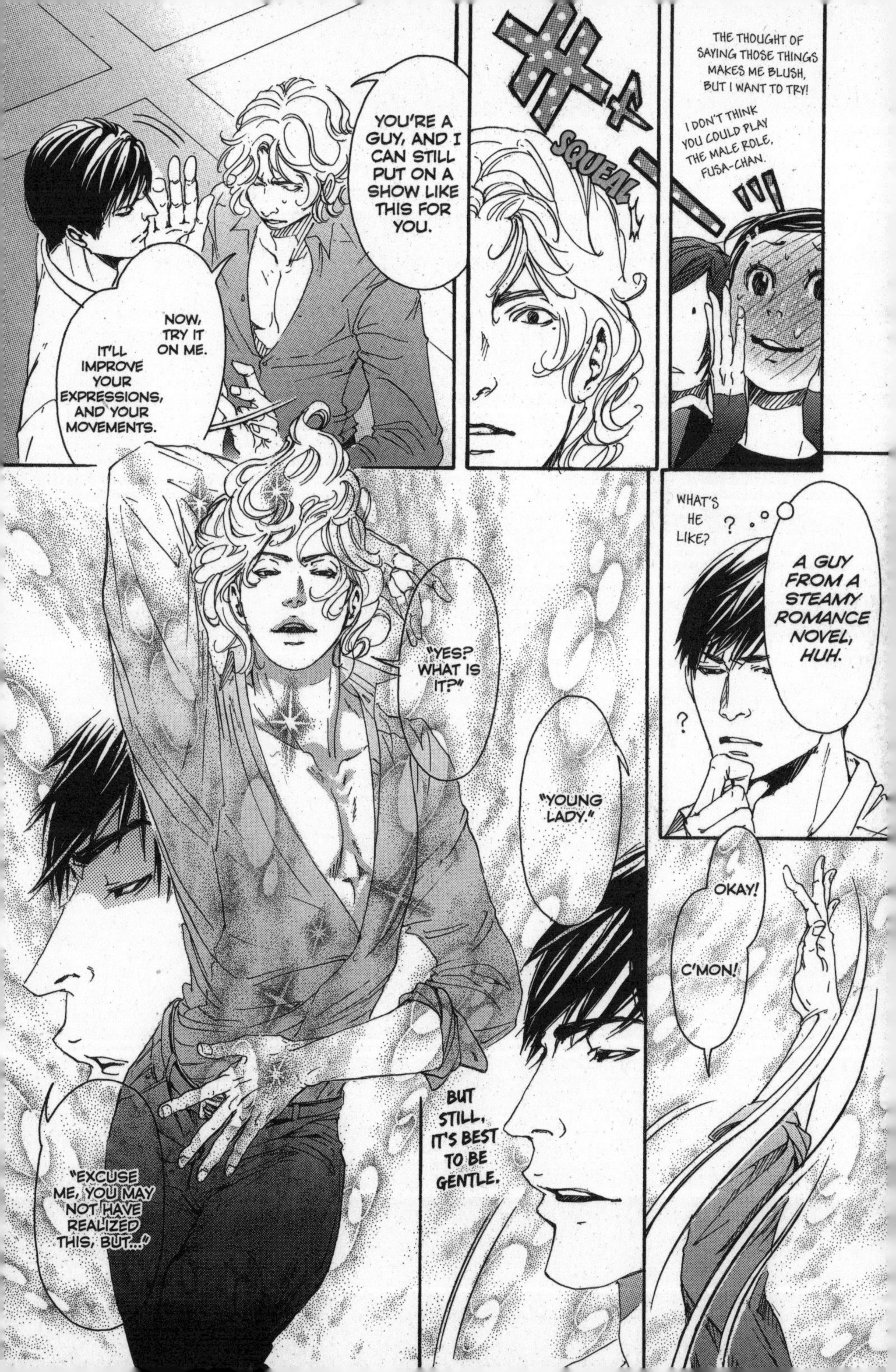
THE THOUGHT OF SAYING THOSE THINGS MAKES ME BLUSH, BUT I WANT TO TRY!
I DON'T THINK YOU COULD PLAY THE MALE ROLE, FUSA-CHAN.
SQUEAL
YOU'RE A GUY, AND I CAN STILL PUT ON A SHOW LIKE THIS FOR YOU.
NOW, TRY IT ON ME.
IT'LL IMPROVE YOUR EXPRESSIONS, AND YOUR MOVEMENTS.
A GUY FROM A STEAMY ROMANCE NOVEL, HUH.
WHAT'S HE LIKE?
OKAY!
C'MON!
"YOUNG LADY."
"YES? WHAT IS IT?"
BUT STILL, IT'S BEST TO BE GENTLE.
"EXCUSE ME, YOU MAY NOT HAVE REALIZED THIS, BUT..."

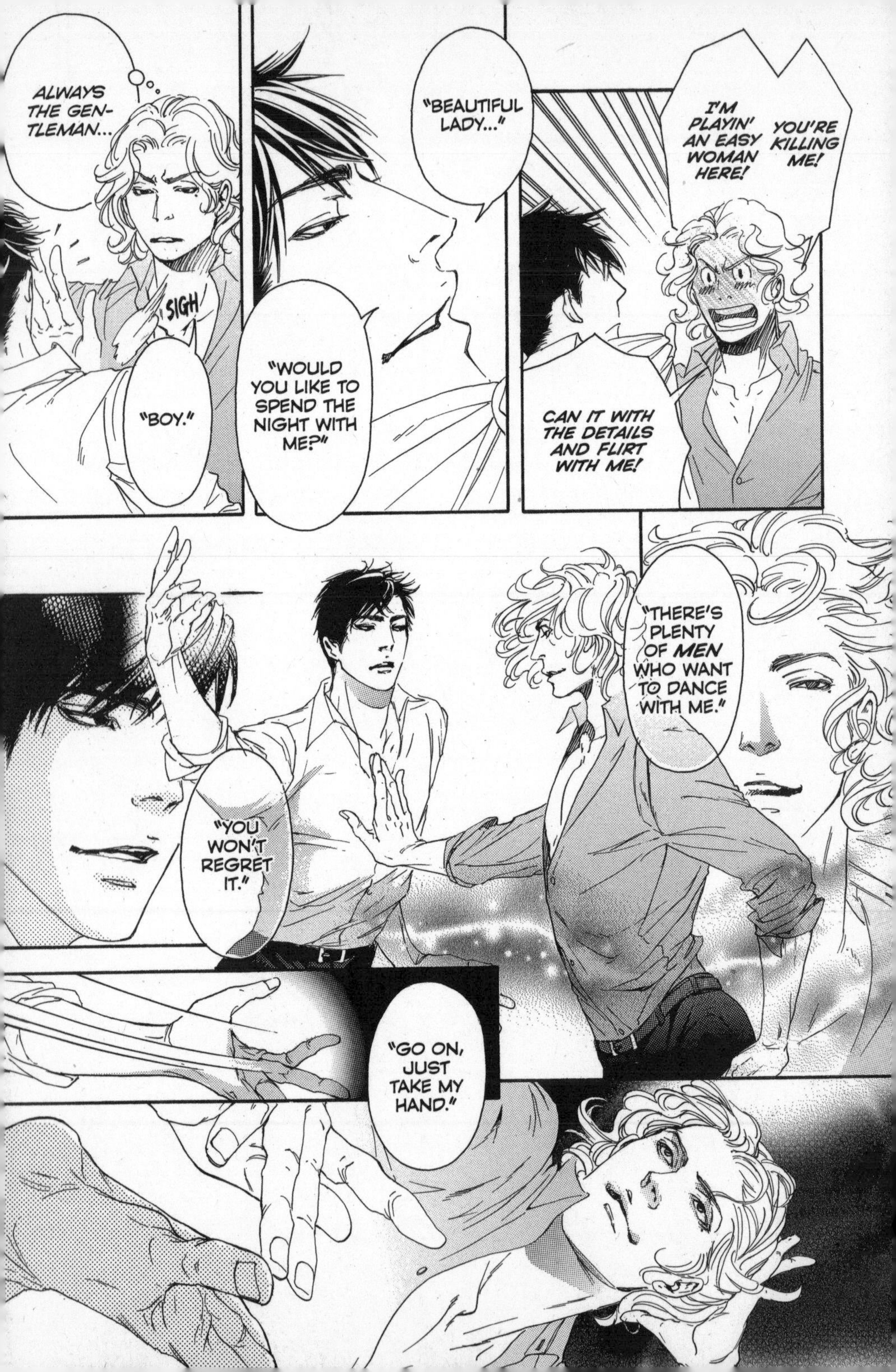
YOU'RE KILLING ME!
I'M PLAYIN' AN EASY WOMAN HERE!
CAN IT WITH THE DETAILS AND FLIRT WITH ME!
"BEAUTIFUL LADY..."
"WOULD YOU LIKE TO SPEND THE NIGHT WITH ME?"
ALWAYS THE GEN-TLEMAN...
SIGH
"BOY."
"THERE'S PLENTY OF *MEN* WHO WANT TO DANCE WITH ME."
"YOU WON'T REGRET IT."
"GO ON, JUST TAKE MY HAND."

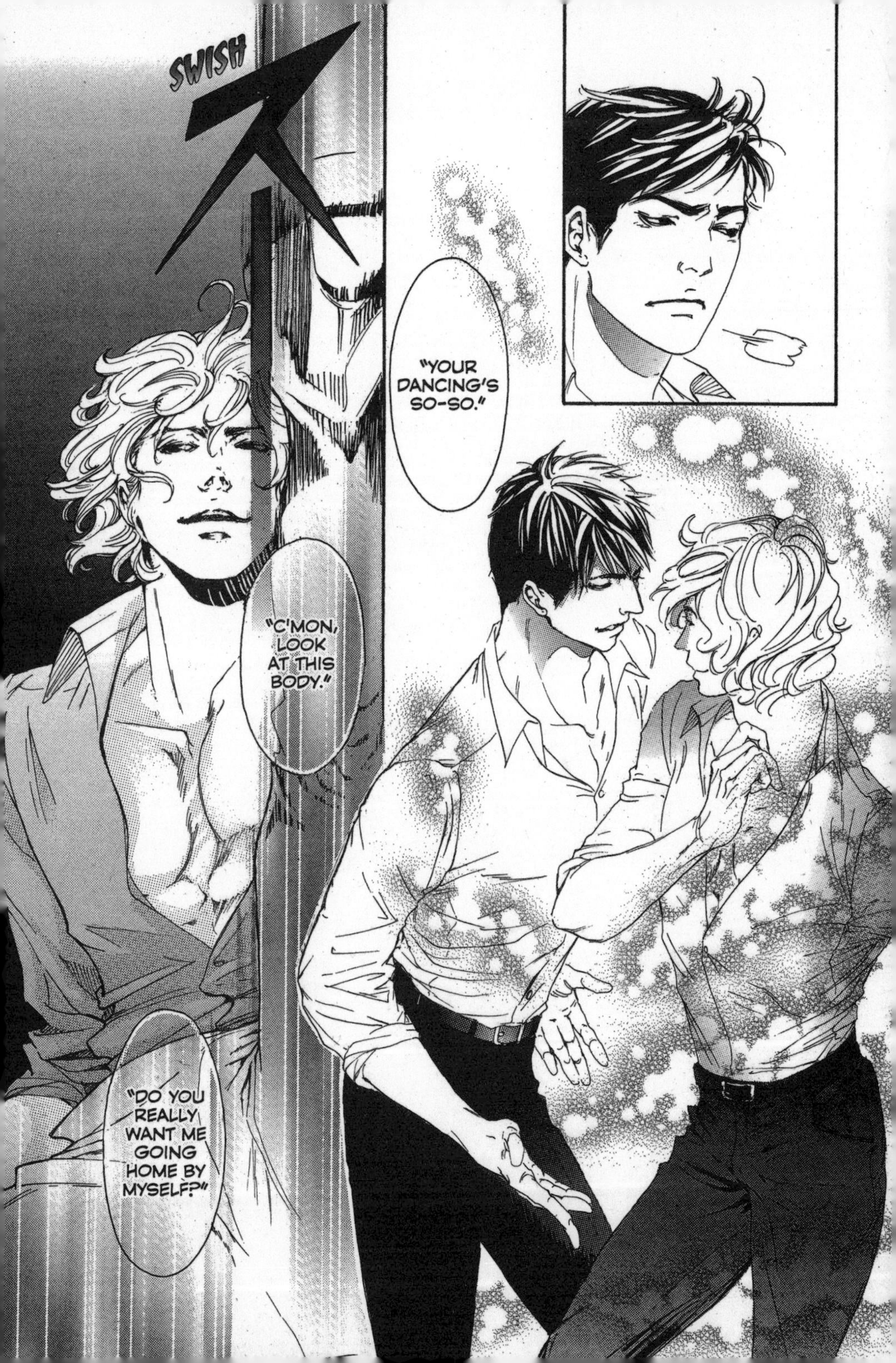
"YOUR DANCING'S SO-SO."
SWISH
"C'MON, LOOK AT THIS BODY."
"DO YOU REALLY WANT ME GOING HOME BY MYSELF?"

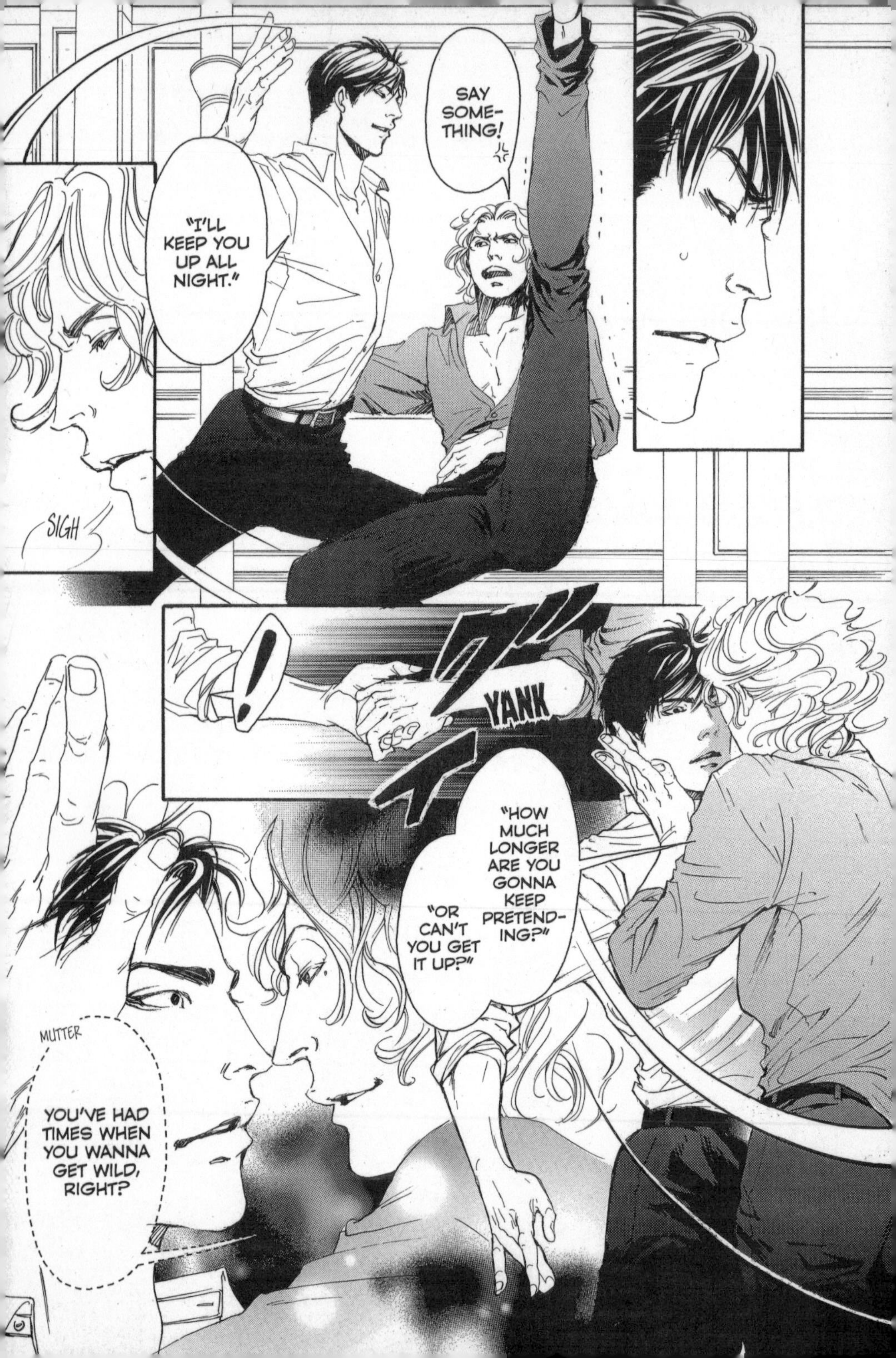
SAY SOMETHING!
"I'LL KEEP YOU UP ALL NIGHT."
SIGH
!
YANK
"HOW MUCH LONGER ARE YOU GONNA KEEP PRETENDING?"
"OR CAN'T YOU GET IT UP?"
MUTTER
YOU'VE HAD TIMES WHEN YOU WANNA GET WILD, RIGHT?

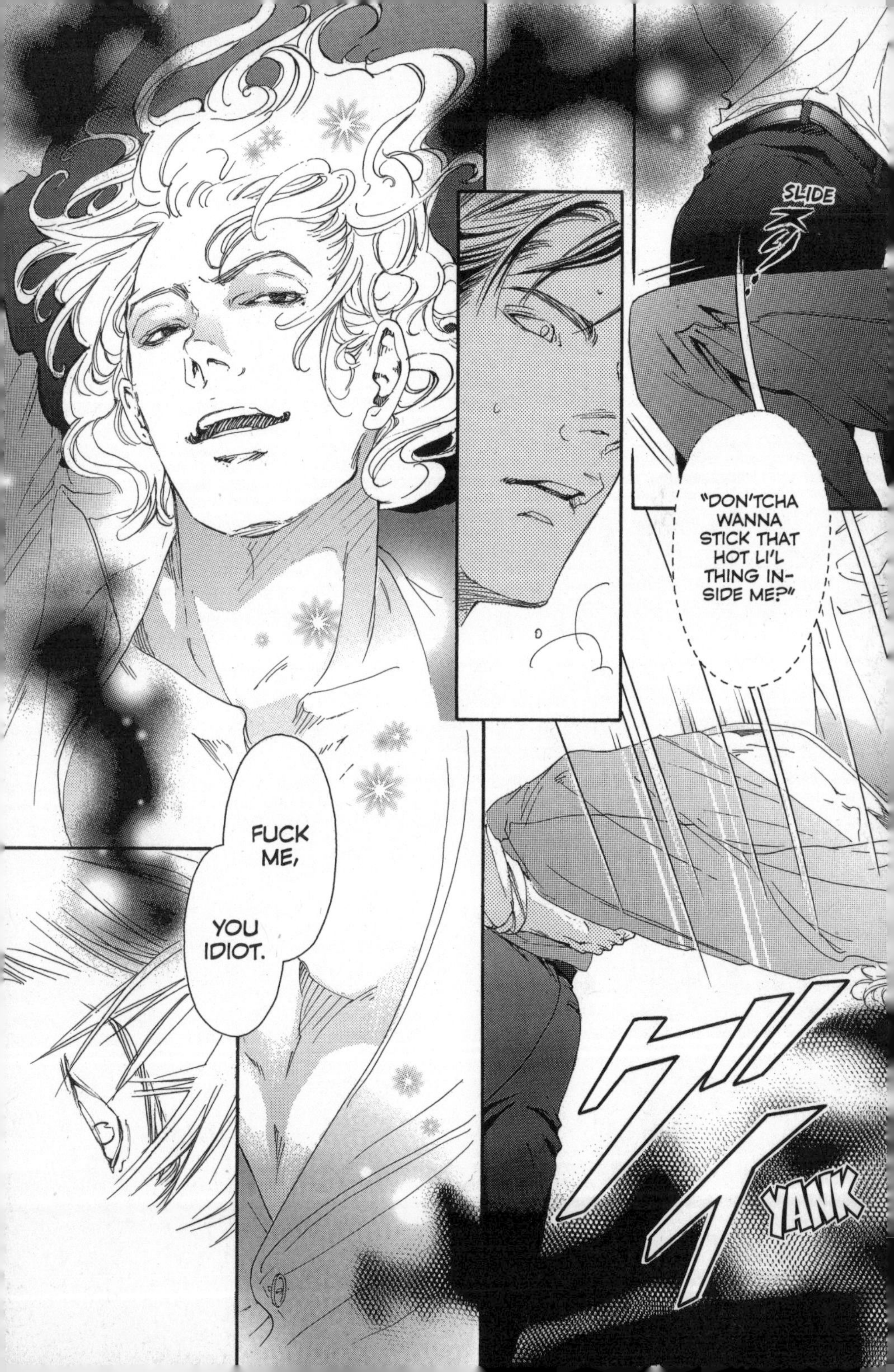
SLIDE
"DON'TCHA WANNA STICK THAT HOT LI'L THING IN-SIDE ME?"
FUCK ME,
YOU IDIOT.
YANK

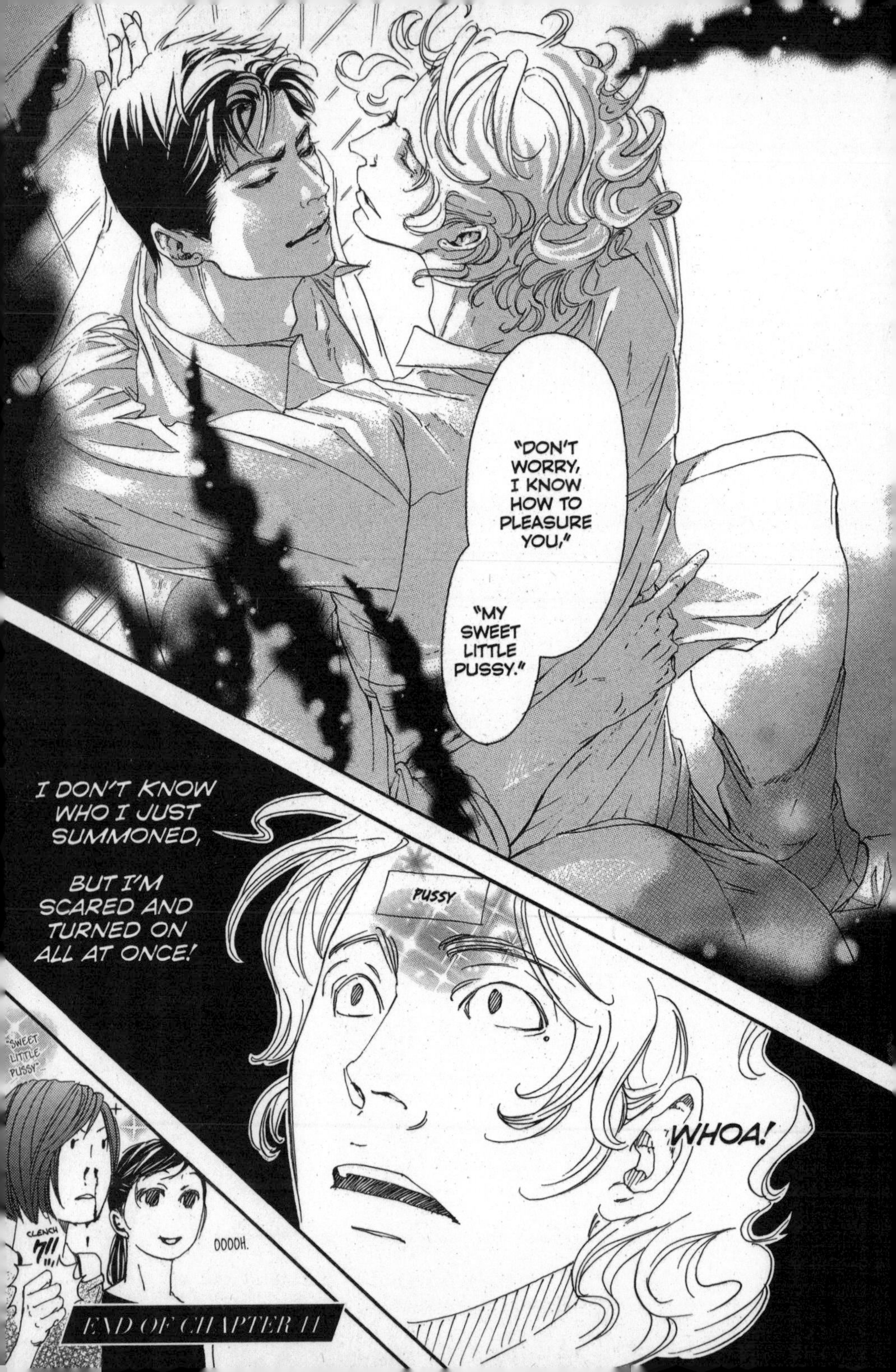
"DON'T WORRY, I KNOW HOW TO PLEASURE YOU,"
"MY SWEET LITTLE PUSSY."
I DON'T KNOW WHO I JUST SUMMONED,
BUT I'M SCARED AND TURNED ON ALL AT ONCE!
PUSSY
WHOA!
"SWEET LITTLE PUSSY"...
CLENCH
OOOOH.
END OF CHAPTER 11

#12
MY FAVORITE THINGS

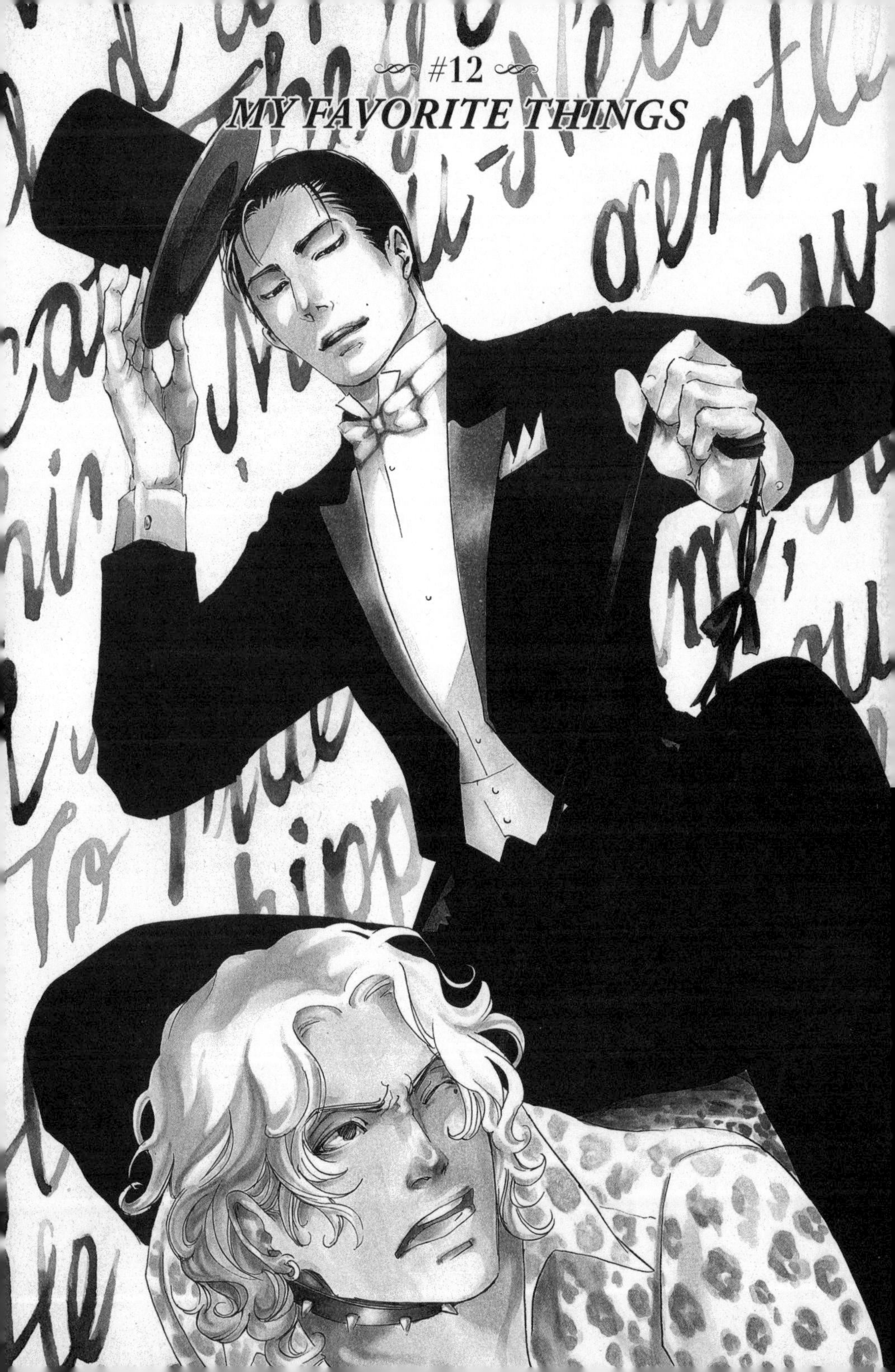

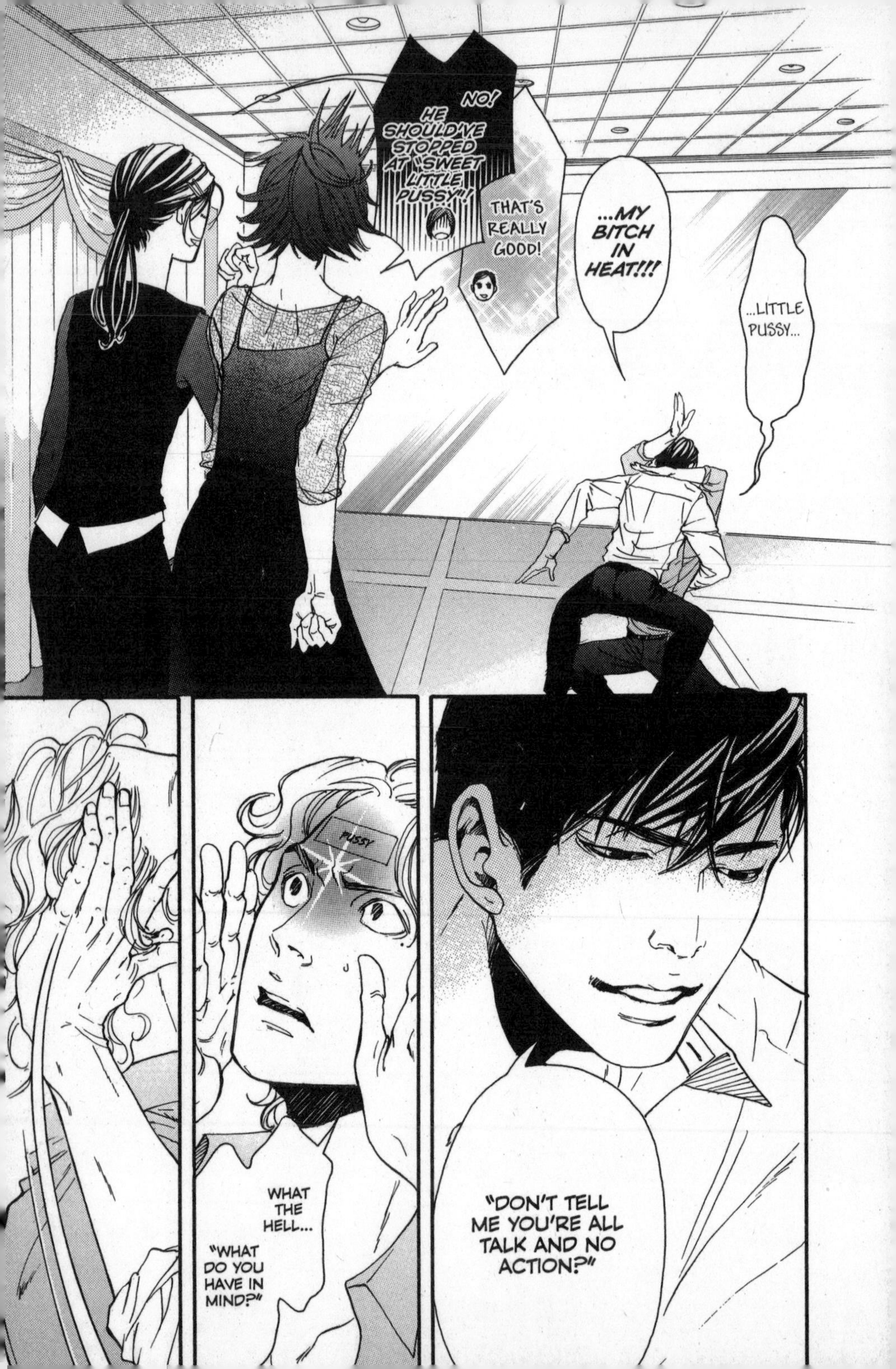
...LITTLE PUSSY...
...MY BITCH IN HEAT!!!
THAT'S REALLY GOOD!
NO! HE SHOULD'VE STOPPED AT "SWEET LITTLE PUSSY"!!
"DON'T TELL ME YOU'RE ALL TALK AND NO ACTION?"
PUSSY
WHAT THE HELL...
"WHAT DO YOU HAVE IN MIND?"

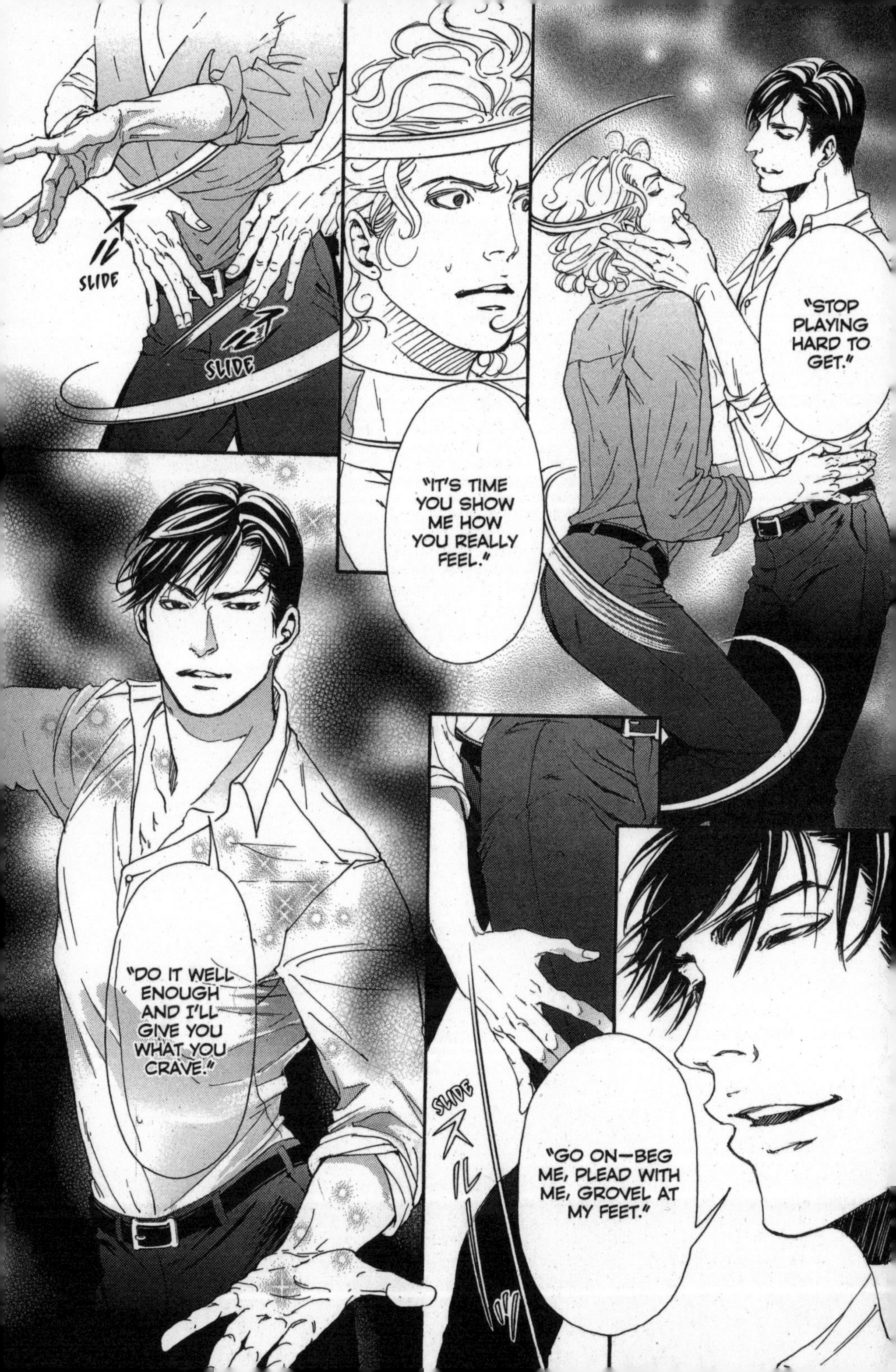
"STOP PLAYING HARD TO GET."
"IT'S TIME YOU SHOW ME HOW YOU REALLY FEEL."
スル SLIDE
スル SLIDE
"GO ON—BEG ME, PLEAD WITH ME, GROVEL AT MY FEET."
SLIDE スル
"DO IT WELL ENOUGH AND I'LL GIVE YOU WHAT YOU CRAVE."

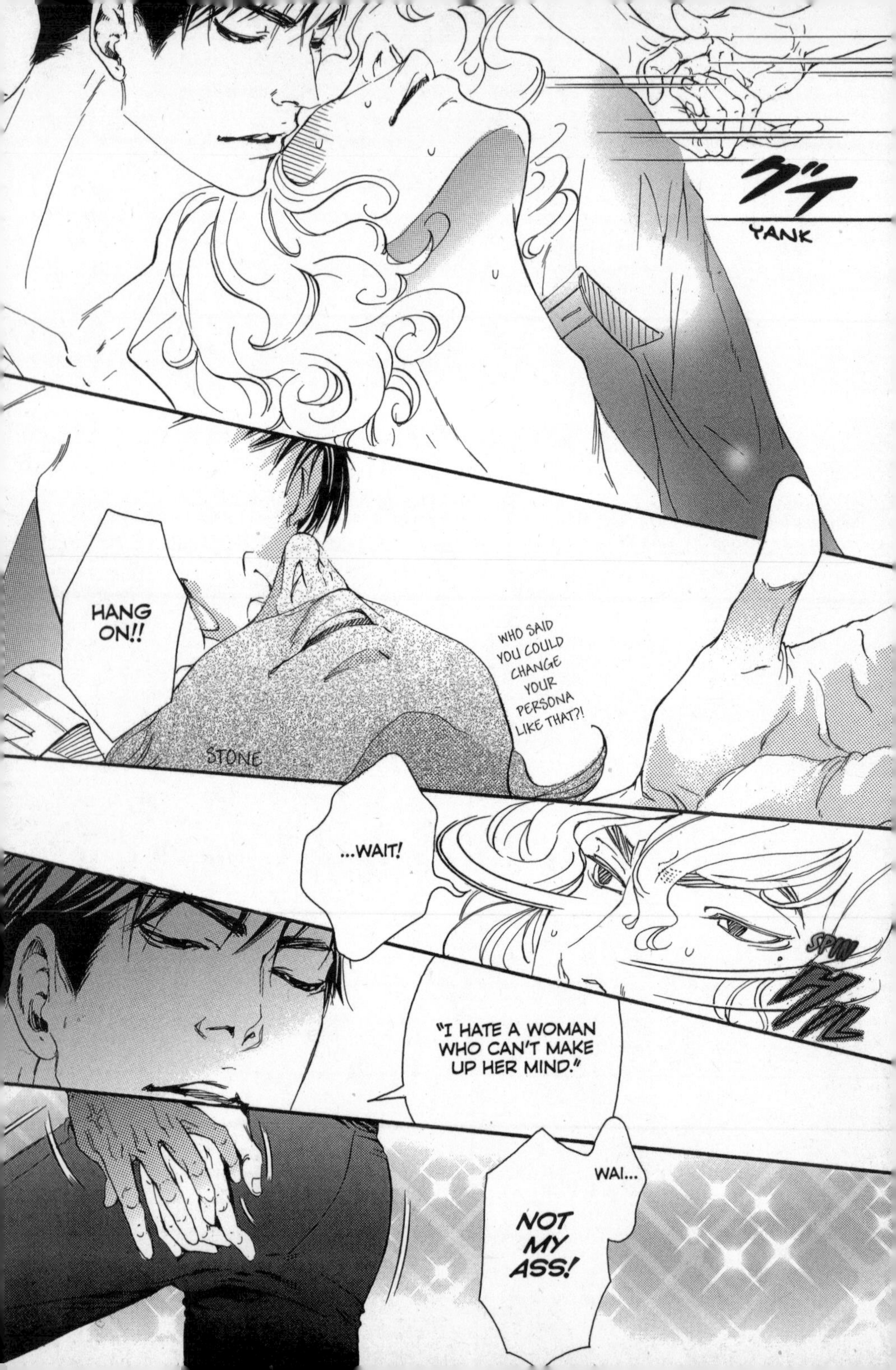
グイ
YANK
WHO SAID YOU COULD CHANGE YOUR PERSONA LIKE THAT?!
HANG ON!!
STONE
...WAIT!
SPIN
"I HATE A WOMAN WHO CAN'T MAKE UP HER MIND."
WAI...
NOT MY ASS!

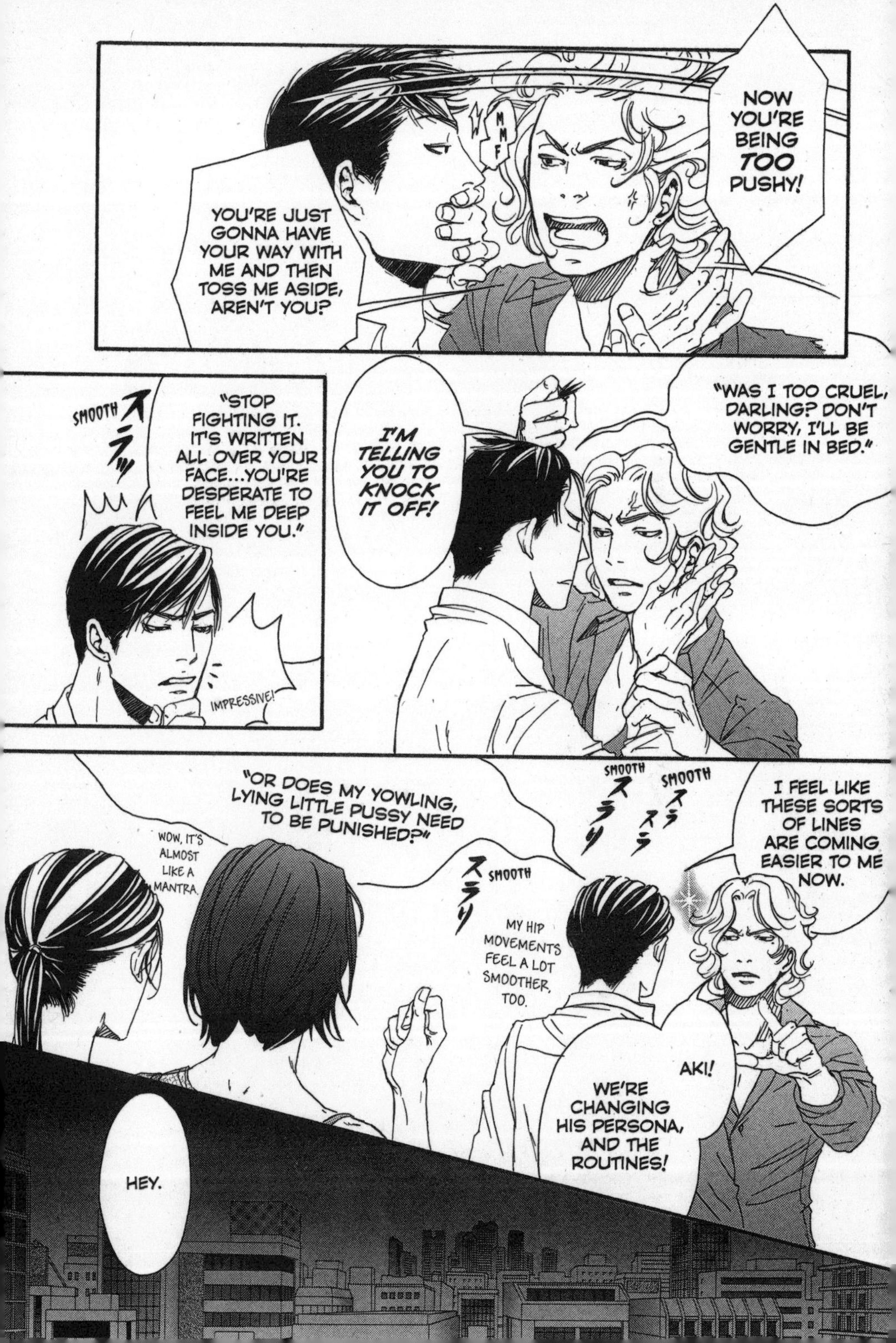
NOW YOU'RE BEING *TOO* PUSHY!
MMF
YOU'RE JUST GONNA HAVE YOUR WAY WITH ME AND THEN TOSS ME ASIDE, AREN'T YOU?
"WAS I TOO CRUEL, DARLING? DON'T WORRY, I'LL BE GENTLE IN BED."
I'M TELLING YOU TO KNOCK IT OFF!
SMOOTH スラッ
"STOP FIGHTING IT. IT'S WRITTEN ALL OVER YOUR FACE...YOU'RE DESPERATE TO FEEL ME DEEP INSIDE YOU."
IMPRESSIVE!
I FEEL LIKE THESE SORTS OF LINES ARE COMING EASIER TO ME NOW.
SMOOTH スラスラ
SMOOTH スラリ
"OR DOES MY YOWLING, LYING LITTLE PUSSY NEED TO BE PUNISHED?"
MY HIP MOVEMENTS FEEL A LOT SMOOTHER, TOO.
SMOOTH スラリ
WOW, IT'S ALMOST LIKE A MANTRA.
AKI!
WE'RE CHANGING HIS PERSONA, AND THE ROUTINES!
HEY.

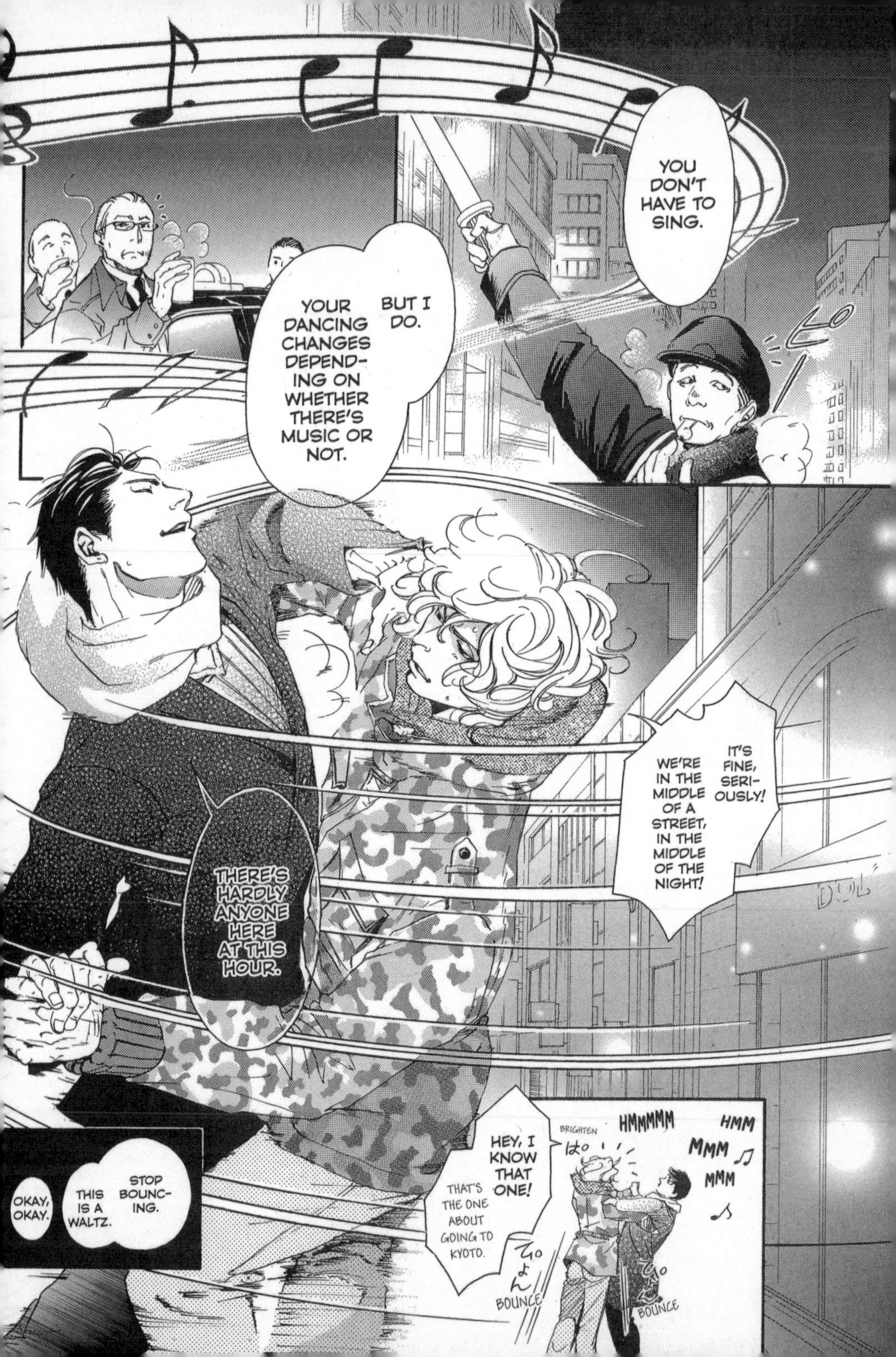
YOU DON'T HAVE TO SING.
BUT I DO.
YOUR DANCING CHANGES DEPENDING ON WHETHER THERE'S MUSIC OR NOT.
IT'S FINE, SERIOUSLY!
WE'RE IN THE MIDDLE OF A STREET, IN THE MIDDLE OF THE NIGHT!
THERE'S HARDLY ANYONE HERE AT THIS HOUR.
HMM MMM MMM
HMMMMM
BRIGHTEN
HEY, I KNOW THAT ONE!
THAT'S THE ONE ABOUT GOING TO KYOTO.
BOUNCE
BOUNCE
STOP BOUNCING.
THIS IS A WALTZ.
OKAY, OKAY.

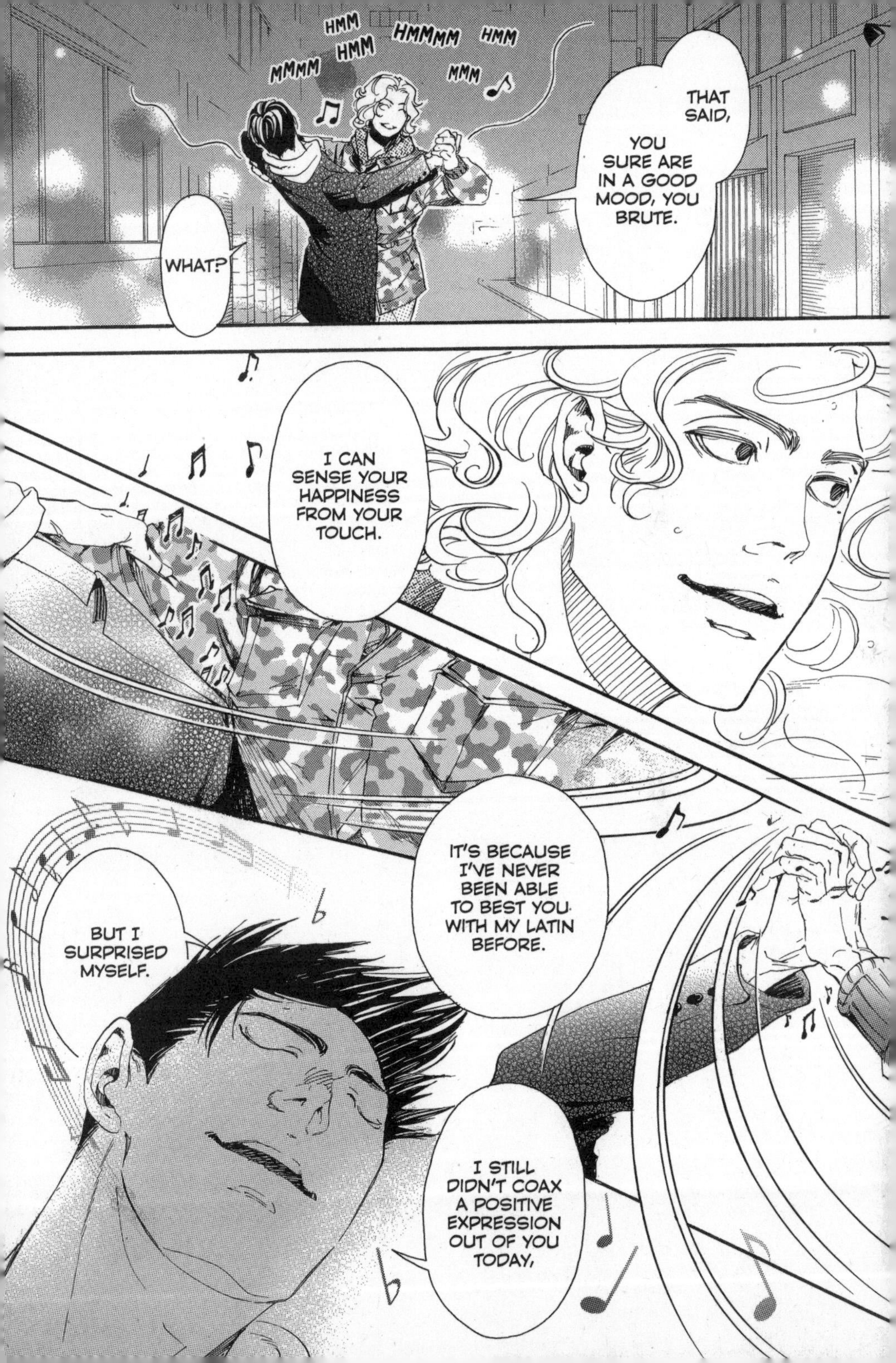
THAT SAID, YOU SURE ARE IN A GOOD MOOD, YOU BRUTE.
HMM HMMMM HMM
HMM HMM
MMMM MMM
WHAT?
I CAN SENSE YOUR HAPPINESS FROM YOUR TOUCH.
IT'S BECAUSE I'VE NEVER BEEN ABLE TO BEST YOU WITH MY LATIN BEFORE.
I STILL DIDN'T COAX A POSITIVE EXPRESSION OUT OF YOU TODAY,
BUT I SURPRISED MYSELF.

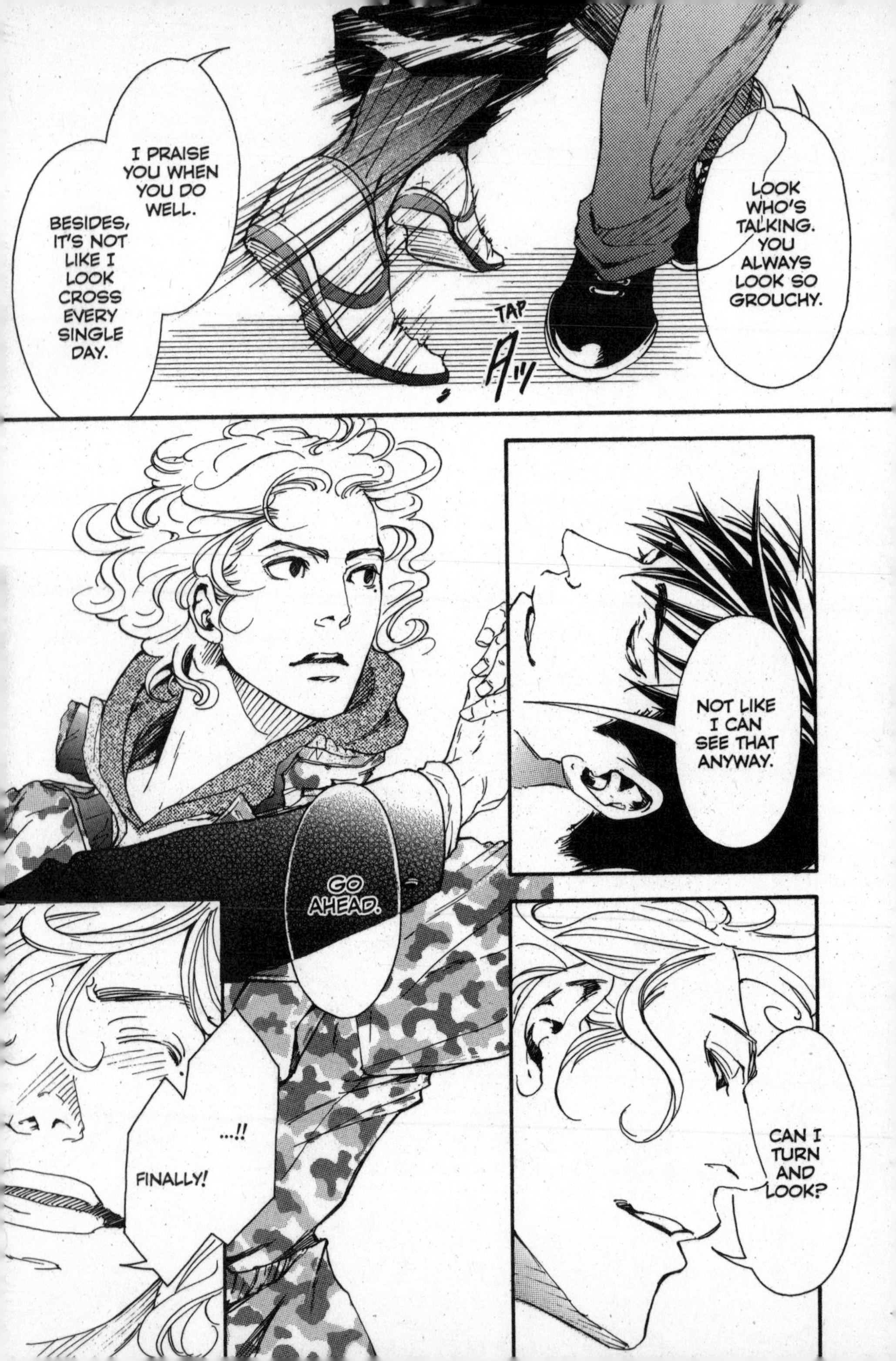
I PRAISE YOU WHEN YOU DO WELL.
BESIDES, IT'S NOT LIKE I LOOK CROSS EVERY SINGLE DAY.
LOOK WHO'S TALKING. YOU ALWAYS LOOK SO GROUCHY.
TAP
NOT LIKE I CAN SEE THAT ANYWAY.
CAN I TURN AND LOOK?
GO AHEAD.
...!!
FINALLY!

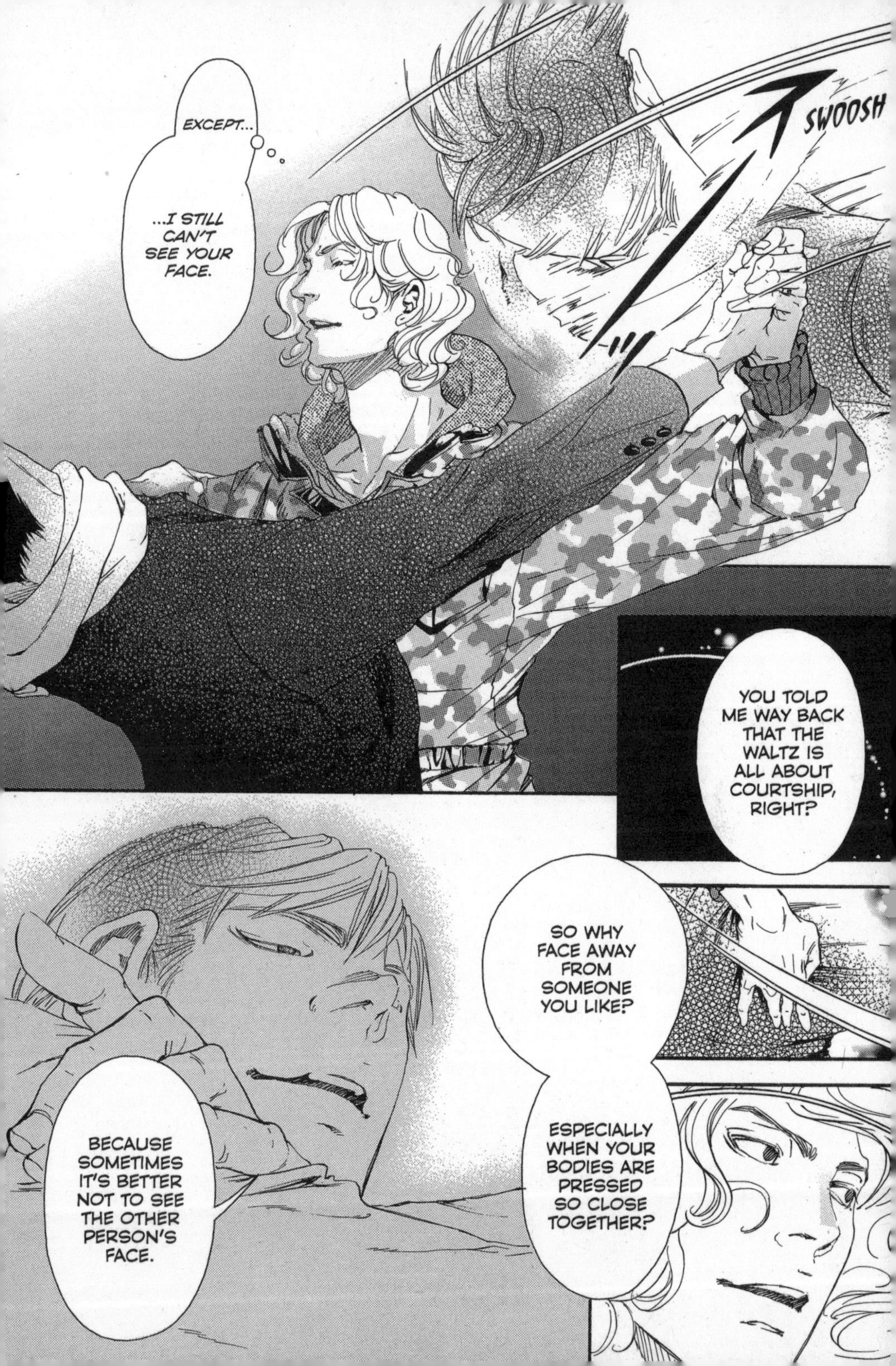
SWOOSH
EXCEPT...
...I STILL CAN'T SEE YOUR FACE.
YOU TOLD ME WAY BACK THAT THE WALTZ IS ALL ABOUT COURTSHIP, RIGHT?
SO WHY FACE AWAY FROM SOMEONE YOU LIKE?
ESPECIALLY WHEN YOUR BODIES ARE PRESSED SO CLOSE TOGETHER?
BECAUSE SOMETIMES IT'S BETTER NOT TO SEE THE OTHER PERSON'S FACE.

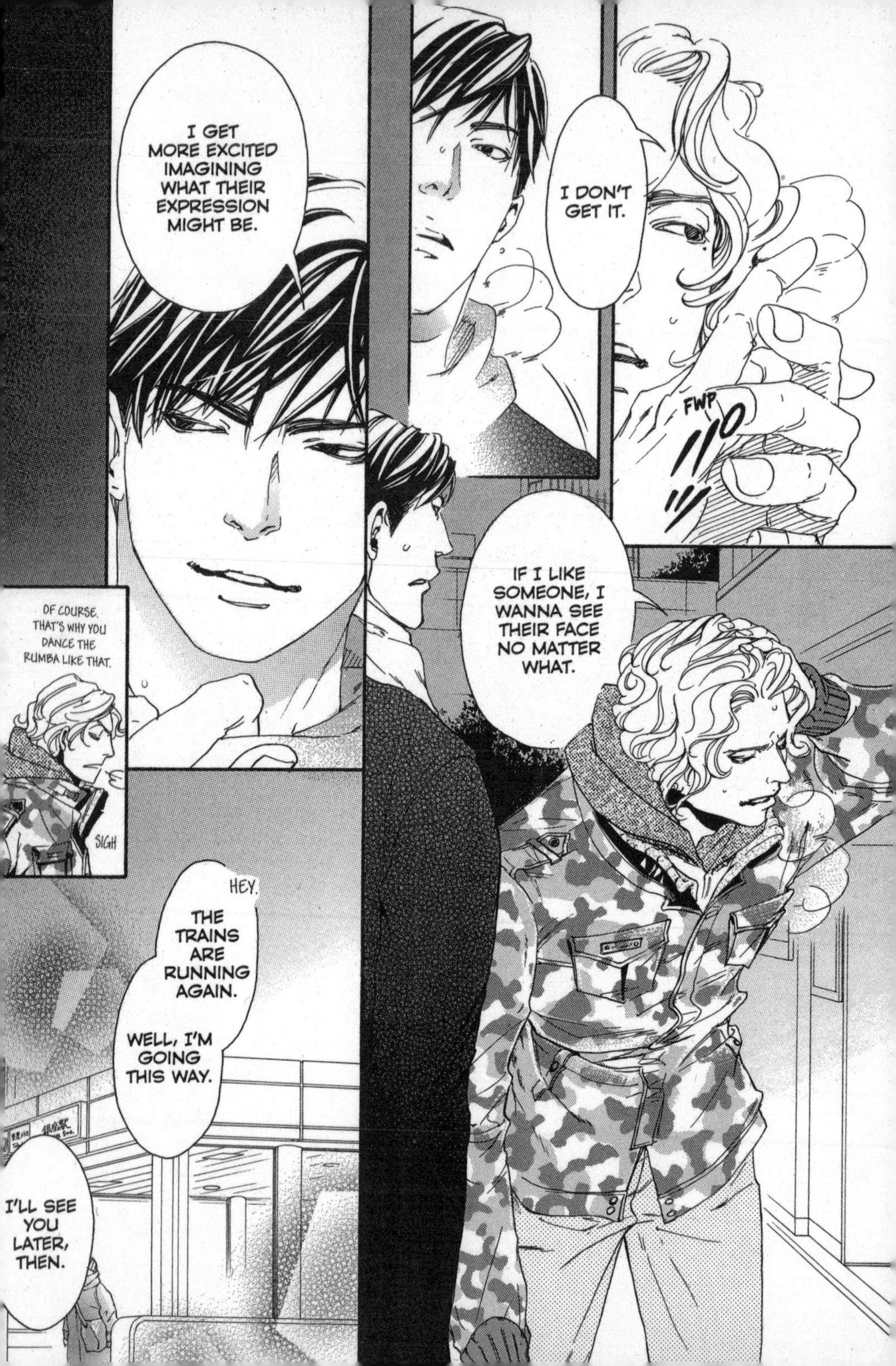
I GET MORE EXCITED IMAGINING WHAT THEIR EXPRESSION MIGHT BE.
I DON'T GET IT.
FWP
IF I LIKE SOMEONE, I WANNA SEE THEIR FACE NO MATTER WHAT.
OF COURSE. THAT'S WHY YOU DANCE THE RUMBA LIKE THAT.
SIGH
HEY.
THE TRAINS ARE RUNNING AGAIN.
WELL, I'M GOING THIS WAY.
I'LL SEE YOU LATER, THEN.

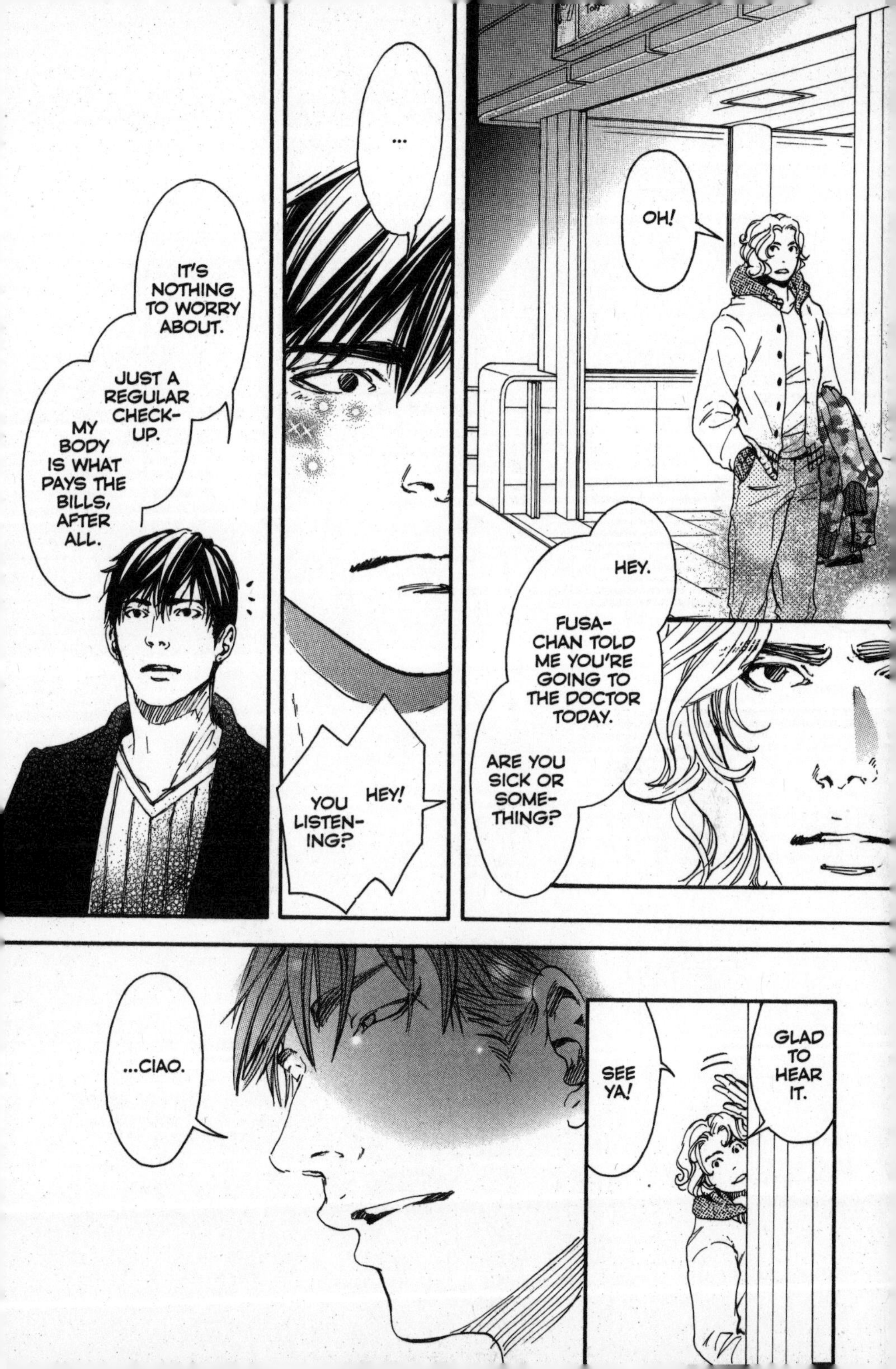
OH!
HEY.
FUSA-CHAN TOLD ME YOU'RE GOING TO THE DOCTOR TODAY.
ARE YOU SICK OR SOME-THING?
...
HEY!
YOU LISTEN-ING?
IT'S NOTHING TO WORRY ABOUT.
JUST A REGULAR CHECK-UP.
MY BODY IS WHAT PAYS THE BILLS, AFTER ALL.
GLAD TO HEAR IT.
SEE YA!
...CIAO.

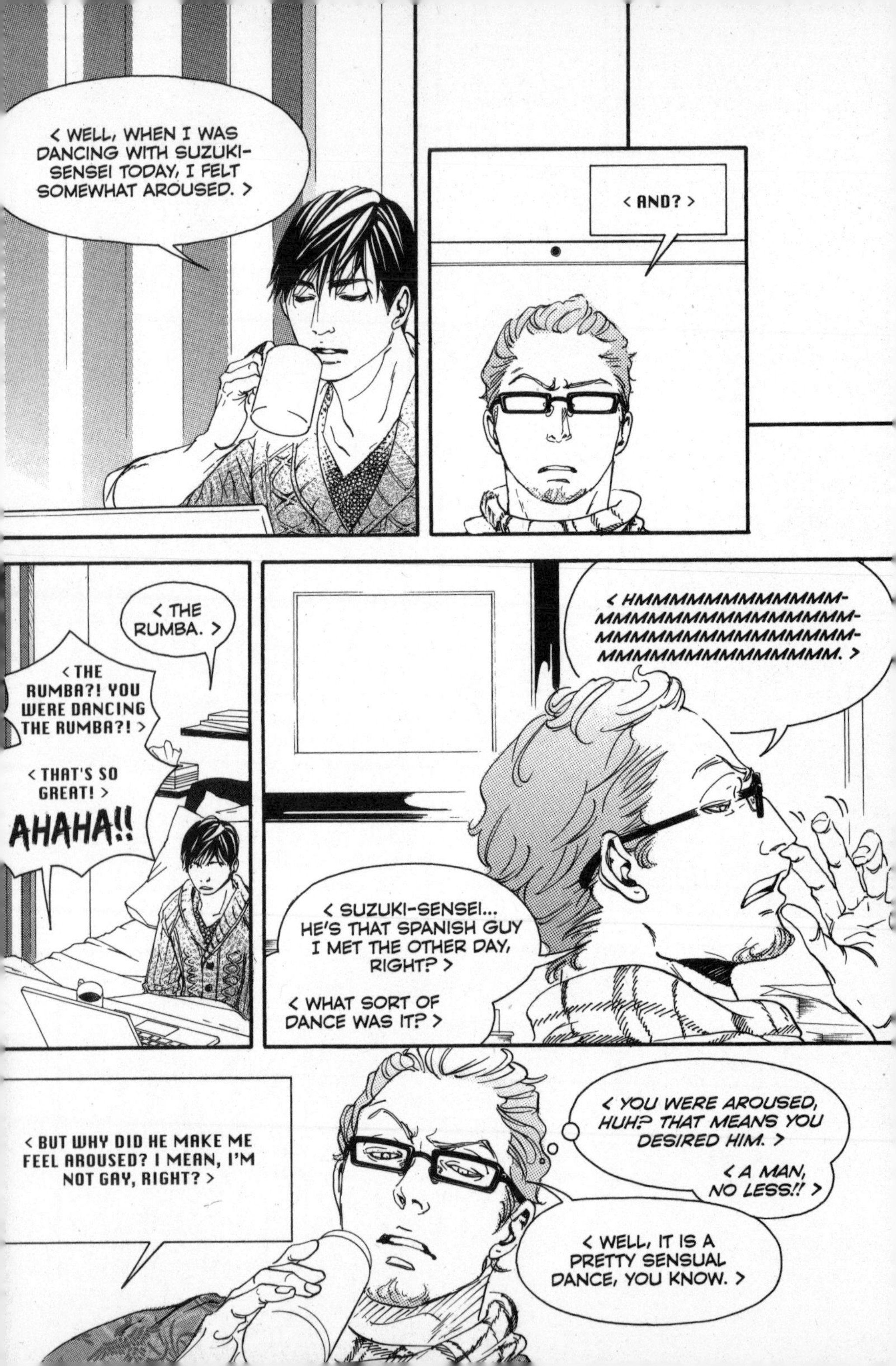

< AND? >
< WELL, WHEN I WAS DANCING WITH SUZUKI-SENSEI TODAY, I FELT SOMEWHAT AROUSED. >
< HMMMMMMMMMMMMMM-MMMMMMMMMMMMMMMMM-MMMMMMMMMMMMMMMMM-MMMMMMMMMMMMMMM. >
< SUZUKI-SENSEI... HE'S THAT SPANISH GUY I MET THE OTHER DAY, RIGHT? >
< WHAT SORT OF DANCE WAS IT? >
< THE RUMBA. >
< THE RUMBA?! YOU WERE DANCING THE RUMBA?! >
< THAT'S SO GREAT! >
AHAHA!!
< YOU WERE AROUSED, HUH? THAT MEANS YOU DESIRED HIM. >
< A MAN, NO LESS!! >
< BUT WHY DID HE MAKE ME FEEL AROUSED? I MEAN, I'M NOT GAY, RIGHT? >
< WELL, IT IS A PRETTY SENSUAL DANCE, YOU KNOW. >

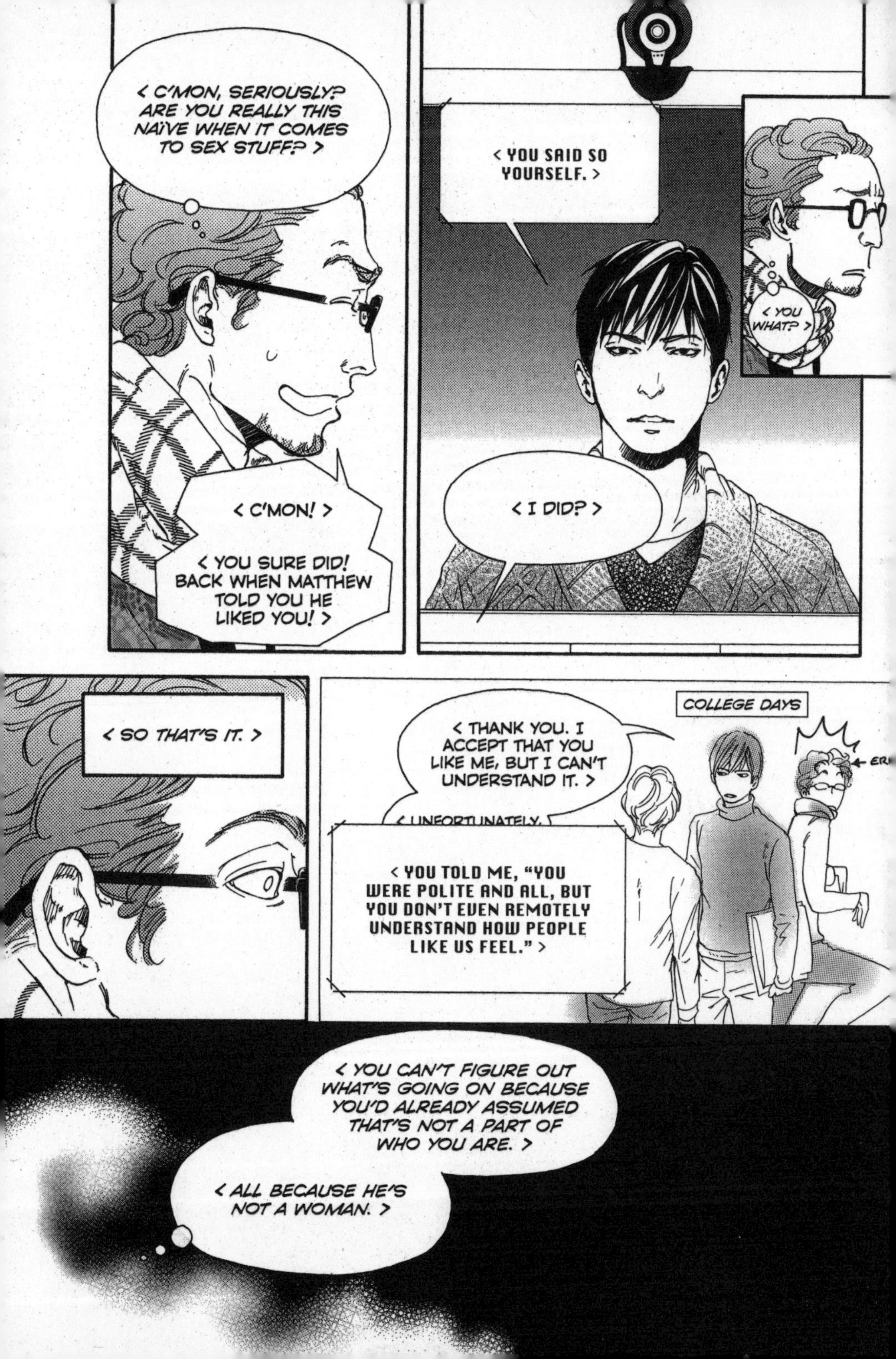
< YOU SAID SO YOURSELF. >
< YOU WHAT? >
< I DID? >
< C'MON, SERIOUSLY? ARE YOU REALLY THIS NAÏVE WHEN IT COMES TO SEX STUFF? >
< C'MON! >
< YOU SURE DID! BACK WHEN MATTHEW TOLD YOU HE LIKED YOU! >
COLLEGE DAYS
< THANK YOU. I ACCEPT THAT YOU LIKE ME, BUT I CAN'T UNDERSTAND IT. >
< UNFORTUNATELY,
< YOU TOLD ME, "YOU WERE POLITE AND ALL, BUT YOU DON'T EVEN REMOTELY UNDERSTAND HOW PEOPLE LIKE US FEEL." >
< SO THAT'S IT. >
< YOU CAN'T FIGURE OUT WHAT'S GOING ON BECAUSE YOU'D ALREADY ASSUMED THAT'S NOT A PART OF WHO YOU ARE. >
< ALL BECAUSE HE'S NOT A WOMAN. >

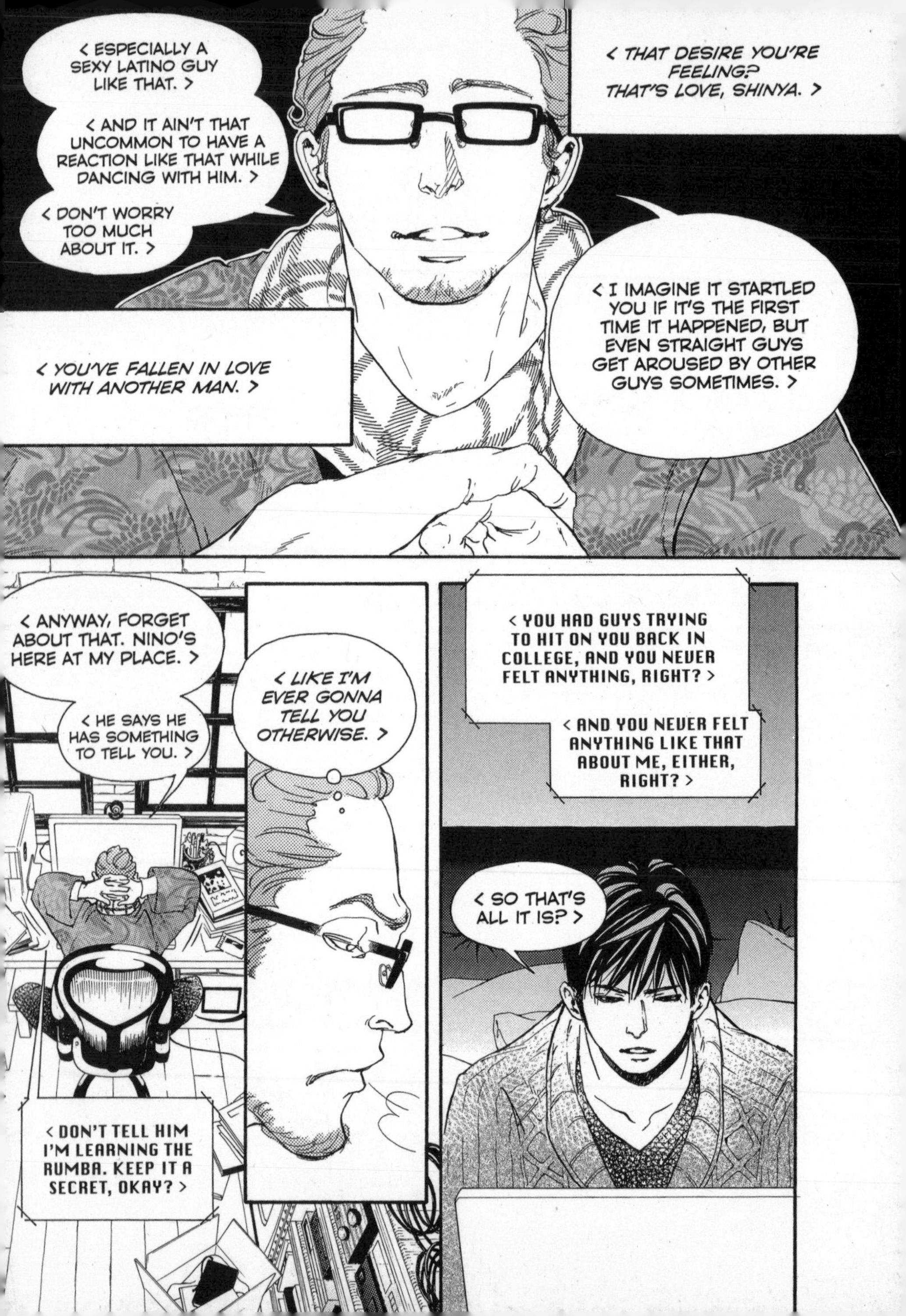
< THAT DESIRE YOU'RE FEELING? THAT'S LOVE, SHINYA. >
< ESPECIALLY A SEXY LATINO GUY LIKE THAT. >
< AND IT AIN'T THAT UNCOMMON TO HAVE A REACTION LIKE THAT WHILE DANCING WITH HIM. >
< DON'T WORRY TOO MUCH ABOUT IT. >
< I IMAGINE IT STARTLED YOU IF IT'S THE FIRST TIME IT HAPPENED, BUT EVEN STRAIGHT GUYS GET AROUSED BY OTHER GUYS SOMETIMES. >
< YOU'VE FALLEN IN LOVE WITH ANOTHER MAN. >
< YOU HAD GUYS TRYING TO HIT ON YOU BACK IN COLLEGE, AND YOU NEVER FELT ANYTHING, RIGHT? >
< AND YOU NEVER FELT ANYTHING LIKE THAT ABOUT ME, EITHER, RIGHT? >
< SO THAT'S ALL IT IS? >
< LIKE I'M EVER GONNA TELL YOU OTHERWISE. >
< ANYWAY, FORGET ABOUT THAT. NINO'S HERE AT MY PLACE. >
< HE SAYS HE HAS SOMETHING TO TELL YOU. >
< DON'T TELL HIM I'M LEARNING THE RUMBA. KEEP IT A SECRET, OKAY? >

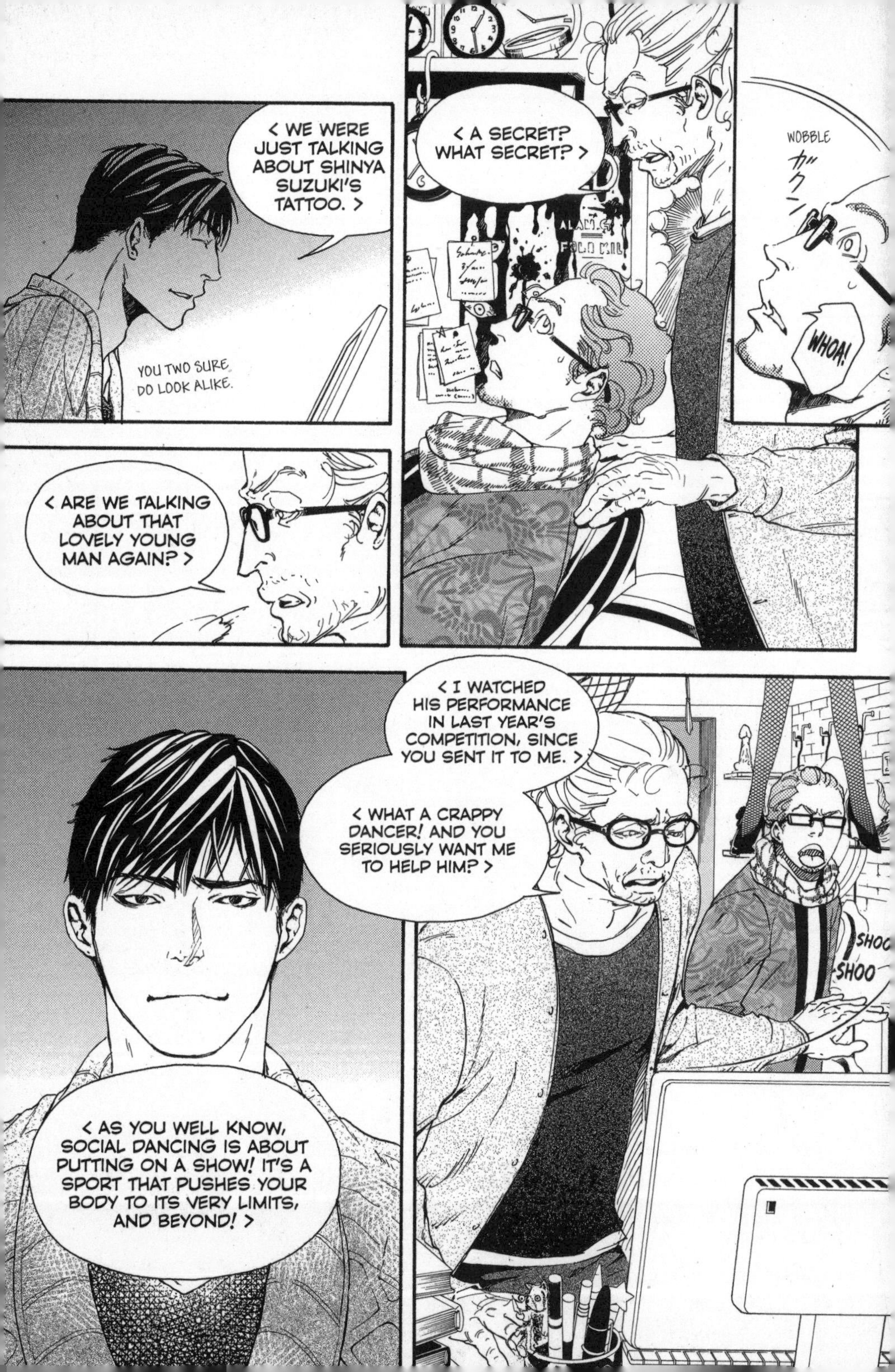
WOBBLE
ガクン
WHOA!
< A SECRET? WHAT SECRET? >
< WE WERE JUST TALKING ABOUT SHINYA SUZUKI'S TATTOO. >
YOU TWO SURE DO LOOK ALIKE.
< ARE WE TALKING ABOUT THAT LOVELY YOUNG MAN AGAIN? >
< I WATCHED HIS PERFORMANCE IN LAST YEAR'S COMPETITION, SINCE YOU SENT IT TO ME. >
< WHAT A CRAPPY DANCER! AND YOU SERIOUSLY WANT ME TO HELP HIM? >
SHOO
SHOO
< AS YOU WELL KNOW, SOCIAL DANCING IS ABOUT PUTTING ON A SHOW! IT'S A SPORT THAT PUSHES YOUR BODY TO ITS VERY LIMITS, AND BEYOND! >

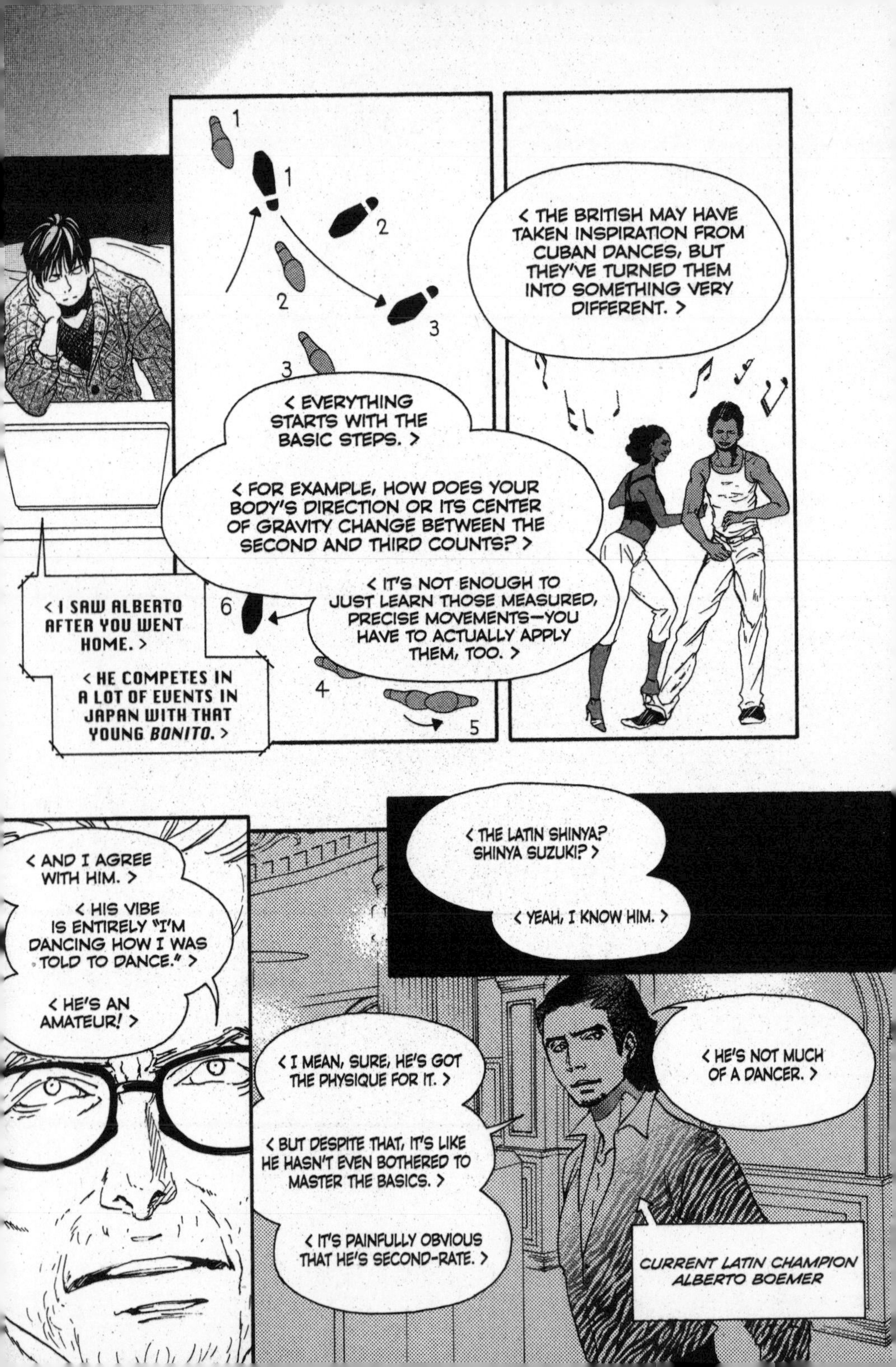
< THE BRITISH MAY HAVE TAKEN INSPIRATION FROM CUBAN DANCES, BUT THEY'VE TURNED THEM INTO SOMETHING VERY DIFFERENT. >
< EVERYTHING STARTS WITH THE BASIC STEPS. >
< FOR EXAMPLE, HOW DOES YOUR BODY'S DIRECTION OR ITS CENTER OF GRAVITY CHANGE BETWEEN THE SECOND AND THIRD COUNTS? >
< IT'S NOT ENOUGH TO JUST LEARN THOSE MEASURED, PRECISE MOVEMENTS—YOU HAVE TO ACTUALLY APPLY THEM, TOO. >
< I SAW ALBERTO AFTER YOU WENT HOME. >
< HE COMPETES IN A LOT OF EVENTS IN JAPAN WITH THAT YOUNG *BONITO*. >
< THE LATIN SHINYA? SHINYA SUZUKI? >
< YEAH, I KNOW HIM. >
< HE'S NOT MUCH OF A DANCER. >
< I MEAN, SURE, HE'S GOT THE PHYSIQUE FOR IT. >
< BUT DESPITE THAT, IT'S LIKE HE HASN'T EVEN BOTHERED TO MASTER THE BASICS. >
< IT'S PAINFULLY OBVIOUS THAT HE'S SECOND-RATE. >
CURRENT LATIN CHAMPION ALBERTO BOEMER
< AND I AGREE WITH HIM. >
< HIS VIBE IS ENTIRELY "I'M DANCING HOW I WAS TOLD TO DANCE." >
< HE'S AN AMATEUR! >

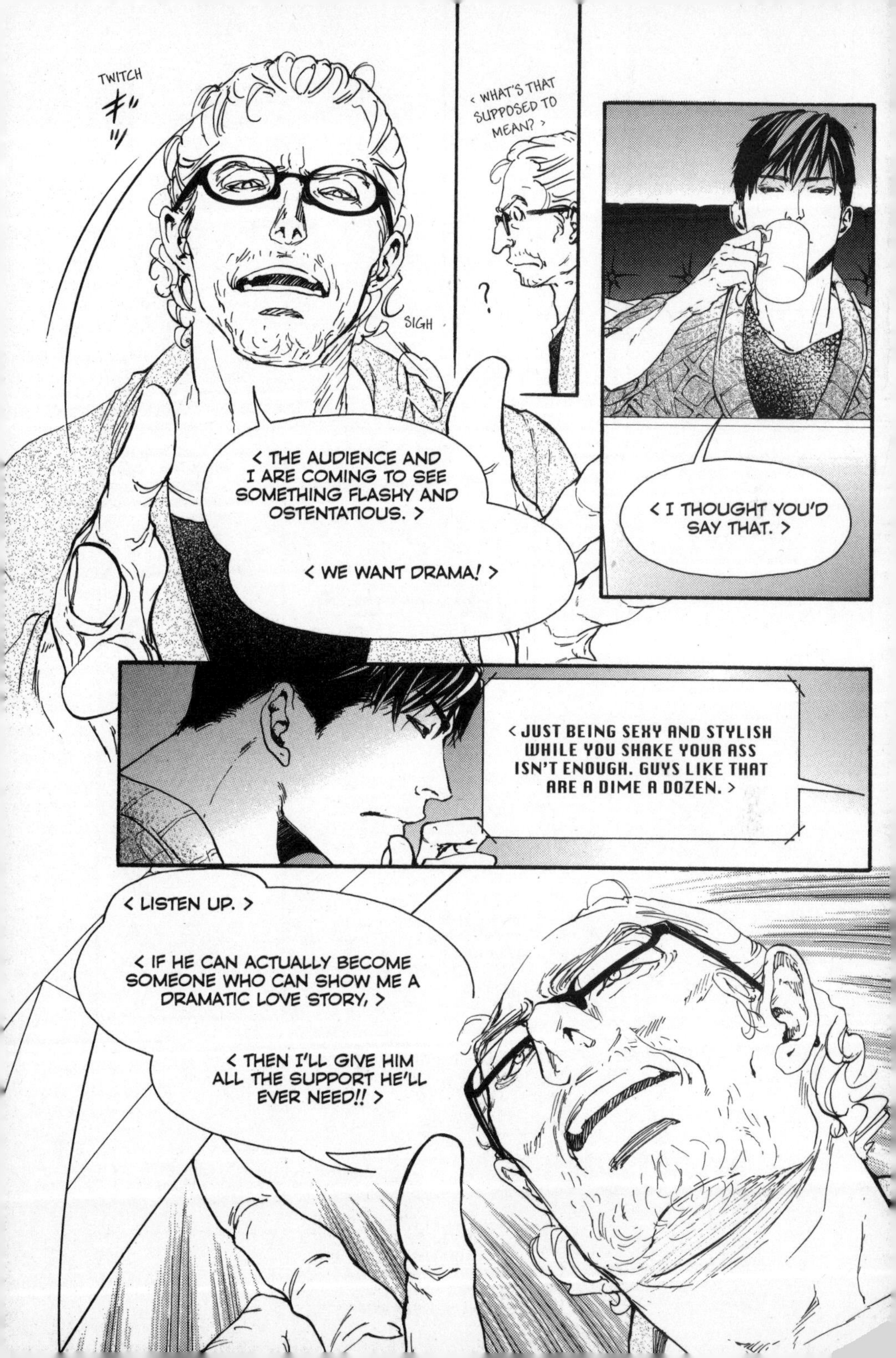
< I THOUGHT YOU'D SAY THAT. >
< WHAT'S THAT SUPPOSED TO MEAN? >
?
TWITCH
ギッ
SIGH
< THE AUDIENCE AND I ARE COMING TO SEE SOMETHING FLASHY AND OSTENTATIOUS. >
< WE WANT DRAMA! >
< JUST BEING SEXY AND STYLISH WHILE YOU SHAKE YOUR ASS ISN'T ENOUGH. GUYS LIKE THAT ARE A DIME A DOZEN. >
< LISTEN UP. >
< IF HE CAN ACTUALLY BECOME SOMEONE WHO CAN SHOW ME A DRAMATIC LOVE STORY, >
< THEN I'LL GIVE HIM ALL THE SUPPORT HE'LL EVER NEED!! >

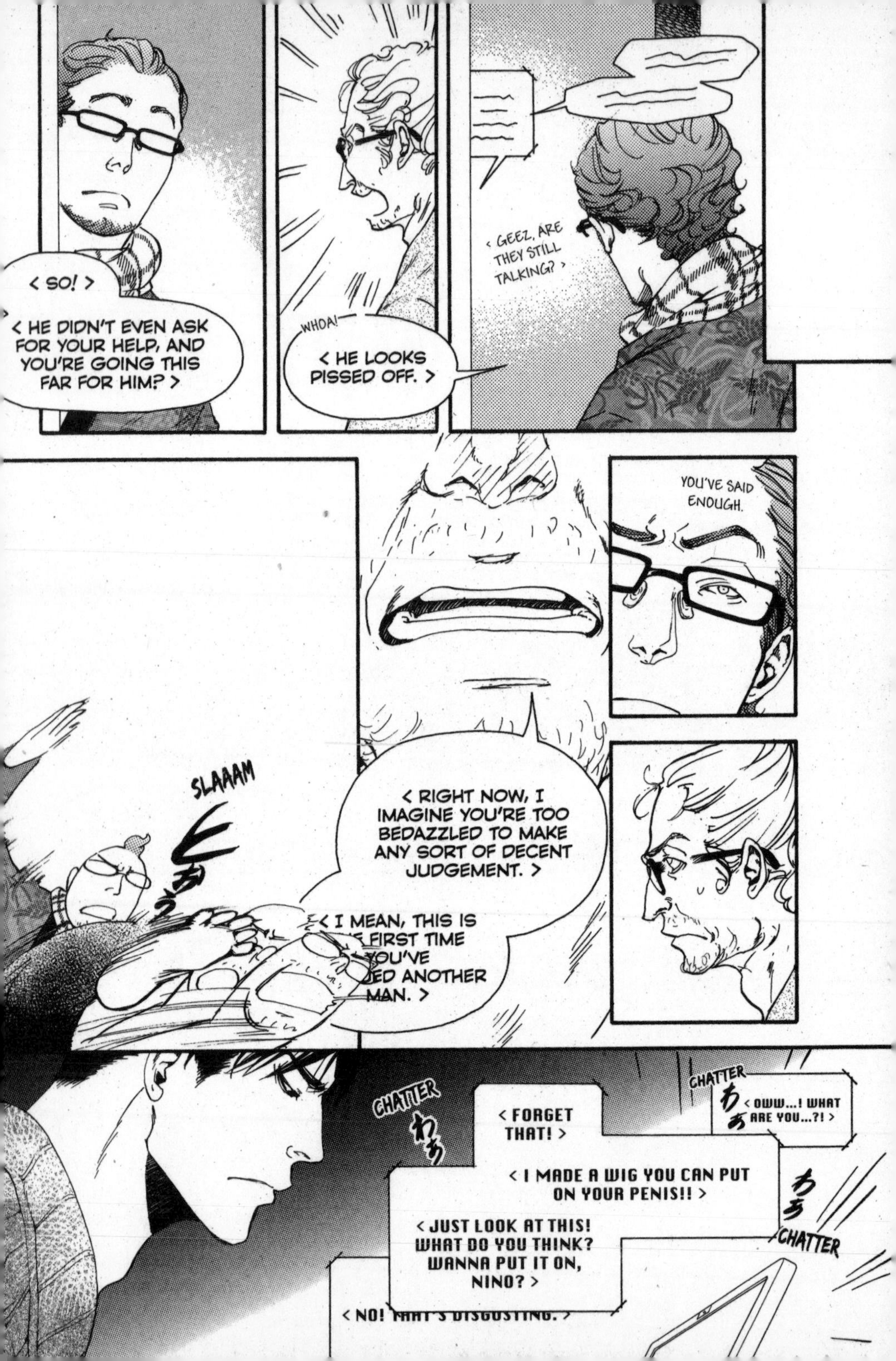

< GEEZ, ARE THEY STILL TALKING? >
WHOA!
< HE LOOKS PISSED OFF. >
< SO! >
< HE DIDN'T EVEN ASK FOR YOUR HELP, AND YOU'RE GOING THIS FAR FOR HIM? >
YOU'VE SAID ENOUGH.
< RIGHT NOW, I IMAGINE YOU'RE TOO BEDAZZLED TO MAKE ANY SORT OF DECENT JUDGEMENT. >
< I MEAN, THIS IS FIRST TIME YOU'VE ED ANOTHER MAN. >
SLAAAM
CHATTER
あ あ
< OWW...! WHAT ARE YOU...?! >
わ ち
CHATTER
< FORGET THAT! >
< I MADE A WIG YOU CAN PUT ON YOUR PENIS!! >
< JUST LOOK AT THIS! WHAT DO YOU THINK? WANNA PUT IT ON, NINO? >
< NO! THAT'S DISGUSTING. >
CHATTER
わあ

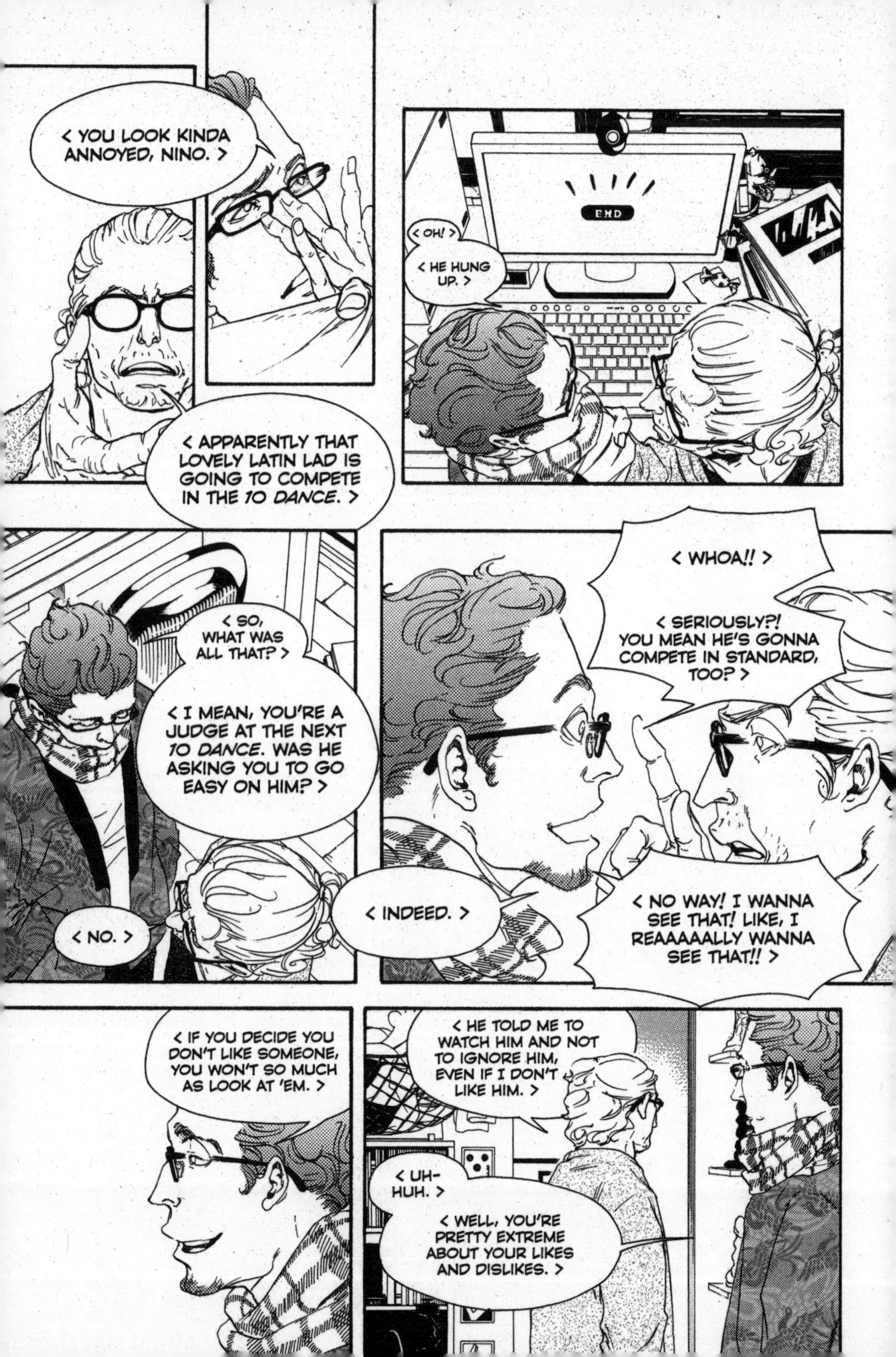
END
< OH! >
< HE HUNG UP. >
< YOU LOOK KINDA ANNOYED, NINO. >
< APPARENTLY THAT LOVELY LATIN LAD IS GOING TO COMPETE IN THE *10 DANCE*. >
< WHOA!! >
< SERIOUSLY?! YOU MEAN HE'S GONNA COMPETE IN STANDARD, TOO? >
< INDEED. >
< NO WAY! I WANNA SEE THAT! LIKE, I REAAAAALLY WANNA SEE THAT!! >
< SO, WHAT WAS ALL THAT? >
< I MEAN, YOU'RE A JUDGE AT THE NEXT *10 DANCE*. WAS HE ASKING YOU TO GO EASY ON HIM? >
< NO. >
< HE TOLD ME TO WATCH HIM AND NOT TO IGNORE HIM, EVEN IF I DON'T LIKE HIM. >
< UH-HUH. >
< WELL, YOU'RE PRETTY EXTREME ABOUT YOUR LIKES AND DISLIKES. >
< IF YOU DECIDE YOU DON'T LIKE SOMEONE, YOU WON'T SO MUCH AS LOOK AT 'EM. >

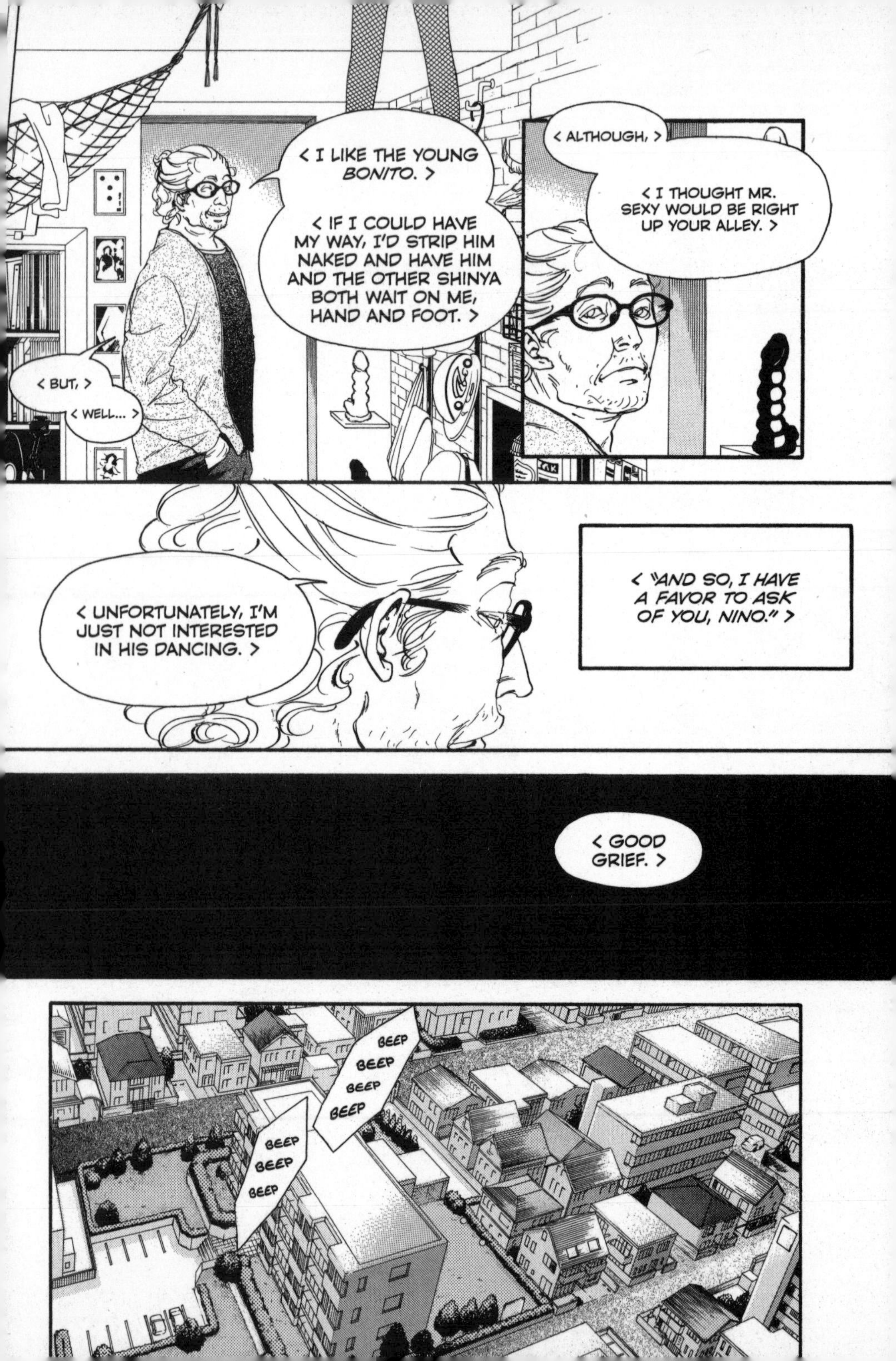
< ALTHOUGH, >
< I THOUGHT MR. SEXY WOULD BE RIGHT UP YOUR ALLEY. >
< I LIKE THE YOUNG *BONITO*. >
< IF I COULD HAVE MY WAY, I'D STRIP HIM NAKED AND HAVE HIM AND THE OTHER SHINYA BOTH WAIT ON ME, HAND AND FOOT. >
< BUT, >
< WELL... >
< *"AND SO, I HAVE A FAVOR TO ASK OF YOU, NINO."* >
< UNFORTUNATELY, I'M JUST NOT INTERESTED IN HIS DANCING. >
< GOOD GRIEF. >
BEEP BEEP BEEP BEEP
BEEP BEEP BEEP

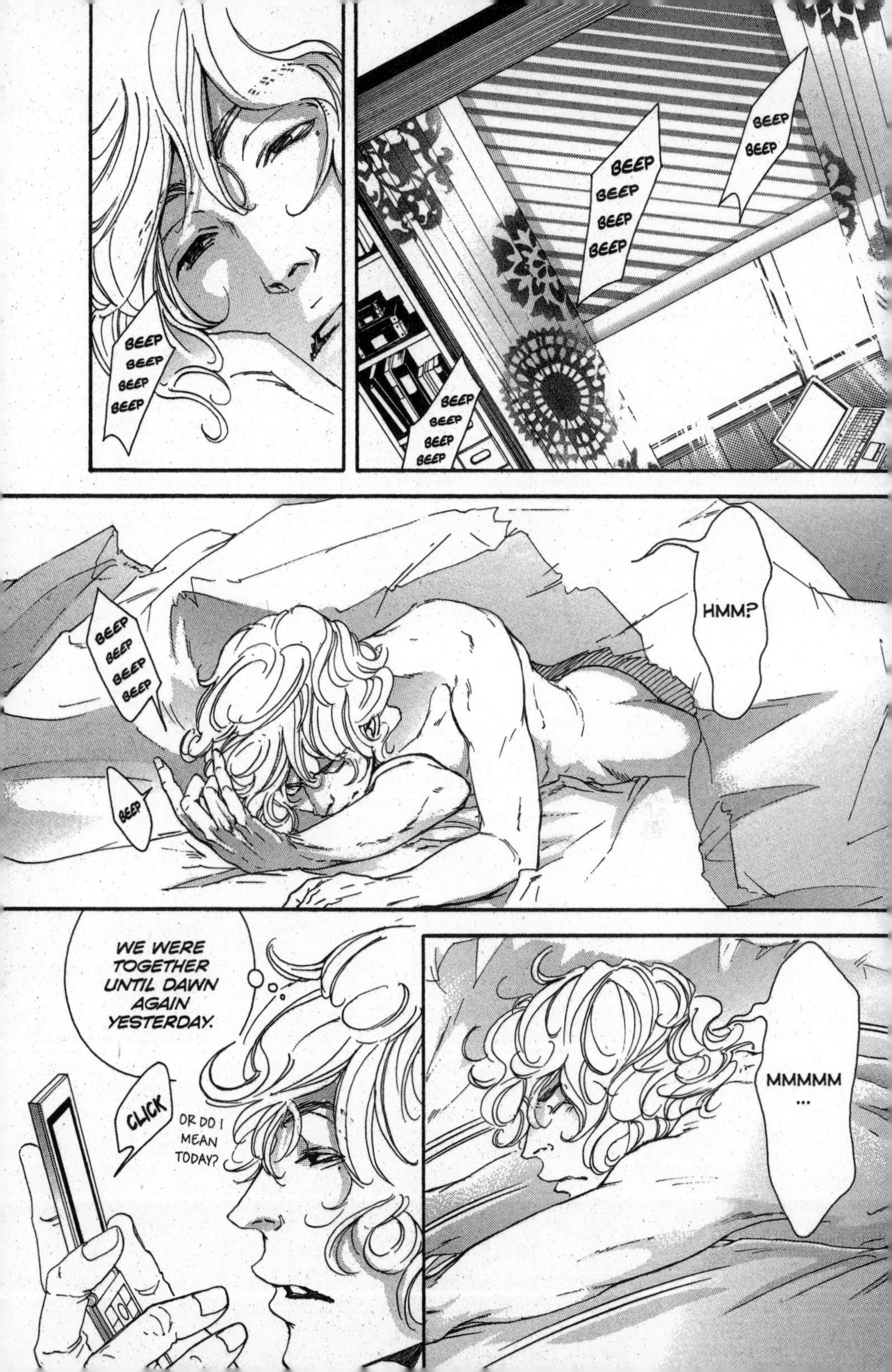
BEEP BEEP
BEEP BEEP BEEP BEEP
BEEP BEEP BEEP BEEP
BEEP BEEP BEEP BEEP
HMM?
BEEP BEEP BEEP BEEP
BEEP
MMMMM ...
WE WERE TOGETHER UNTIL DAWN AGAIN YESTERDAY.
CLICK
OR DO I MEAN TODAY?

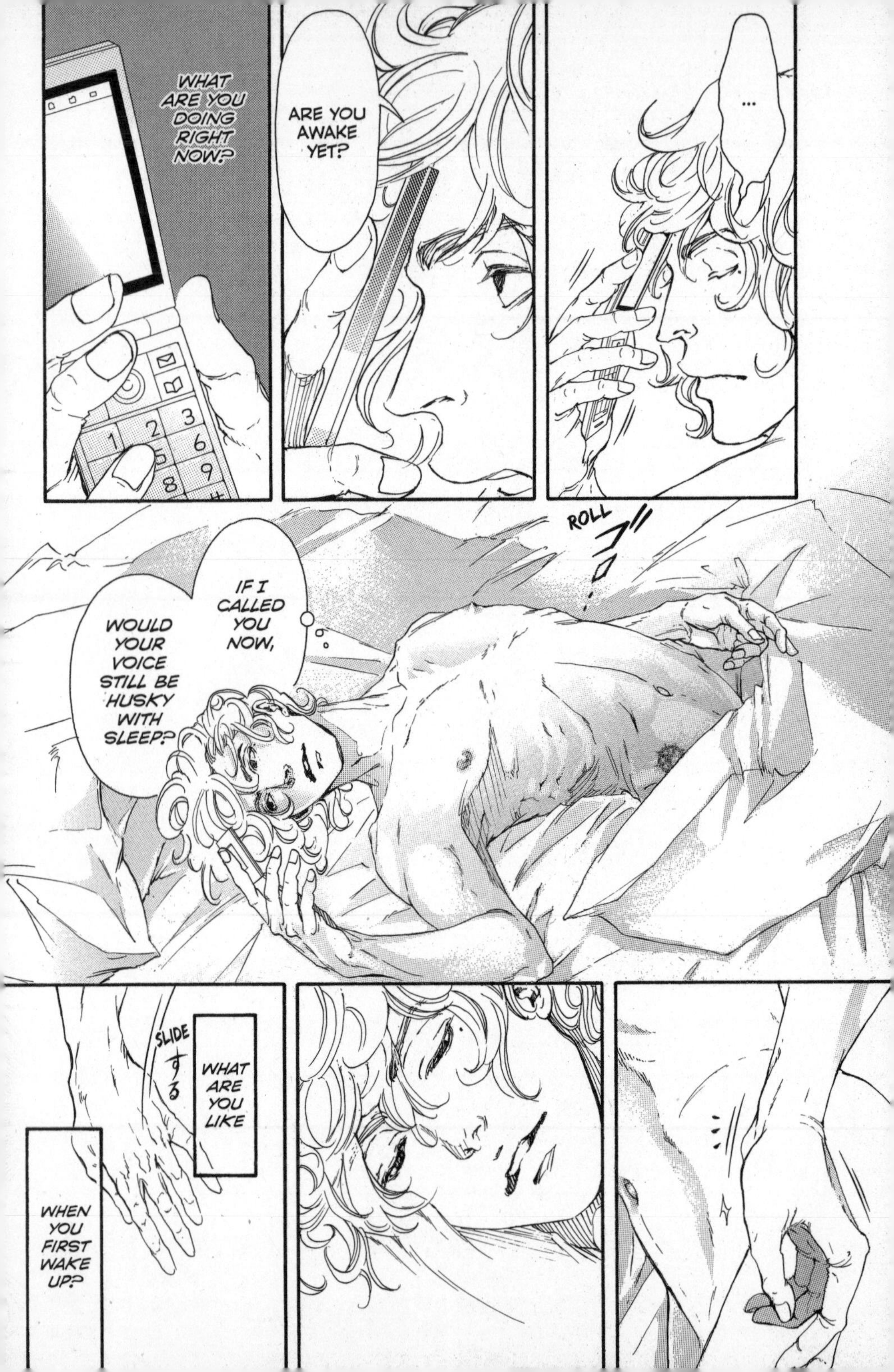
...
ARE YOU AWAKE YET?
WHAT ARE YOU DOING RIGHT NOW?
ROLL
IF I CALLED YOU NOW,
WOULD YOUR VOICE STILL BE HUSKY WITH SLEEP?
SLIDE
WHAT ARE YOU LIKE
WHEN YOU FIRST WAKE UP?

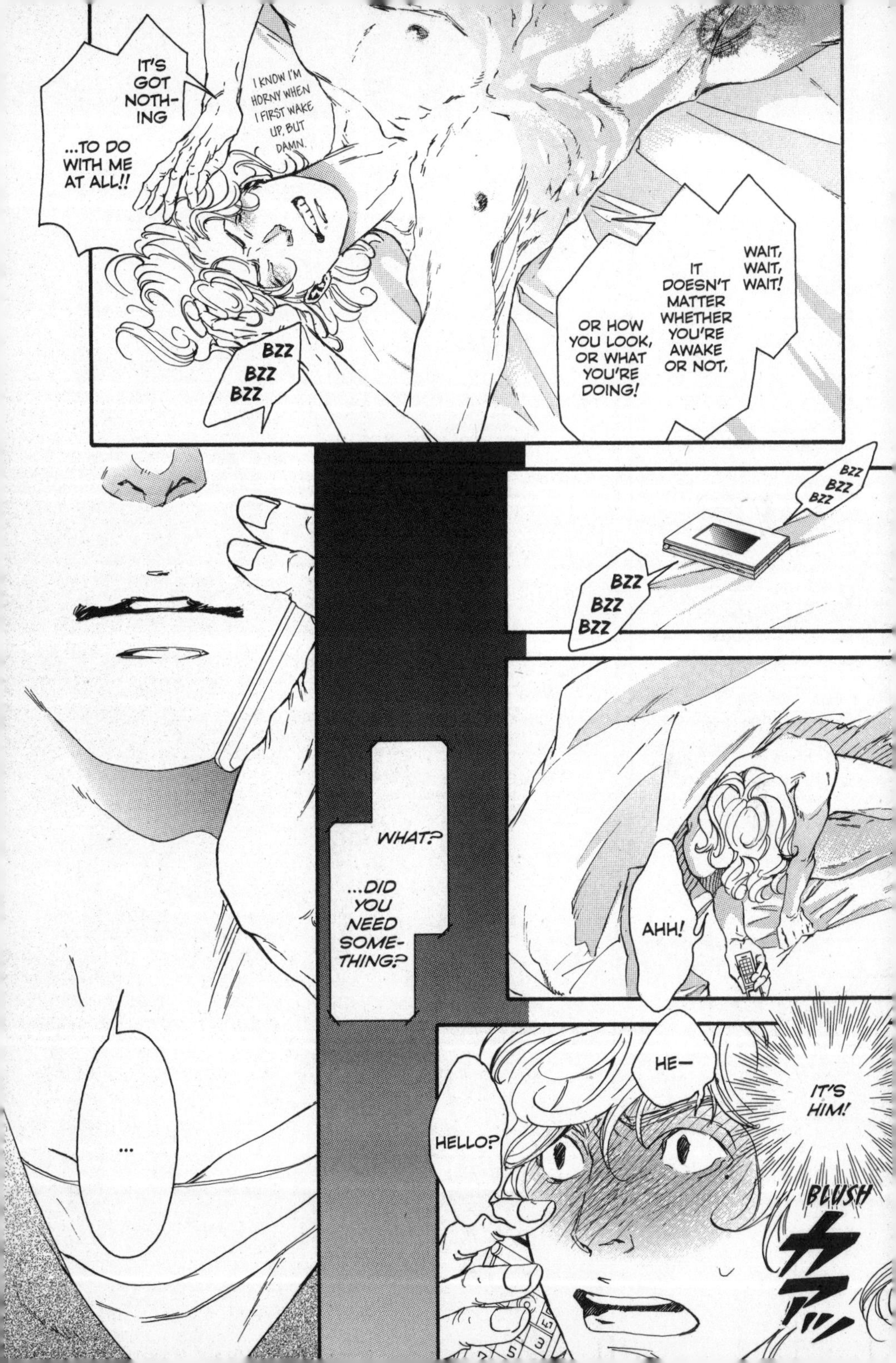
WAIT, WAIT, WAIT!
IT DOESN'T MATTER WHETHER YOU'RE AWAKE OR NOT,
OR HOW YOU LOOK, OR WHAT YOU'RE DOING!
BZZ BZZ BZZ
I KNOW I'M HORNY WHEN I FIRST WAKE UP, BUT DAMN.
IT'S GOT NOTHING
...TO DO WITH ME AT ALL!!
BZZ BZZ BZZ
BZZ BZZ BZZ
AHH!
HE—
IT'S HIM!
BLUSH
HELLO?
WHAT?
...DID YOU NEED SOMETHING?
...

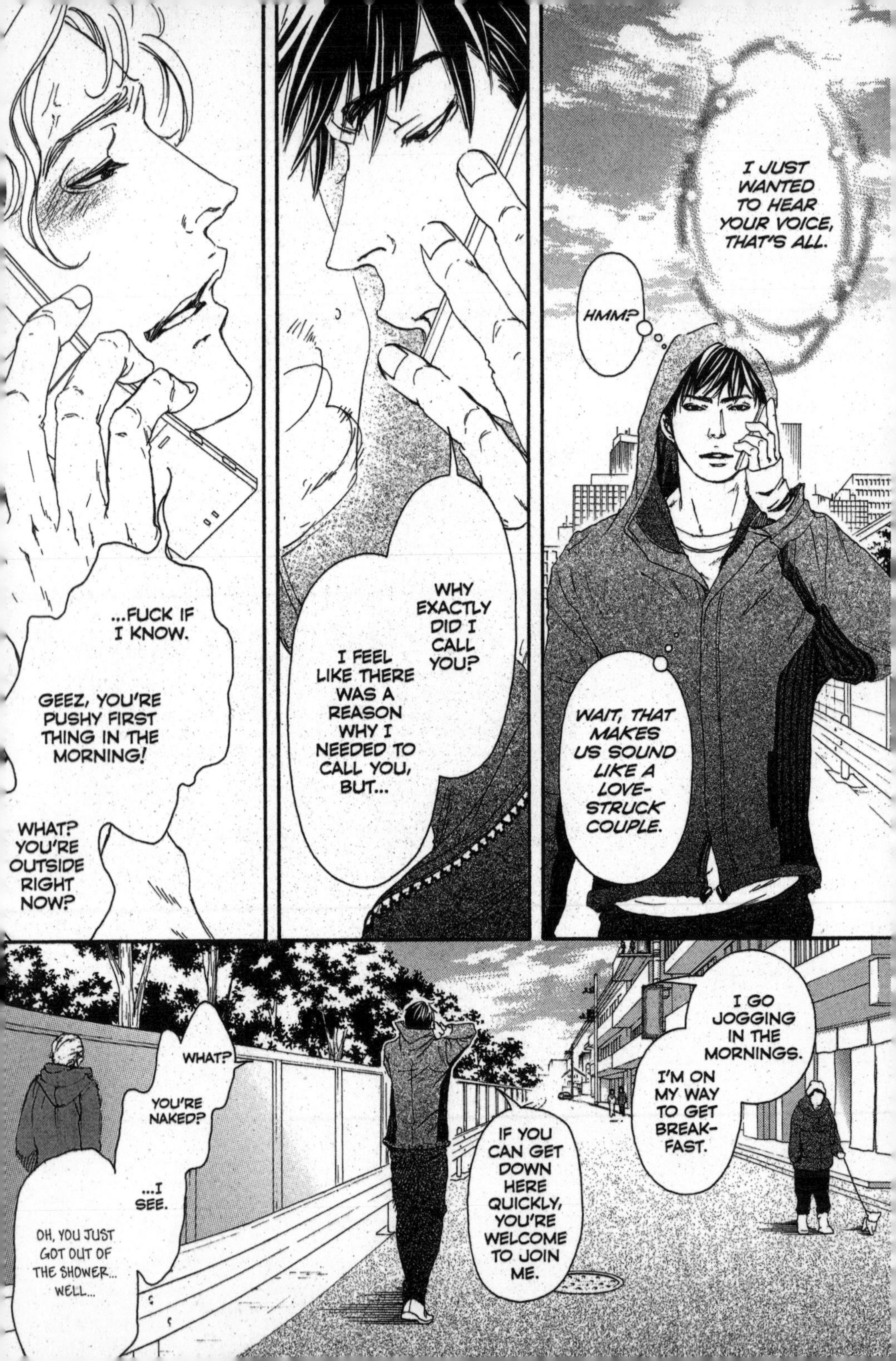
I JUST WANTED TO HEAR YOUR VOICE, THAT'S ALL.
HMM?
WAIT, THAT MAKES US SOUND LIKE A LOVE-STRUCK COUPLE.
WHY EXACTLY DID I CALL YOU?
I FEEL LIKE THERE WAS A REASON WHY I NEEDED TO CALL YOU, BUT...
...FUCK IF I KNOW.
GEEZ, YOU'RE PUSHY FIRST THING IN THE MORNING!
WHAT? YOU'RE OUTSIDE RIGHT NOW?
I GO JOGGING IN THE MORNINGS.
I'M ON MY WAY TO GET BREAK-FAST.
IF YOU CAN GET DOWN HERE QUICKLY, YOU'RE WELCOME TO JOIN ME.
WHAT?
YOU'RE NAKED?
...I SEE.
OH, YOU JUST GOT OUT OF THE SHOWER... WELL...

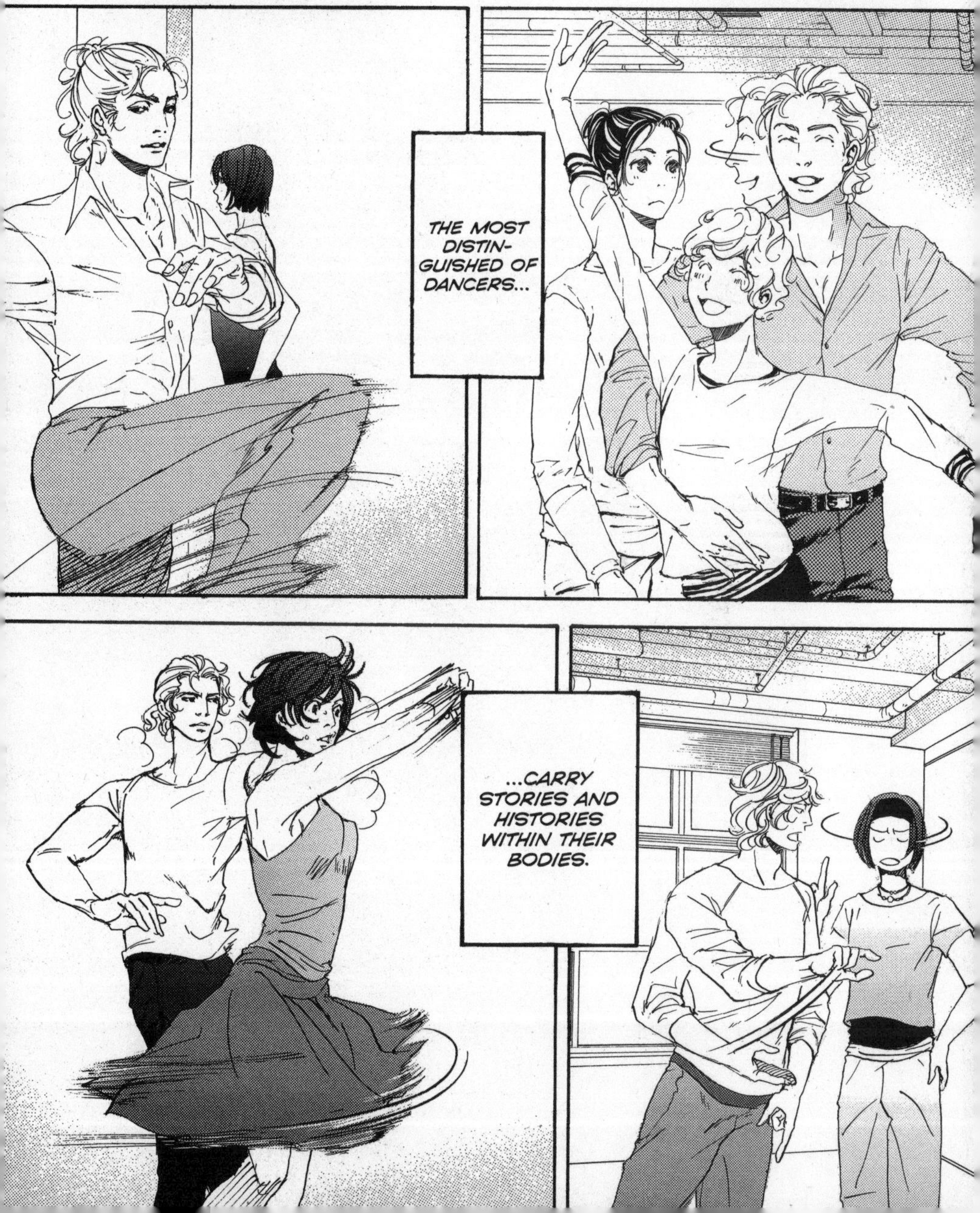
THE MOST DISTIN- GUISHED OF DANCERS...
...CARRY STORIES AND HISTORIES WITHIN THEIR BODIES.

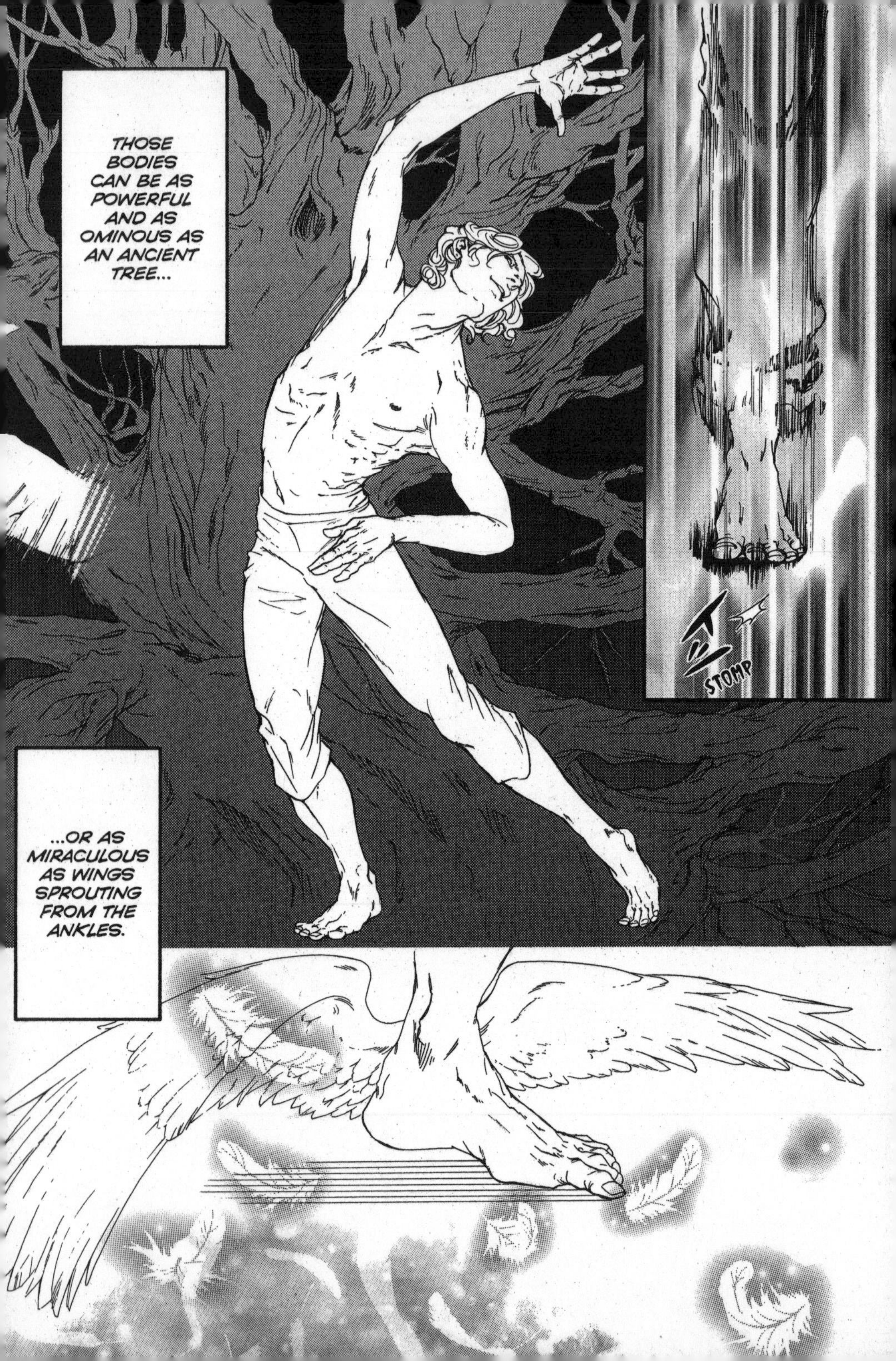
STOMP
THOSE BODIES CAN BE AS POWERFUL AND AS OMINOUS AS AN ANCIENT TREE...
...OR AS MIRACULOUS AS WINGS SPROUTING FROM THE ANKLES.

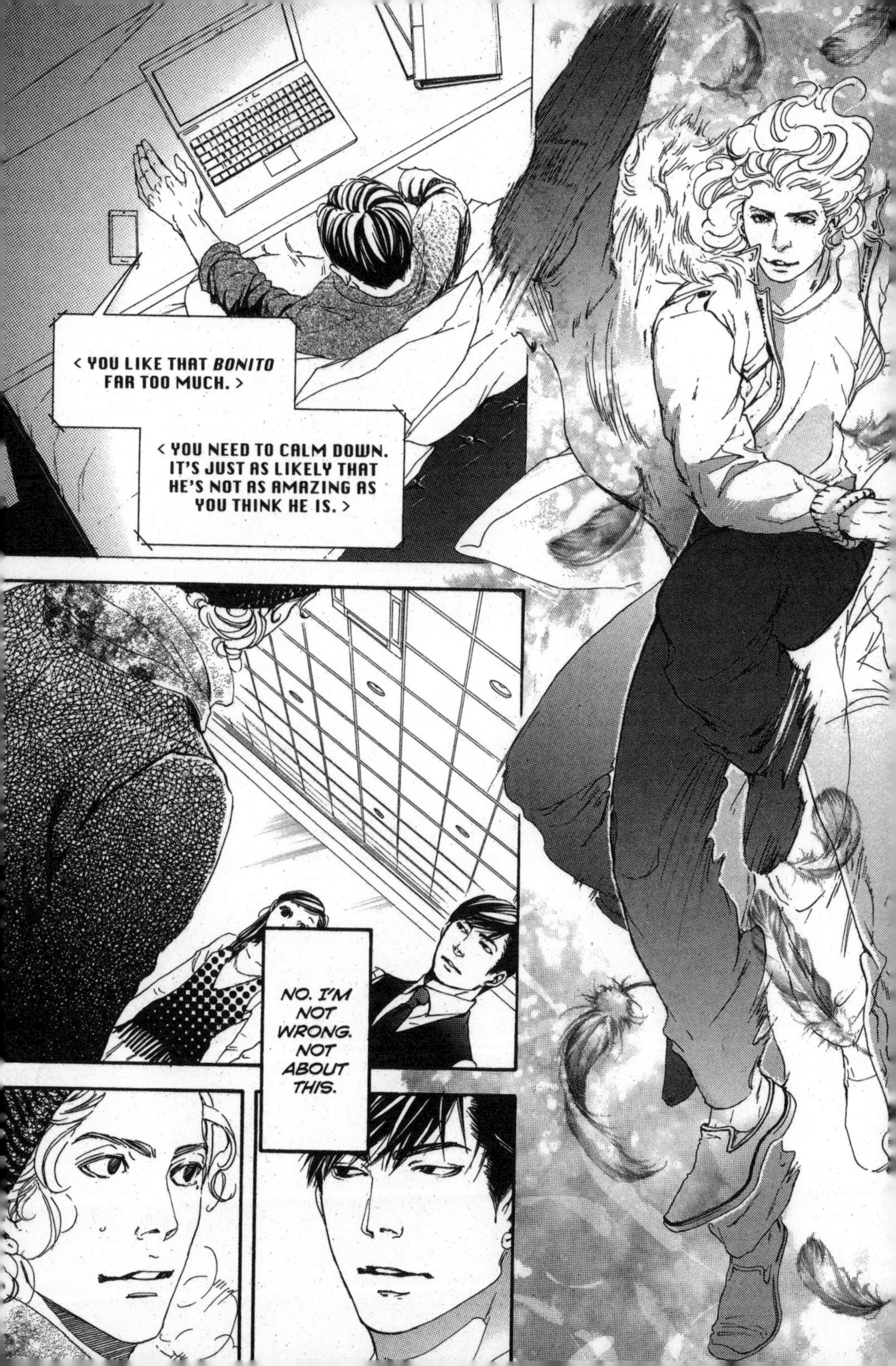
< YOU LIKE THAT *BONITO* FAR TOO MUCH. >
< YOU NEED TO CALM DOWN. IT'S JUST AS LIKELY THAT HE'S NOT AS AMAZING AS YOU THINK HE IS. >
NO. I'M NOT WRONG. NOT ABOUT THIS.

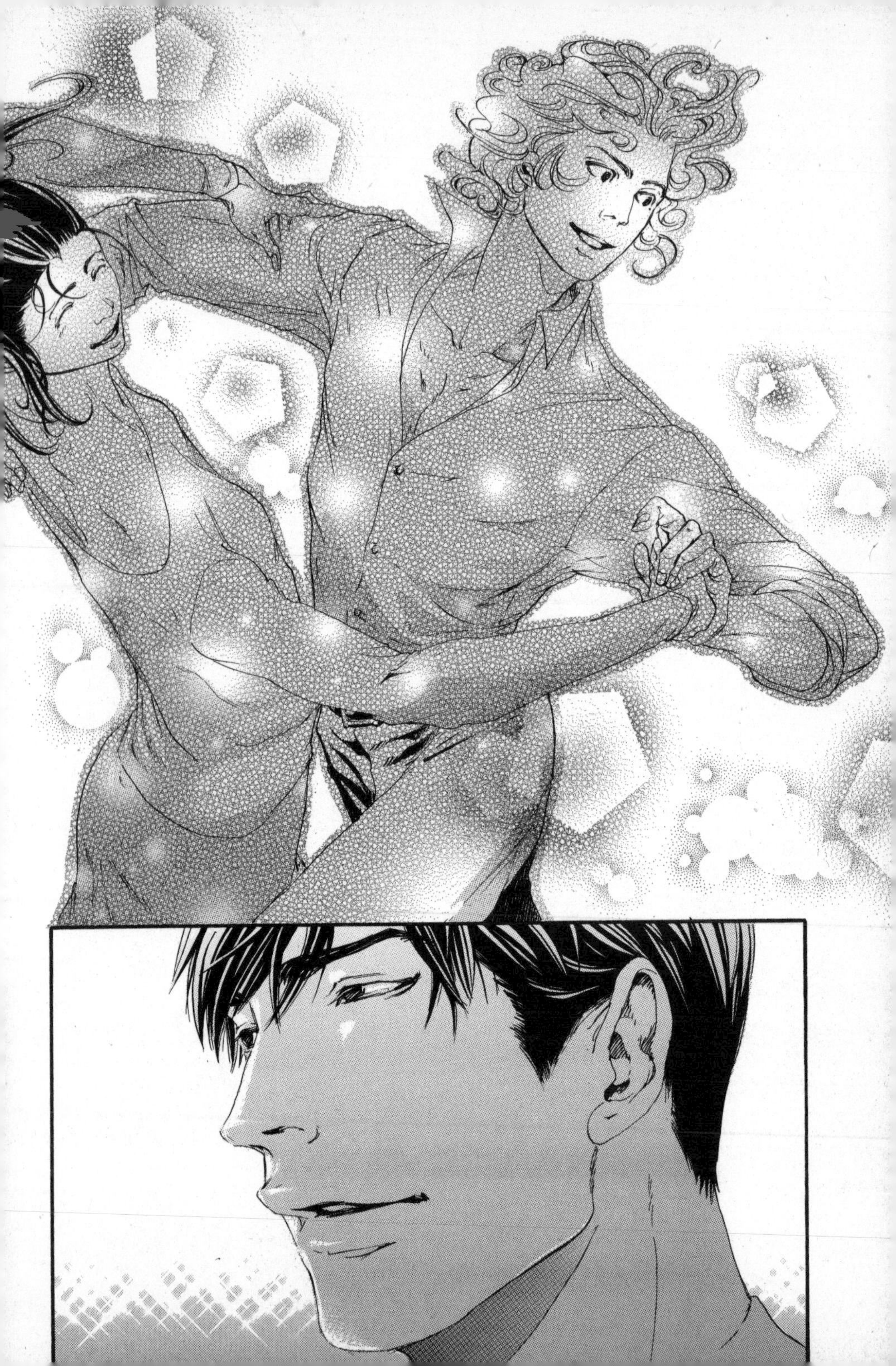

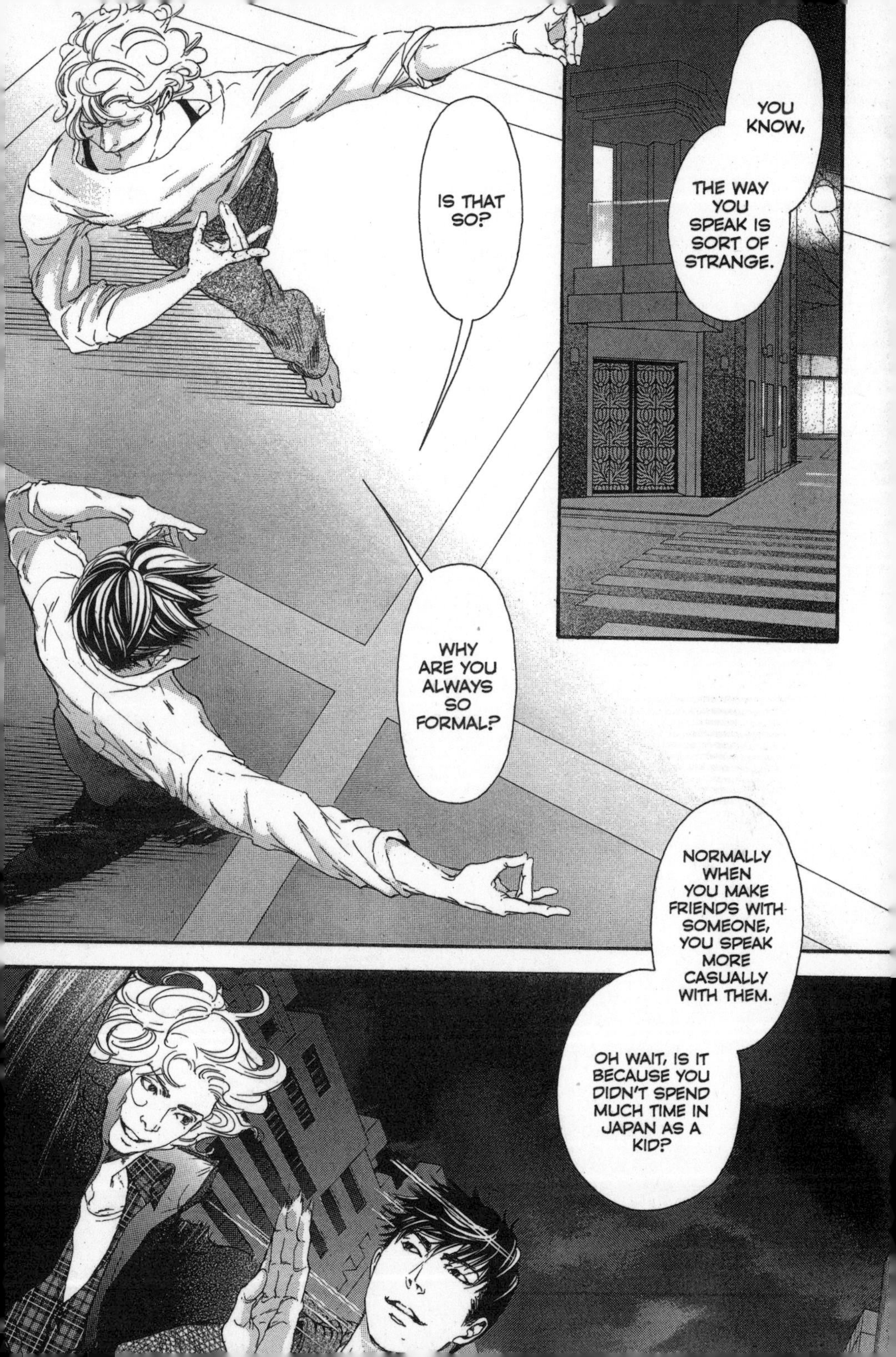
YOU KNOW,
THE WAY YOU SPEAK IS SORT OF STRANGE.
IS THAT SO?
WHY ARE YOU ALWAYS SO FORMAL?
NORMALLY WHEN YOU MAKE FRIENDS WITH SOMEONE, YOU SPEAK MORE CASUALLY WITH THEM.
OH WAIT, IS IT BECAUSE YOU DIDN'T SPEND MUCH TIME IN JAPAN AS A KID?

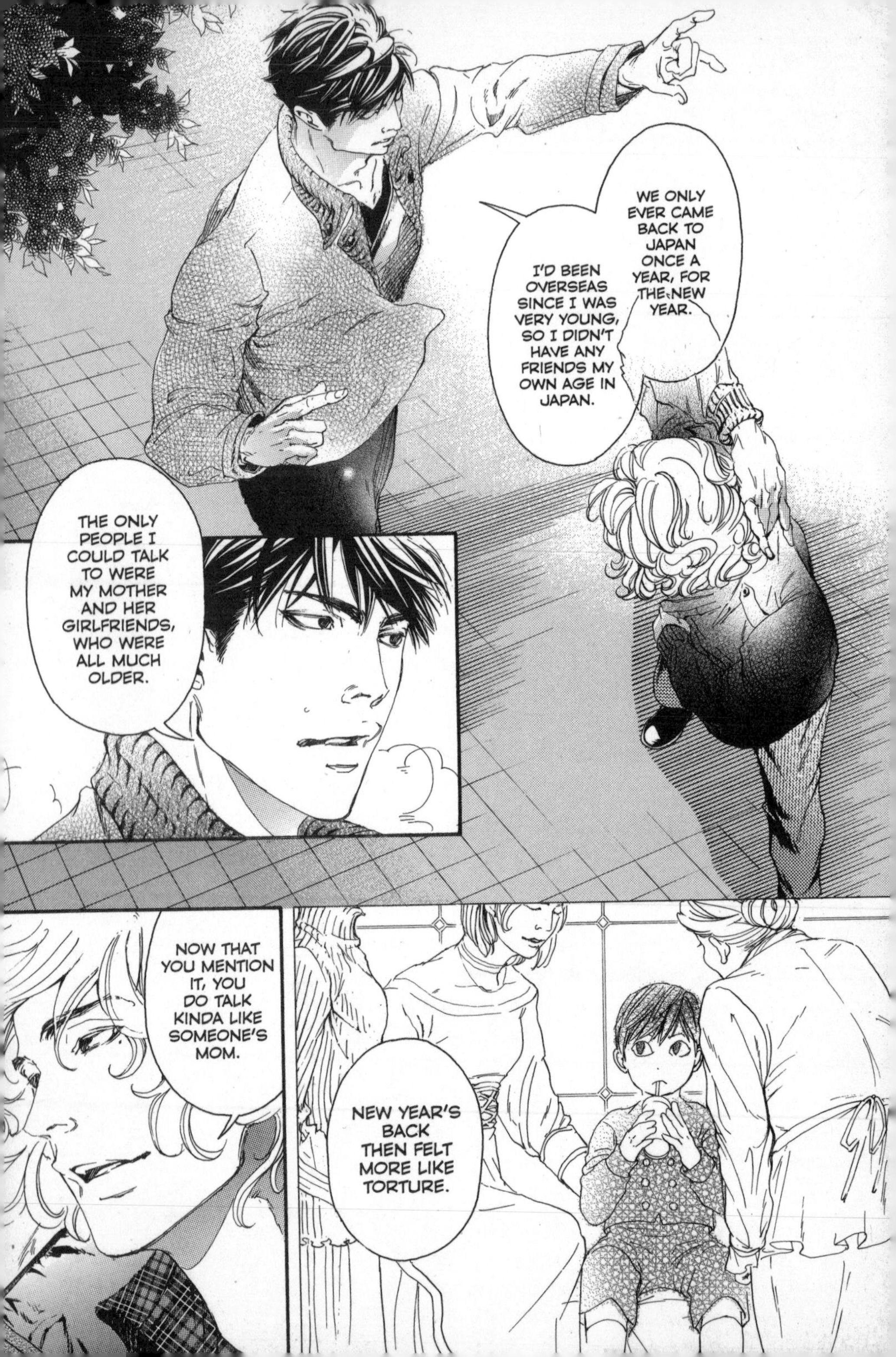
I'D BEEN OVERSEAS SINCE I WAS VERY YOUNG, SO I DIDN'T HAVE ANY FRIENDS MY OWN AGE IN JAPAN.
WE ONLY EVER CAME BACK TO JAPAN ONCE A YEAR, FOR THE NEW YEAR.
THE ONLY PEOPLE I COULD TALK TO WERE MY MOTHER AND HER GIRLFRIENDS, WHO WERE ALL MUCH OLDER.
NEW YEAR'S BACK THEN FELT MORE LIKE TORTURE.
NOW THAT YOU MENTION IT, YOU DO TALK KINDA LIKE SOMEONE'S MOM.

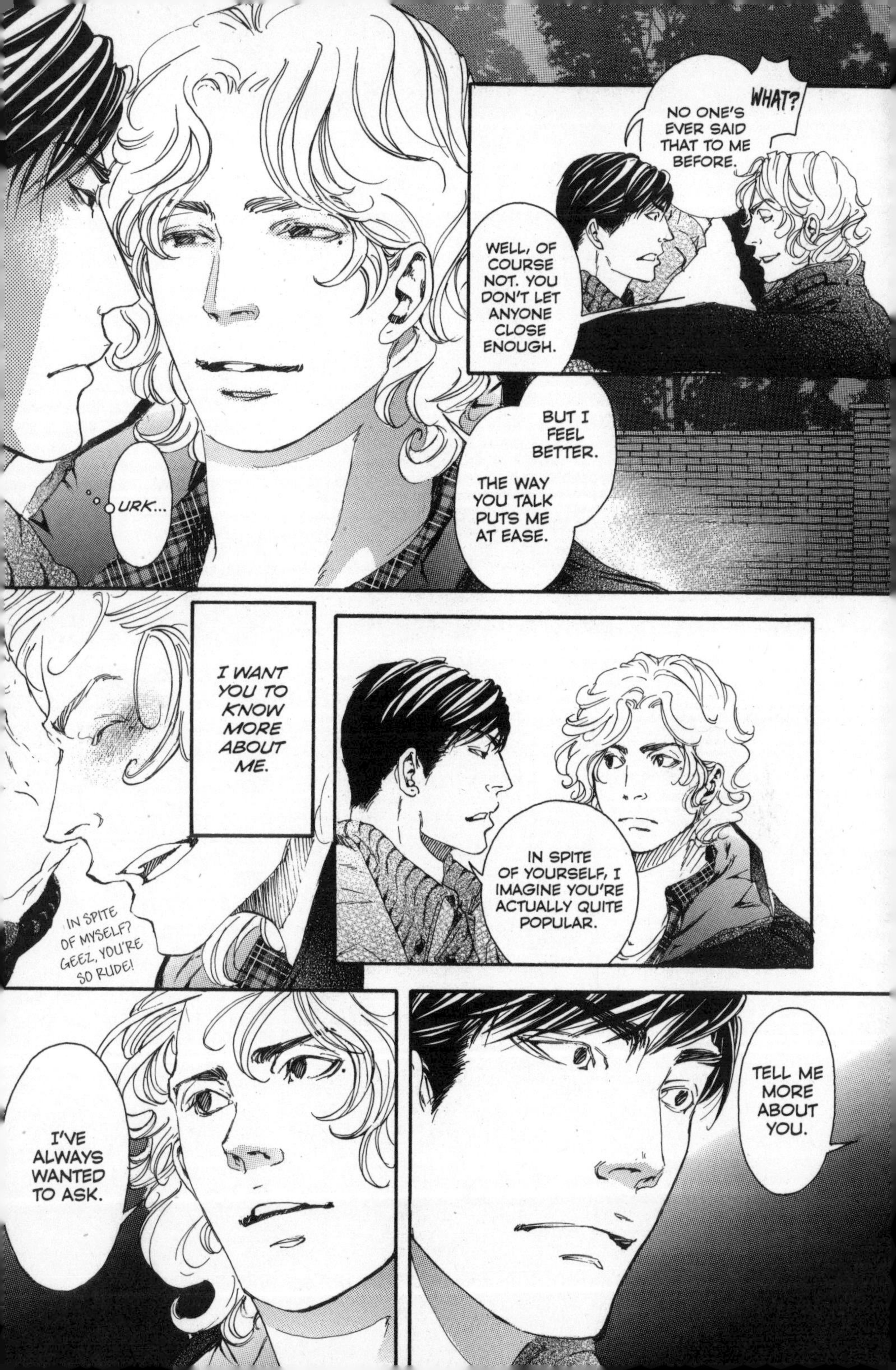
WHAT?
NO ONE'S EVER SAID THAT TO ME BEFORE.
WELL, OF COURSE NOT. YOU DON'T LET ANYONE CLOSE ENOUGH.
BUT I FEEL BETTER.
THE WAY YOU TALK PUTS ME AT EASE.
URK...
IN SPITE OF YOURSELF, I IMAGINE YOU'RE ACTUALLY QUITE POPULAR.
I WANT YOU TO KNOW MORE ABOUT ME.
IN SPITE OF MYSELF? GEEZ, YOU'RE SO RUDE!
TELL ME MORE ABOUT YOU.
I'VE ALWAYS WANTED TO ASK.

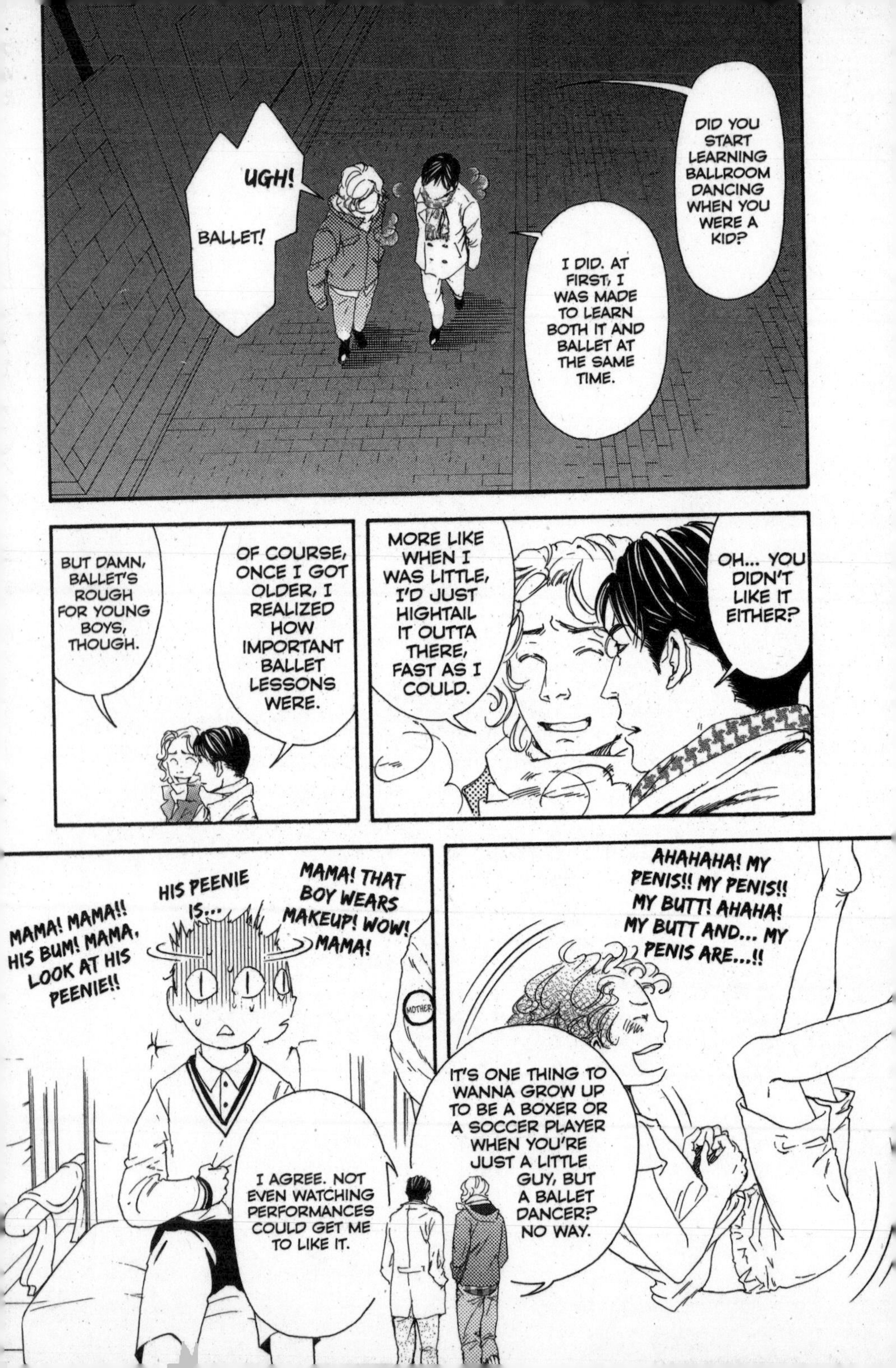
DID YOU START LEARNING BALLROOM DANCING WHEN YOU WERE A KID?
I DID. AT FIRST, I WAS MADE TO LEARN BOTH IT AND BALLET AT THE SAME TIME.
UGH! BALLET!
OH... YOU DIDN'T LIKE IT EITHER?
MORE LIKE WHEN I WAS LITTLE, I'D JUST HIGHTAIL IT OUTTA THERE, FAST AS I COULD.
OF COURSE, ONCE I GOT OLDER, I REALIZED HOW IMPORTANT BALLET LESSONS WERE.
BUT DAMN, BALLET'S ROUGH FOR YOUNG BOYS, THOUGH.
AHAHAHA! MY PENIS!! MY PENIS!! MY BUTT! AHAHA! MY BUTT AND... MY PENIS ARE...!!
IT'S ONE THING TO WANNA GROW UP TO BE A BOXER OR A SOCCER PLAYER WHEN YOU'RE JUST A LITTLE GUY, BUT A BALLET DANCER? NO WAY.
MAMA! THAT BOY WEARS MAKEUP! WOW! MAMA!
HIS PEENIE IS...
MAMA! MAMA!! HIS BUM! MAMA, LOOK AT HIS PEENIE!!
MOTHER
I AGREE. NOT EVEN WATCHING PERFORMANCES COULD GET ME TO LIKE IT.

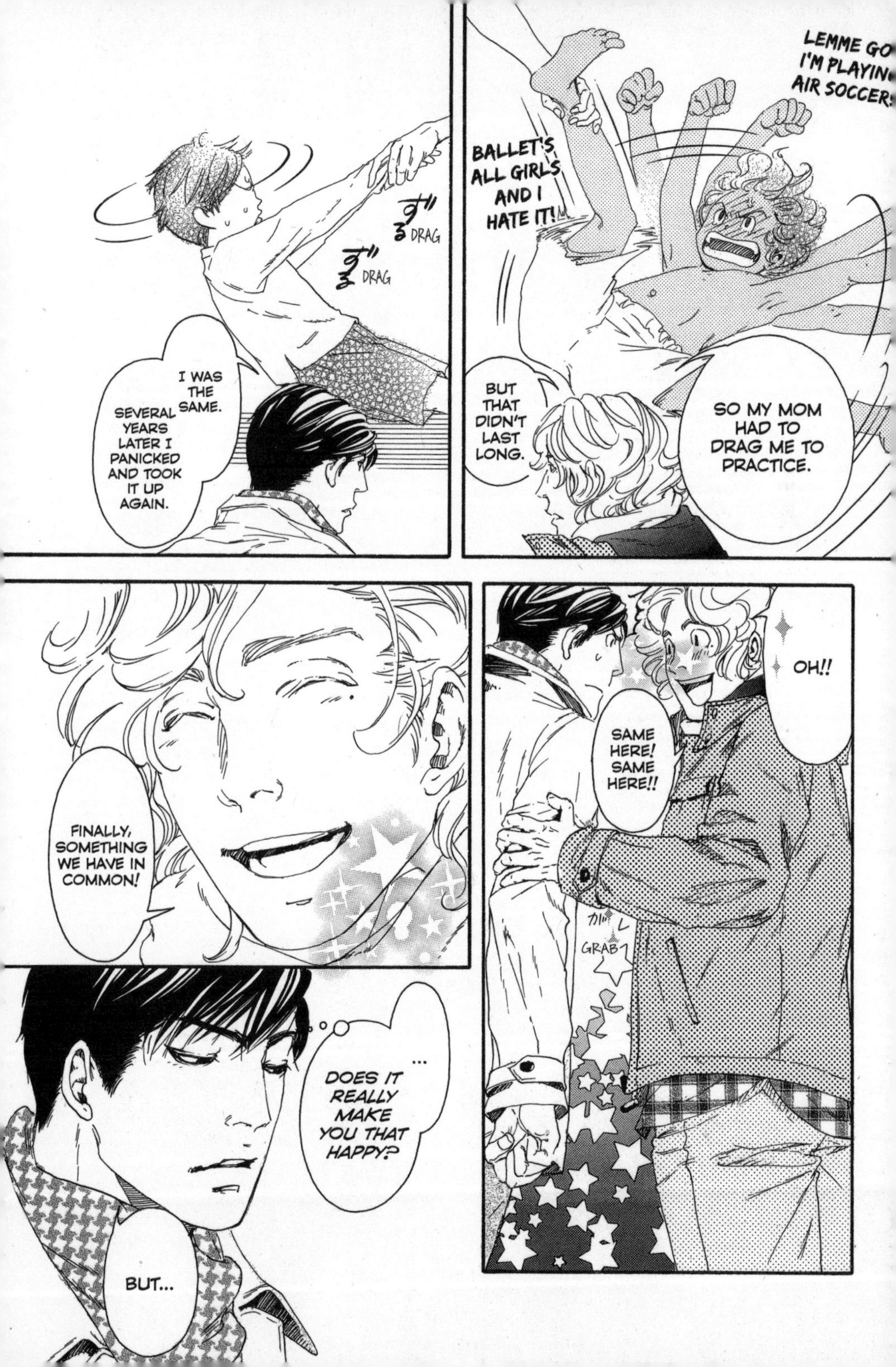
LEMME GO
I'M PLAYIN
AIR SOCCER
BALLET'S ALL GIRLS AND I HATE IT!
SO MY MOM HAD TO DRAG ME TO PRACTICE.
BUT THAT DIDN'T LAST LONG.
ずる DRAG
ずる DRAG
I WAS THE SAME.
SEVERAL YEARS LATER I PANICKED AND TOOK IT UP AGAIN.
OH!!
SAME HERE! SAME HERE!!
GRAB
FINALLY, SOMETHING WE HAVE IN COMMON!
...DOES IT REALLY MAKE YOU THAT HAPPY?
BUT...

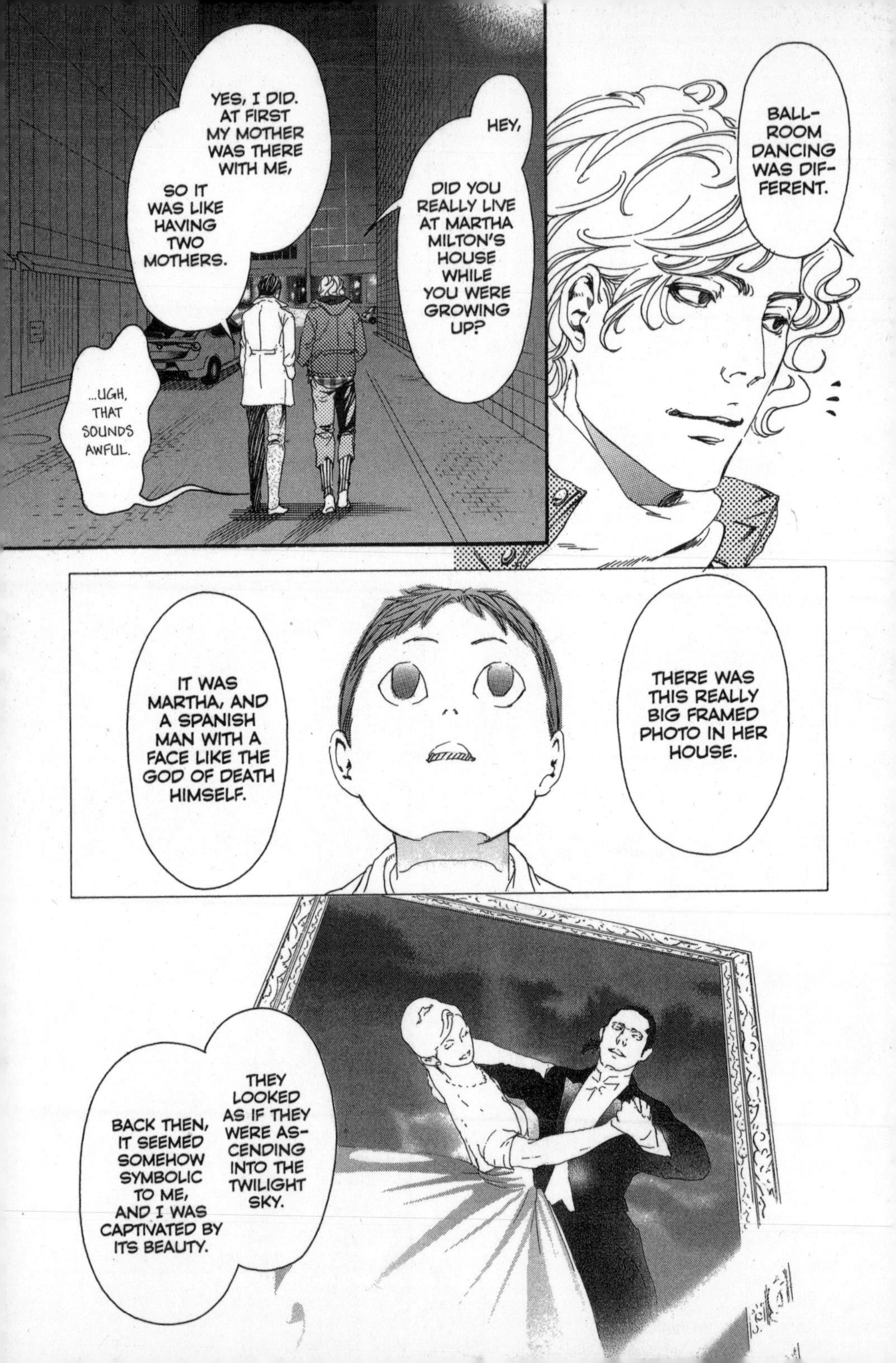
BALLROOM DANCING WAS DIFFERENT.
HEY,
DID YOU REALLY LIVE AT MARTHA MILTON'S HOUSE WHILE YOU WERE GROWING UP?
YES, I DID. AT FIRST MY MOTHER WAS THERE WITH ME,
SO IT WAS LIKE HAVING TWO MOTHERS.
...UGH, THAT SOUNDS AWFUL.
THERE WAS THIS REALLY BIG FRAMED PHOTO IN HER HOUSE.
IT WAS MARTHA, AND A SPANISH MAN WITH A FACE LIKE THE GOD OF DEATH HIMSELF.
THEY LOOKED AS IF THEY WERE ASCENDING INTO THE TWILIGHT SKY.
BACK THEN, IT SEEMED SOMEHOW SYMBOLIC TO ME, AND I WAS CAPTIVATED BY ITS BEAUTY.

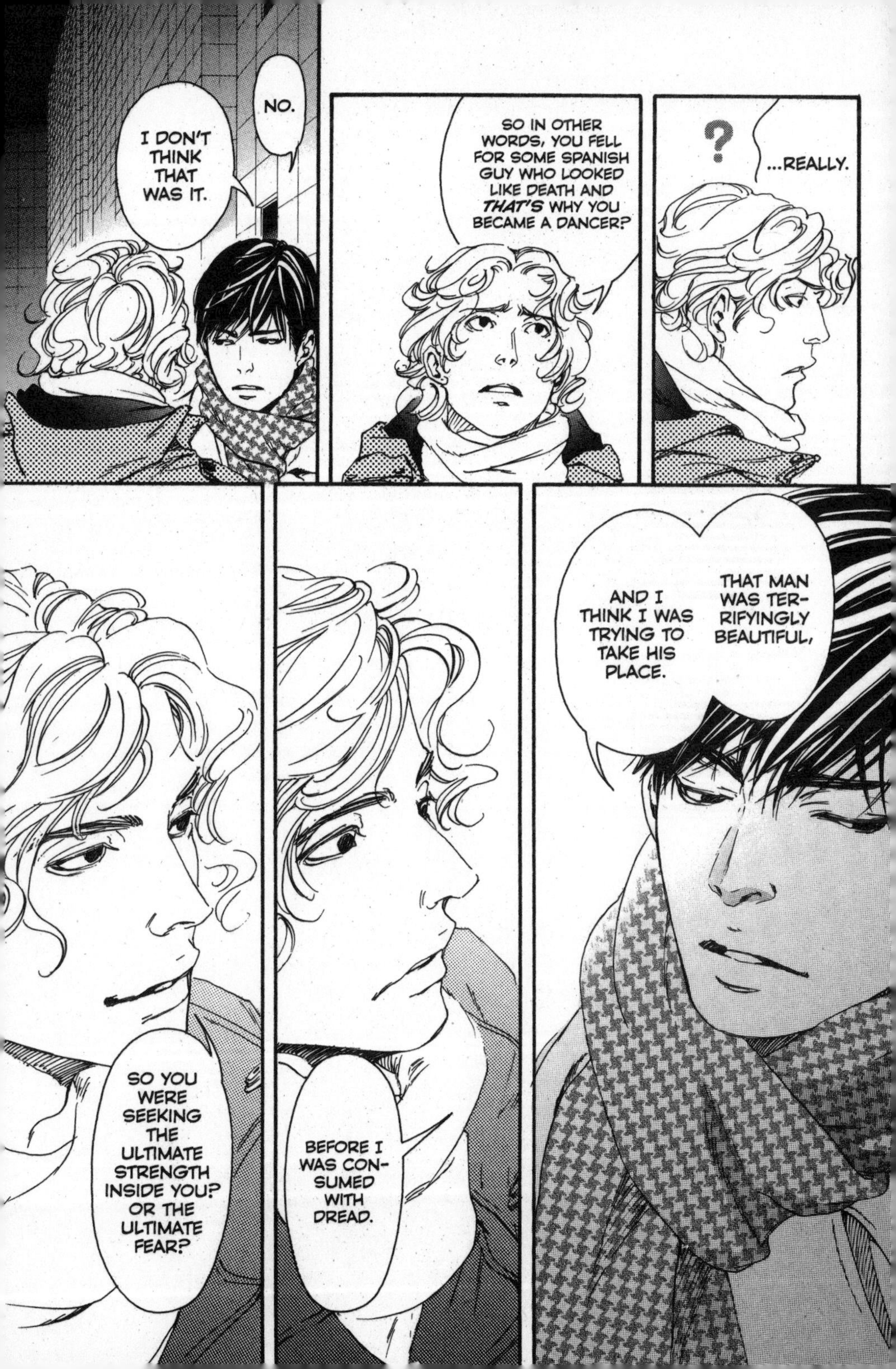
?
...REALLY.
SO IN OTHER WORDS, YOU FELL FOR SOME SPANISH GUY WHO LOOKED LIKE DEATH AND *THAT'S* WHY YOU BECAME A DANCER?
NO.
I DON'T THINK THAT WAS IT.
THAT MAN WAS TERRIFYINGLY BEAUTIFUL,
AND I THINK I WAS TRYING TO TAKE HIS PLACE.
BEFORE I WAS CONSUMED WITH DREAD.
SO YOU WERE SEEKING THE ULTIMATE STRENGTH INSIDE YOU? OR THE ULTIMATE FEAR?

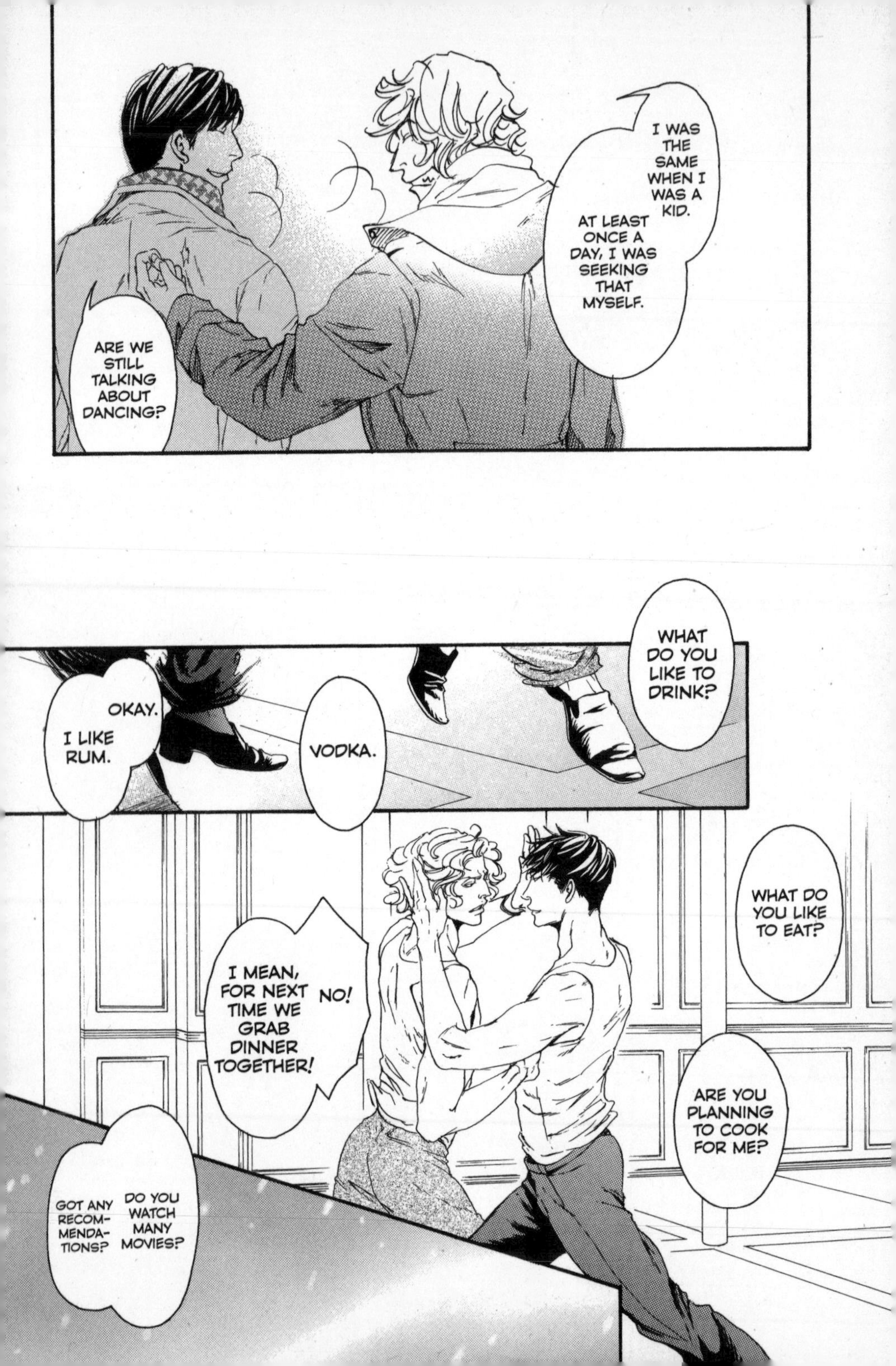
I WAS THE SAME WHEN I WAS A KID.
AT LEAST ONCE A DAY, I WAS SEEKING THAT MYSELF.
ARE WE STILL TALKING ABOUT DANCING?
WHAT DO YOU LIKE TO DRINK?
VODKA.
OKAY.
I LIKE RUM.
WHAT DO YOU LIKE TO EAT?
ARE YOU PLANNING TO COOK FOR ME?
NO!
I MEAN, FOR NEXT TIME WE GRAB DINNER TOGETHER!
DO YOU WATCH MANY MOVIES?
GOT ANY RECOMMENDATIONS?

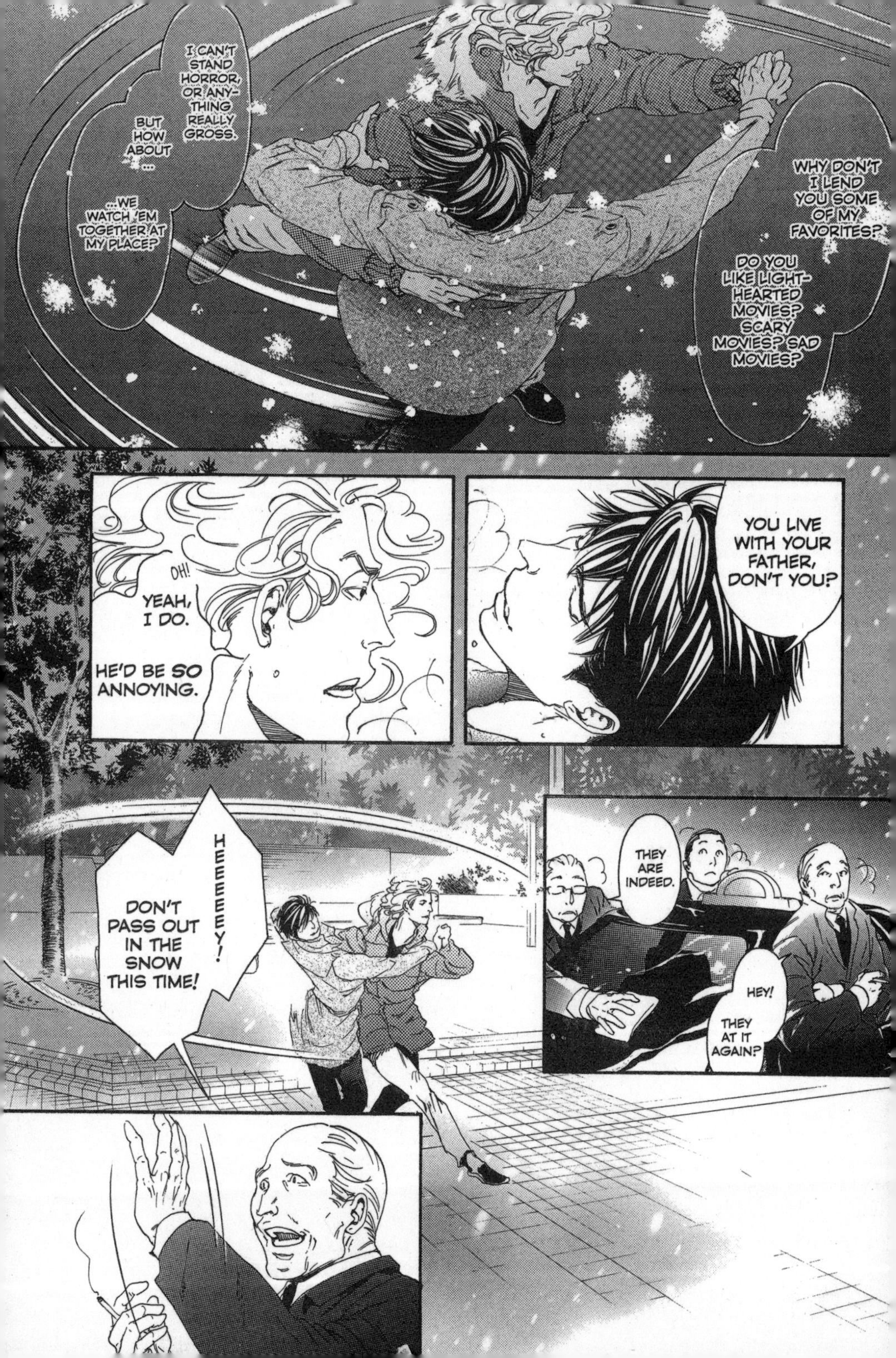
WHY DON'T I LEND YOU SOME OF MY FAVORITES?
DO YOU LIKE LIGHT-HEARTED MOVIES? SCARY MOVIES? SAD MOVIES?
I CAN'T STAND HORROR, OR ANY-THING REALLY GROSS.
BUT HOW ABOUT ...
...WE WATCH 'EM TOGETHER AT MY PLACE?
YOU LIVE WITH YOUR FATHER, DON'T YOU?
OH!
YEAH, I DO.
HE'D BE SO ANNOYING.
HEY!
THEY AT IT AGAIN?
THEY ARE INDEED.
HEEEEEEY!
DON'T PASS OUT IN THE SNOW THIS TIME!

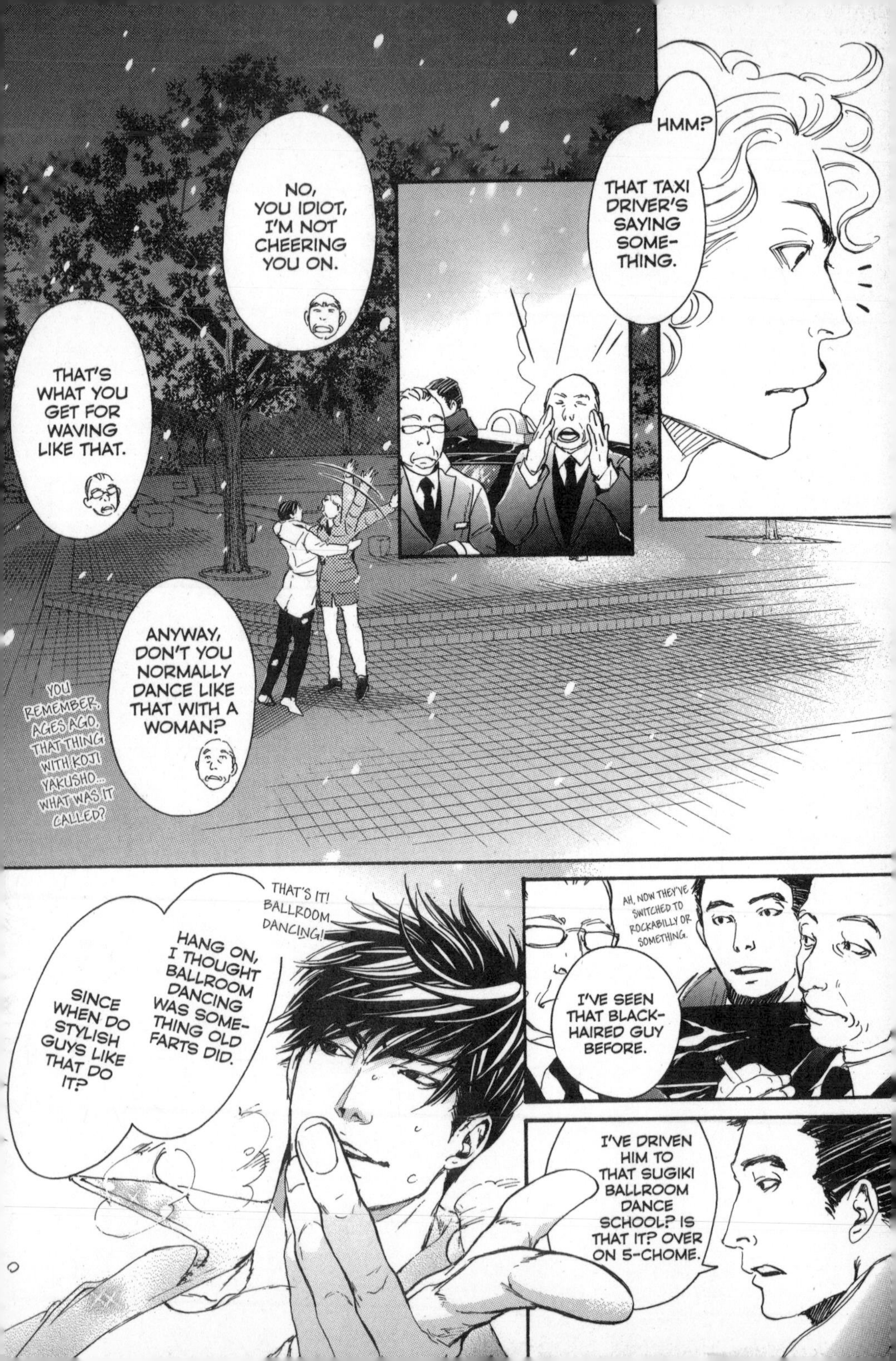
HMM?
THAT TAXI DRIVER'S SAYING SOME-THING.
NO, YOU IDIOT, I'M NOT CHEERING YOU ON.
THAT'S WHAT YOU GET FOR WAVING LIKE THAT.
ANYWAY, DON'T YOU NORMALLY DANCE LIKE THAT WITH A WOMAN?
YOU REMEMBER, AGES AGO, THAT THING WITH KOJI YAKUSHO... WHAT WAS IT CALLED?
AH, NOW THEY'VE SWITCHED TO ROCKABILLY OR SOMETHING.
I'VE SEEN THAT BLACK-HAIRED GUY BEFORE.
I'VE DRIVEN HIM TO THAT SUGIKI BALLROOM DANCE SCHOOL? IS THAT IT? OVER ON 5-CHOME.
THAT'S IT! BALLROOM DANCING!
HANG ON, I THOUGHT BALLROOM DANCING WAS SOME-THING OLD FARTS DID.
SINCE WHEN DO STYLISH GUYS LIKE THAT DO IT?

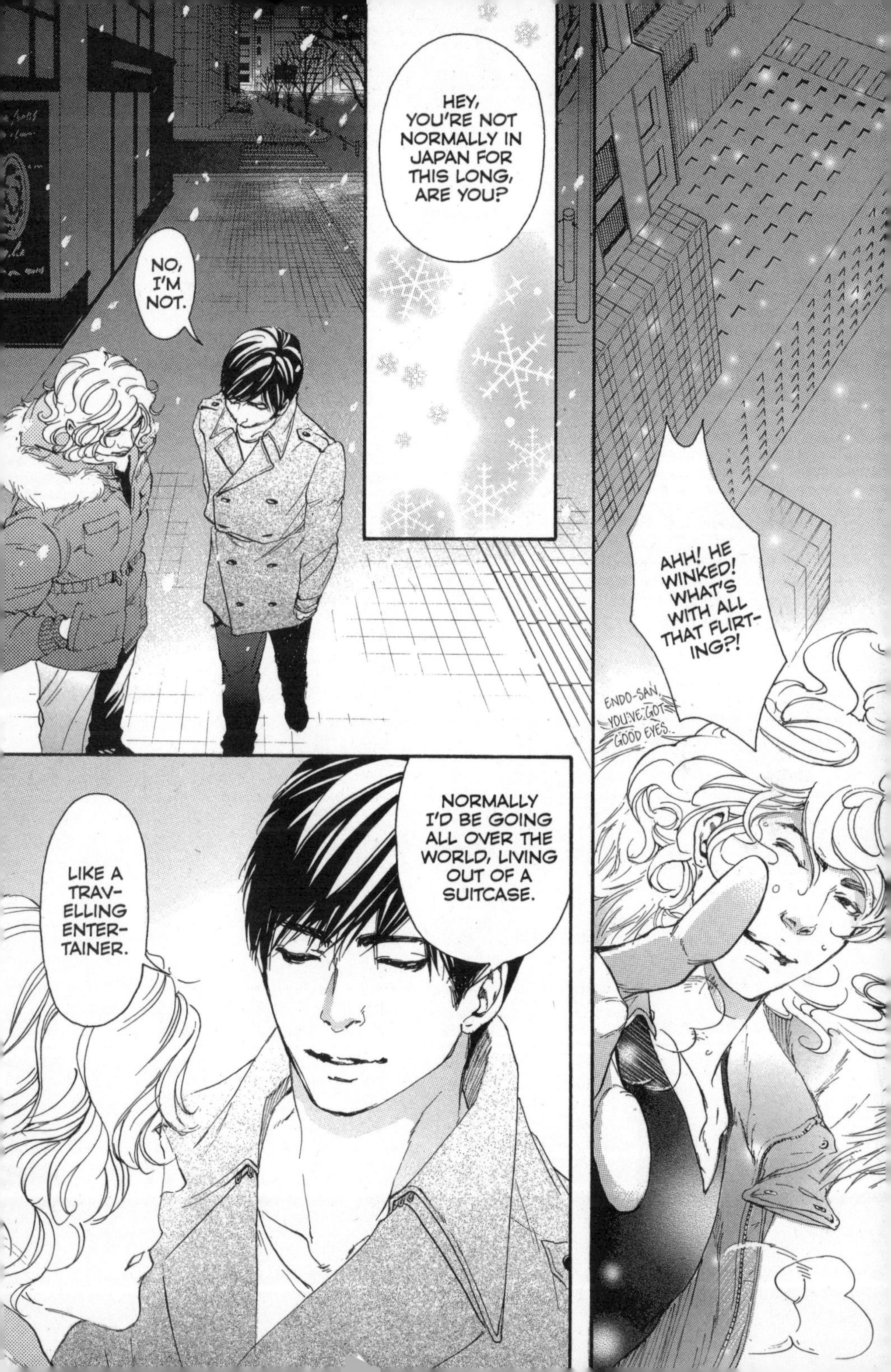
AHH! HE WINKED! WHAT'S WITH ALL THAT FLIRT-ING?!
ENDO-SAN, YOU'VE GOT GOOD EYES.
HEY, YOU'RE NOT NORMALLY IN JAPAN FOR THIS LONG, ARE YOU?
NO, I'M NOT.
NORMALLY I'D BE GOING ALL OVER THE WORLD, LIVING OUT OF A SUITCASE.
LIKE A TRAV-ELLING ENTER-TAINER.

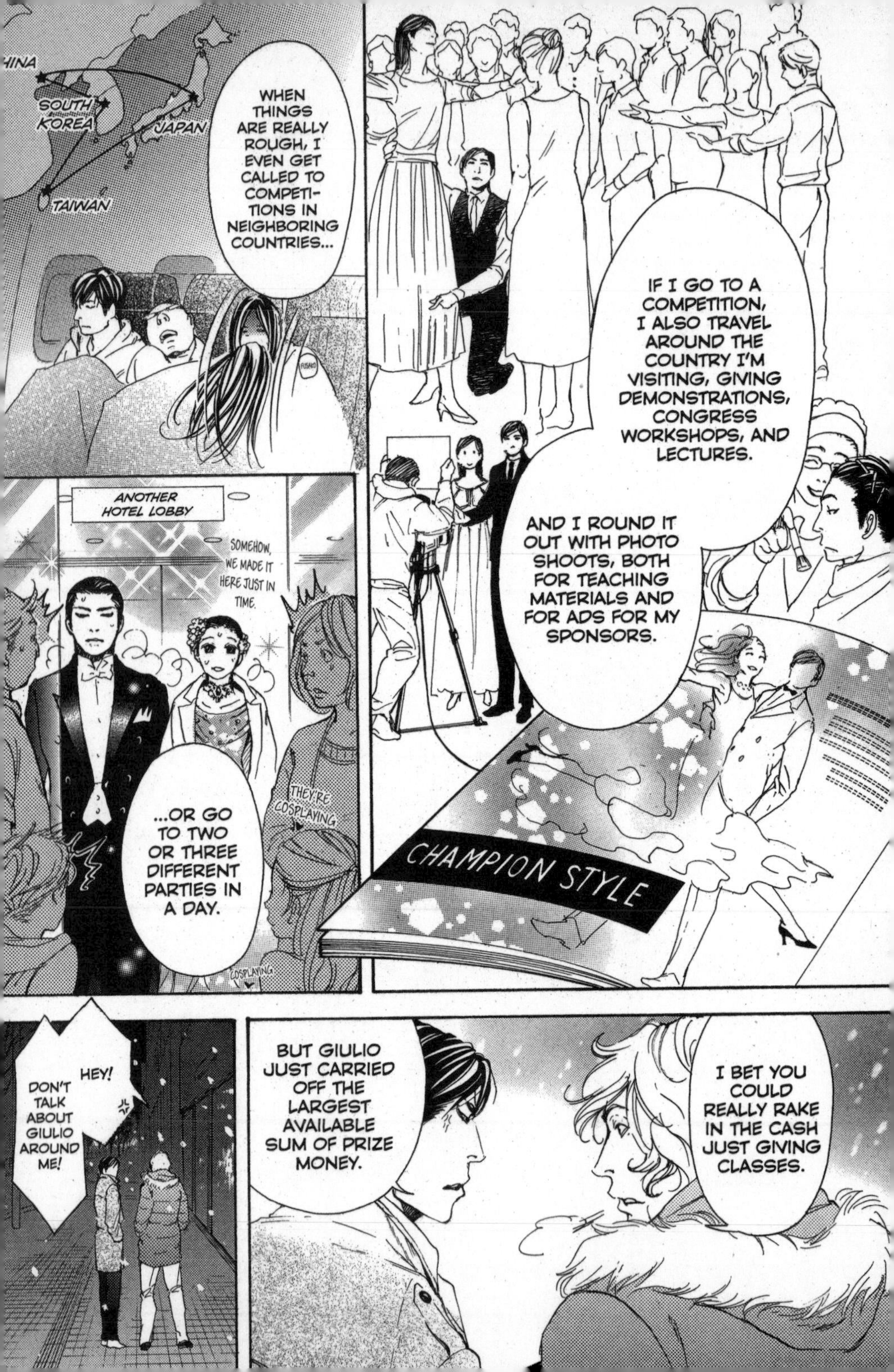
IF I GO TO A COMPETITION, I ALSO TRAVEL AROUND THE COUNTRY I'M VISITING, GIVING DEMONSTRATIONS, CONGRESS WORKSHOPS, AND LECTURES.
AND I ROUND IT OUT WITH PHOTO SHOOTS, BOTH FOR TEACHING MATERIALS AND FOR ADS FOR MY SPONSORS.
CHAMPION STYLE
HINA
SOUTH KOREA
JAPAN
TAIWAN
WHEN THINGS ARE REALLY ROUGH, I EVEN GET CALLED TO COMPETITIONS IN NEIGHBORING COUNTRIES...
ANOTHER HOTEL LOBBY
SOMEHOW, WE MADE IT HERE JUST IN TIME.
THEY'RE COSPLAYING
...OR GO TO TWO OR THREE DIFFERENT PARTIES IN A DAY.
COSPLAYING
I BET YOU COULD REALLY RAKE IN THE CASH JUST GIVING CLASSES.
BUT GIULIO JUST CARRIED OFF THE LARGEST AVAILABLE SUM OF PRIZE MONEY.
HEY!
DON'T TALK ABOUT GIULIO AROUND ME!

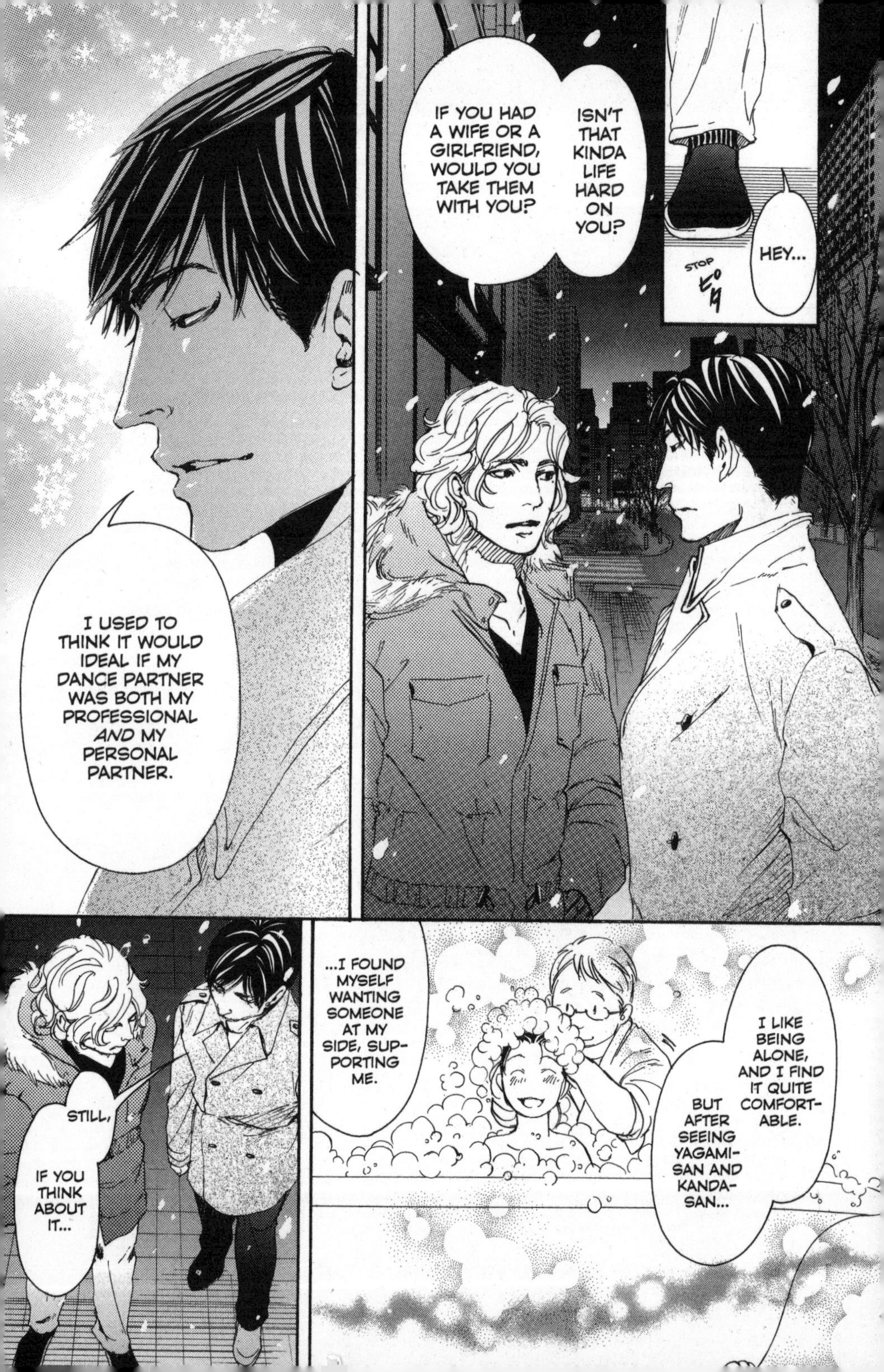
HEY...
STOP
ISN'T THAT KINDA LIFE HARD ON YOU?
IF YOU HAD A WIFE OR A GIRLFRIEND, WOULD YOU TAKE THEM WITH YOU?
I USED TO THINK IT WOULD IDEAL IF MY DANCE PARTNER WAS BOTH MY PROFESSIONAL *AND* MY PERSONAL PARTNER.
I LIKE BEING ALONE, AND I FIND IT QUITE COMFORTABLE.
BUT AFTER SEEING YAGAMI-SAN AND KANDA-SAN...
...I FOUND MYSELF WANTING SOMEONE AT MY SIDE, SUPPORTING ME.
STILL,
IF YOU THINK ABOUT IT...

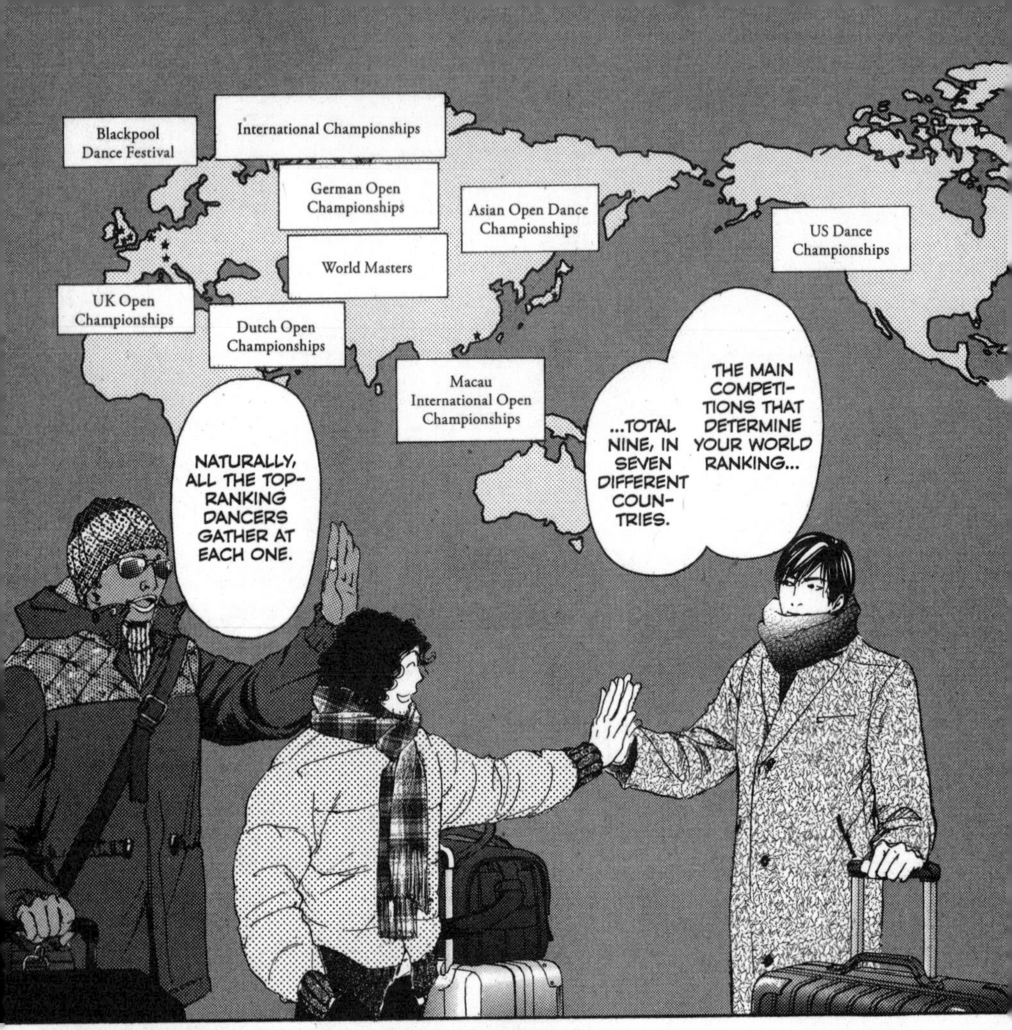
Blackpool Dance Festival
International Championships
German Open Championships
Asian Open Dance Championships
US Dance Championships
World Masters
UK Open Championships
Dutch Open Championships
Macau International Open Championships
THE MAIN COMPETI-TIONS THAT DETERMINE YOUR WORLD RANKING...
...TOTAL NINE, IN SEVEN DIFFERENT COUN-TRIES.
NATURALLY, ALL THE TOP-RANKING DANCERS GATHER AT EACH ONE.

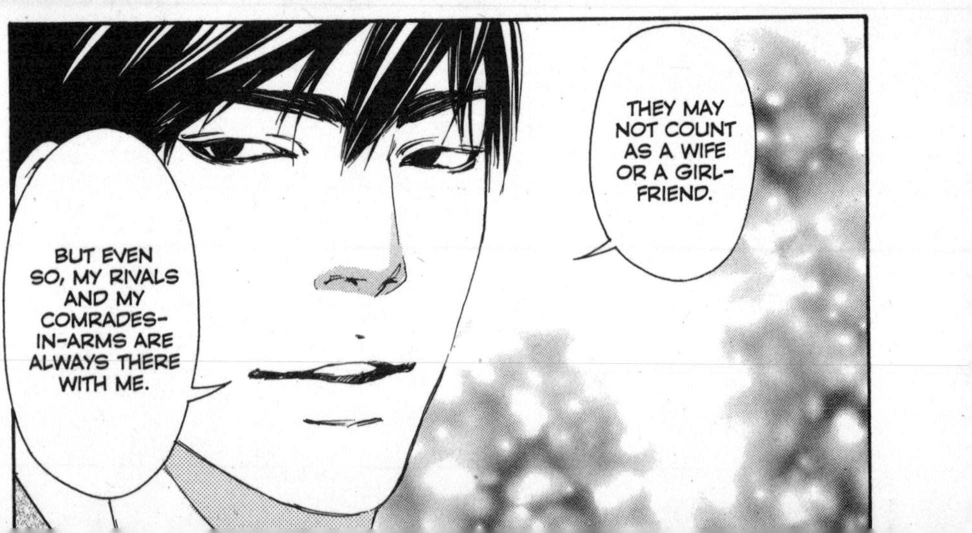
THEY MAY NOT COUNT AS A WIFE OR A GIRL-FRIEND.
BUT EVEN SO, MY RIVALS AND MY COMRADES-IN-ARMS ARE ALWAYS THERE WITH ME.

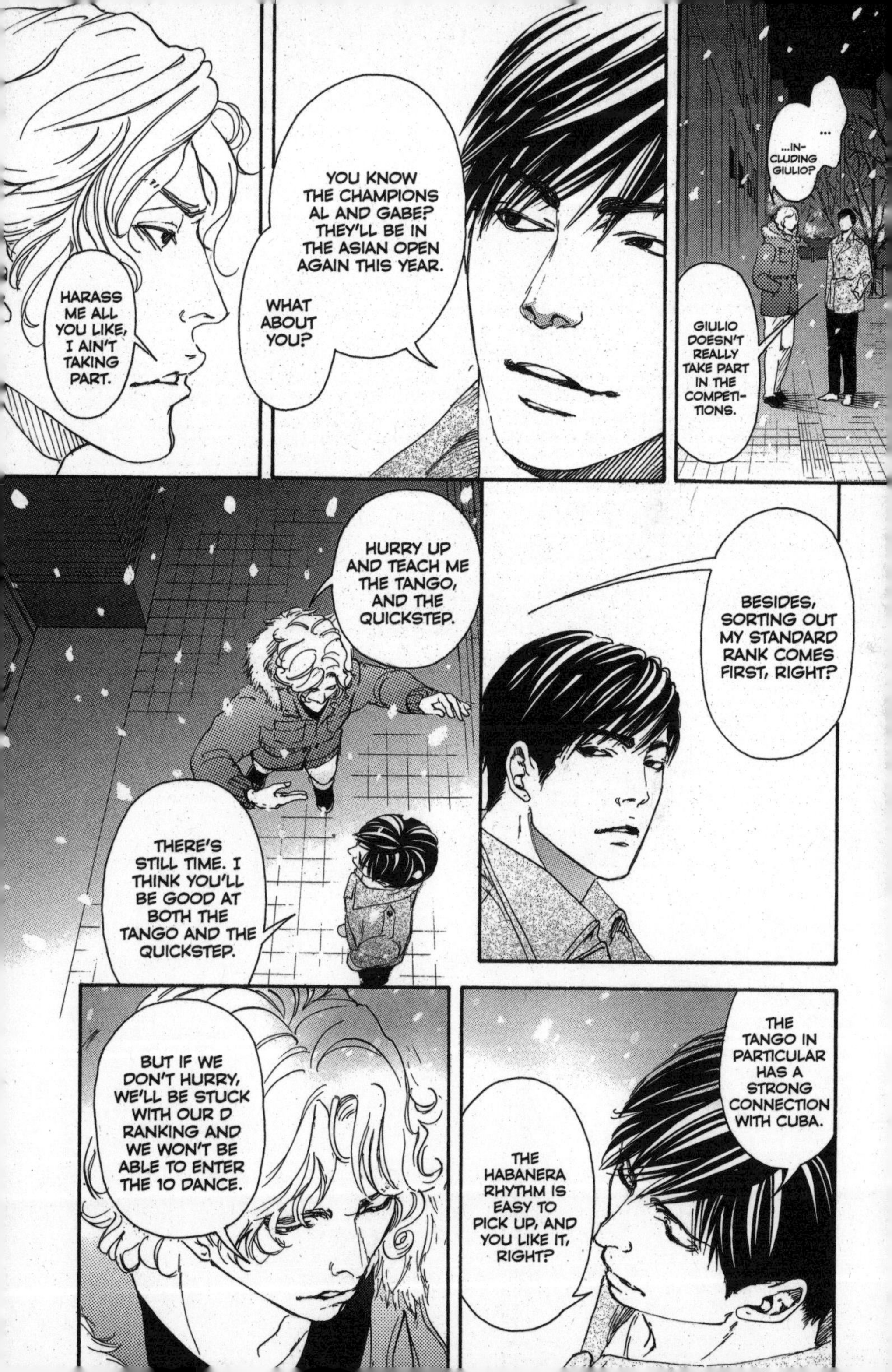
...
...IN-CLUDING GIULIO?
GIULIO DOESN'T REALLY TAKE PART IN THE COMPETI-TIONS.
YOU KNOW THE CHAMPIONS AL AND GABE? THEY'LL BE IN THE ASIAN OPEN AGAIN THIS YEAR.
WHAT ABOUT YOU?
HARASS ME ALL YOU LIKE, I AIN'T TAKING PART.
BESIDES, SORTING OUT MY STANDARD RANK COMES FIRST, RIGHT?
HURRY UP AND TEACH ME THE TANGO, AND THE QUICKSTEP.
THERE'S STILL TIME. I THINK YOU'LL BE GOOD AT BOTH THE TANGO AND THE QUICKSTEP.
THE TANGO IN PARTICULAR HAS A STRONG CONNECTION WITH CUBA.
THE HABANERA RHYTHM IS EASY TO PICK UP, AND YOU LIKE IT, RIGHT?
BUT IF WE DON'T HURRY, WE'LL BE STUCK WITH OUR D RANKING AND WE WON'T BE ABLE TO ENTER THE 10 DANCE.

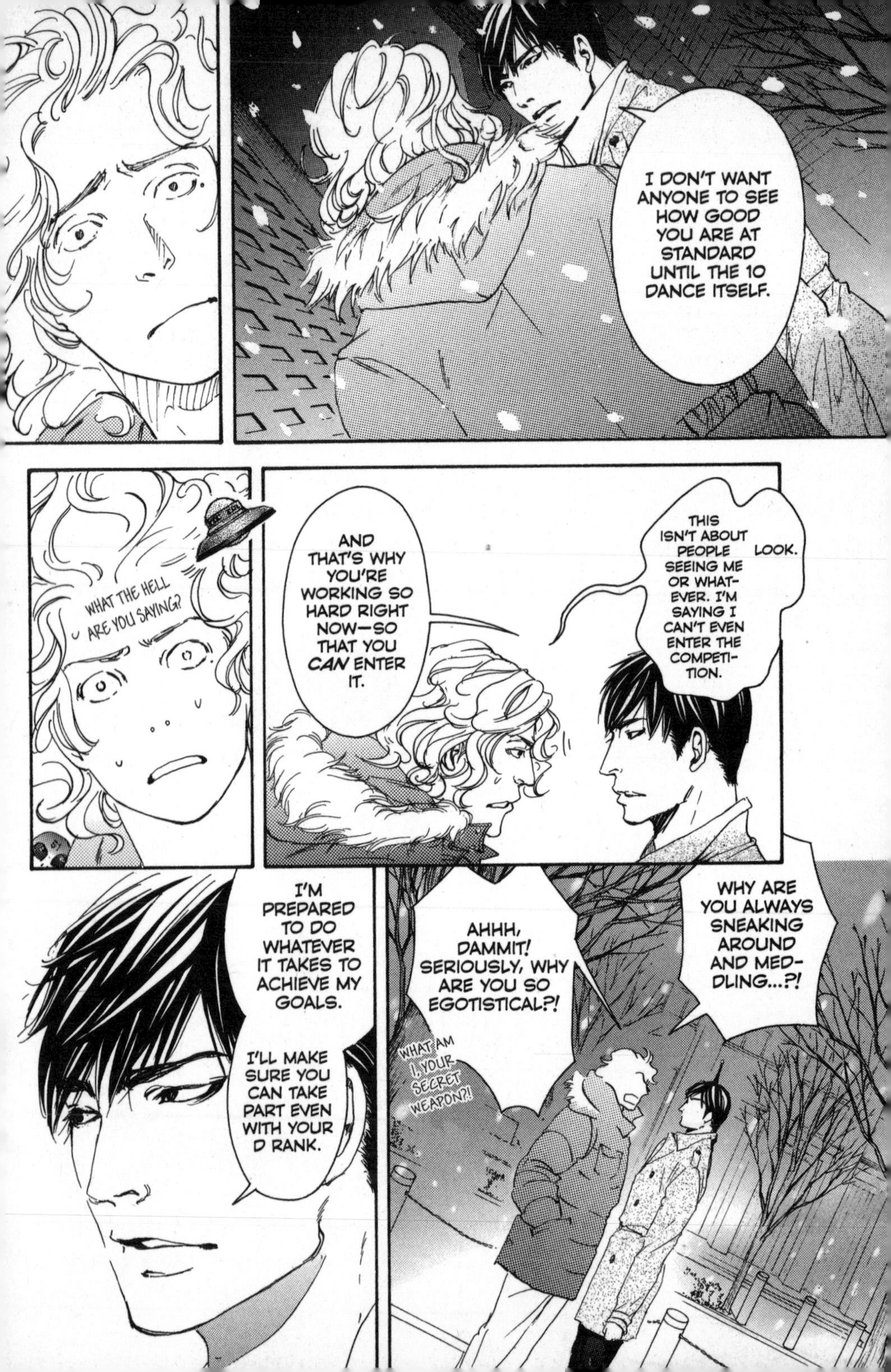
I DON'T WANT ANYONE TO SEE HOW GOOD YOU ARE AT STANDARD UNTIL THE 10 DANCE ITSELF.
LOOK.
THIS ISN'T ABOUT PEOPLE SEEING ME OR WHAT-EVER. I'M SAYING I CAN'T EVEN ENTER THE COMPETI-TION.
AND THAT'S WHY YOU'RE WORKING SO HARD RIGHT NOW—SO THAT YOU *CAN* ENTER IT.
WHAT THE HELL ARE YOU SAYING?
WHY ARE YOU ALWAYS SNEAKING AROUND AND MED-DLING...?!
AHHH, DAMMIT! SERIOUSLY, WHY ARE YOU SO EGOTISTICAL?!
WHAT AM I, YOUR SECRET WEAPON?!
I'M PREPARED TO DO WHATEVER IT TAKES TO ACHIEVE MY GOALS.
I'LL MAKE SURE YOU CAN TAKE PART EVEN WITH YOUR D RANK.

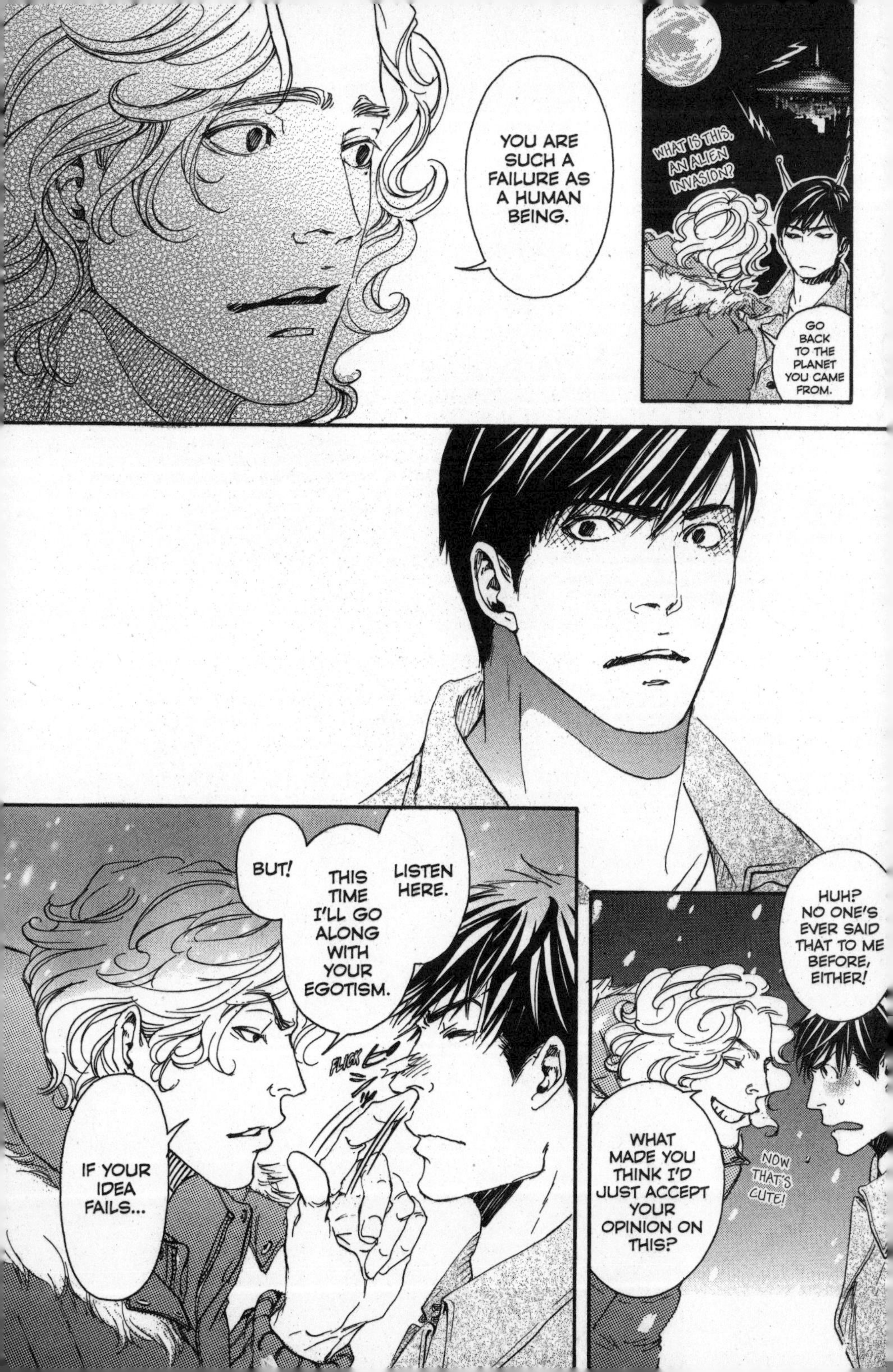
WHAT IS THIS. AN ALIEN INVASION?
GO BACK TO THE PLANET YOU CAME FROM.
YOU ARE SUCH A FAILURE AS A HUMAN BEING.
HUH? NO ONE'S EVER SAID THAT TO ME BEFORE, EITHER!
NOW THAT'S CUTE!
WHAT MADE YOU THINK I'D JUST ACCEPT YOUR OPINION ON THIS?
LISTEN HERE.
THIS TIME I'LL GO ALONG WITH YOUR EGOTISM.
BUT!
FLICK
IF YOUR IDEA FAILS...

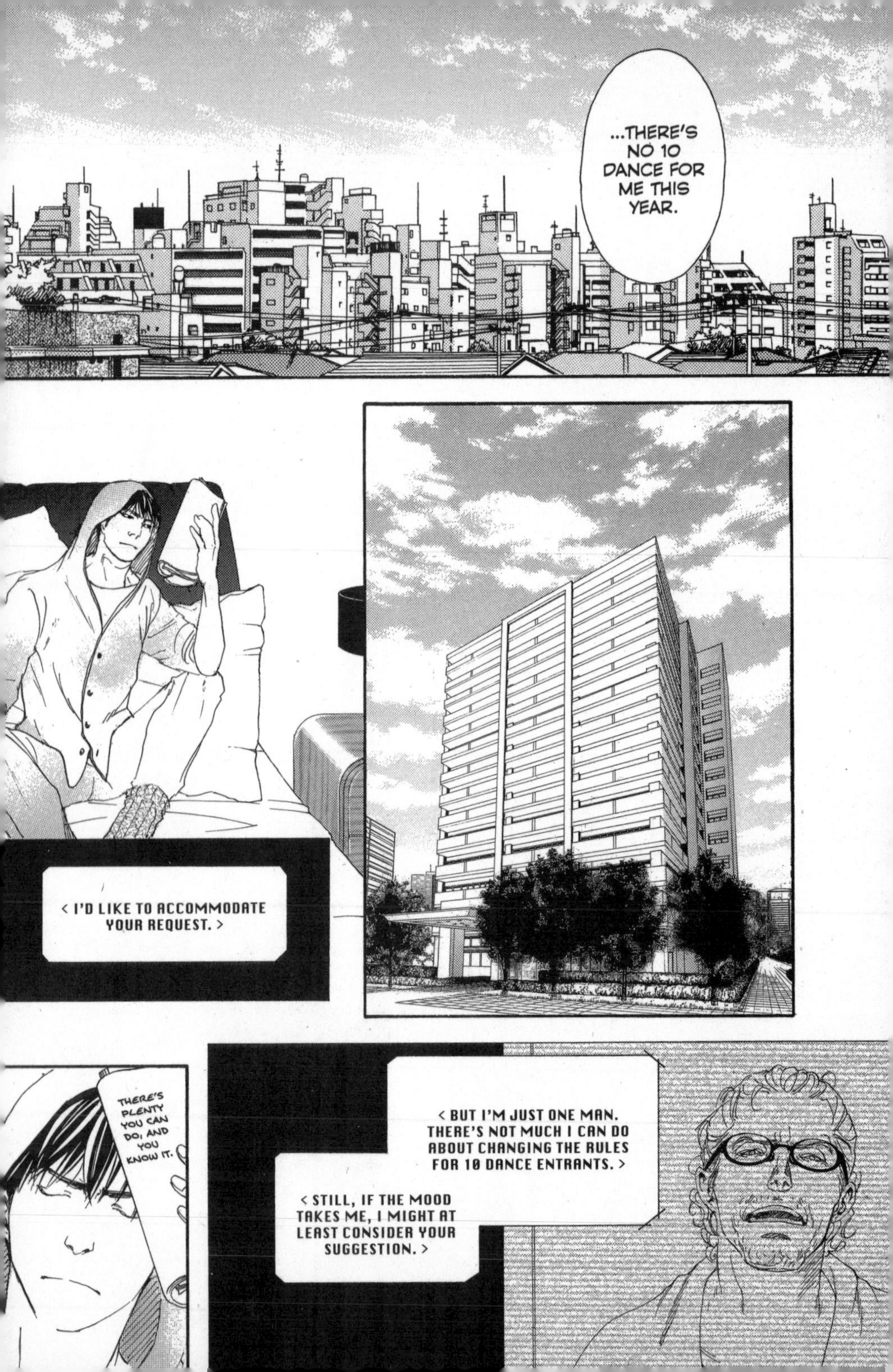
...THERE'S NO 10 DANCE FOR ME THIS YEAR.
< I'D LIKE TO ACCOMMODATE YOUR REQUEST. >
< BUT I'M JUST ONE MAN. THERE'S NOT MUCH I CAN DO ABOUT CHANGING THE RULES FOR 10 DANCE ENTRANTS. >
< STILL, IF THE MOOD TAKES ME, I MIGHT AT LEAST CONSIDER YOUR SUGGESTION. >
THERE'S PLENTY YOU CAN DO, AND YOU KNOW IT.

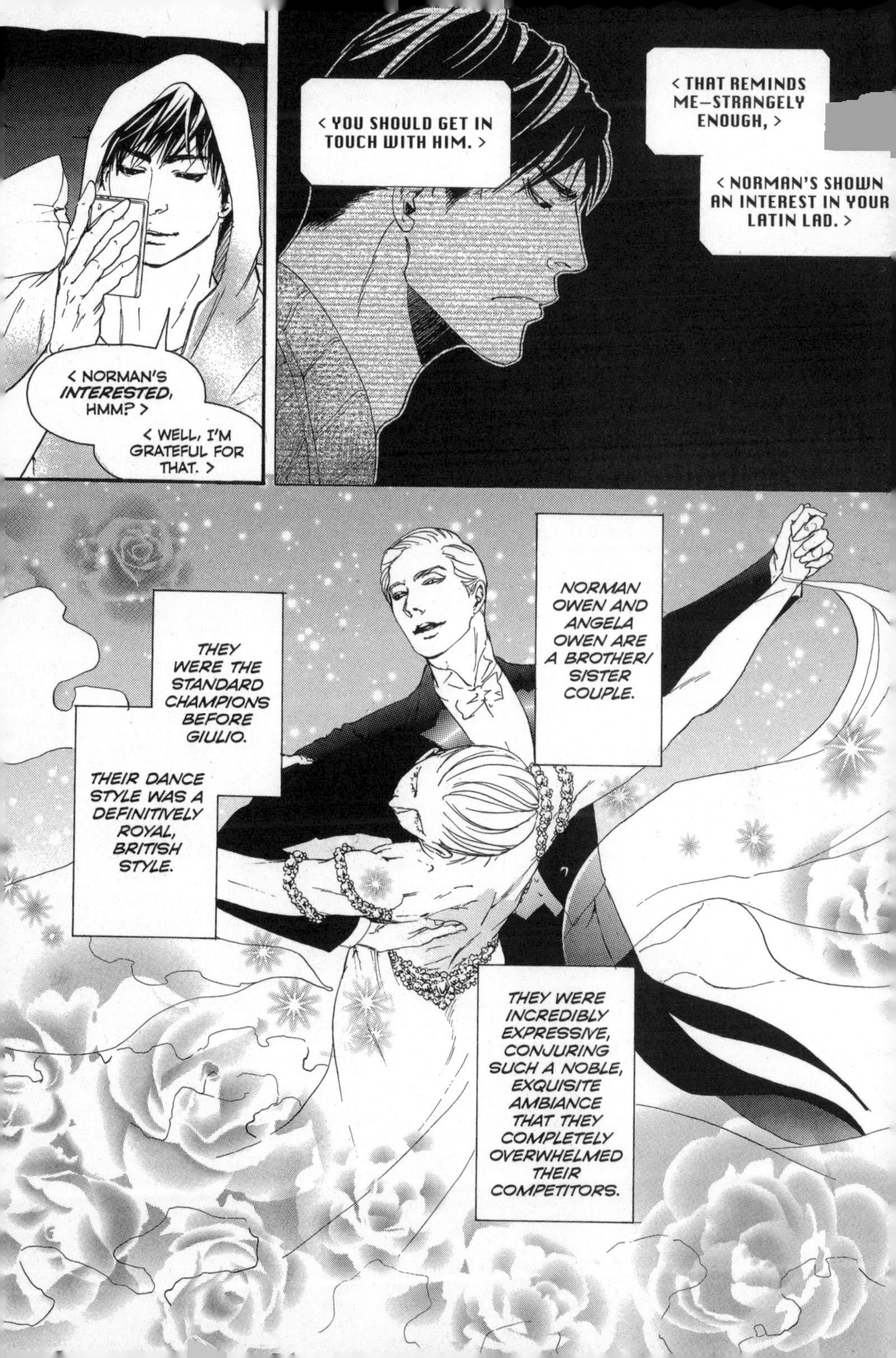
< THAT REMINDS ME—STRANGELY ENOUGH, >
< NORMAN'S SHOWN AN INTEREST IN YOUR LATIN LAD. >
< YOU SHOULD GET IN TOUCH WITH HIM. >
< NORMAN'S *INTERESTED*, HMM? >
< WELL, I'M GRATEFUL FOR THAT. >
NORMAN OWEN AND ANGELA OWEN ARE A BROTHER/SISTER COUPLE.
THEY WERE THE STANDARD CHAMPIONS BEFORE GIULIO.
THEIR DANCE STYLE WAS A DEFINITIVELY ROYAL, BRITISH STYLE.
THEY WERE INCREDIBLY EXPRESSIVE, CONJURING SUCH A NOBLE, EXQUISITE AMBIANCE THAT THEY COMPLETELY OVERWHELMED THEIR COMPETITORS.

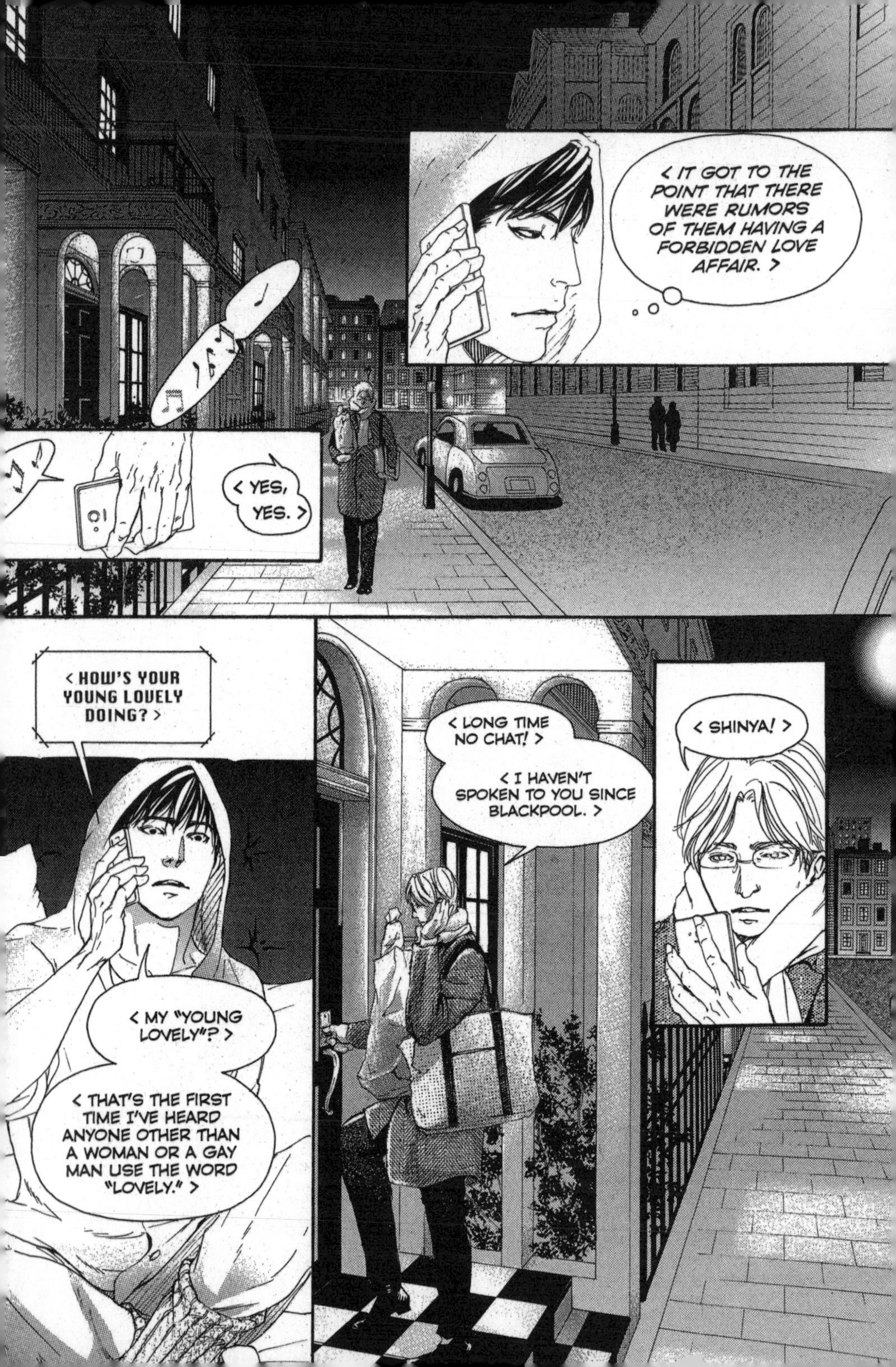

< IT GOT TO THE POINT THAT THERE WERE RUMORS OF THEM HAVING A FORBIDDEN LOVE AFFAIR. >
< YES, YES. >
< SHINYA! >
< LONG TIME NO CHAT! >
< I HAVEN'T SPOKEN TO YOU SINCE BLACKPOOL. >
< HOW'S YOUR YOUNG LOVELY DOING? >
< MY "YOUNG LOVELY"? >
< THAT'S THE FIRST TIME I'VE HEARD ANYONE OTHER THAN A WOMAN OR A GAY MAN USE THE WORD "LOVELY." >

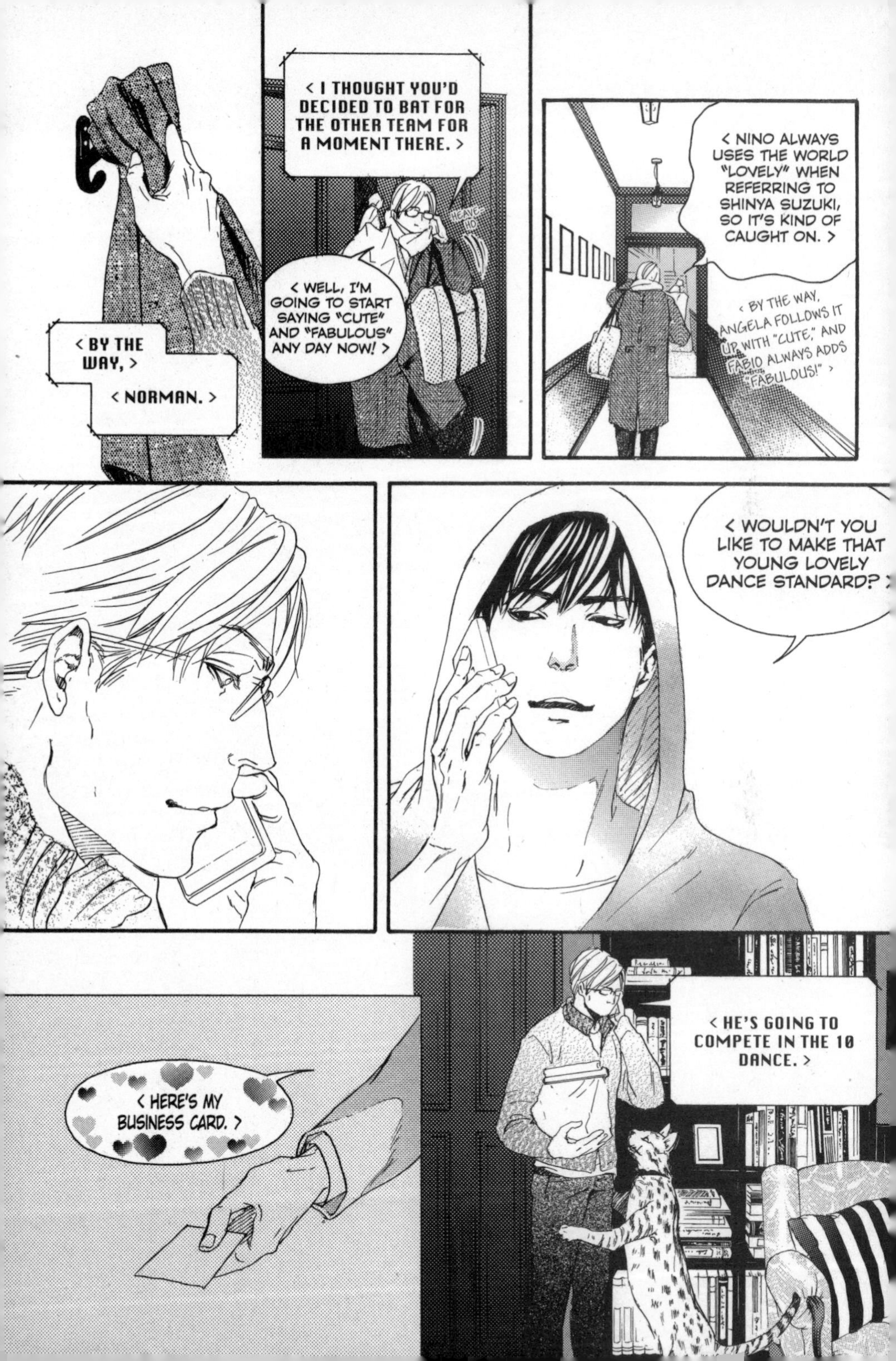
< NINO ALWAYS USES THE WORLD "LOVELY" WHEN REFERRING TO SHINYA SUZUKI, SO IT'S KIND OF CAUGHT ON. >
< BY THE WAY, ANGELA FOLLOWS IT UP WITH "CUTE," AND FABIO ALWAYS ADDS "FABULOUS!" >
< I THOUGHT YOU'D DECIDED TO BAT FOR THE OTHER TEAM FOR A MOMENT THERE. >
HEAVE-HO
< WELL, I'M GOING TO START SAYING "CUTE" AND "FABULOUS" ANY DAY NOW! >
< BY THE WAY, >
< NORMAN. >
< WOULDN'T YOU LIKE TO MAKE THAT YOUNG LOVELY DANCE STANDARD? >
< HE'S GOING TO COMPETE IN THE 10 DANCE. >
< HERE'S MY BUSINESS CARD. >

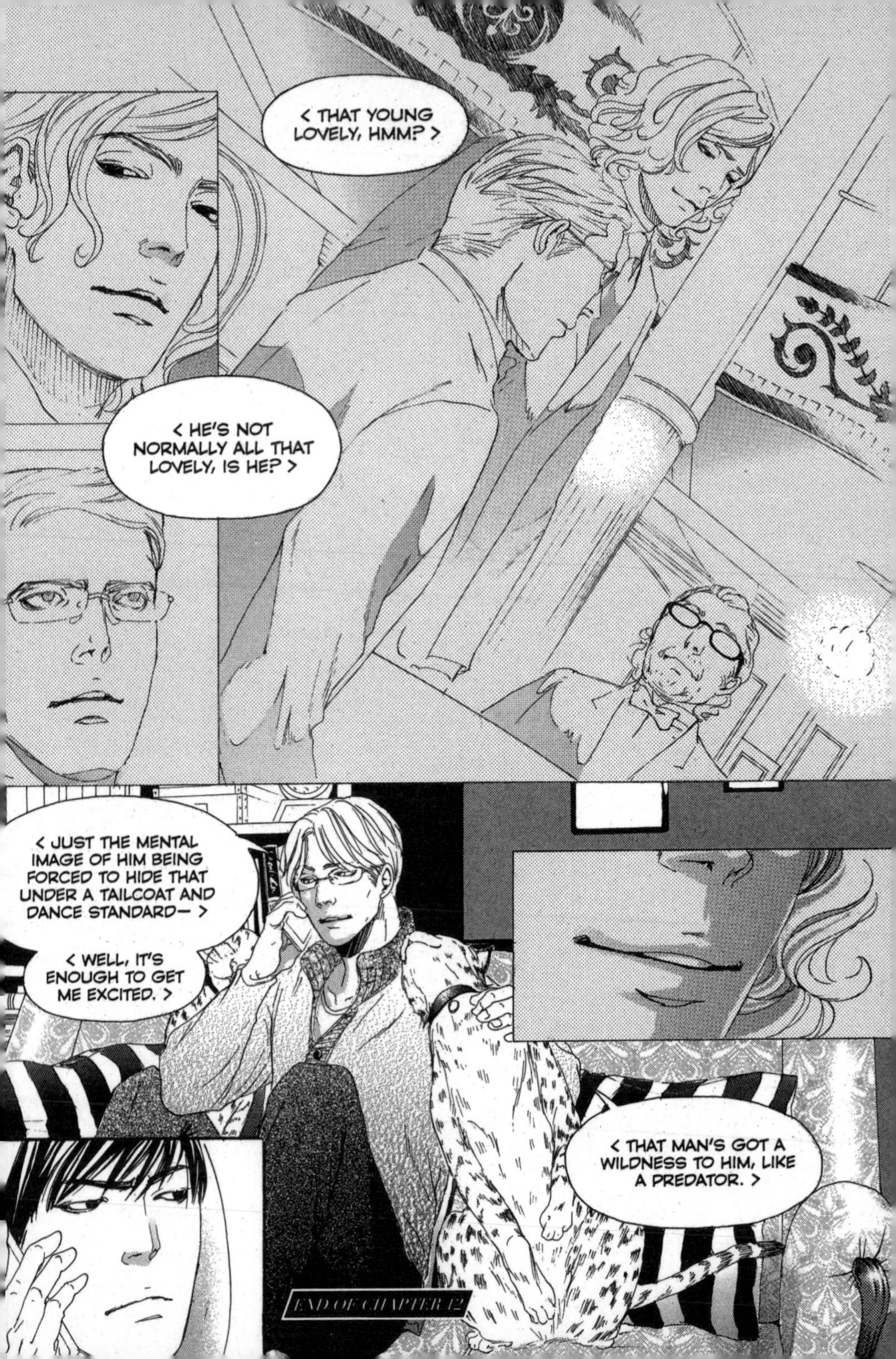
< THAT YOUNG LOVELY, HMM? >
< HE'S NOT NORMALLY ALL THAT LOVELY, IS HE? >
< THAT MAN'S GOT A WILDNESS TO HIM, LIKE A PREDATOR. >
< JUST THE MENTAL IMAGE OF HIM BEING FORCED TO HIDE THAT UNDER A TAILCOAT AND DANCE STANDARD— >
< WELL, IT'S ENOUGH TO GET ME EXCITED. >
END OF CHAPTER 12

Bonus Comic

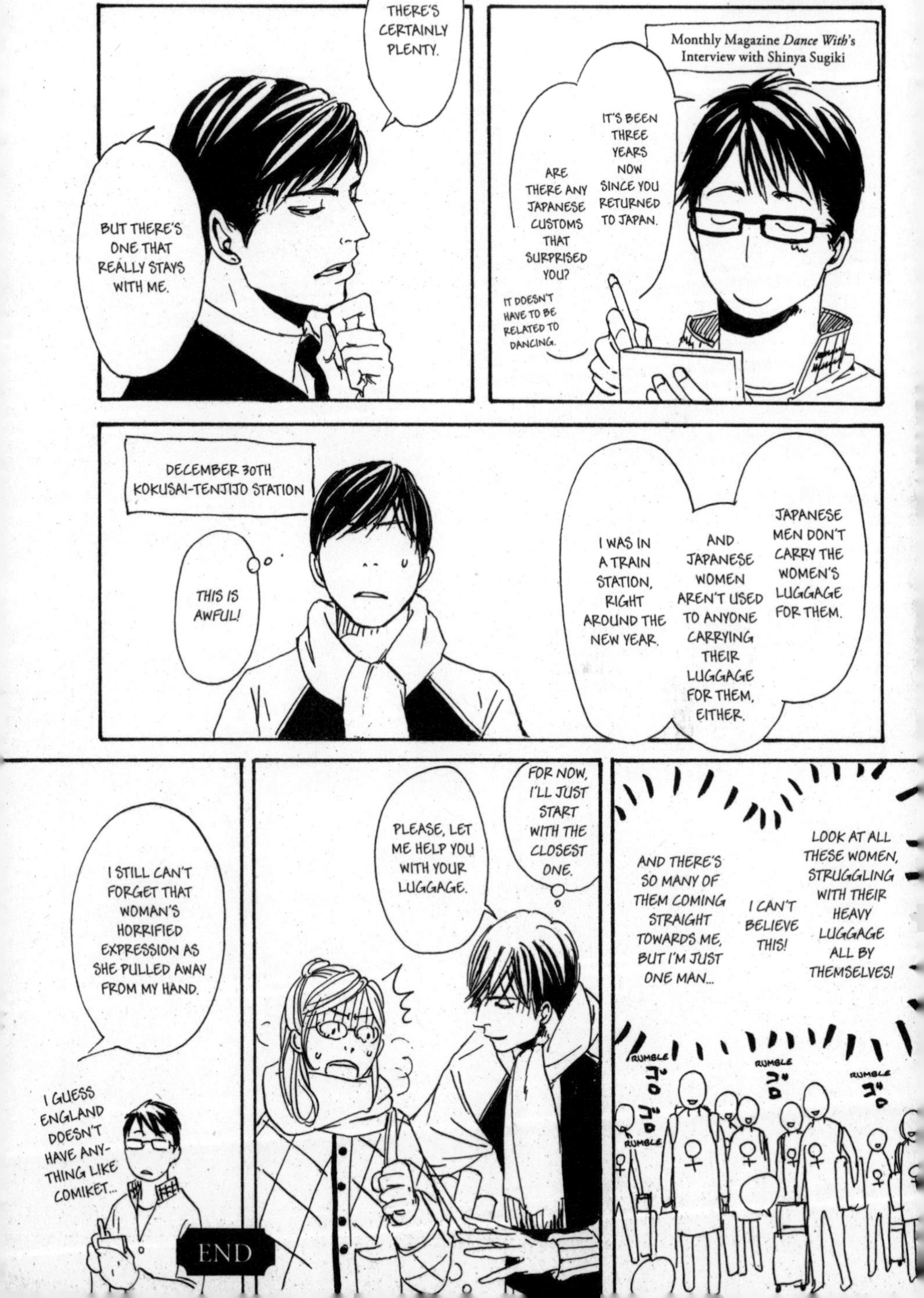
Monthly Magazine *Dance With*'s Interview with Shinya Sugiki
IT'S BEEN THREE YEARS NOW SINCE YOU RETURNED TO JAPAN.
ARE THERE ANY JAPANESE CUSTOMS THAT SURPRISED YOU?
IT DOESN'T HAVE TO BE RELATED TO DANCING.
THERE'S CERTAINLY PLENTY.
BUT THERE'S ONE THAT REALLY STAYS WITH ME.
DECEMBER 30TH KOKUSAI-TENJIJO STATION
JAPANESE MEN DON'T CARRY THE WOMEN'S LUGGAGE FOR THEM.
AND JAPANESE WOMEN AREN'T USED TO ANYONE CARRYING THEIR LUGGAGE FOR THEM, EITHER.
I WAS IN A TRAIN STATION, RIGHT AROUND THE NEW YEAR.
THIS IS AWFUL!
LOOK AT ALL THESE WOMEN, STRUGGLING WITH THEIR HEAVY LUGGAGE ALL BY THEMSELVES!
I CAN'T BELIEVE THIS!
AND THERE'S SO MANY OF THEM COMING STRAIGHT TOWARDS ME, BUT I'M JUST ONE MAN...
RUMBLE
RUMBLE
RUMBLE
RUMBLE
FOR NOW, I'LL JUST START WITH THE CLOSEST ONE.
PLEASE, LET ME HELP YOU WITH YOUR LUGGAGE.
I STILL CAN'T FORGET THAT WOMAN'S HORRIFIED EXPRESSION AS SHE PULLED AWAY FROM MY HAND.
I GUESS ENGLAND DOESN'T HAVE ANYTHING LIKE COMIKET...
END

10 DANCE

YOU AND THE GINZA NIGHT AND THE MUSIC

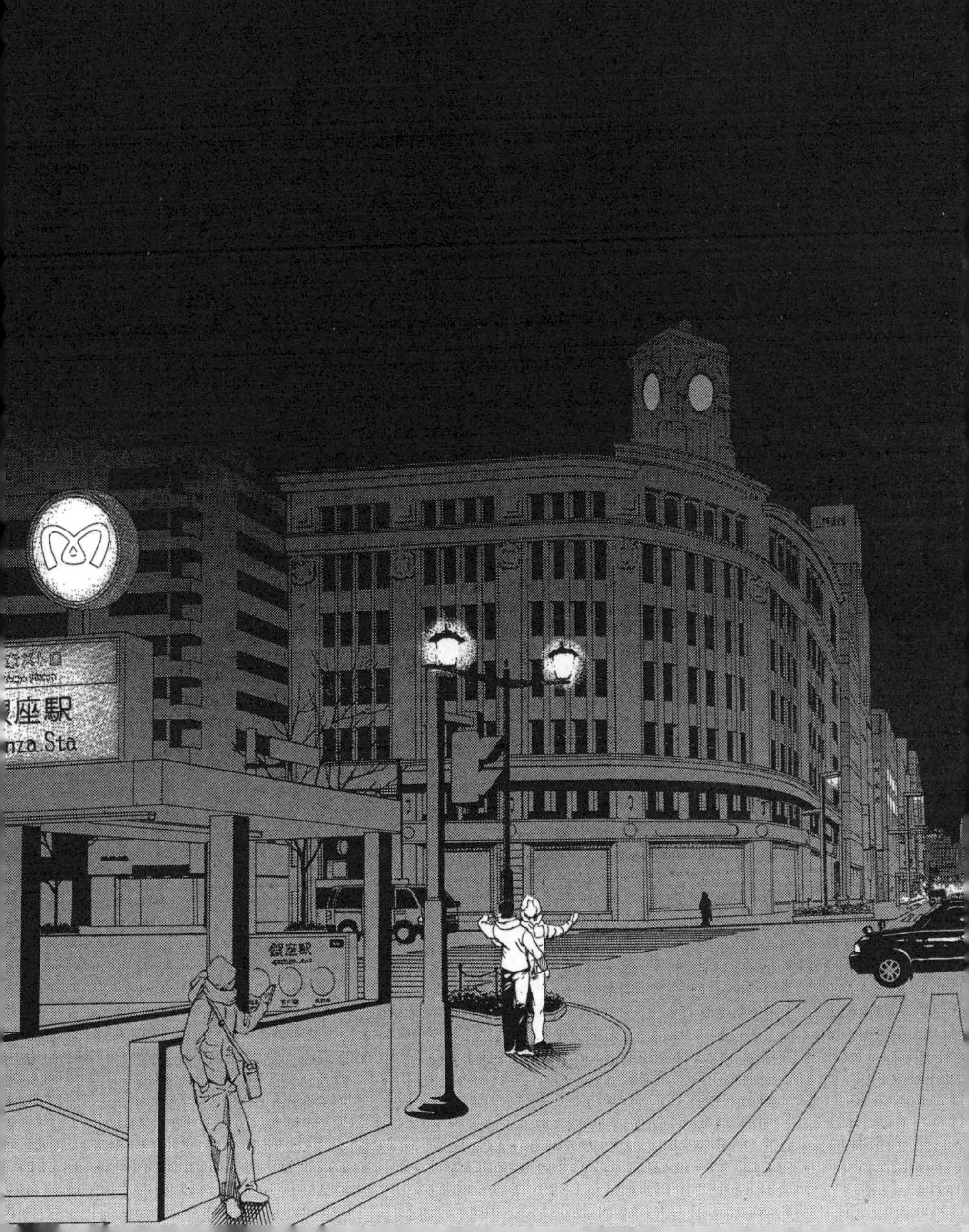
銀座駅

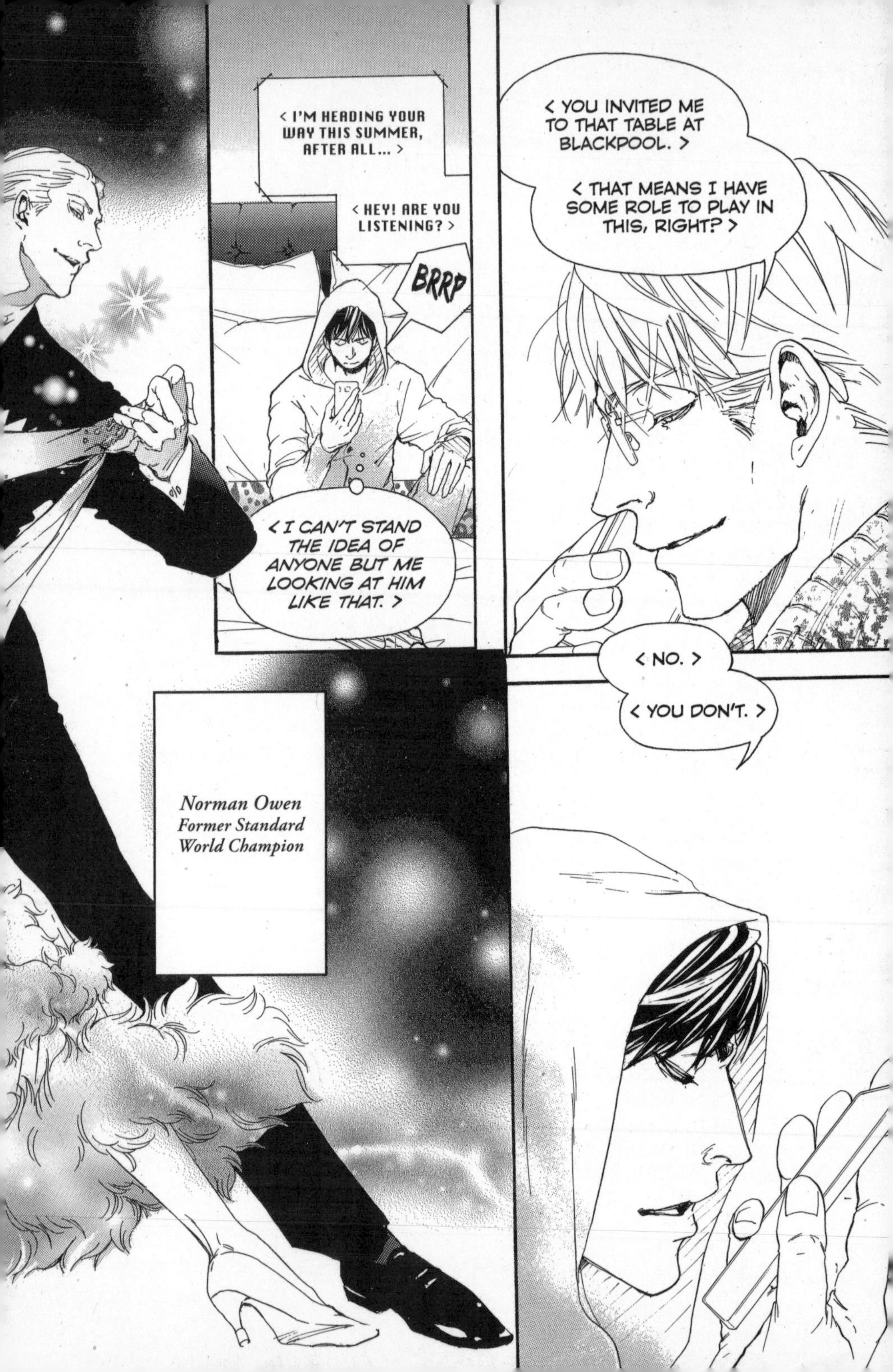
< YOU INVITED ME TO THAT TABLE AT BLACKPOOL. >
< THAT MEANS I HAVE SOME ROLE TO PLAY IN THIS, RIGHT? >
< NO. >
< YOU DON'T. >
< I'M HEADING YOUR WAY THIS SUMMER, AFTER ALL... >
< HEY! ARE YOU LISTENING? >
BRRP
< I CAN'T STAND THE IDEA OF ANYONE BUT ME LOOKING AT HIM LIKE THAT. >
Norman Owen
Former Standard
World Champion

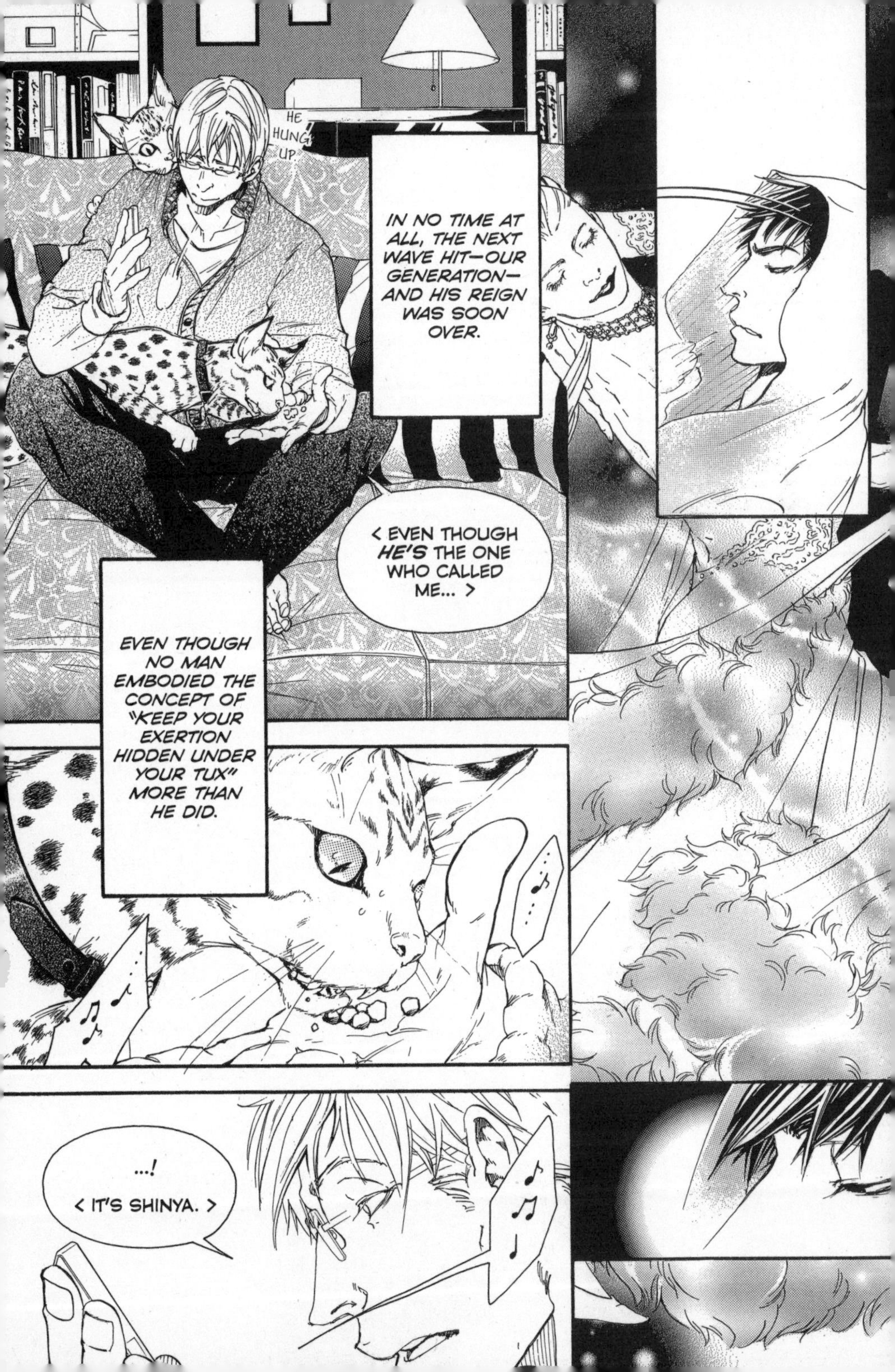
IN NO TIME AT ALL, THE NEXT WAVE HIT—OUR GENERATION—AND HIS REIGN WAS SOON OVER.
HE HUNG UP
< EVEN THOUGH HE'S THE ONE WHO CALLED ME... >
EVEN THOUGH NO MAN EMBODIED THE CONCEPT OF "KEEP YOUR EXERTION HIDDEN UNDER YOUR TUX" MORE THAN HE DID.
...!
< IT'S SHINYA. >

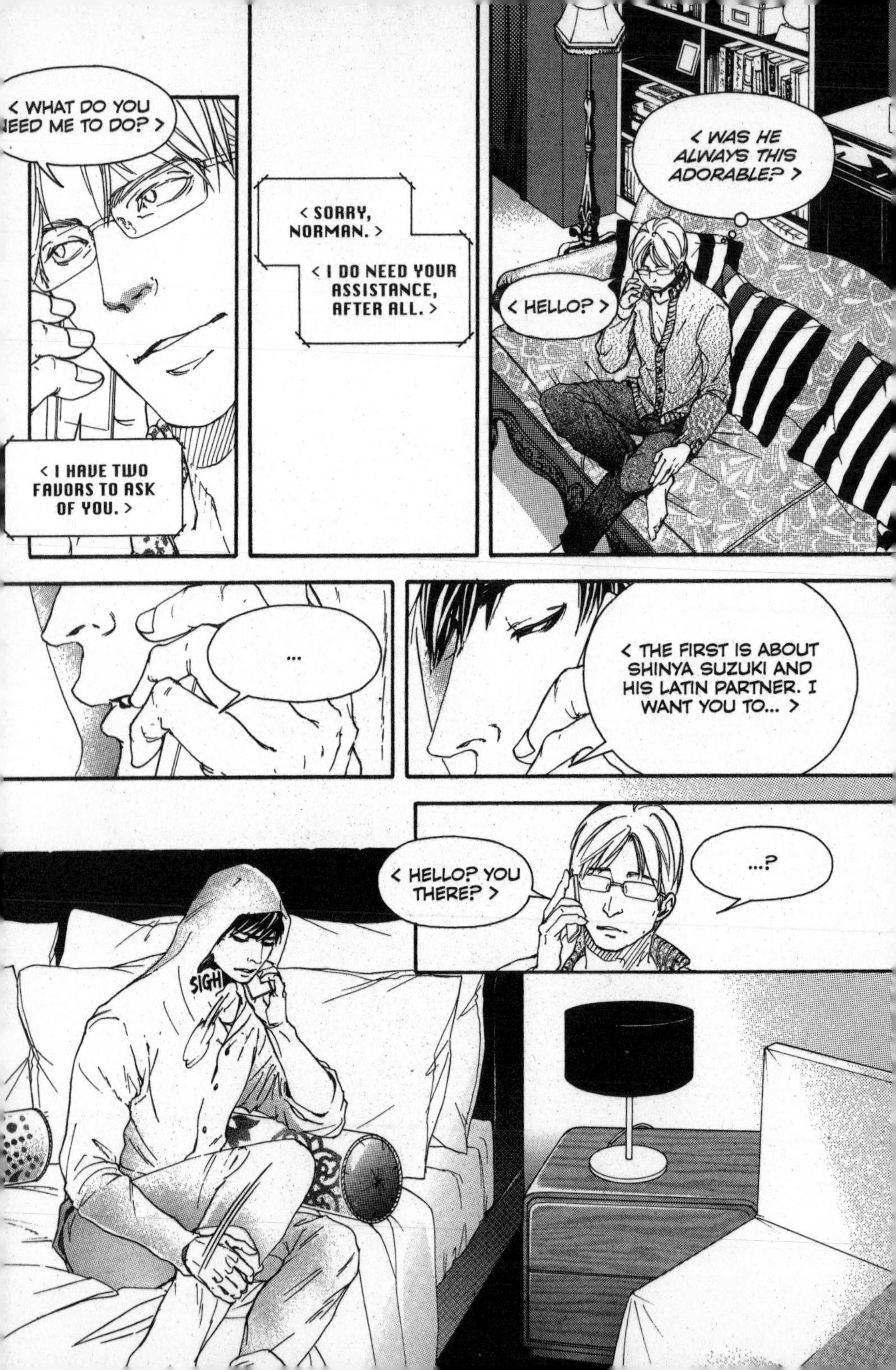
< WAS HE ALWAYS THIS ADORABLE? >
< HELLO? >
< SORRY, NORMAN. >
< I DO NEED YOUR ASSISTANCE, AFTER ALL. >
< WHAT DO YOU NEED ME TO DO? >
< I HAVE TWO FAVORS TO ASK OF YOU. >
< THE FIRST IS ABOUT SHINYA SUZUKI AND HIS LATIN PARTNER. I WANT YOU TO... >
...
...?
< HELLO? YOU THERE? >
SIGH

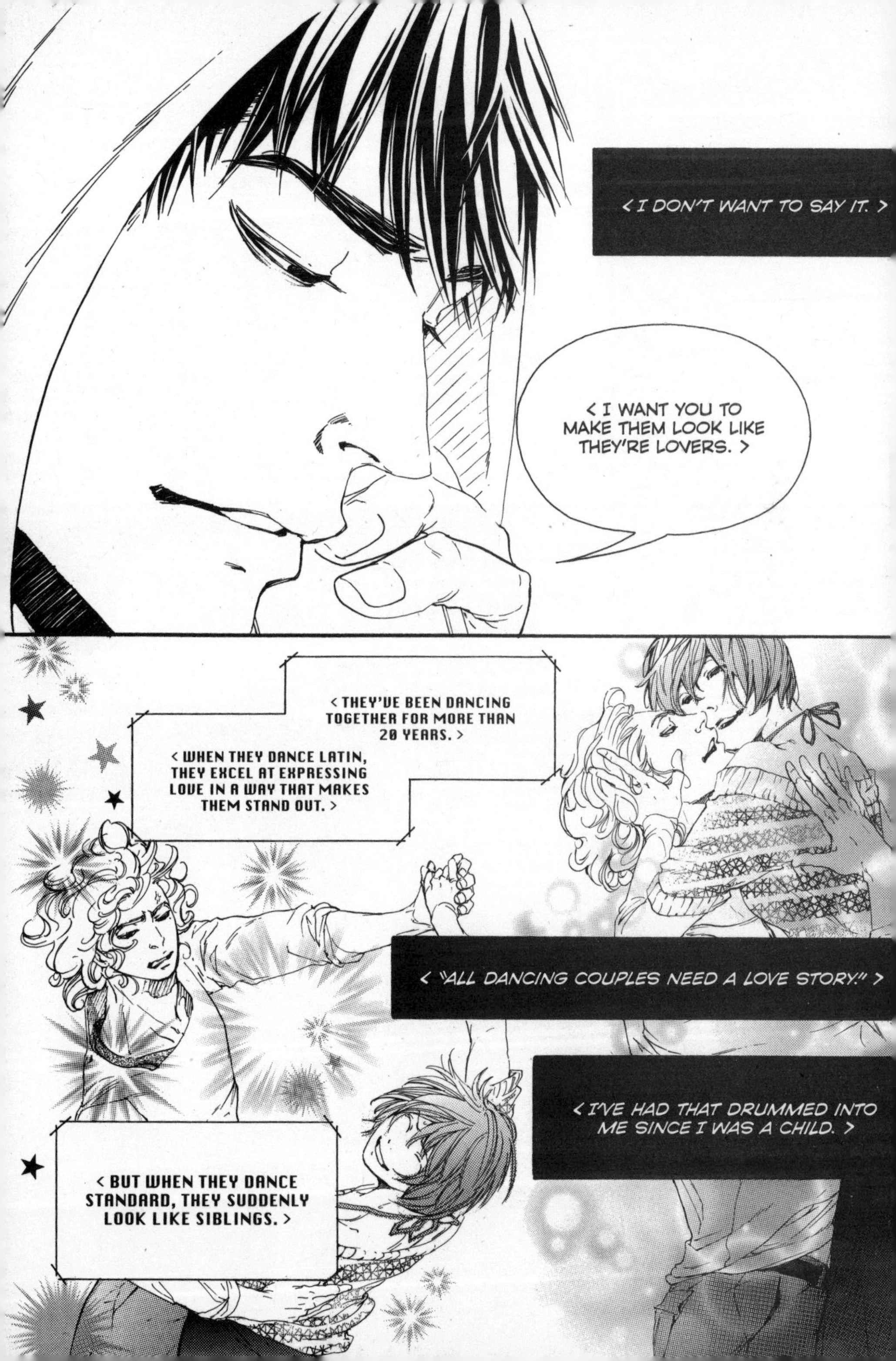
< I DON'T WANT TO SAY IT. >
< I WANT YOU TO MAKE THEM LOOK LIKE THEY'RE LOVERS. >
< THEY'VE BEEN DANCING TOGETHER FOR MORE THAN 20 YEARS. >
< WHEN THEY DANCE LATIN, THEY EXCEL AT EXPRESSING LOVE IN A WAY THAT MAKES THEM STAND OUT. >
< BUT WHEN THEY DANCE STANDARD, THEY SUDDENLY LOOK LIKE SIBLINGS. >
< "ALL DANCING COUPLES NEED A LOVE STORY." >
< I'VE HAD THAT DRUMMED INTO ME SINCE I WAS A CHILD. >

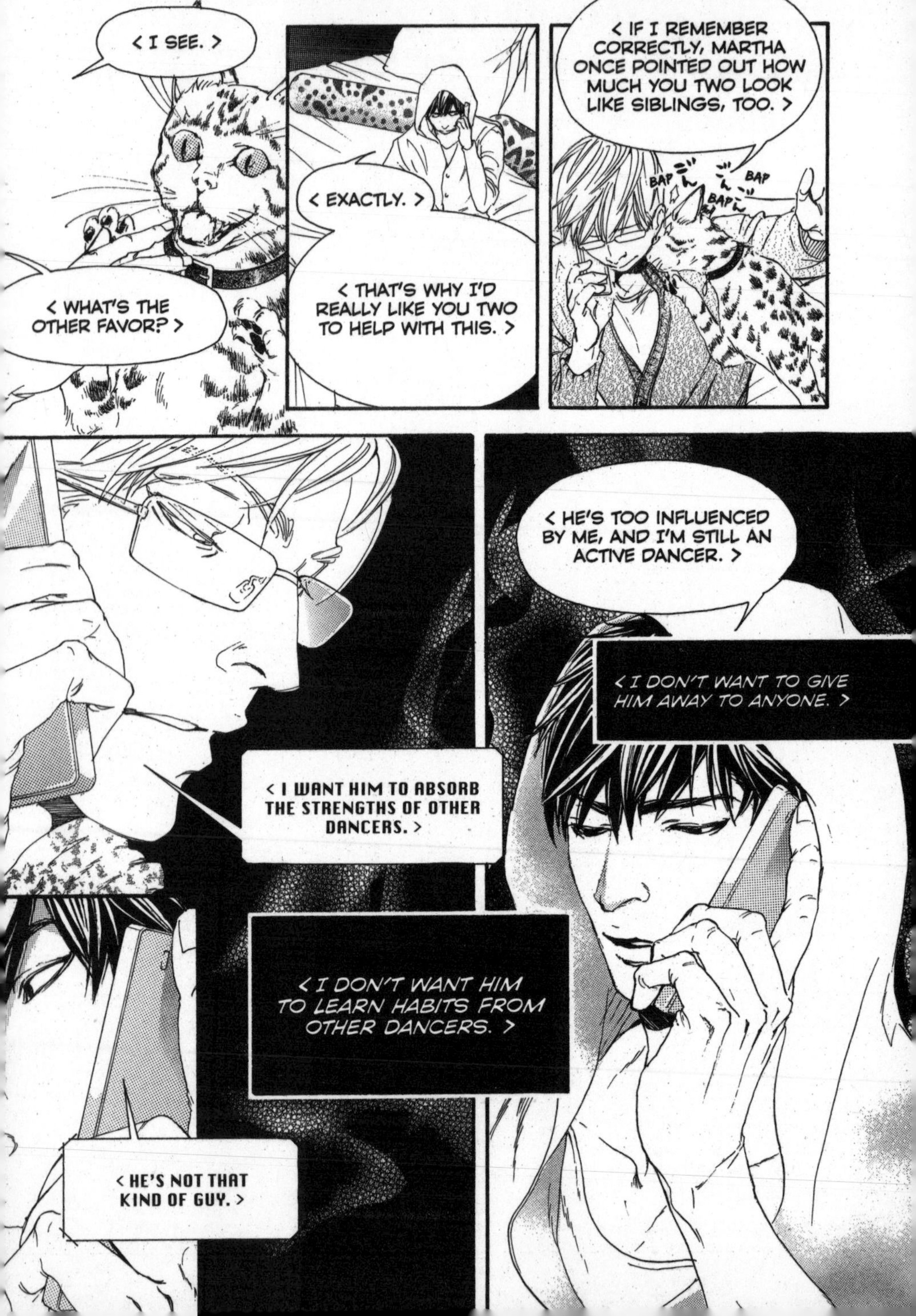
< IF I REMEMBER CORRECTLY, MARTHA ONCE POINTED OUT HOW MUCH YOU TWO LOOK LIKE SIBLINGS, TOO. >
BAP
BAP
BAP
< EXACTLY. >
< THAT'S WHY I'D REALLY LIKE YOU TWO TO HELP WITH THIS. >
< I SEE. >
< WHAT'S THE OTHER FAVOR? >
< HE'S TOO INFLUENCED BY ME, AND I'M STILL AN ACTIVE DANCER. >
< I DON'T WANT TO GIVE HIM AWAY TO ANYONE. >
< I WANT HIM TO ABSORB THE STRENGTHS OF OTHER DANCERS. >
< I DON'T WANT HIM TO LEARN HABITS FROM OTHER DANCERS. >
< HE'S NOT THAT KIND OF GUY. >

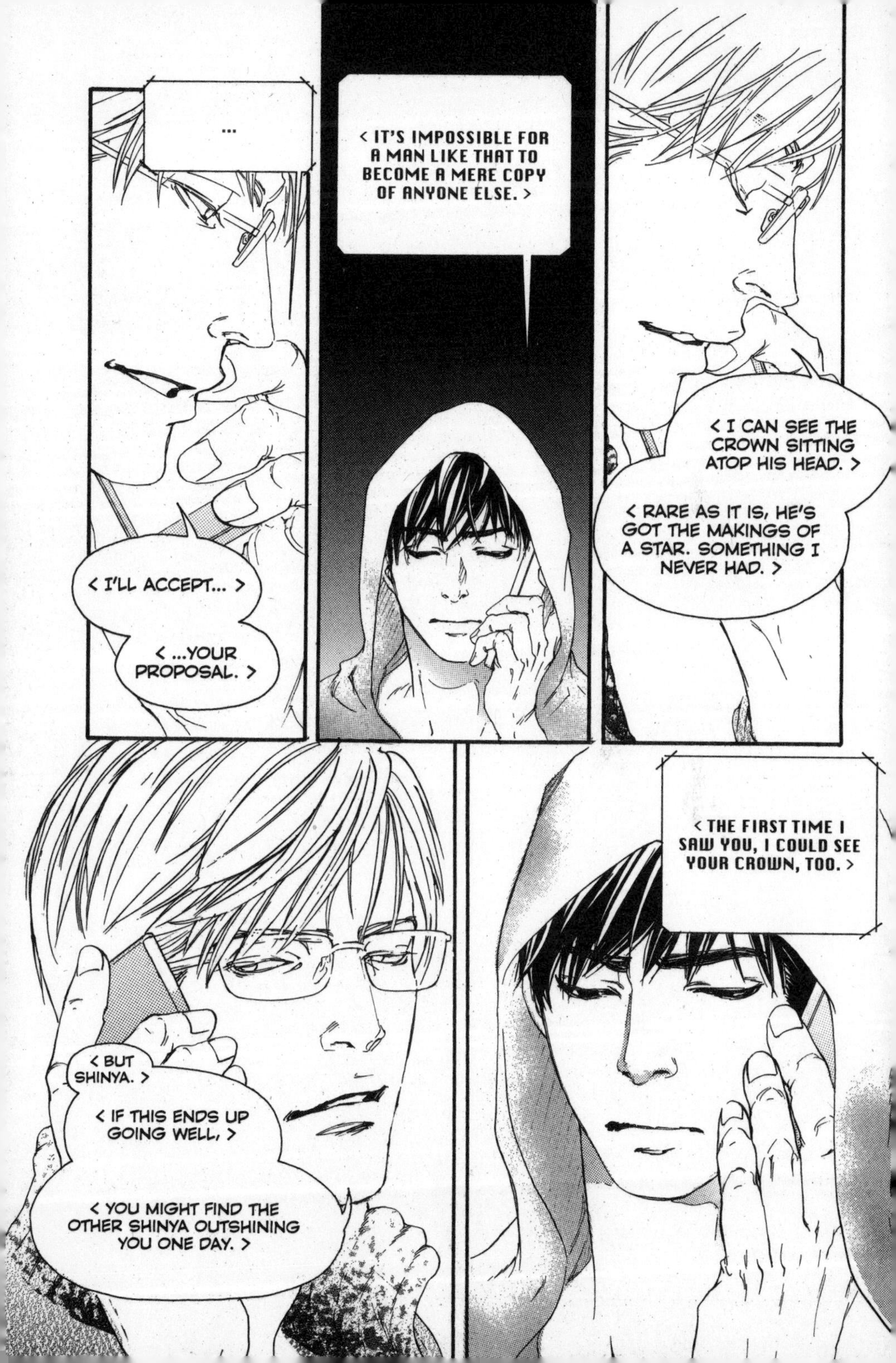
< I CAN SEE THE CROWN SITTING ATOP HIS HEAD. >
< RARE AS IT IS, HE'S GOT THE MAKINGS OF A STAR. SOMETHING I NEVER HAD. >
< IT'S IMPOSSIBLE FOR A MAN LIKE THAT TO BECOME A MERE COPY OF ANYONE ELSE. >
...
< I'LL ACCEPT... >
< ...YOUR PROPOSAL. >
< THE FIRST TIME I SAW YOU, I COULD SEE YOUR CROWN, TOO. >
< BUT SHINYA. >
< IF THIS ENDS UP GOING WELL, >
< YOU MIGHT FIND THE OTHER SHINYA OUTSHINING YOU ONE DAY. >

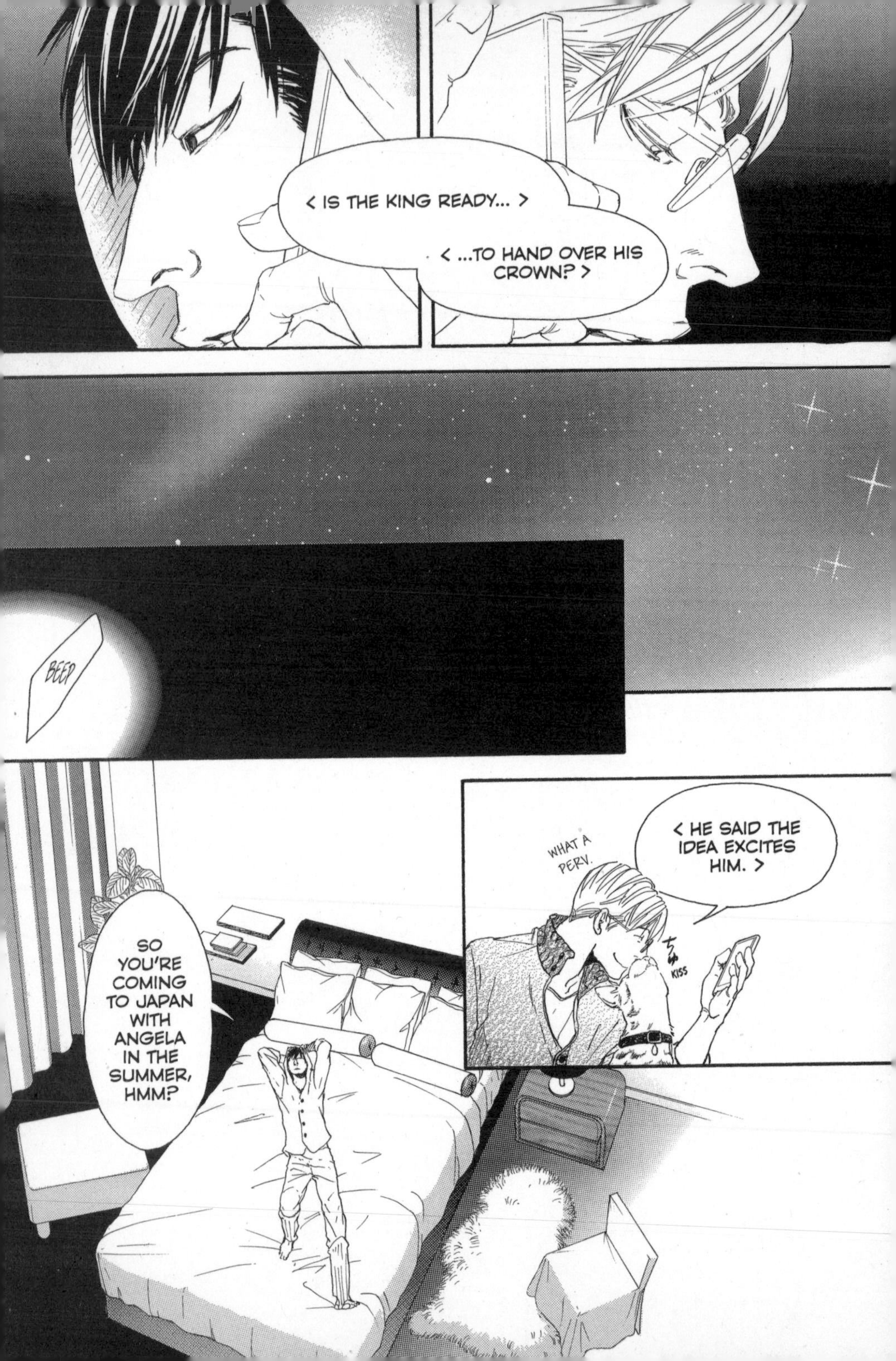

< IS THE KING READY... >
< ...TO HAND OVER HIS CROWN? >
BEEP
< HE SAID THE IDEA EXCITES HIM. >
WHAT A PERV.
ちゅ KISS
SO YOU'RE COMING TO JAPAN WITH ANGELA IN THE SUMMER, HMM?

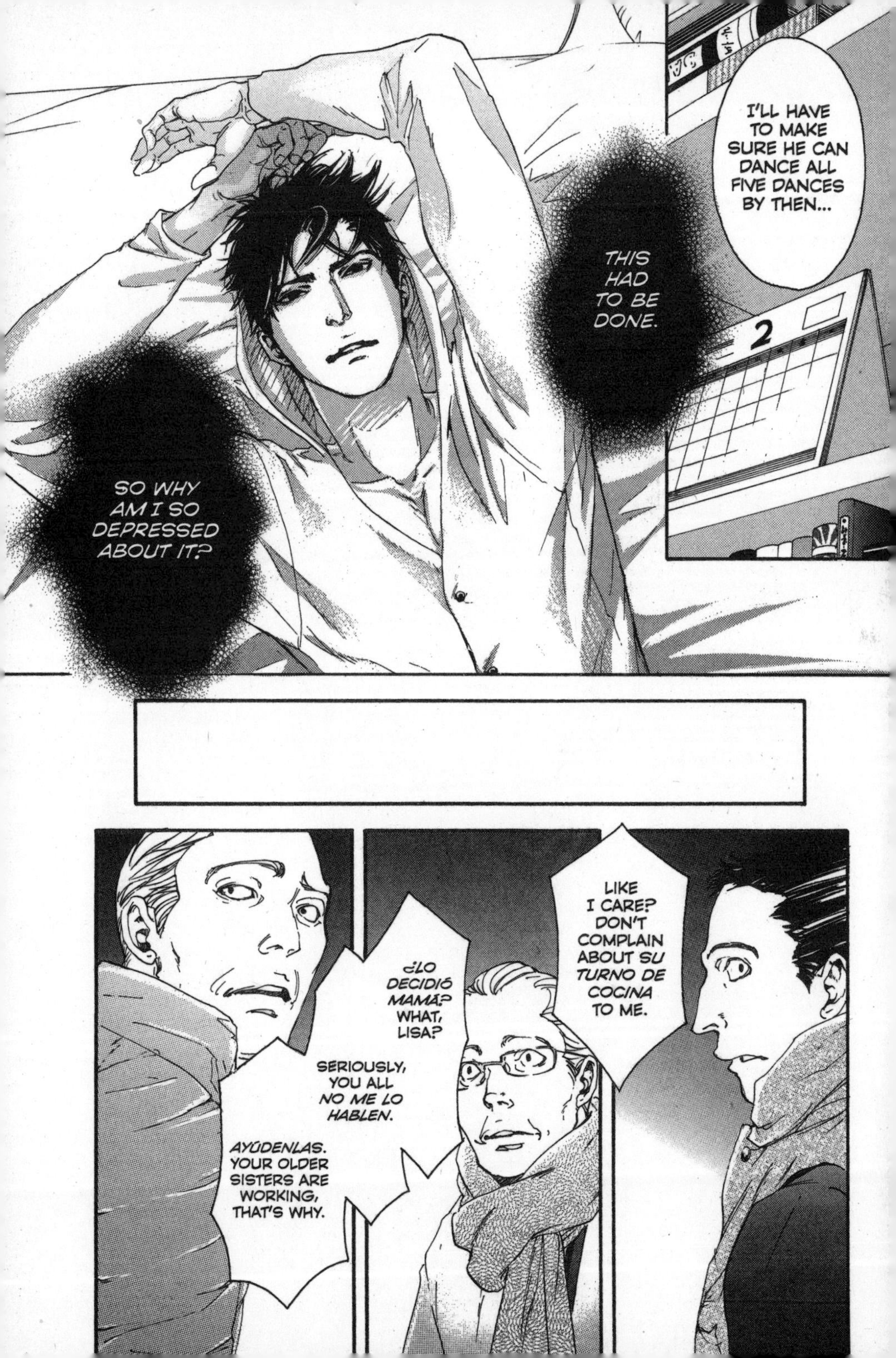
I'LL HAVE TO MAKE SURE HE CAN DANCE ALL FIVE DANCES BY THEN...
THIS HAD TO BE DONE.
SO WHY AM I SO DEPRESSED ABOUT IT?
LIKE I CARE? DON'T COMPLAIN ABOUT SU TURNO DE COCINA TO ME.
¿LO DECIDIÓ MAMÁ? WHAT, LISA?
SERIOUSLY, YOU ALL NO ME LO HABLEN.
AYÚDENLAS. YOUR OLDER SISTERS ARE WORKING, THAT'S WHY.

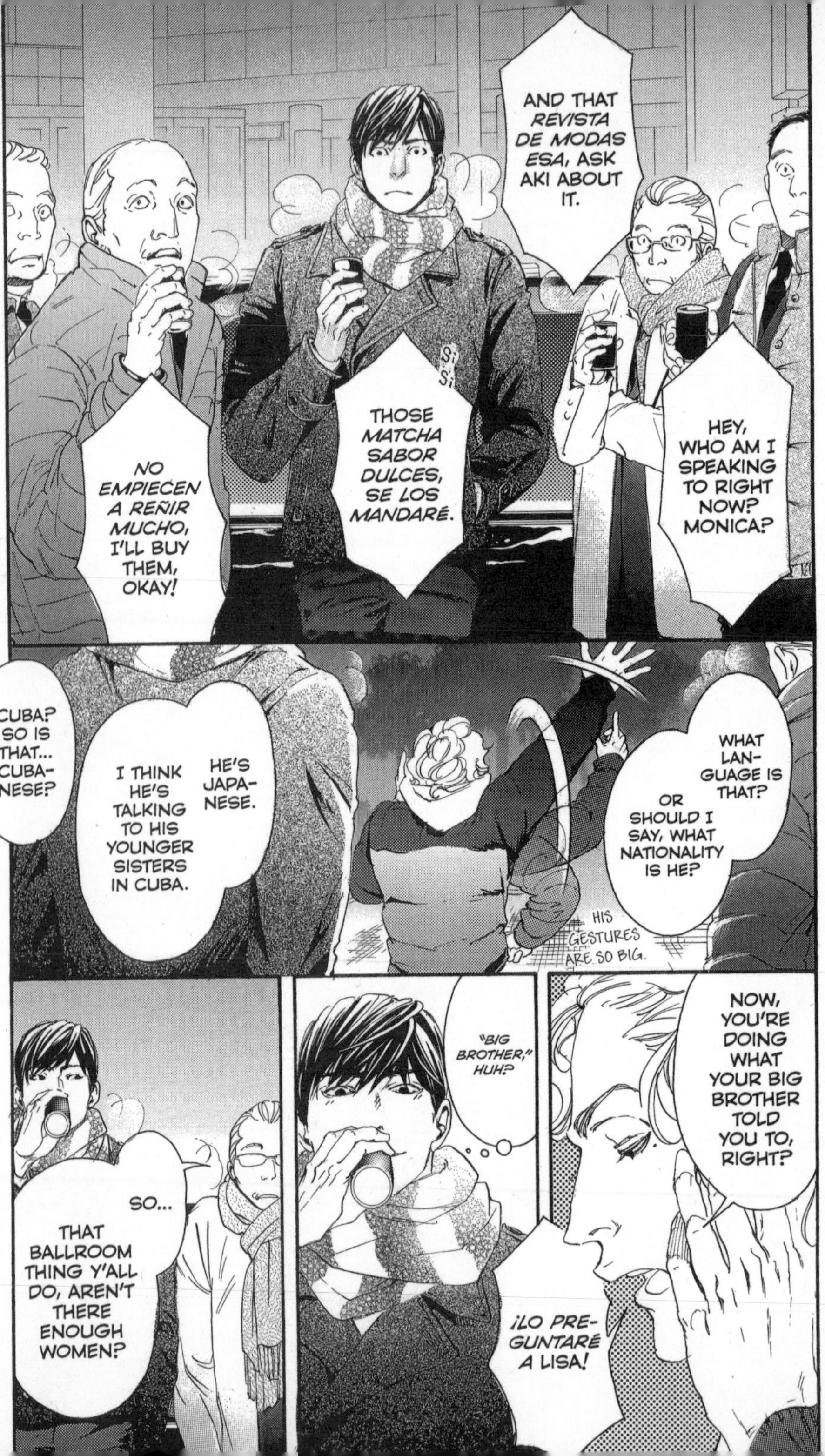
AND THAT *REVISTA DE MODAS ESA*, ASK AKI ABOUT IT.
HEY, WHO AM I SPEAKING TO RIGHT NOW? MONICA?
Sí Sí
THOSE *MATCHA SABOR DULCES, SE LOS MANDARÉ.*
NO EMPIECEN A REÑIR MUCHO, I'LL BUY THEM, OKAY!
WHAT LANGUAGE IS THAT?
OR SHOULD I SAY, WHAT NATIONALITY IS HE?
HIS GESTURES ARE SO BIG.
HE'S JAPANESE.
I THINK HE'S TALKING TO HIS YOUNGER SISTERS IN CUBA.
CUBA? SO IS THAT... CUBANESE?
NOW, YOU'RE DOING WHAT YOUR BIG BROTHER TOLD YOU TO, RIGHT?
¡LO PREGUNTARÉ A LISA!
"BIG BROTHER," HUH?
SO...
THAT BALLROOM THING Y'ALL DO, AREN'T THERE ENOUGH WOMEN?

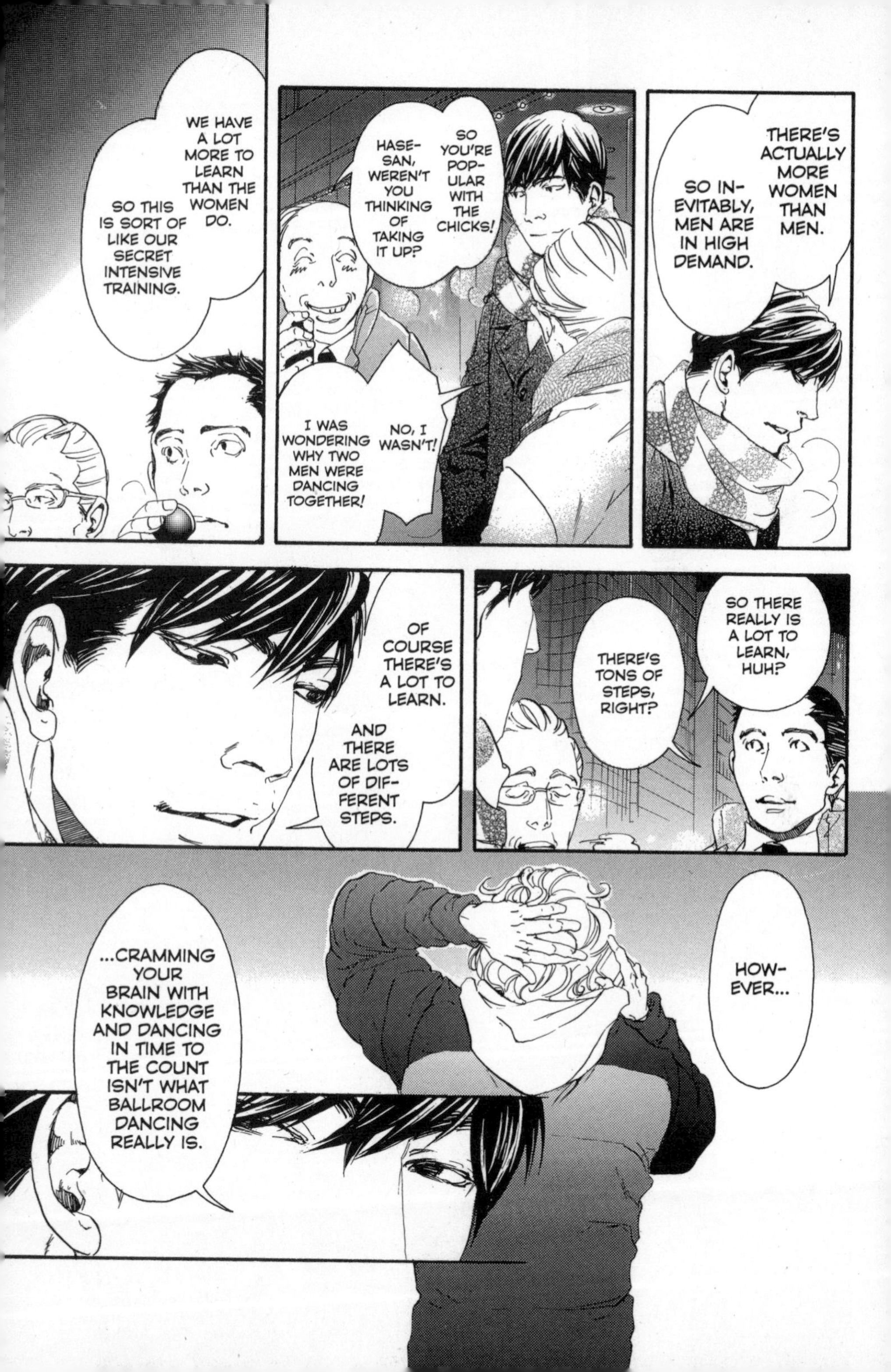
THERE'S ACTUALLY MORE WOMEN THAN MEN.
SO IN-EVITABLY, MEN ARE IN HIGH DEMAND.
SO YOU'RE POP-ULAR WITH THE CHICKS!
HASE-SAN, WEREN'T YOU THINKING OF TAKING IT UP?
NO, I WASN'T!
I WAS WONDERING WHY TWO MEN WERE DANCING TOGETHER!
WE HAVE A LOT MORE TO LEARN THAN THE WOMEN DO.
SO THIS IS SORT OF LIKE OUR SECRET INTENSIVE TRAINING.
SO THERE REALLY IS A LOT TO LEARN, HUH?
THERE'S TONS OF STEPS, RIGHT?
OF COURSE THERE'S A LOT TO LEARN.
AND THERE ARE LOTS OF DIF-FERENT STEPS.
HOW-EVER...
...CRAMMING YOUR BRAIN WITH KNOWLEDGE AND DANCING IN TIME TO THE COUNT ISN'T WHAT BALLROOM DANCING REALLY IS.

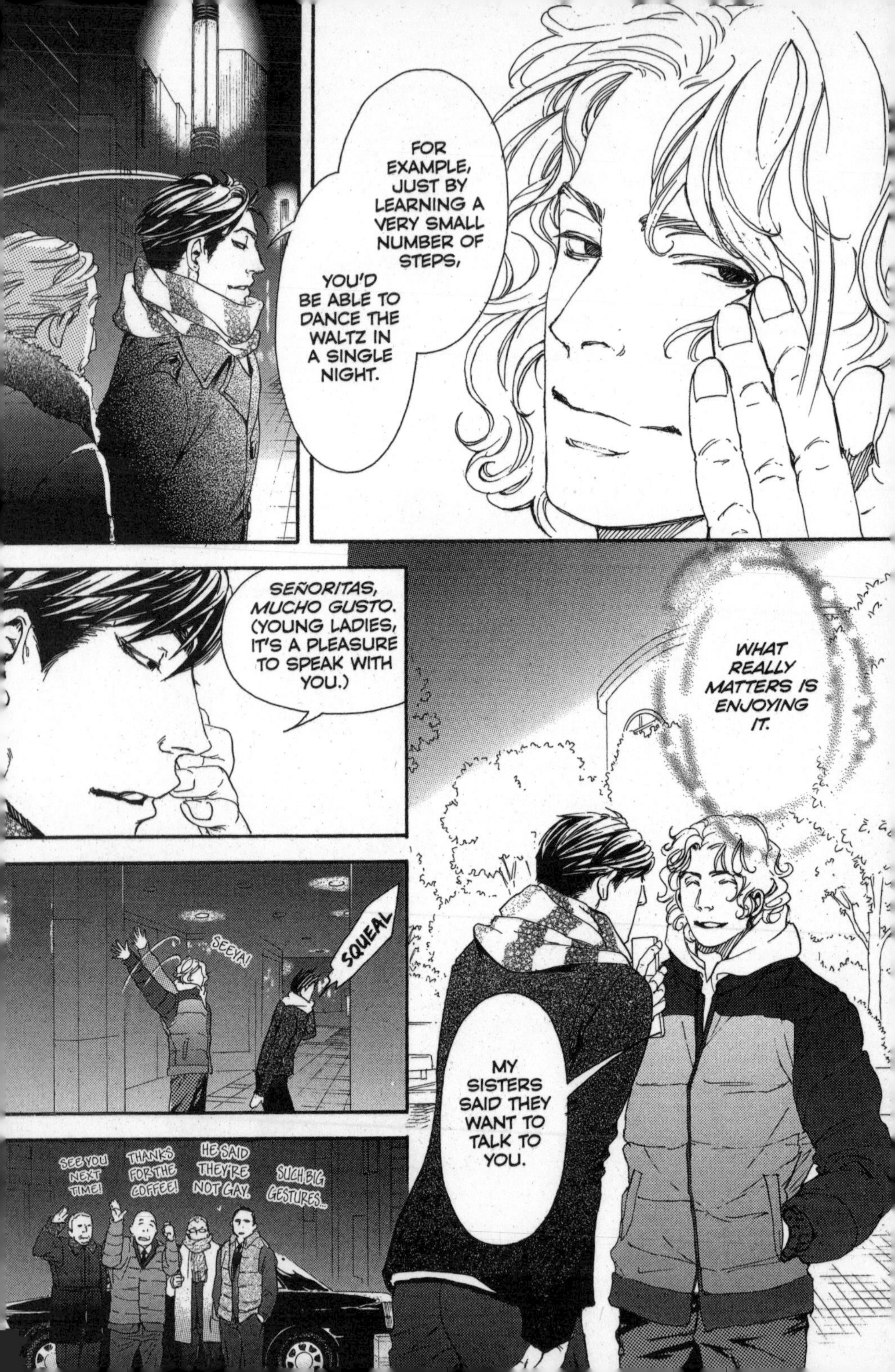
FOR EXAMPLE, JUST BY LEARNING A VERY SMALL NUMBER OF STEPS,
YOU'D BE ABLE TO DANCE THE WALTZ IN A SINGLE NIGHT.
WHAT REALLY MATTERS IS ENJOYING IT.
MY SISTERS SAID THEY WANT TO TALK TO YOU.
SEÑORITAS, MUCHO GUSTO. (YOUNG LADIES, IT'S A PLEASURE TO SPEAK WITH YOU.)
SQUEAL
SEEYA!
SUCH BIG GESTURES...
HE SAID THEY'RE NOT GAY.
THANKS FOR THE COFFEE!
SEE YOU NEXT TIME!

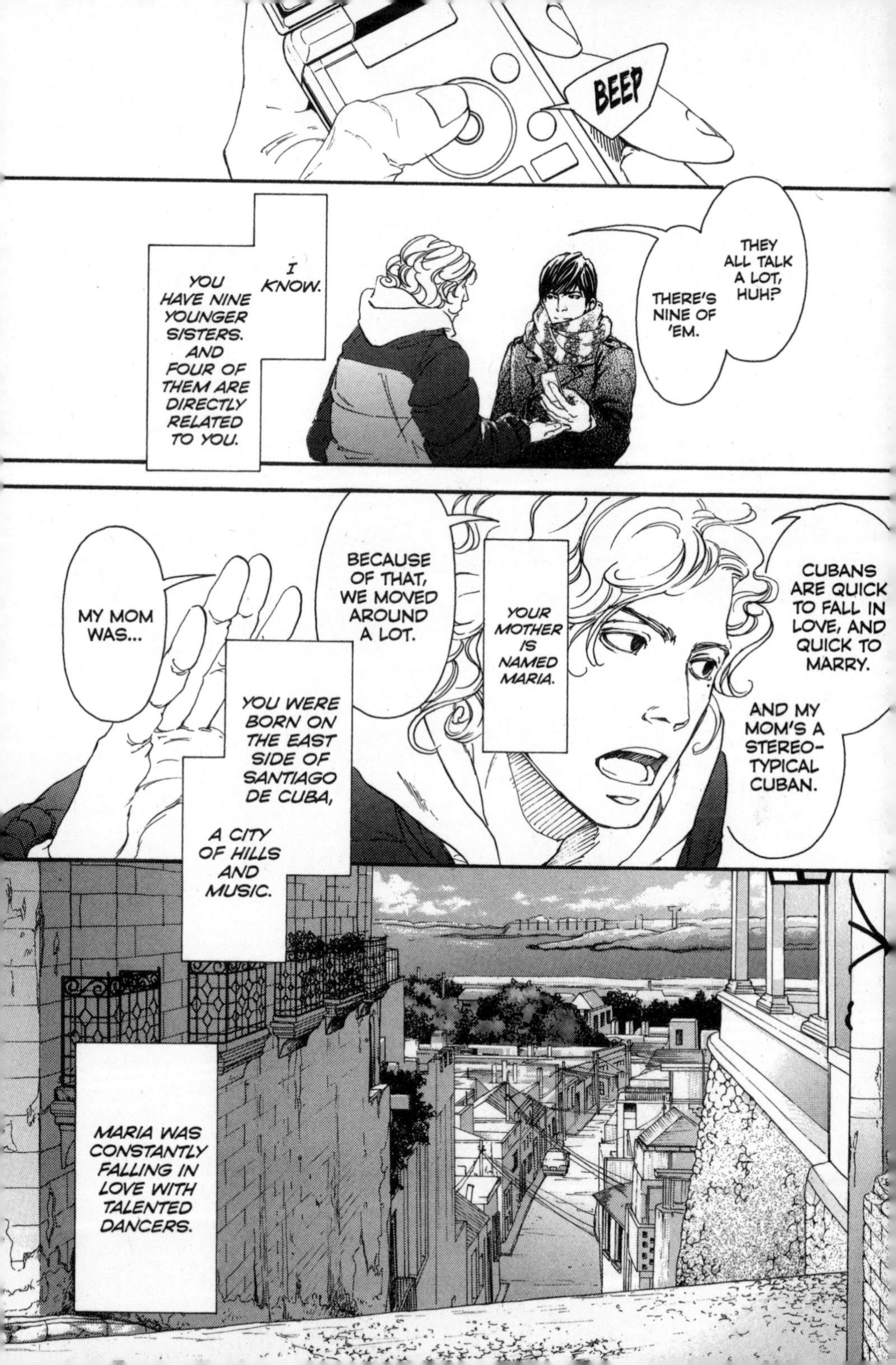
BEEP
THEY ALL TALK A LOT, HUH?
THERE'S NINE OF 'EM.
I KNOW.
YOU HAVE NINE YOUNGER SISTERS. AND FOUR OF THEM ARE DIRECTLY RELATED TO YOU.
CUBANS ARE QUICK TO FALL IN LOVE, AND QUICK TO MARRY.
AND MY MOM'S A STEREOTYPICAL CUBAN.
YOUR MOTHER IS NAMED MARIA.
BECAUSE OF THAT, WE MOVED AROUND A LOT.
MY MOM WAS...
YOU WERE BORN ON THE EAST SIDE OF SANTIAGO DE CUBA,
A CITY OF HILLS AND MUSIC.
MARIA WAS CONSTANTLY FALLING IN LOVE WITH TALENTED DANCERS.

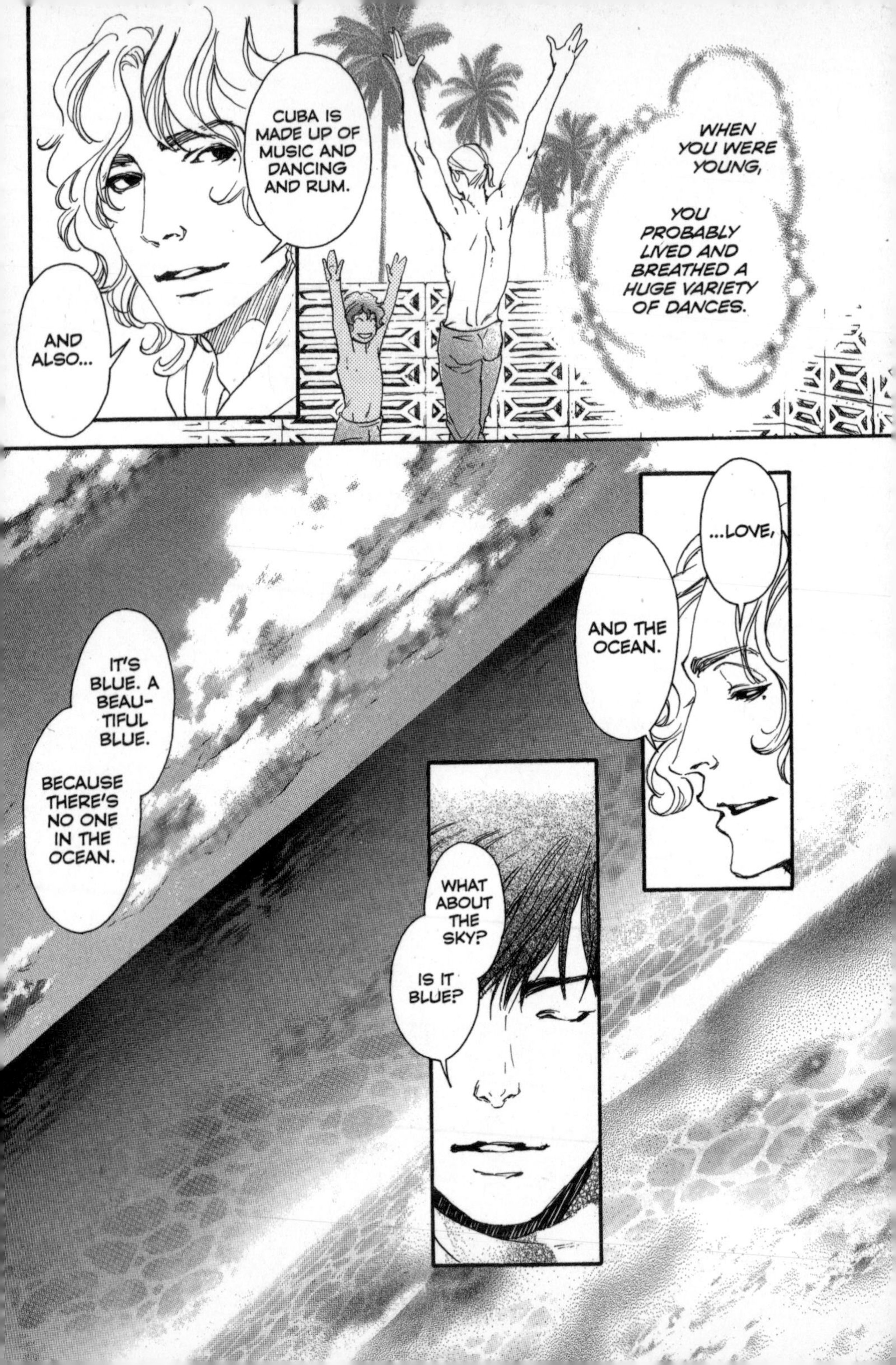
WHEN YOU WERE YOUNG,
YOU PROBABLY LIVED AND BREATHED A HUGE VARIETY OF DANCES.
CUBA IS MADE UP OF MUSIC AND DANCING AND RUM.
AND ALSO...
...LOVE,
AND THE OCEAN.
IT'S BLUE. A BEAU-TIFUL BLUE.
BECAUSE THERE'S NO ONE IN THE OCEAN.
WHAT ABOUT THE SKY?
IS IT BLUE?

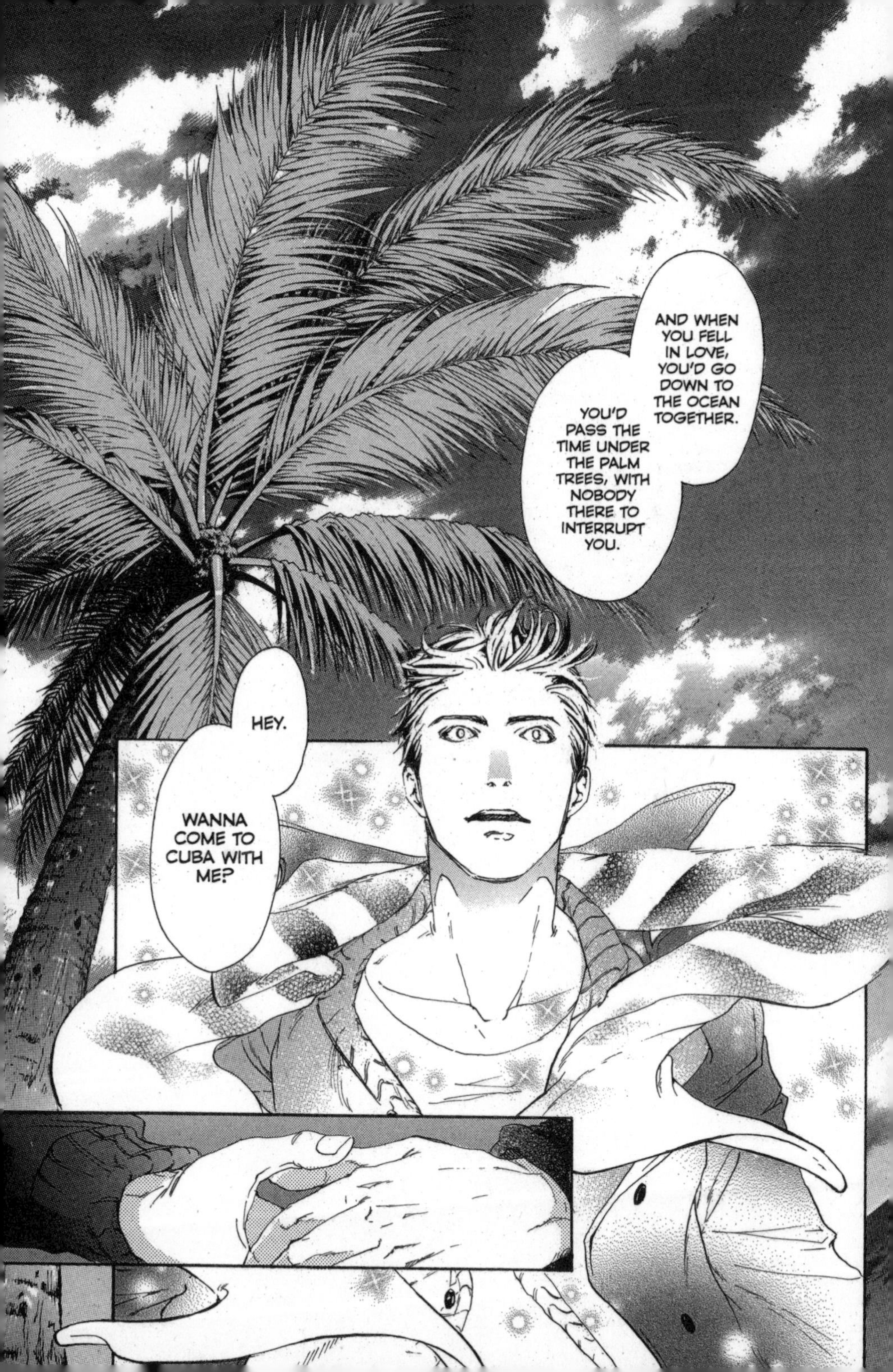
AND WHEN YOU FELL IN LOVE, YOU'D GO DOWN TO THE OCEAN TOGETHER.
YOU'D PASS THE TIME UNDER THE PALM TREES, WITH NOBODY THERE TO INTERRUPT YOU.
HEY.
WANNA COME TO CUBA WITH ME?

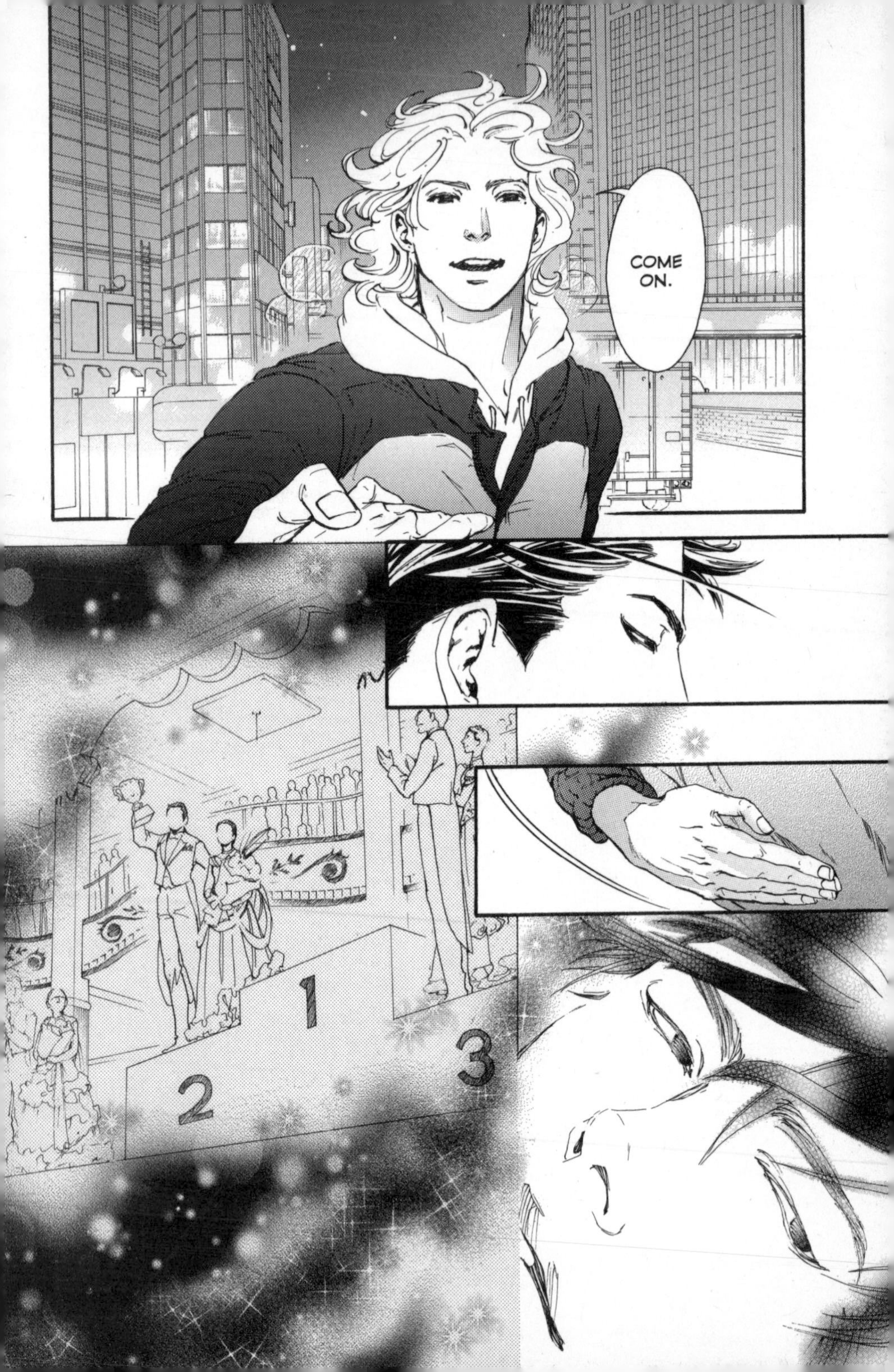
COME ON.
1
2
3

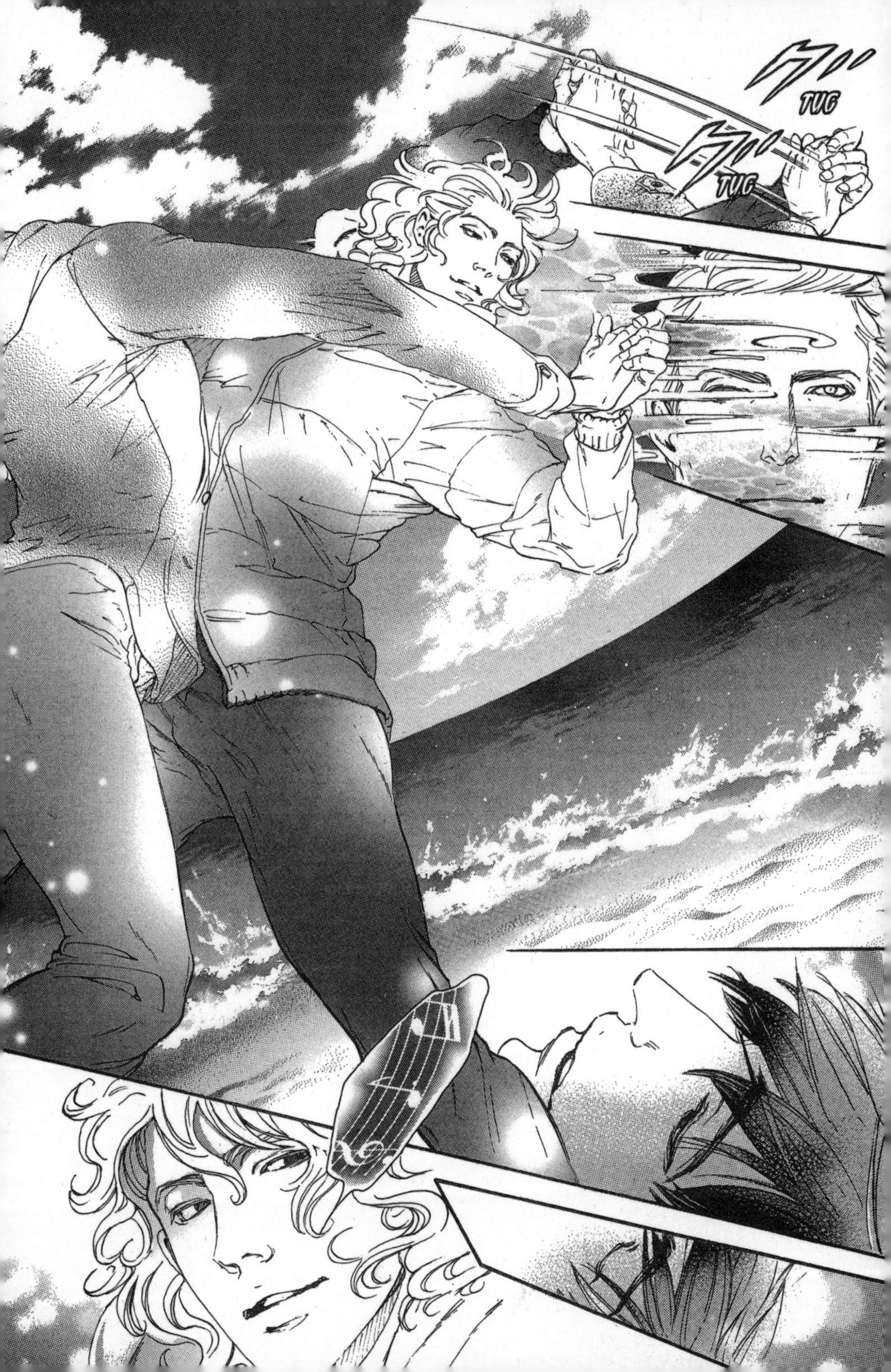
グッ
TUG
グッ
TUG

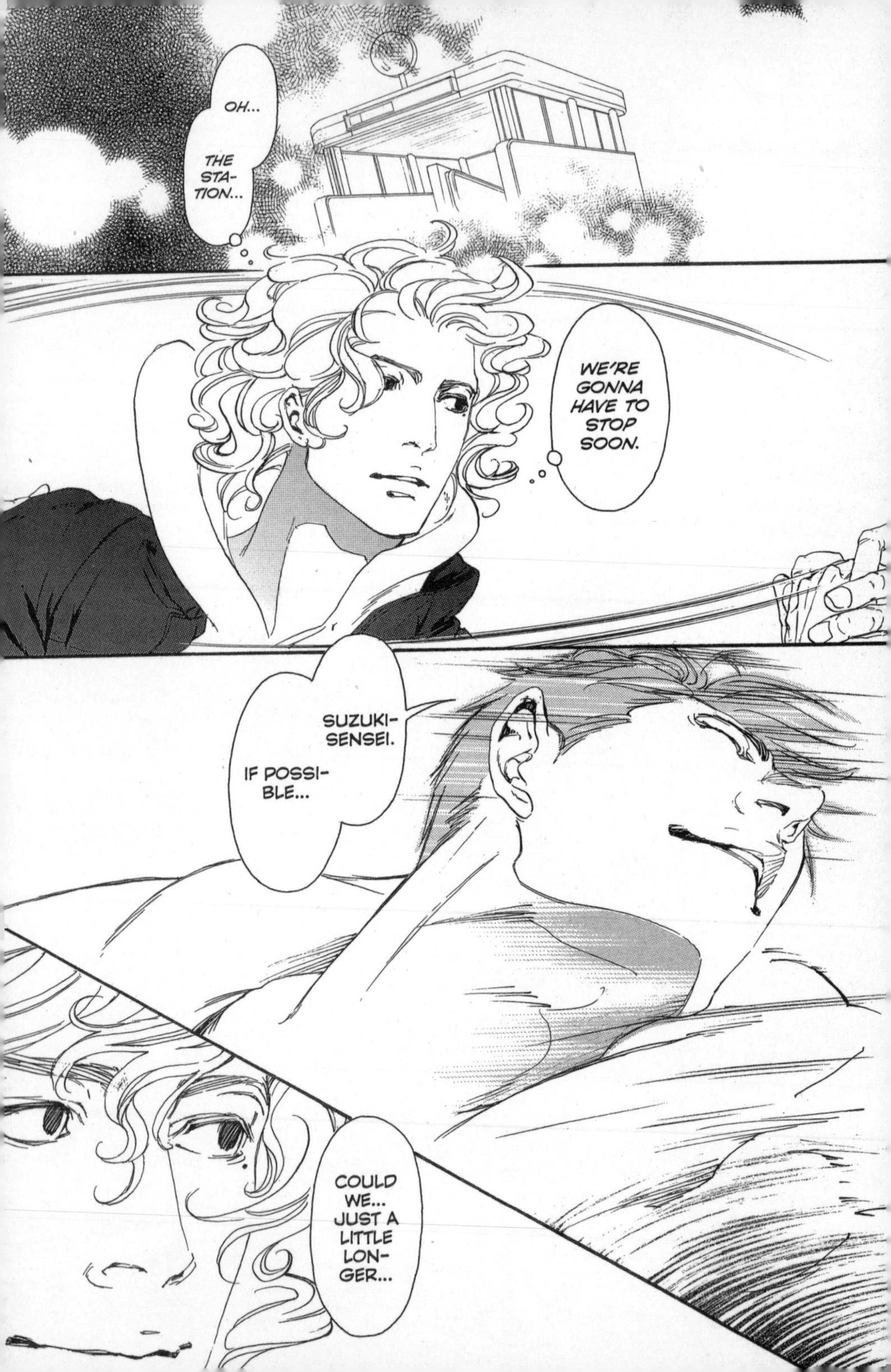
OH... THE STATION...
WE'RE GONNA HAVE TO STOP SOON.
SUZUKI-SENSEI.
IF POSSIBLE...
COULD WE... JUST A LITTLE LONGER...

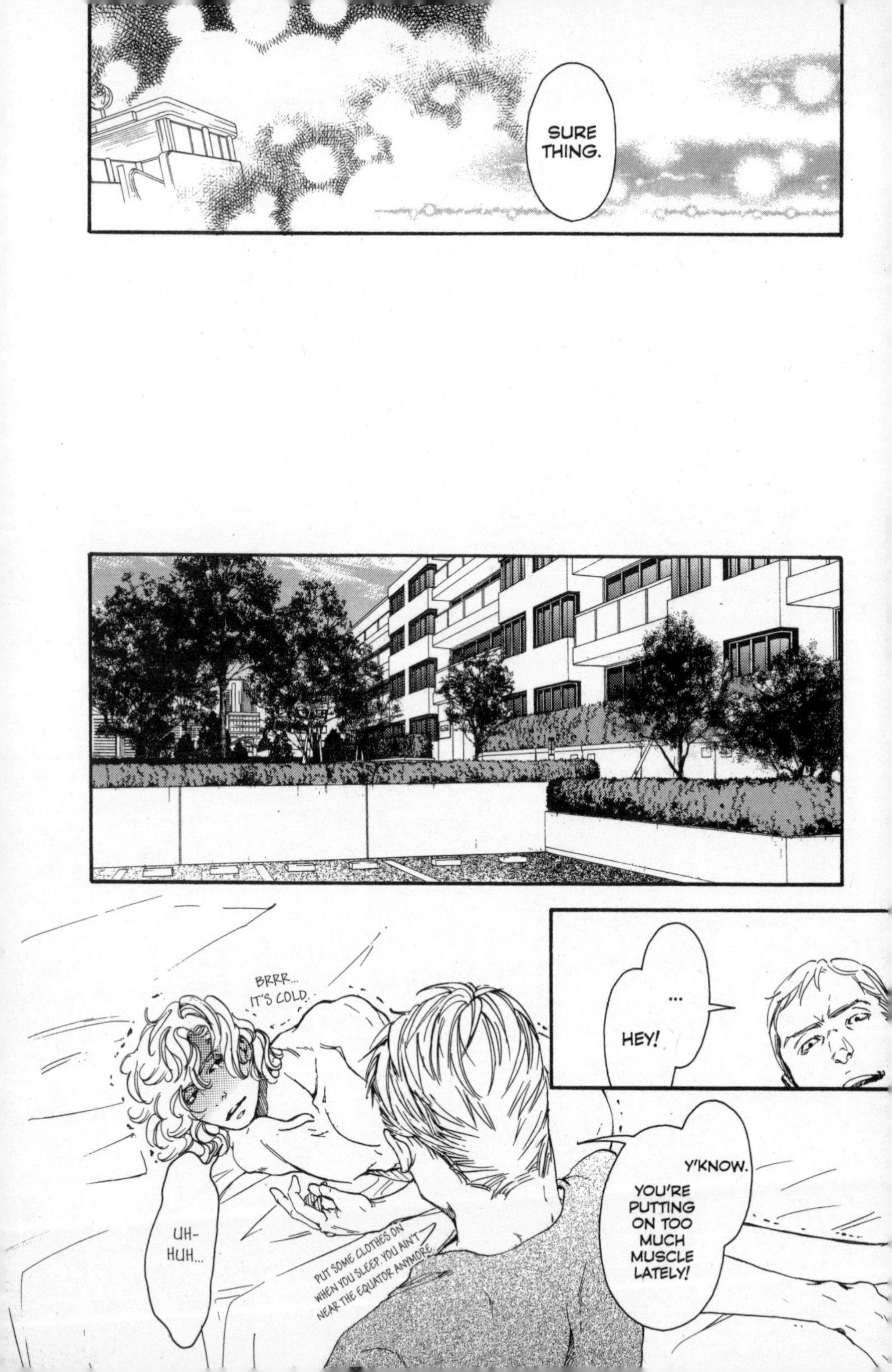
SURE THING.
... HEY!
BRRR... IT'S COLD.
PUT SOME CLOTHES ON WHEN YOU SLEEP. YOU AIN'T NEAR THE EQUATOR ANYMORE.
UH-HUH...
Y'KNOW. YOU'RE PUTTING ON TOO MUCH MUSCLE LATELY!

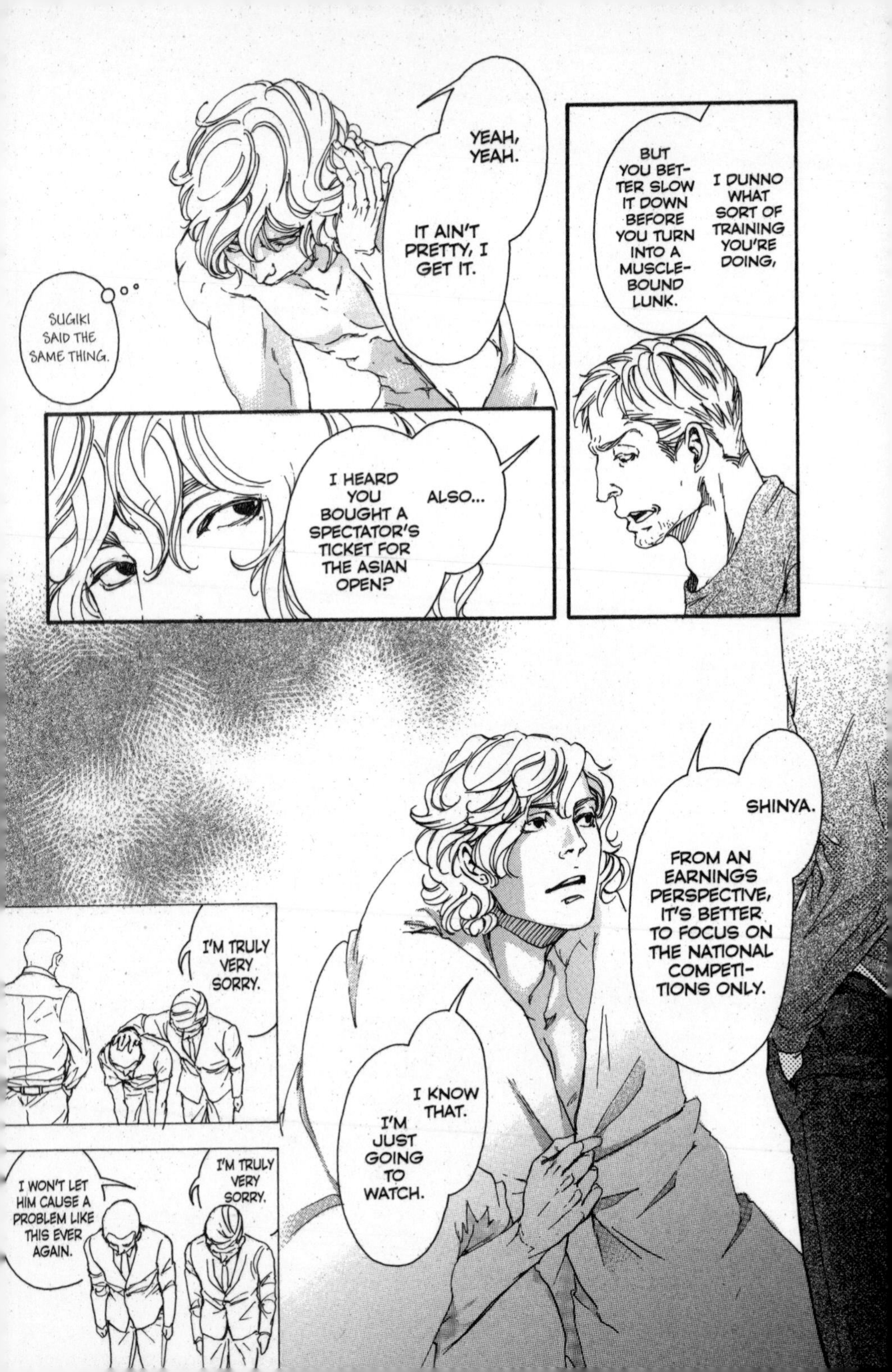
I DUNNO WHAT SORT OF TRAINING YOU'RE DOING,
BUT YOU BETTER SLOW IT DOWN BEFORE YOU TURN INTO A MUSCLE-BOUND LUNK.
YEAH, YEAH.
IT AIN'T PRETTY, I GET IT.
SUGIKI SAID THE SAME THING.
ALSO...
I HEARD YOU BOUGHT A SPECTATOR'S TICKET FOR THE ASIAN OPEN?
SHINYA.
FROM AN EARNINGS PERSPECTIVE, IT'S BETTER TO FOCUS ON THE NATIONAL COMPETI-TIONS ONLY.
I KNOW THAT.
I'M JUST GOING TO WATCH.
I'M TRULY VERY SORRY.
I'M TRULY VERY SORRY.
I WON'T LET HIM CAUSE A PROBLEM LIKE THIS EVER AGAIN.

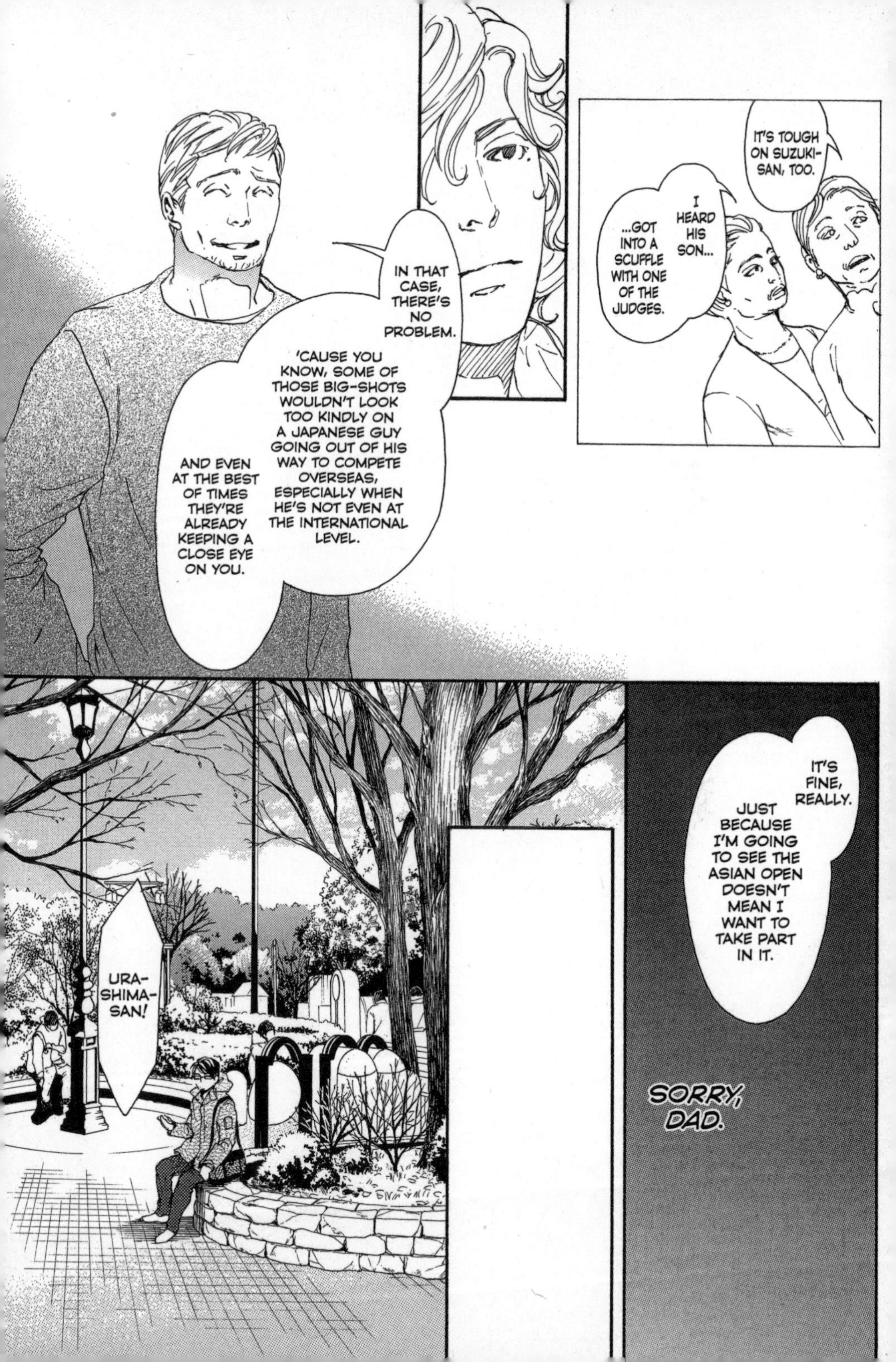
IT'S TOUGH ON SUZUKI-SAN, TOO.
I HEARD HIS SON...
...GOT INTO A SCUFFLE WITH ONE OF THE JUDGES.
IN THAT CASE, THERE'S NO PROBLEM.
'CAUSE YOU KNOW, SOME OF THOSE BIG-SHOTS WOULDN'T LOOK TOO KINDLY ON A JAPANESE GUY GOING OUT OF HIS WAY TO COMPETE OVERSEAS, ESPECIALLY WHEN HE'S NOT EVEN AT THE INTERNATIONAL LEVEL.
AND EVEN AT THE BEST OF TIMES THEY'RE ALREADY KEEPING A CLOSE EYE ON YOU.
IT'S FINE, REALLY.
JUST BECAUSE I'M GOING TO SEE THE ASIAN OPEN DOESN'T MEAN I WANT TO TAKE PART IN IT.
SORRY, DAD.
URA-SHIMA-SAN!

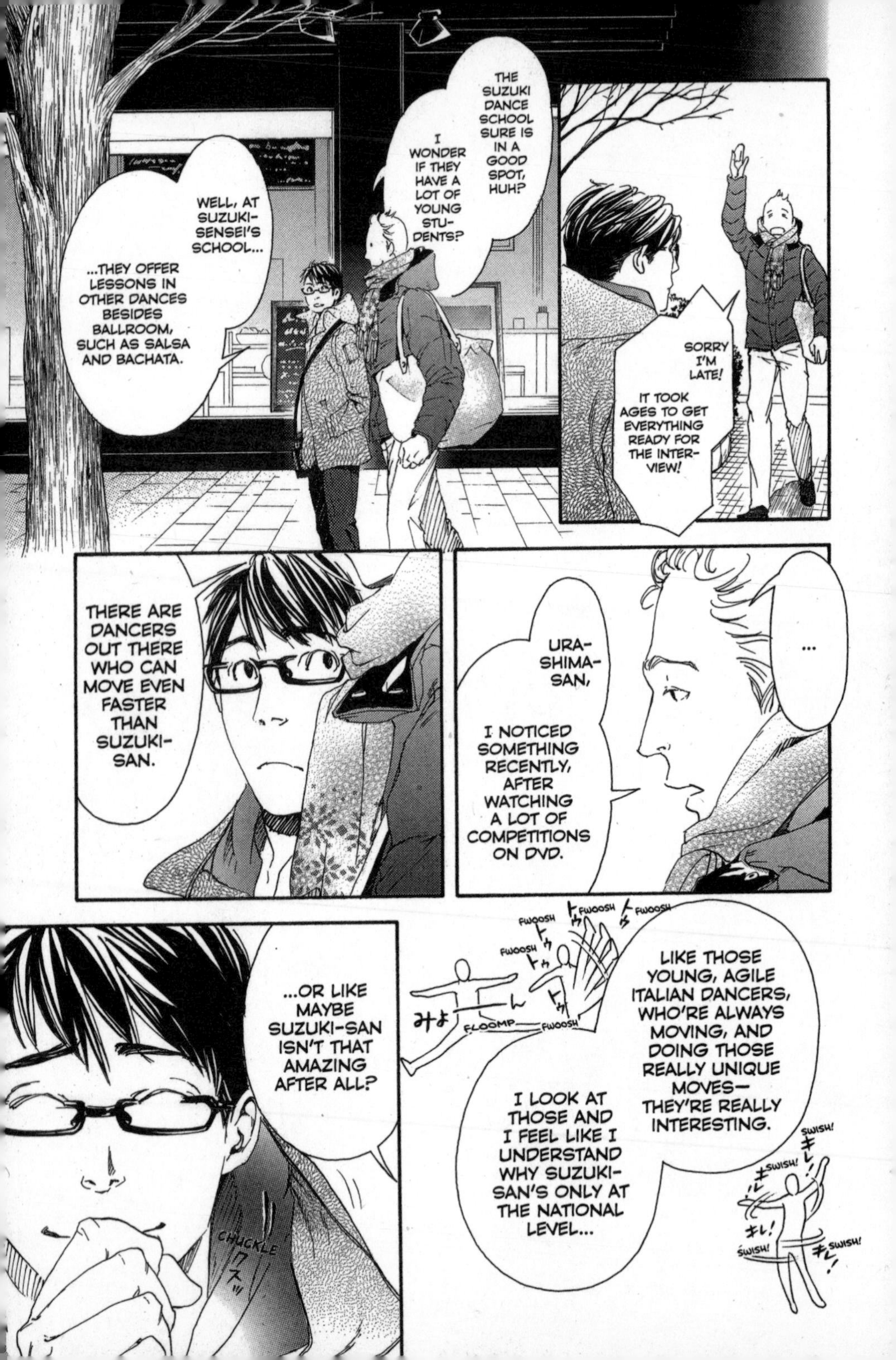
SORRY I'M LATE!
IT TOOK AGES TO GET EVERYTHING READY FOR THE INTERVIEW!
THE SUZUKI DANCE SCHOOL SURE IS IN A GOOD SPOT, HUH?
I WONDER IF THEY HAVE A LOT OF YOUNG STUDENTS?
WELL, AT SUZUKI-SENSEI'S SCHOOL...
...THEY OFFER LESSONS IN OTHER DANCES BESIDES BALLROOM, SUCH AS SALSA AND BACHATA.
...
URASHIMA-SAN,
I NOTICED SOMETHING RECENTLY, AFTER WATCHING A LOT OF COMPETITIONS ON DVD.
THERE ARE DANCERS OUT THERE WHO CAN MOVE EVEN FASTER THAN SUZUKI-SAN.
FWOOSH FWOOSH FWOOSH FWOOSH
FLOOMP FWOOSH
LIKE THOSE YOUNG, AGILE ITALIAN DANCERS, WHO'RE ALWAYS MOVING, AND DOING THOSE REALLY UNIQUE MOVES—THEY'RE REALLY INTERESTING.
SWISH! SWISH! SWISH! SWISH!
I LOOK AT THOSE AND I FEEL LIKE I UNDERSTAND WHY SUZUKI-SAN'S ONLY AT THE NATIONAL LEVEL...
...OR LIKE MAYBE SUZUKI-SAN ISN'T THAT AMAZING AFTER ALL?
CHUCKLE

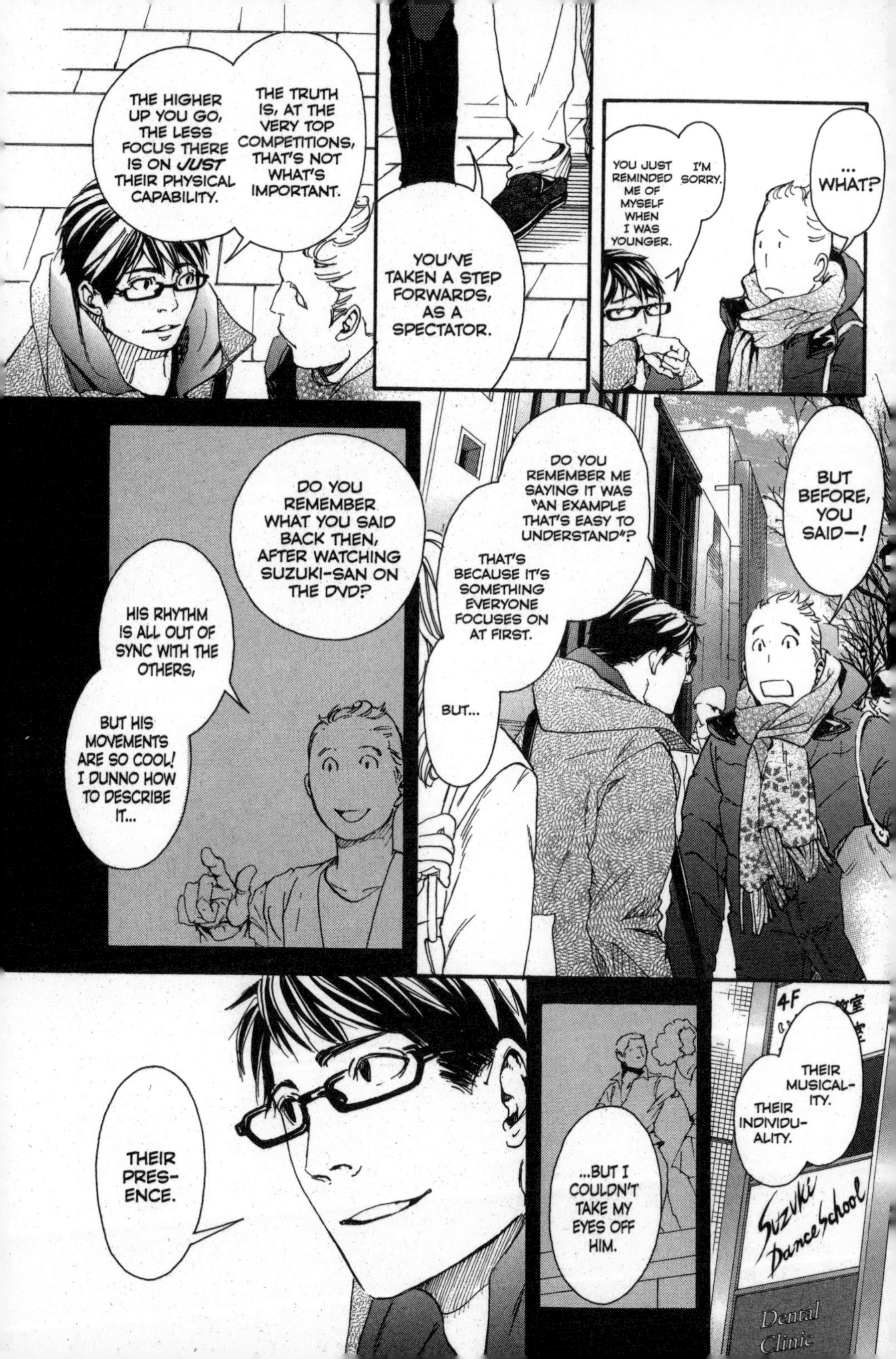
...WHAT?
I'M SORRY.
YOU JUST REMINDED ME OF MYSELF WHEN I WAS YOUNGER.
YOU'VE TAKEN A STEP FORWARDS, AS A SPECTATOR.
THE TRUTH IS, AT THE VERY TOP COMPETITIONS, THAT'S NOT WHAT'S IMPORTANT.
THE HIGHER UP YOU GO, THE LESS FOCUS THERE IS ON *JUST* THEIR PHYSICAL CAPABILITY.
BUT BEFORE, YOU SAID—!
DO YOU REMEMBER ME SAYING IT WAS "AN EXAMPLE THAT'S EASY TO UNDERSTAND"?
THAT'S BECAUSE IT'S SOMETHING EVERYONE FOCUSES ON AT FIRST.
BUT...
DO YOU REMEMBER WHAT YOU SAID BACK THEN, AFTER WATCHING SUZUKI-SAN ON THE DVD?
HIS RHYTHM IS ALL OUT OF SYNC WITH THE OTHERS,
BUT HIS MOVEMENTS ARE SO COOL! I DUNNO HOW TO DESCRIBE IT...
4F
THEIR MUSICALITY.
THEIR INDIVIDUALITY.
Suzuki Dance School
Dental Clinic
...BUT I COULDN'T TAKE MY EYES OFF HIM.
THEIR PRESENCE.

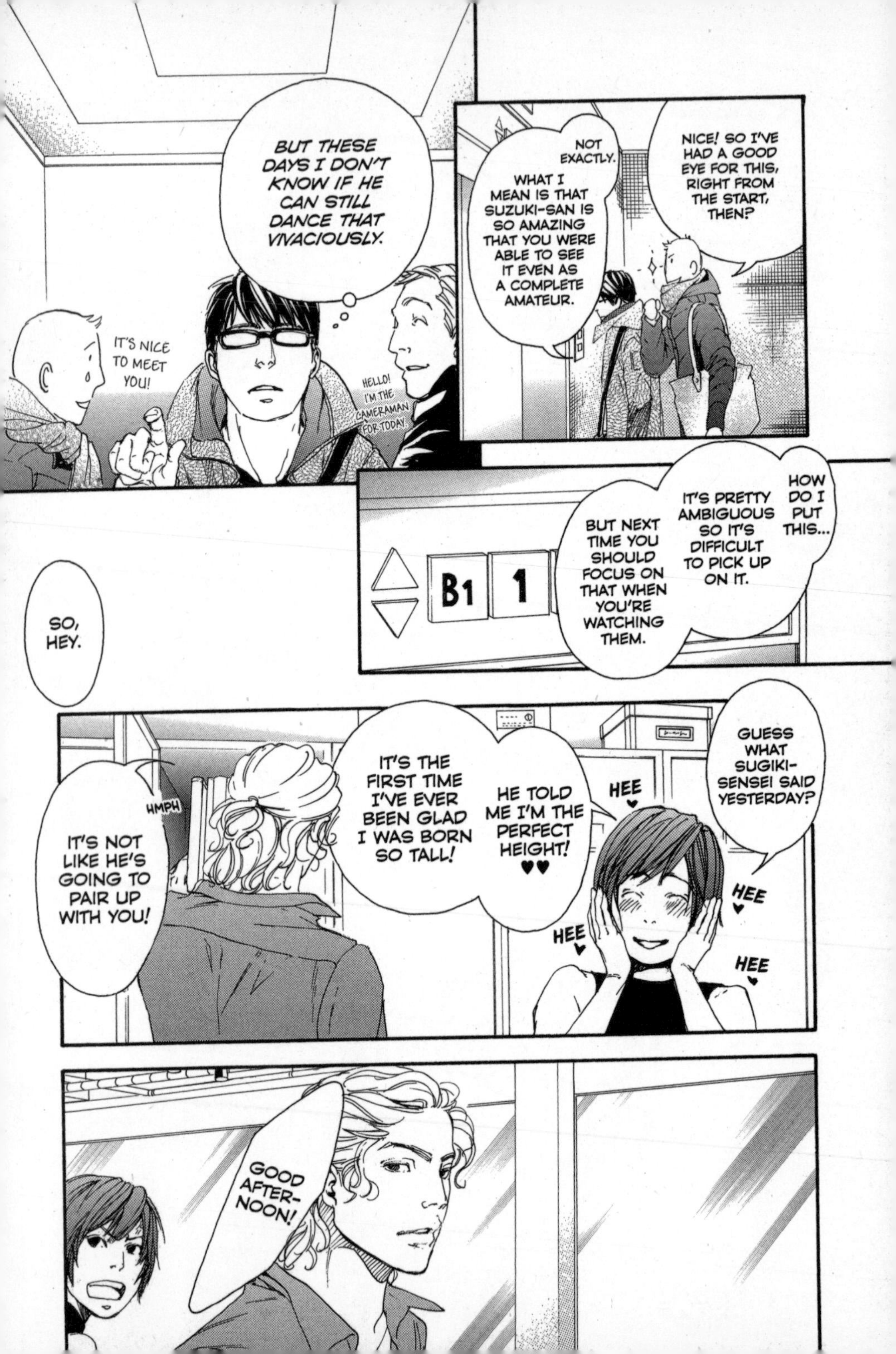
NICE! SO I'VE HAD A GOOD EYE FOR THIS, RIGHT FROM THE START, THEN?
NOT EXACTLY.
WHAT I MEAN IS THAT SUZUKI-SAN IS SO AMAZING THAT YOU WERE ABLE TO SEE IT EVEN AS A COMPLETE AMATEUR.
BUT THESE DAYS I DON'T KNOW IF HE CAN STILL DANCE THAT VIVACIOUSLY.
HELLO! I'M THE CAMERAMAN FOR TODAY.
IT'S NICE TO MEET YOU!
HOW DO I PUT THIS...
IT'S PRETTY AMBIGUOUS SO IT'S DIFFICULT TO PICK UP ON IT.
BUT NEXT TIME YOU SHOULD FOCUS ON THAT WHEN YOU'RE WATCHING THEM.
B1
1
SO, HEY.
GUESS WHAT SUGIKI-SENSEI SAID YESTERDAY?
HEE♥
HEE♥
HEE♥
HEE♥
HE TOLD ME I'M THE PERFECT HEIGHT! ♥♥
IT'S THE FIRST TIME I'VE EVER BEEN GLAD I WAS BORN SO TALL!
HMPH
IT'S NOT LIKE HE'S GOING TO PAIR UP WITH YOU!
GOOD AFTER-NOON!

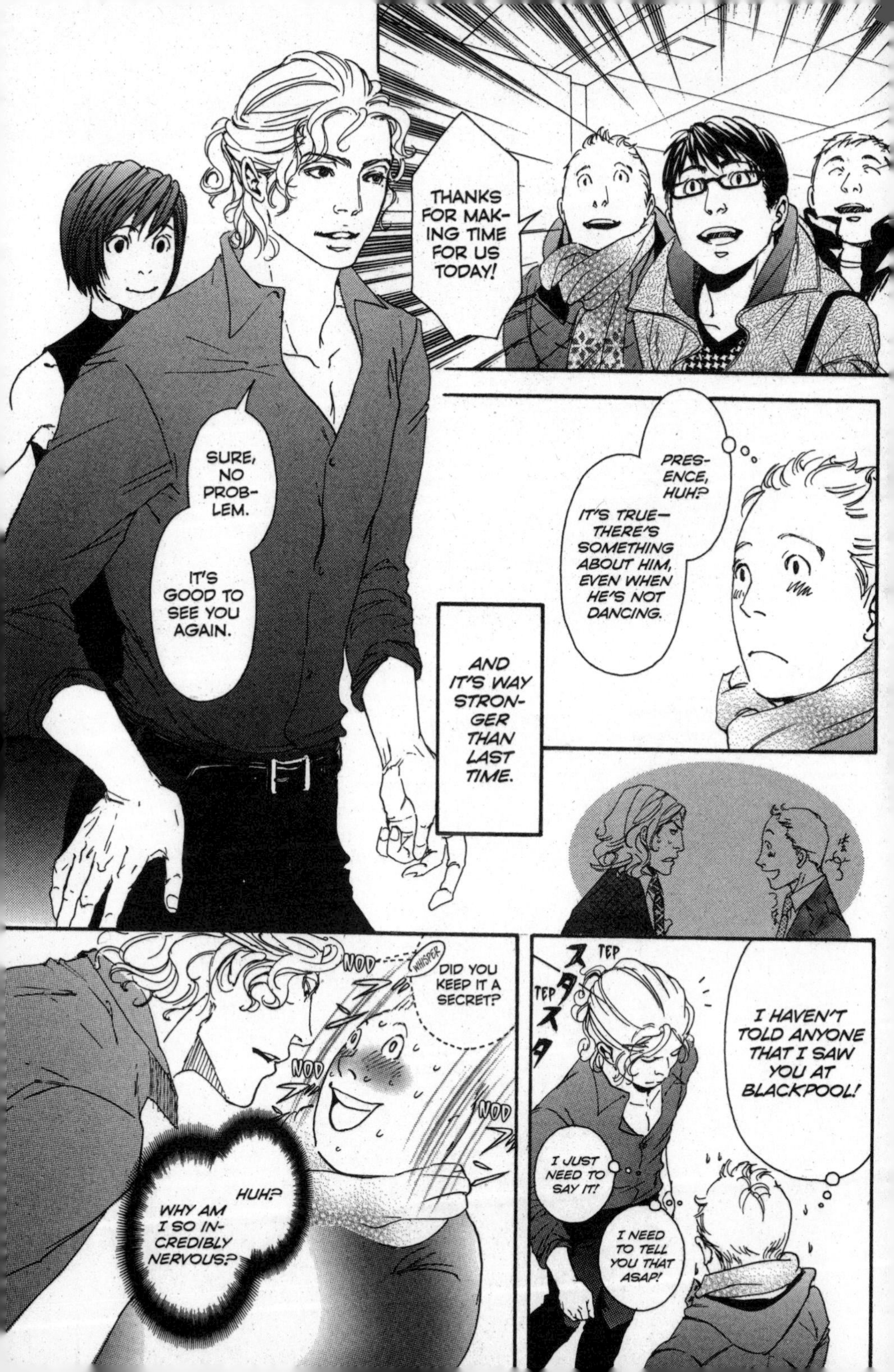
THANKS FOR MAKING TIME FOR US TODAY!
PRESENCE, HUH?
IT'S TRUE—THERE'S SOMETHING ABOUT HIM, EVEN WHEN HE'S NOT DANCING.
AND IT'S WAY STRONGER THAN LAST TIME.
SURE, NO PROBLEM.
IT'S GOOD TO SEE YOU AGAIN.
TEP
TEP
I HAVEN'T TOLD ANYONE THAT I SAW YOU AT BLACKPOOL!
I JUST NEED TO SAY IT!
I NEED TO TELL YOU THAT ASAP!
NOD
WHISPER
DID YOU KEEP IT A SECRET?
NOD
NOD
HUH?
WHY AM I SO INCREDIBLY NERVOUS?

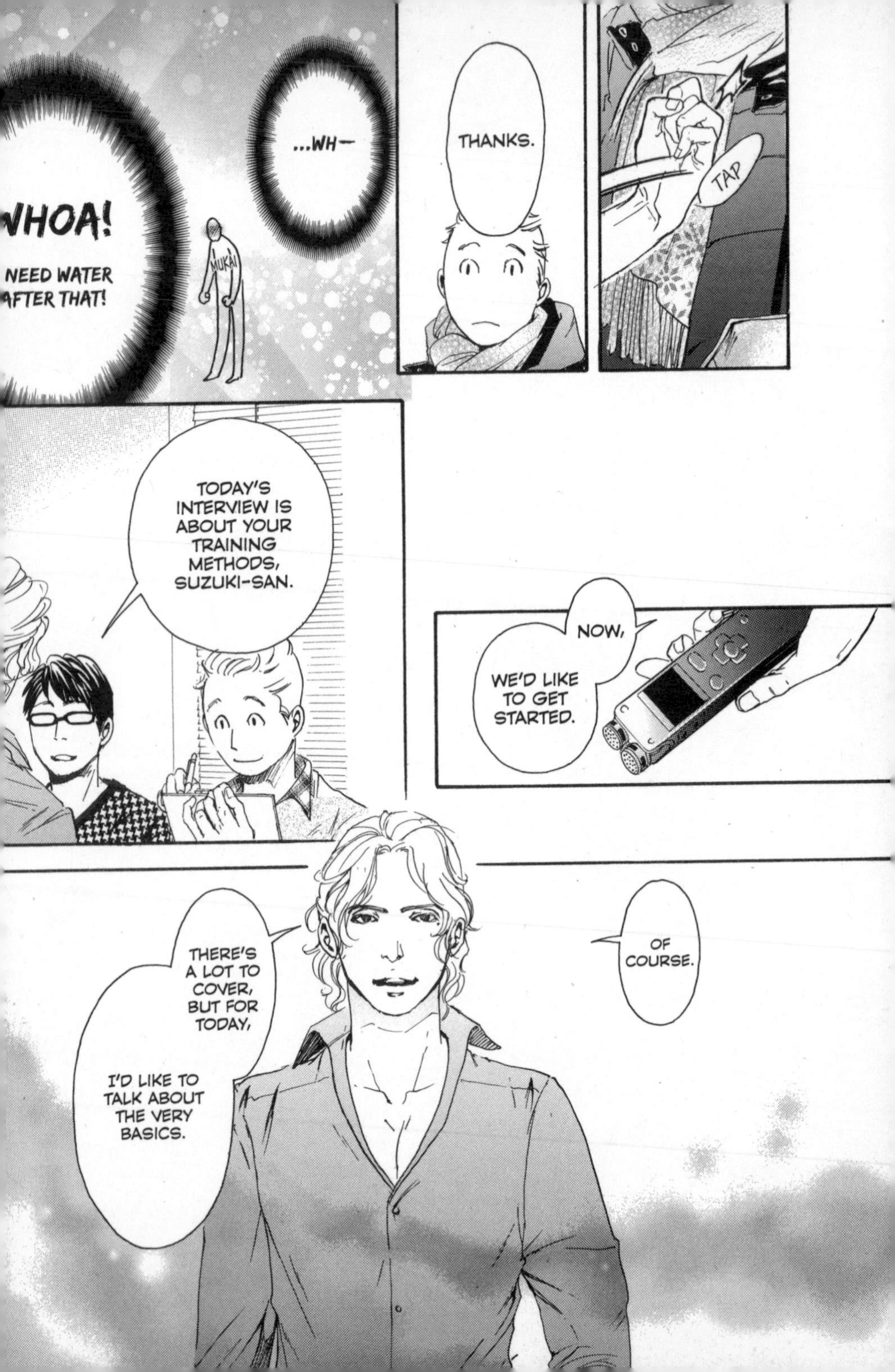
TAP
THANKS.
...WH—
WHOA!
NEED WATER
AFTER THAT!
MUKAI
NOW,
WE'D LIKE TO GET STARTED.
TODAY'S INTERVIEW IS ABOUT YOUR TRAINING METHODS, SUZUKI-SAN.
OF COURSE.
THERE'S A LOT TO COVER, BUT FOR TODAY,
I'D LIKE TO TALK ABOUT THE VERY BASICS.

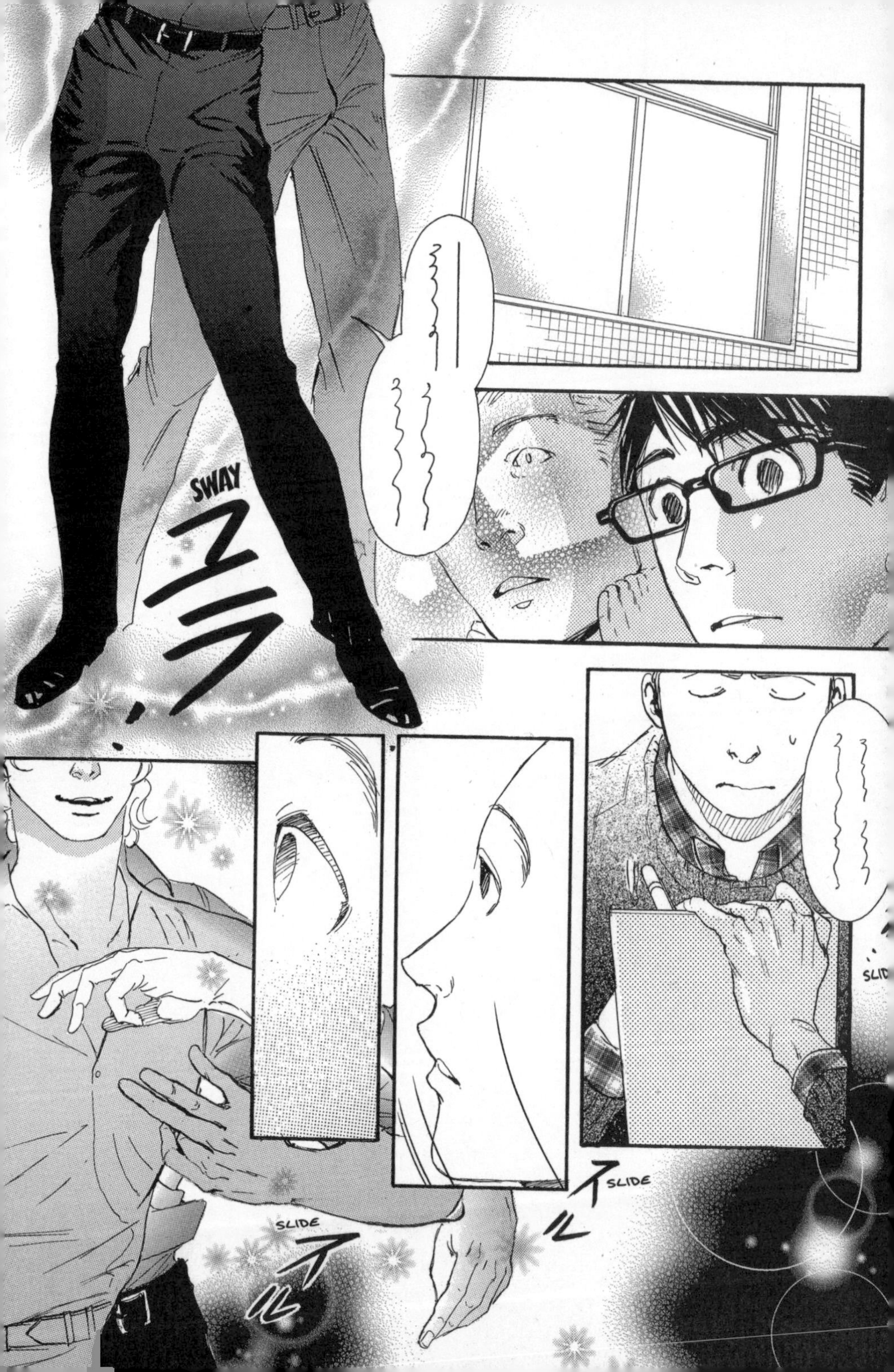

SWAY
ユラ
SLIDE
スル
SLIDE
スル

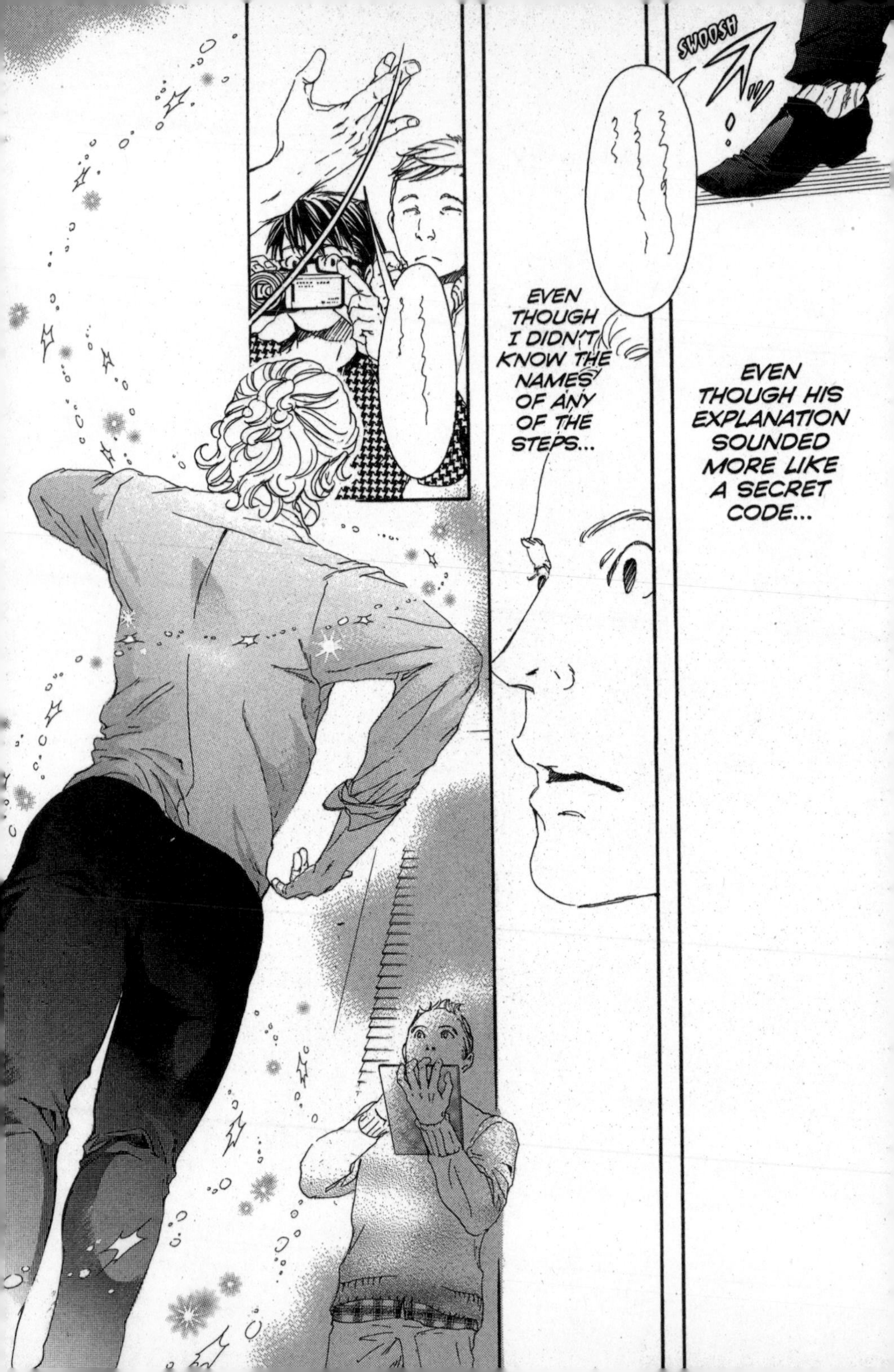
SWOOSH
EVEN THOUGH HIS EXPLANATION SOUNDED MORE LIKE A SECRET CODE...
EVEN THOUGH I DIDN'T KNOW THE NAMES OF ANY OF THE STEPS...

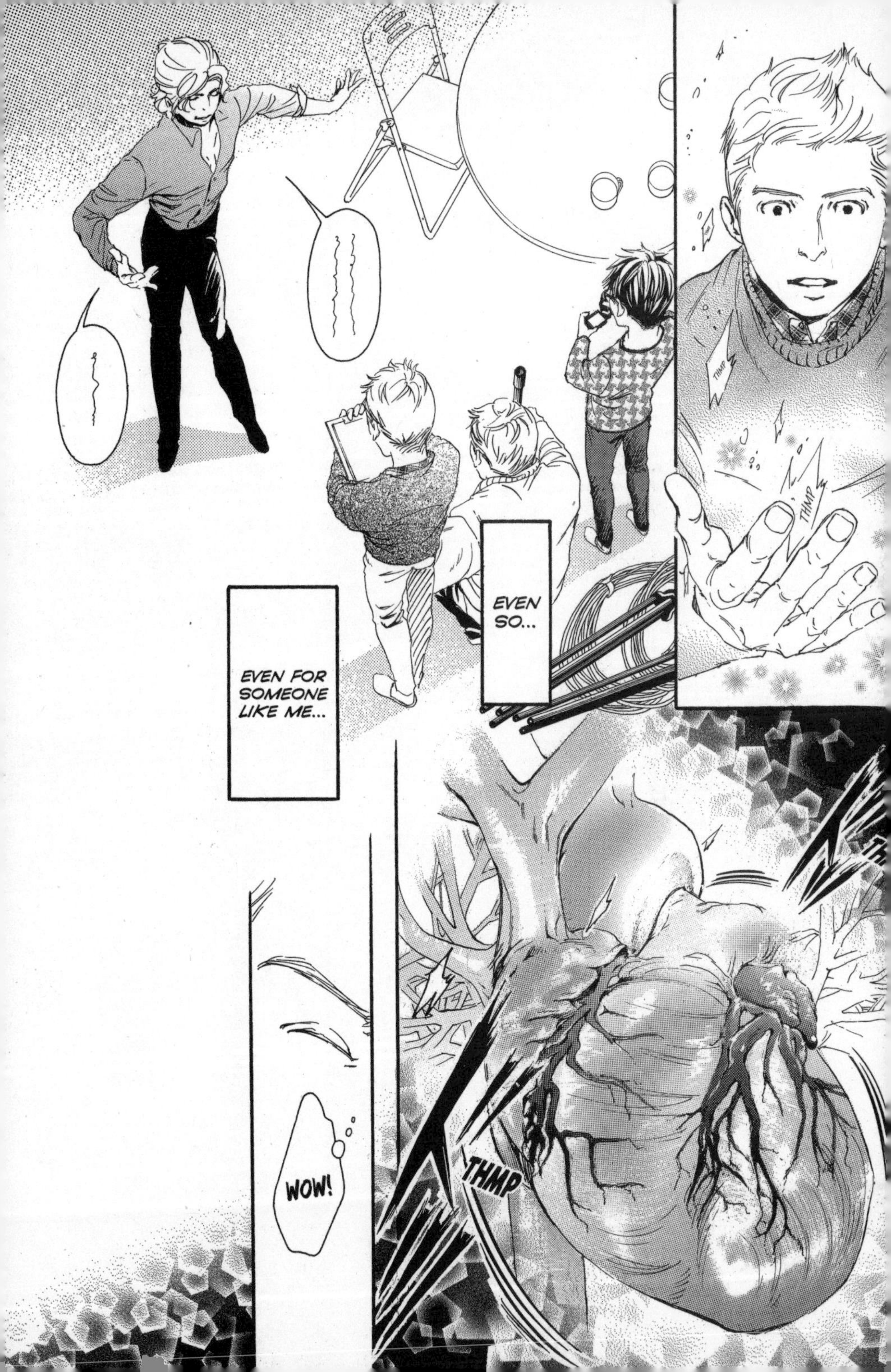
THMP
THMP
EVEN SO...
EVEN FOR SOMEONE LIKE ME...
THMP
WOW!

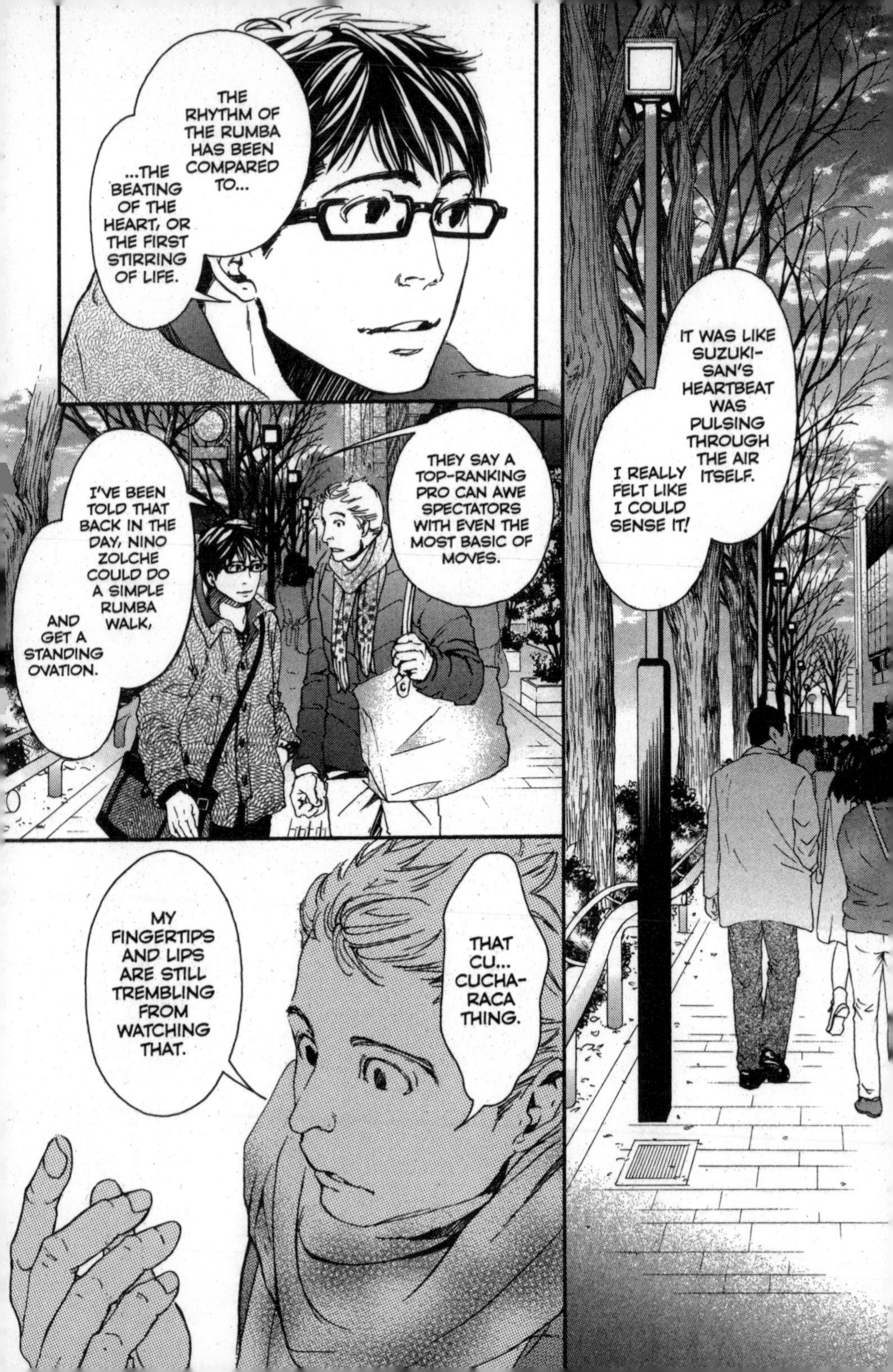
IT WAS LIKE SUZUKI-SAN'S HEARTBEAT WAS PULSING THROUGH THE AIR ITSELF.
I REALLY FELT LIKE I COULD SENSE IT!
THE RHYTHM OF THE RUMBA HAS BEEN COMPARED TO...
...THE BEATING OF THE HEART, OR THE FIRST STIRRING OF LIFE.
THEY SAY A TOP-RANKING PRO CAN AWE SPECTATORS WITH EVEN THE MOST BASIC OF MOVES.
I'VE BEEN TOLD THAT BACK IN THE DAY, NINO ZOLCHE COULD DO A SIMPLE RUMBA WALK,
AND GET A STANDING OVATION.
THAT CU... CUCHA-RACA THING.
MY FINGERTIPS AND LIPS ARE STILL TREMBLING FROM WATCHING THAT.

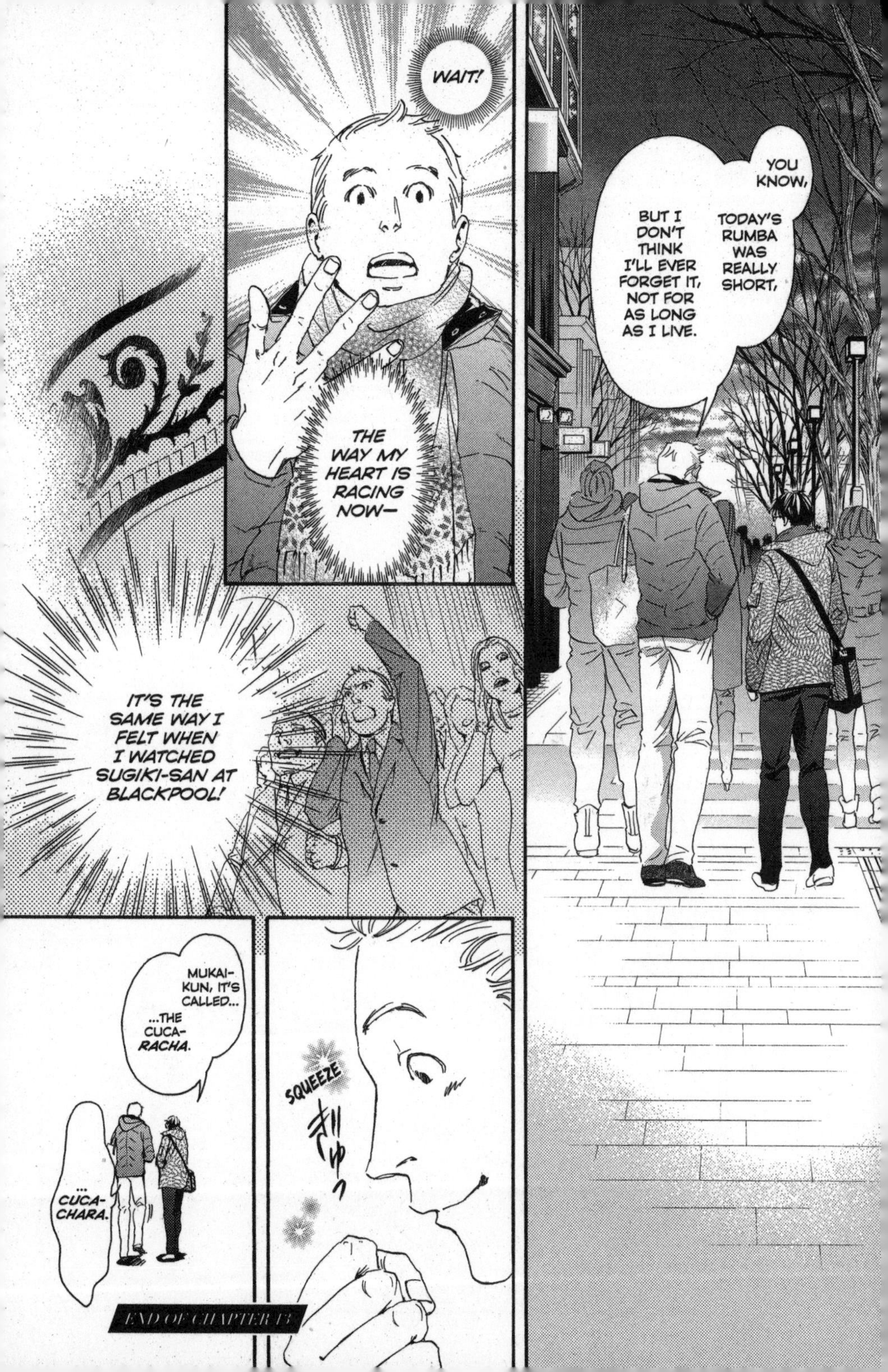
YOU KNOW,
TODAY'S RUMBA WAS REALLY SHORT,
BUT I DON'T THINK I'LL EVER FORGET IT, NOT FOR AS LONG AS I LIVE.
WAIT!
THE WAY MY HEART IS RACING NOW—
IT'S THE SAME WAY I FELT WHEN I WATCHED SUGIKI-SAN AT BLACKPOOL!
SQUEEZE
ぎゅっ
MUKAI-KUN, IT'S CALLED...
...THE CUCA-RACHA.
...CUCA-CHARA.
END OF CHAPTER 13

10 DANCE

#14
MASQUERADE

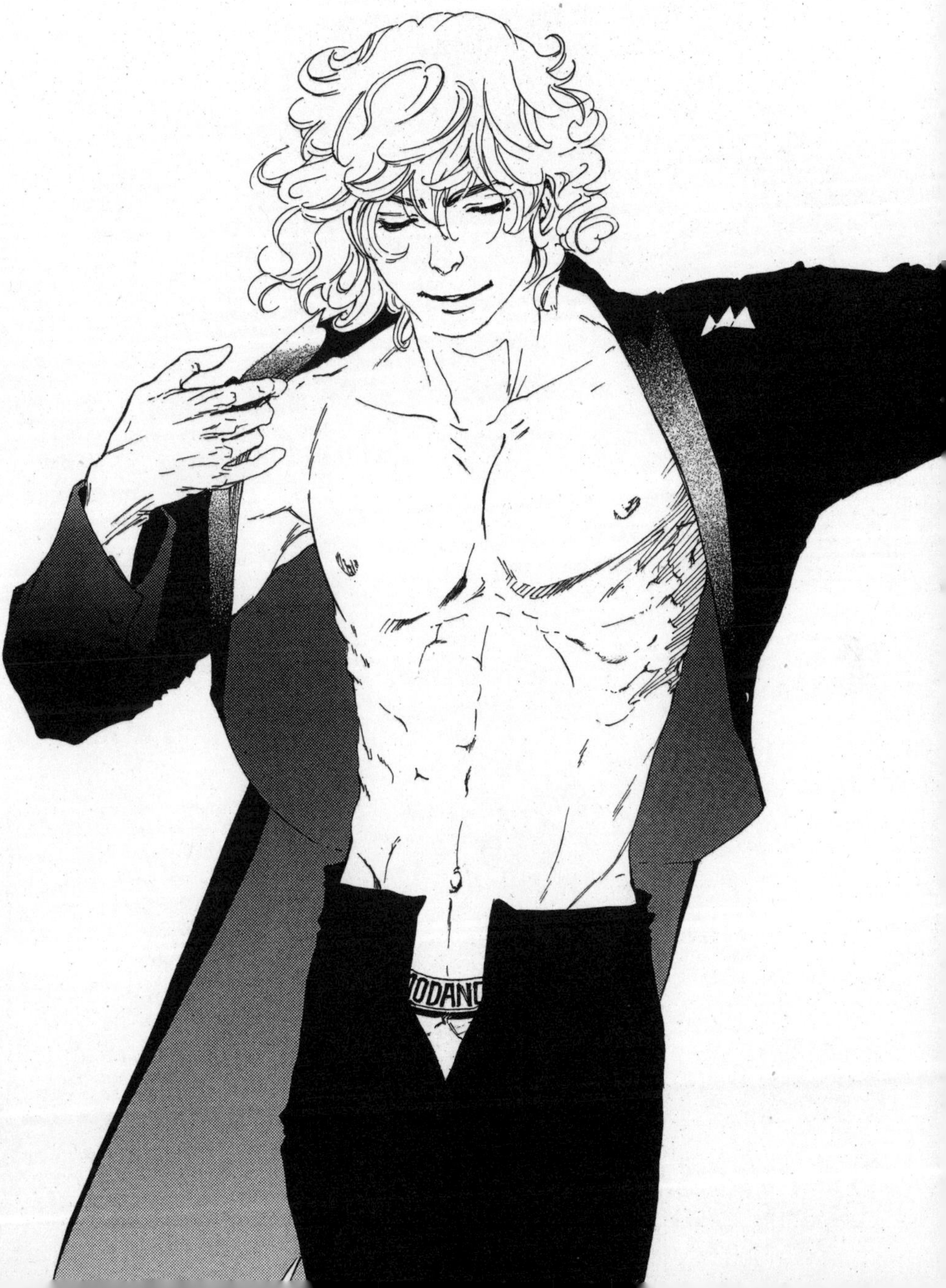

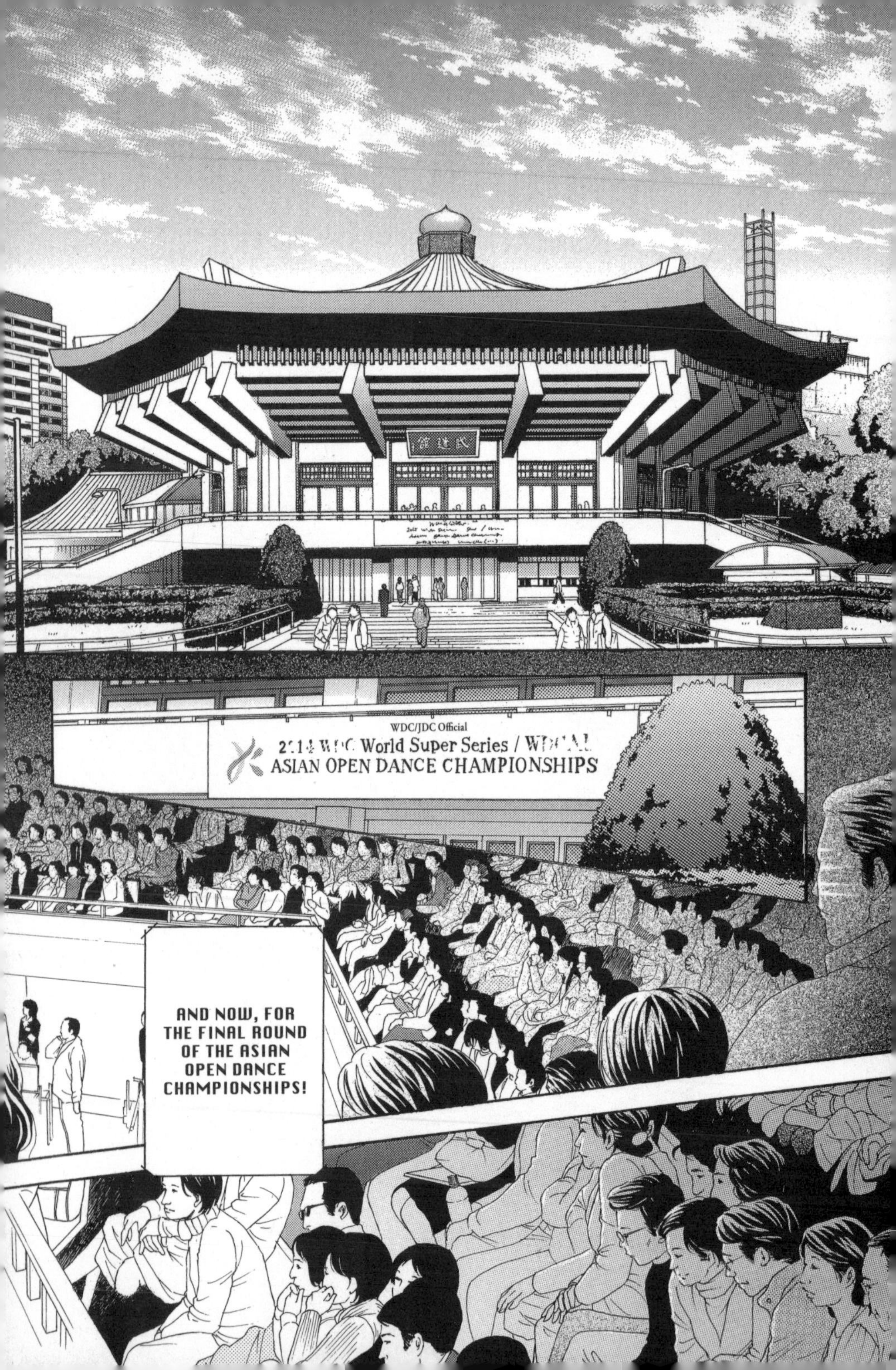
WDC/JDC Official
World Super Series /
ASIAN OPEN DANCE CHAMPIONSHIPS
AND NOW, FOR THE FINAL ROUND OF THE ASIAN OPEN DANCE CHAMPIONSHIPS!

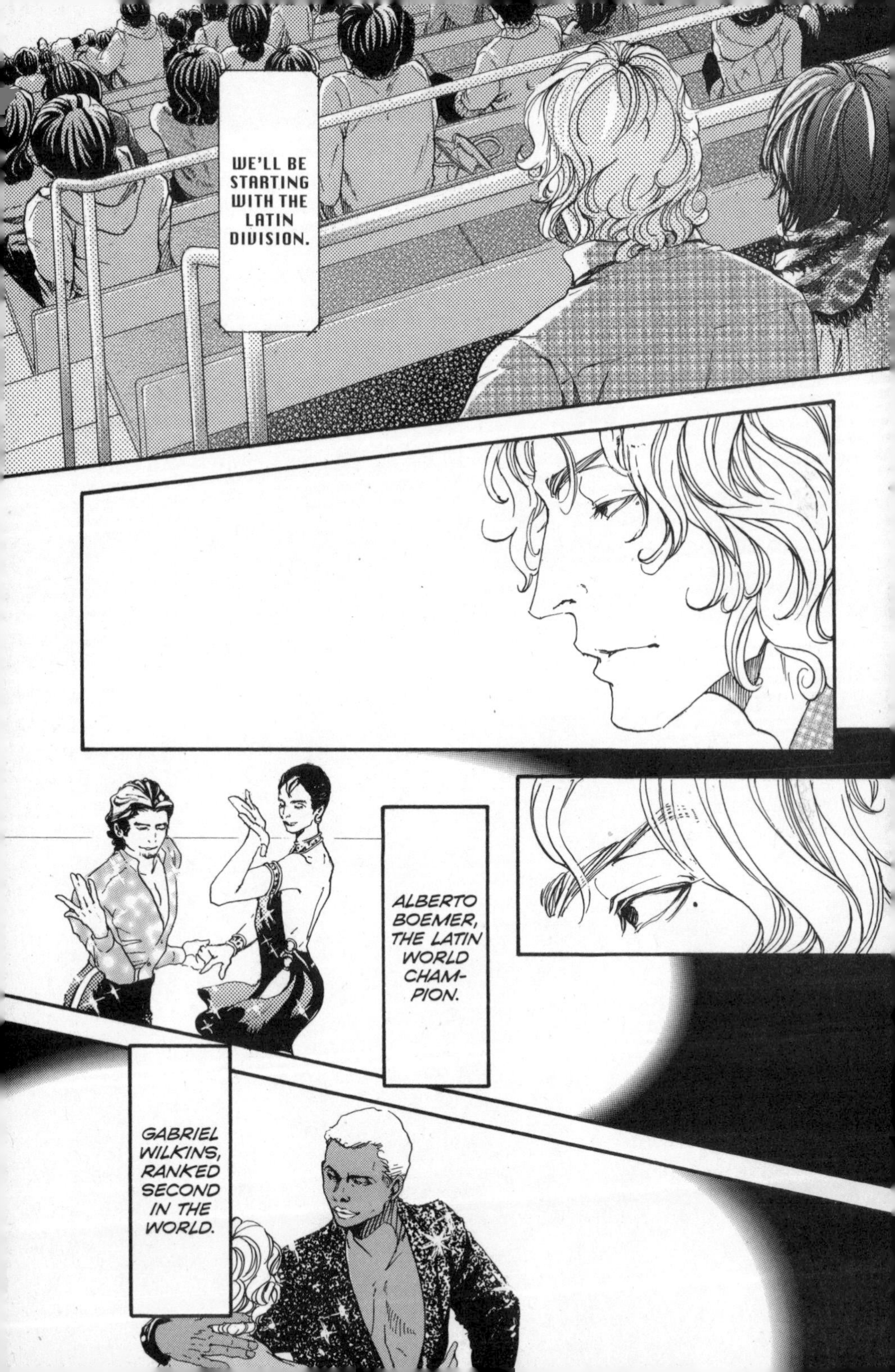
WE'LL BE STARTING WITH THE LATIN DIVISION.
ALBERTO BOEMER, THE LATIN WORLD CHAM-PION.
GABRIEL WILKINS, RANKED SECOND IN THE WORLD.

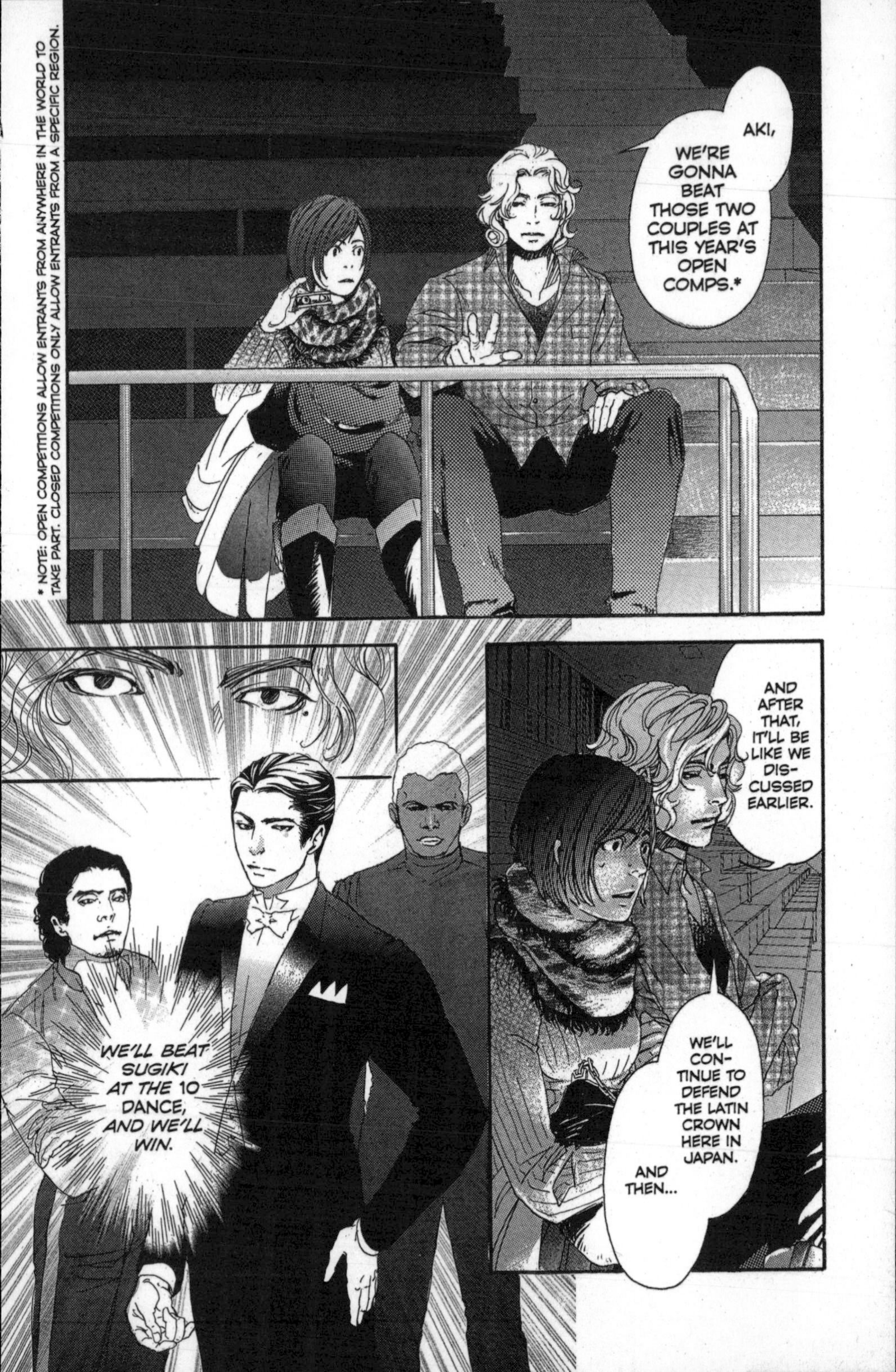
AKI, WE'RE GONNA BEAT THOSE TWO COUPLES AT THIS YEAR'S OPEN COMPS.*
AND AFTER THAT, IT'LL BE LIKE WE DIS-CUSSED EARLIER.
WE'LL CON-TINUE TO DEFEND THE LATIN CROWN HERE IN JAPAN.
AND THEN...
WE'LL BEAT SUGIKI AT THE 10 DANCE, AND WE'LL WIN.

* NOTE: OPEN COMPETITIONS ALLOW ENTRANTS FROM ANYWHERE IN THE WORLD TO TAKE PART. CLOSED COMPETITIONS ONLY ALLOW ENTRANTS FROM A SPECIFIC REGION.

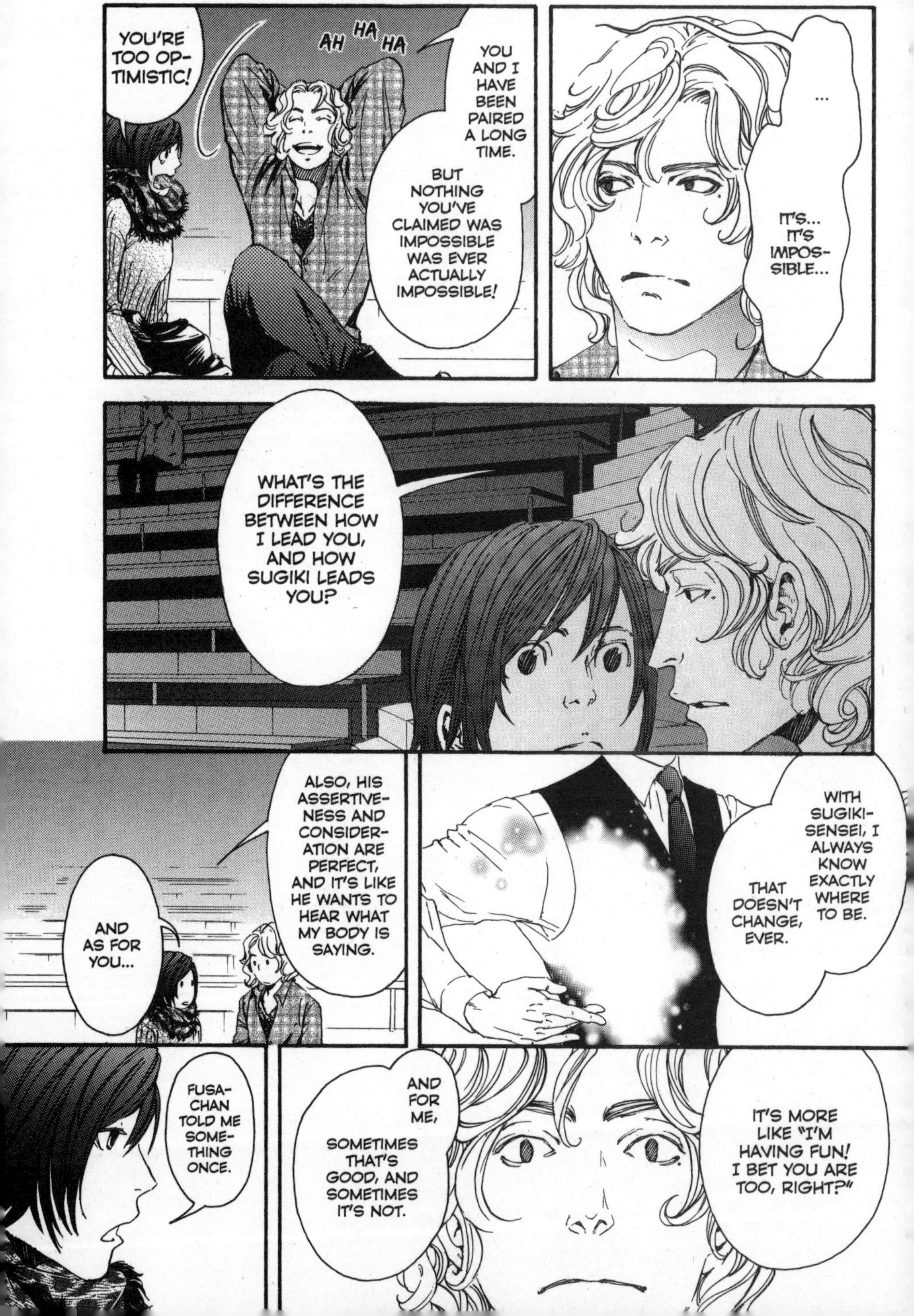
...
IT'S... IT'S IMPOSSIBLE...
YOU AND I HAVE BEEN PAIRED A LONG TIME.
BUT NOTHING YOU'VE CLAIMED WAS IMPOSSIBLE WAS EVER ACTUALLY IMPOSSIBLE!
AH HA HA
YOU'RE TOO OPTIMISTIC!
WHAT'S THE DIFFERENCE BETWEEN HOW I LEAD YOU, AND HOW SUGIKI LEADS YOU?
WITH SUGIKI-SENSEI, I ALWAYS KNOW EXACTLY WHERE TO BE.
THAT DOESN'T CHANGE, EVER.
ALSO, HIS ASSERTIVENESS AND CONSIDERATION ARE PERFECT, AND IT'S LIKE HE WANTS TO HEAR WHAT MY BODY IS SAYING.
AND AS FOR YOU...
IT'S MORE LIKE "I'M HAVING FUN! I BET YOU ARE TOO, RIGHT?"
AND FOR ME,
SOMETIMES THAT'S GOOD, AND SOMETIMES IT'S NOT.
FUSA-CHAN TOLD ME SOMETHING ONCE.

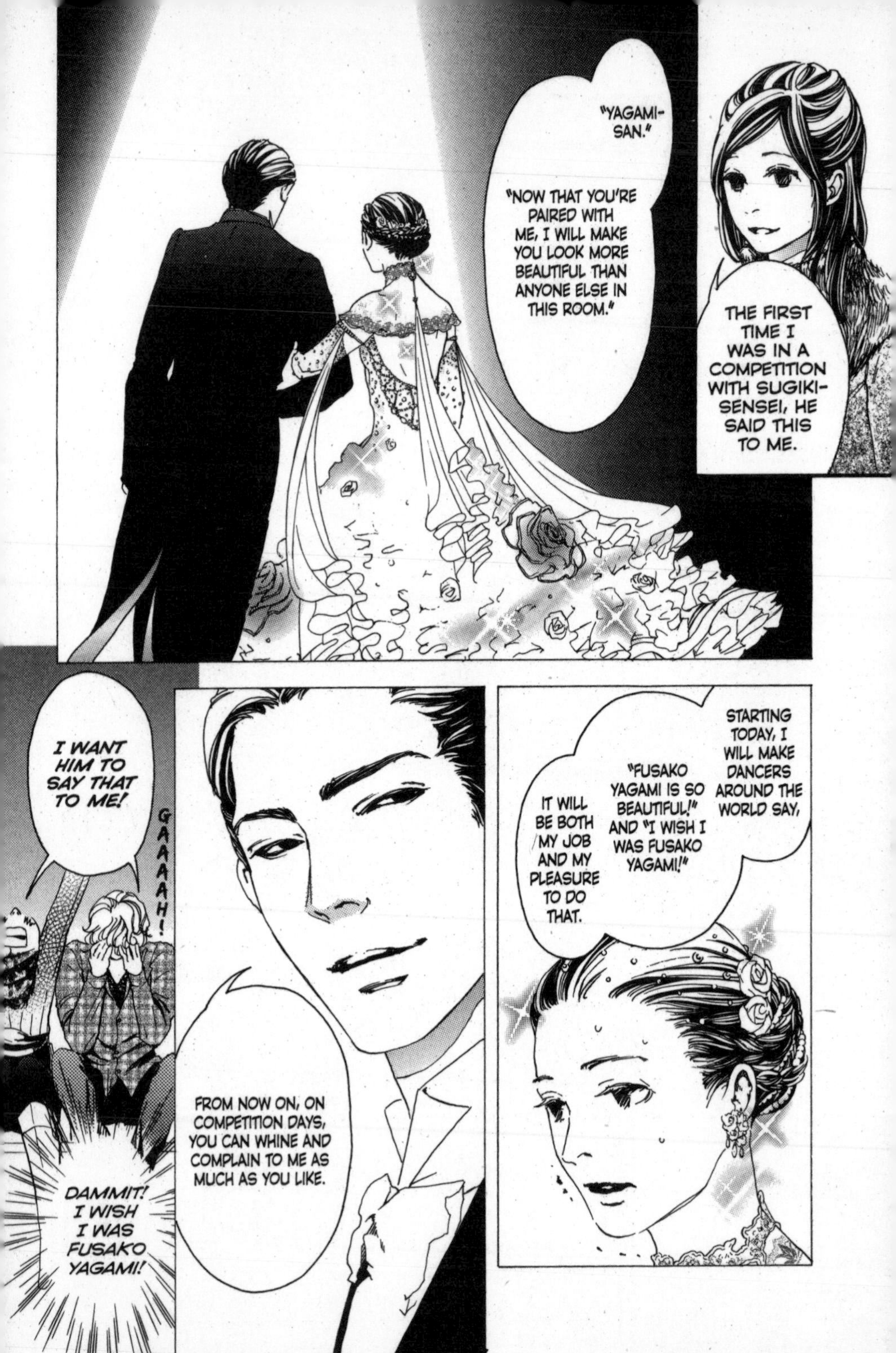
THE FIRST TIME I WAS IN A COMPETITION WITH SUGIKI-SENSEI, HE SAID THIS TO ME.
"YAGAMI-SAN."
"NOW THAT YOU'RE PAIRED WITH ME, I WILL MAKE YOU LOOK MORE BEAUTIFUL THAN ANYONE ELSE IN THIS ROOM."
STARTING TODAY, I WILL MAKE DANCERS AROUND THE WORLD SAY,
"FUSAKO YAGAMI IS SO BEAUTIFUL!" AND "I WISH I WAS FUSAKO YAGAMI!"
IT WILL BE BOTH MY JOB AND MY PLEASURE TO DO THAT.
FROM NOW ON, ON COMPETITION DAYS, YOU CAN WHINE AND COMPLAIN TO ME AS MUCH AS YOU LIKE.
I WANT HIM TO SAY THAT TO ME!
GAAAAAH!
DAMMIT! I WISH I WAS FUSAKO YAGAMI!

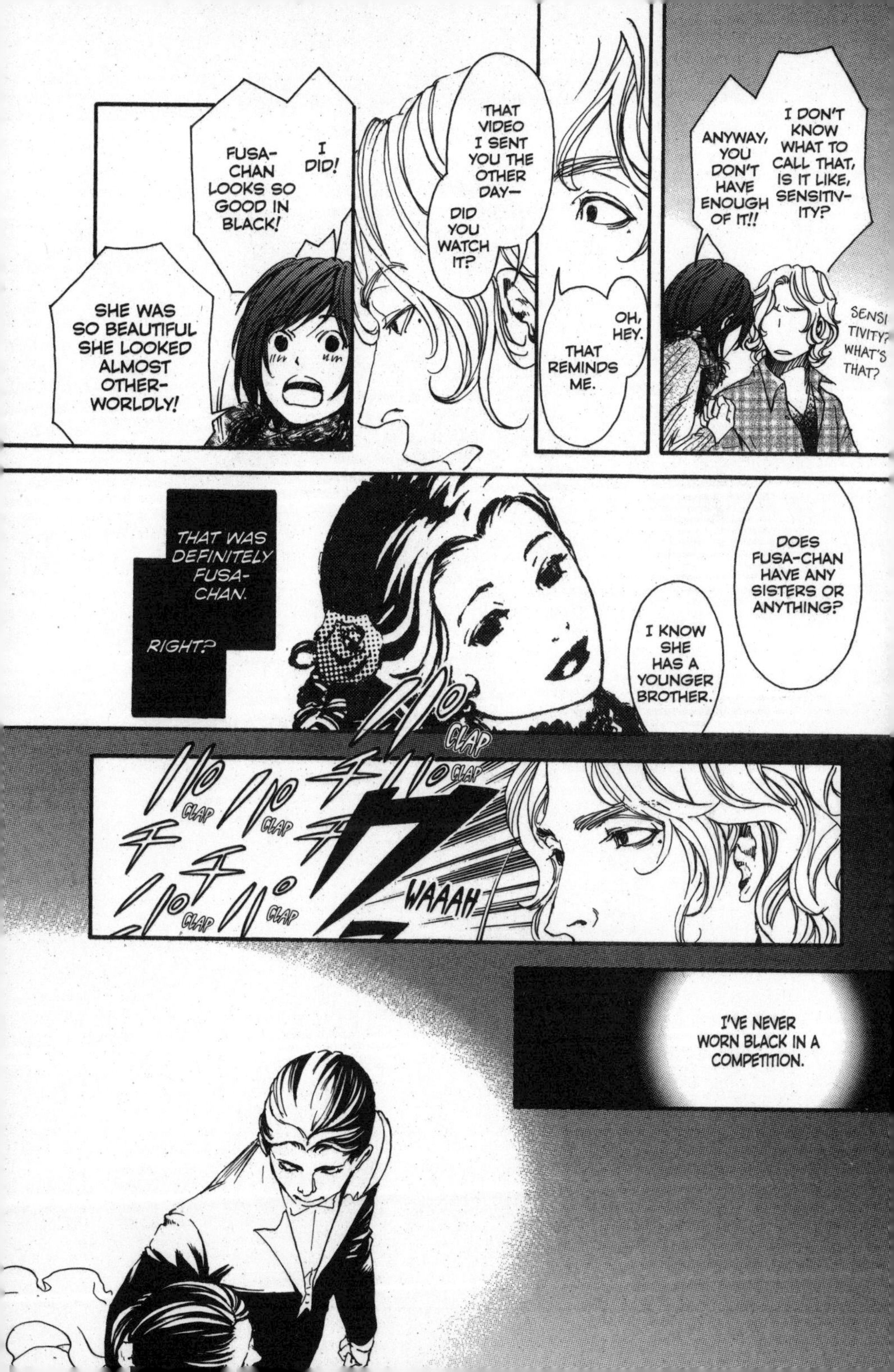
I DON'T KNOW WHAT TO CALL THAT, IS IT LIKE, SENSITIVITY?
ANYWAY, YOU DON'T HAVE ENOUGH OF IT!!
SENSITIVITY? WHAT'S THAT?
OH, HEY. THAT REMINDS ME.
THAT VIDEO I SENT YOU THE OTHER DAY—
DID YOU WATCH IT?
I DID!
FUSA-CHAN LOOKS SO GOOD IN BLACK!
SHE WAS SO BEAUTIFUL SHE LOOKED ALMOST OTHER-WORLDLY!
DOES FUSA-CHAN HAVE ANY SISTERS OR ANYTHING?
I KNOW SHE HAS A YOUNGER BROTHER.
THAT WAS DEFINITELY FUSA-CHAN.
RIGHT?
CLAP CLAP
WAAAH
CLAP CLAP CLAP CLAP CLAP
I'VE NEVER WORN BLACK IN A COMPETITION.

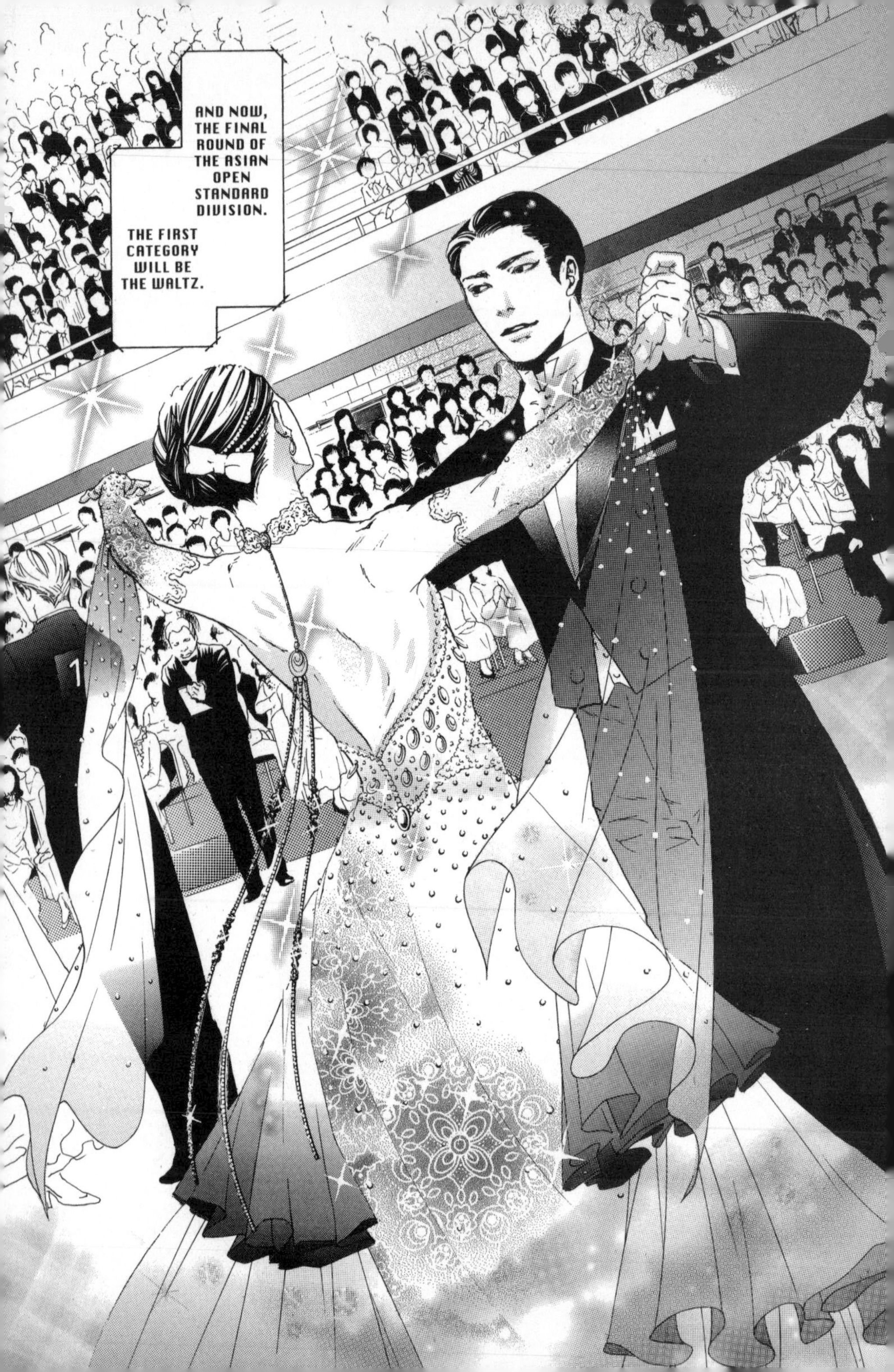
AND NOW, THE FINAL ROUND OF THE ASIAN OPEN STANDARD DIVISION.
THE FIRST CATEGORY WILL BE THE WALTZ.

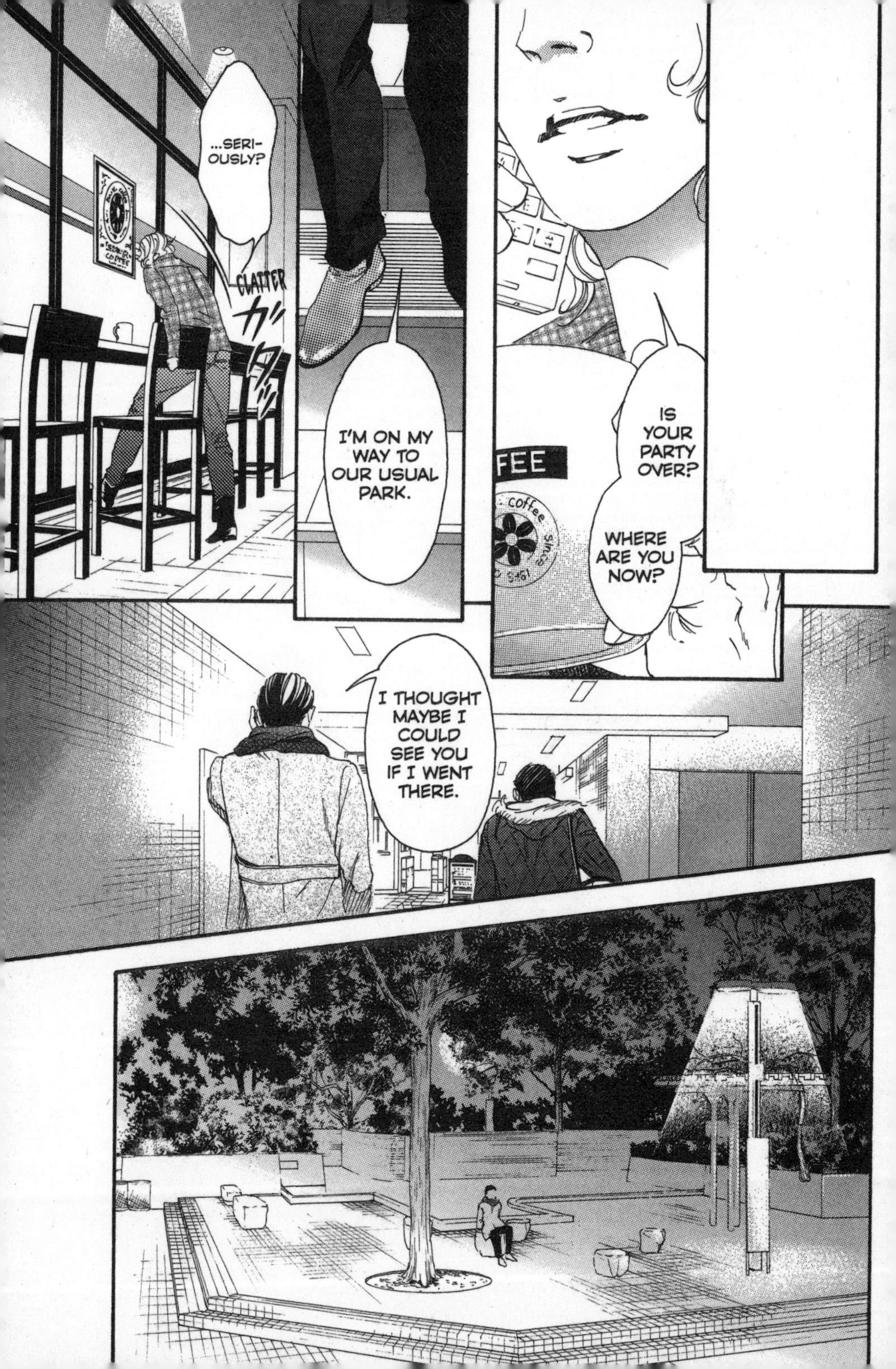
IS YOUR PARTY OVER?
WHERE ARE YOU NOW?
I'M ON MY WAY TO OUR USUAL PARK.
...SERI-OUSLY?
CLATTER
I THOUGHT MAYBE I COULD SEE YOU IF I WENT THERE.

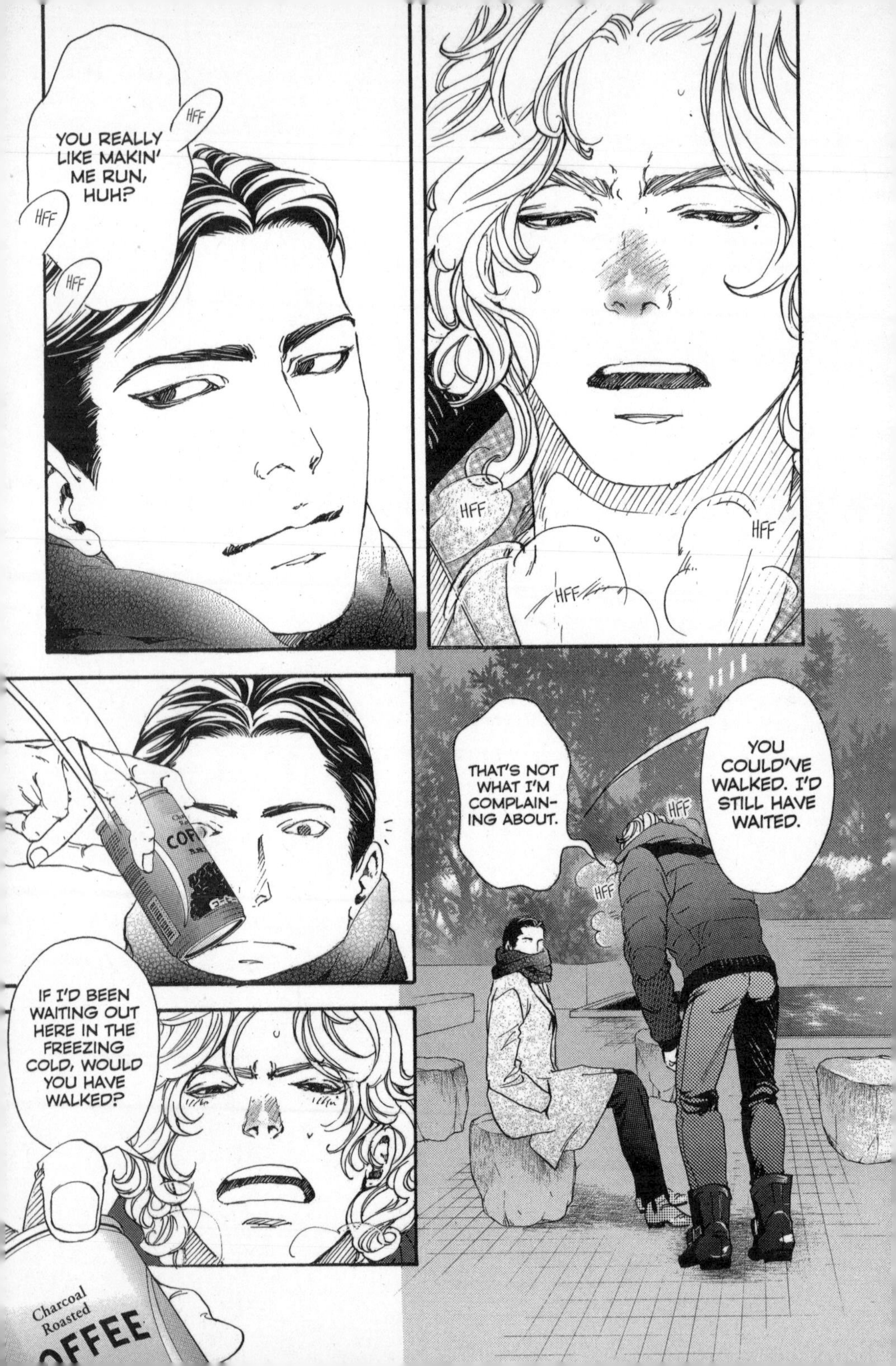
HFF
HFF
HFF
HFF
YOU REALLY LIKE MAKIN' ME RUN, HUH?
HFF
HFF
YOU COULD'VE WALKED. I'D STILL HAVE WAITED.
HFF
THAT'S NOT WHAT I'M COMPLAINING ABOUT.
HFF
IF I'D BEEN WAITING OUT HERE IN THE FREEZING COLD, WOULD YOU HAVE WALKED?
Charcoal Roasted
OFFEE

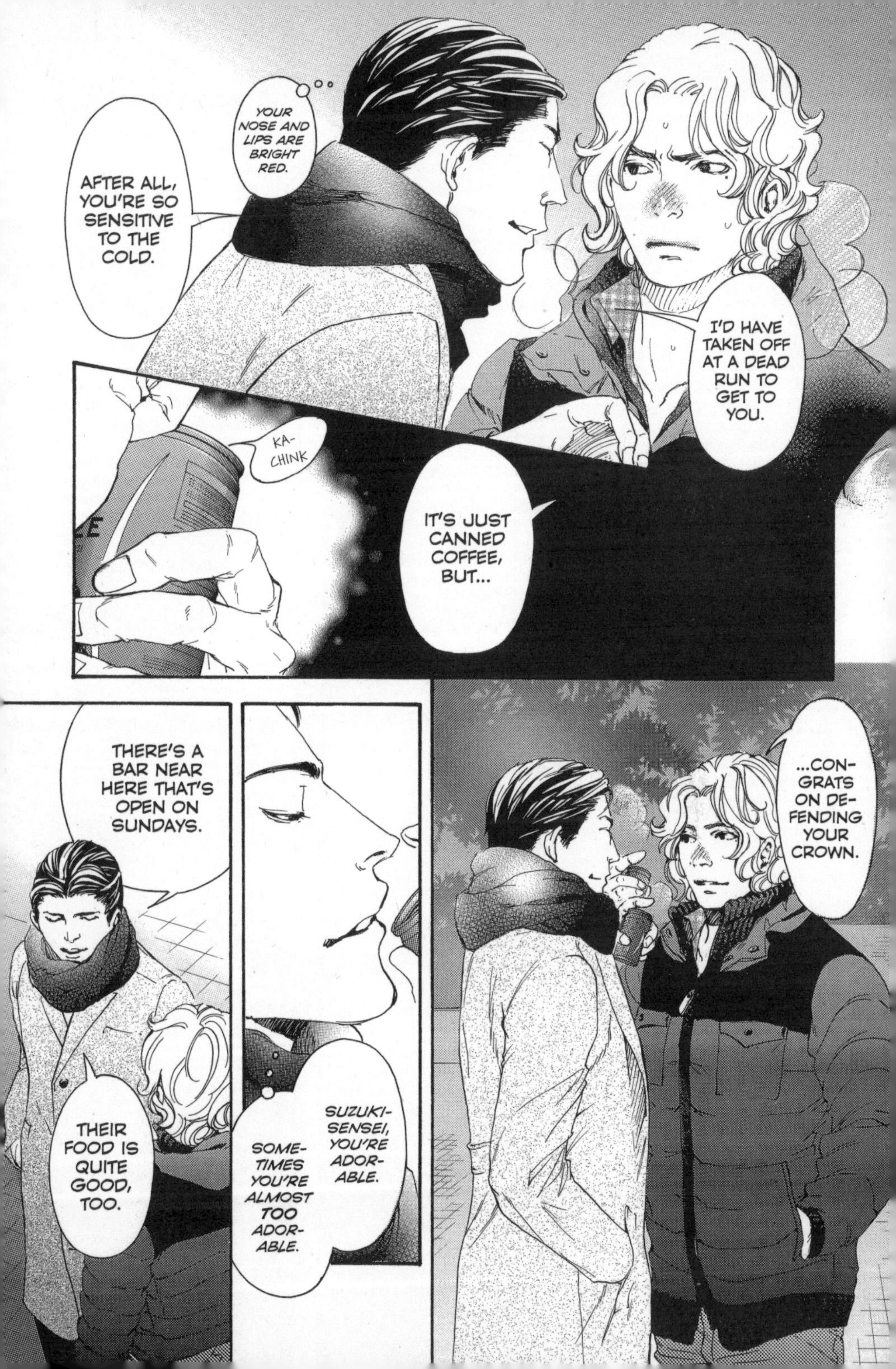
YOUR NOSE AND LIPS ARE BRIGHT RED.
AFTER ALL, YOU'RE SO SENSITIVE TO THE COLD.
I'D HAVE TAKEN OFF AT A DEAD RUN TO GET TO YOU.
KA-CHINK
IT'S JUST CANNED COFFEE, BUT...
...CON-GRATS ON DE-FENDING YOUR CROWN.
SUZUKI-SENSEI, YOU'RE ADOR-ABLE.
SOME-TIMES YOU'RE ALMOST TOO ADOR-ABLE.
THERE'S A BAR NEAR HERE THAT'S OPEN ON SUNDAYS.
THEIR FOOD IS QUITE GOOD, TOO.

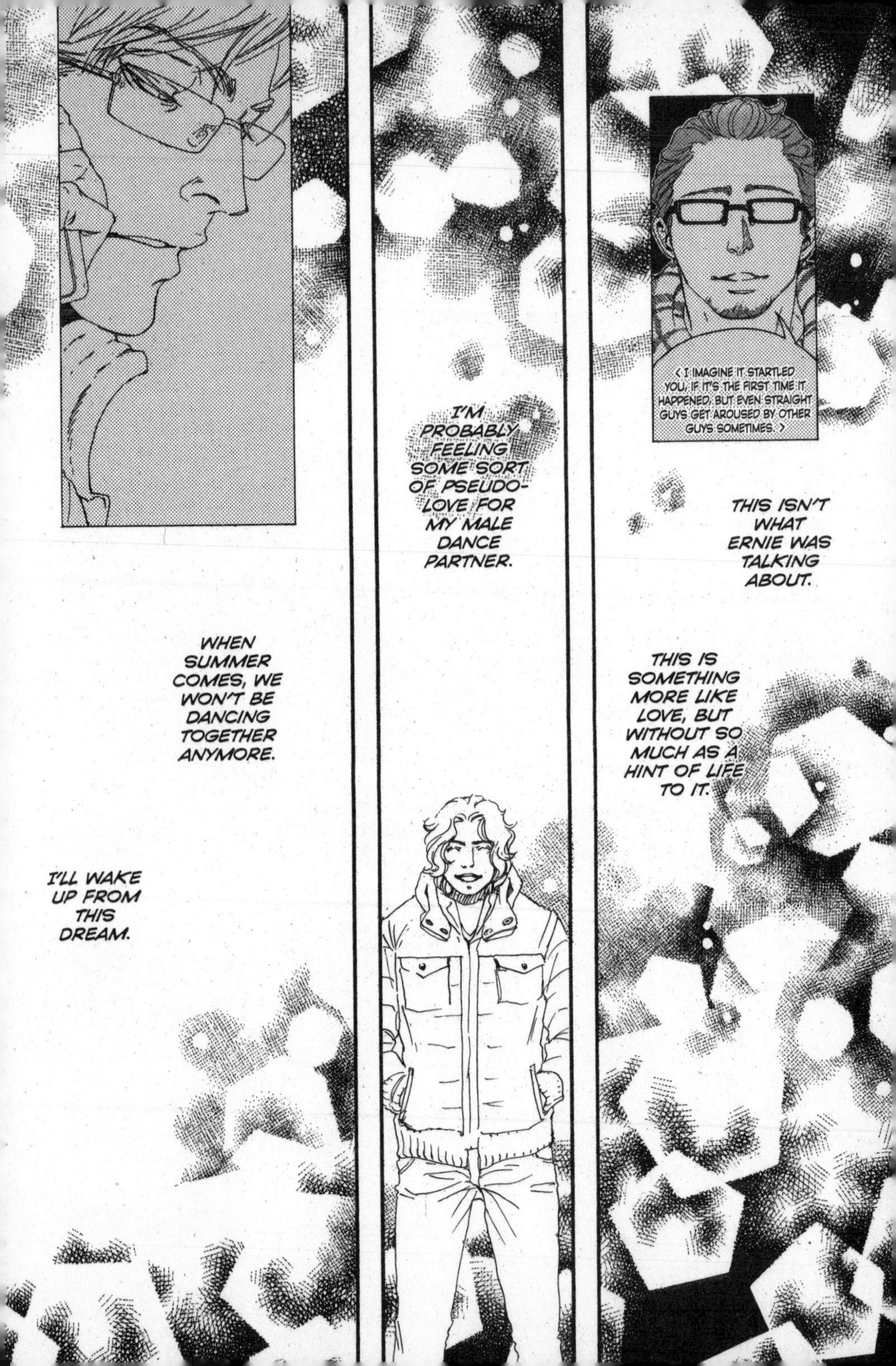
< I IMAGINE IT STARTLED YOU, IF IT'S THE FIRST TIME IT HAPPENED, BUT EVEN STRAIGHT GUYS GET AROUSED BY OTHER GUYS SOMETIMES. >
THIS ISN'T WHAT ERNIE WAS TALKING ABOUT.
THIS IS SOMETHING MORE LIKE LOVE, BUT WITHOUT SO MUCH AS A HINT OF LIFE TO IT.
I'M PROBABLY FEELING SOME SORT OF PSEUDO-LOVE FOR MY MALE DANCE PARTNER.
WHEN SUMMER COMES, WE WON'T BE DANCING TOGETHER ANYMORE.
I'LL WAKE UP FROM THIS DREAM.

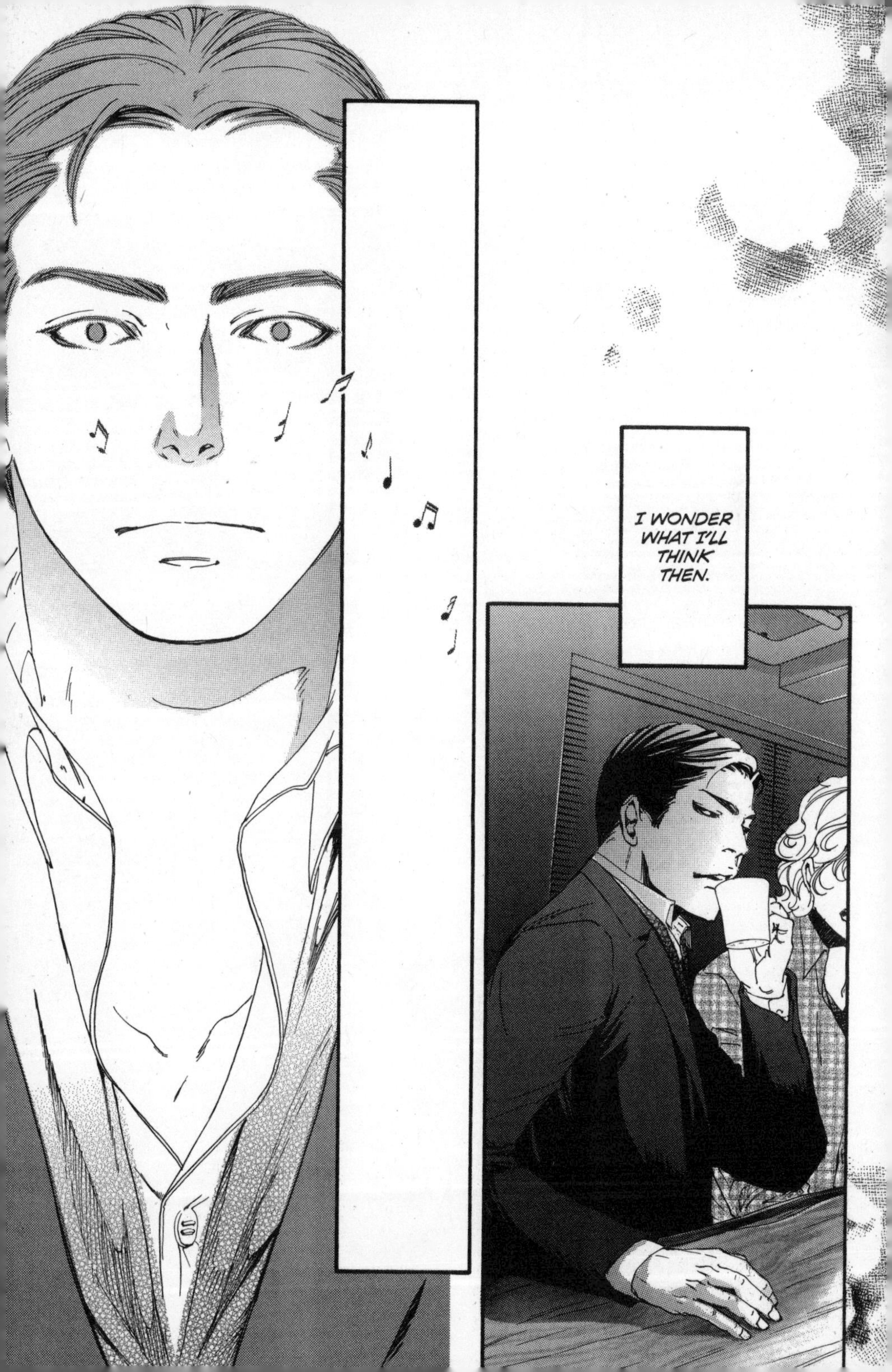
I WONDER WHAT I'LL THINK THEN.

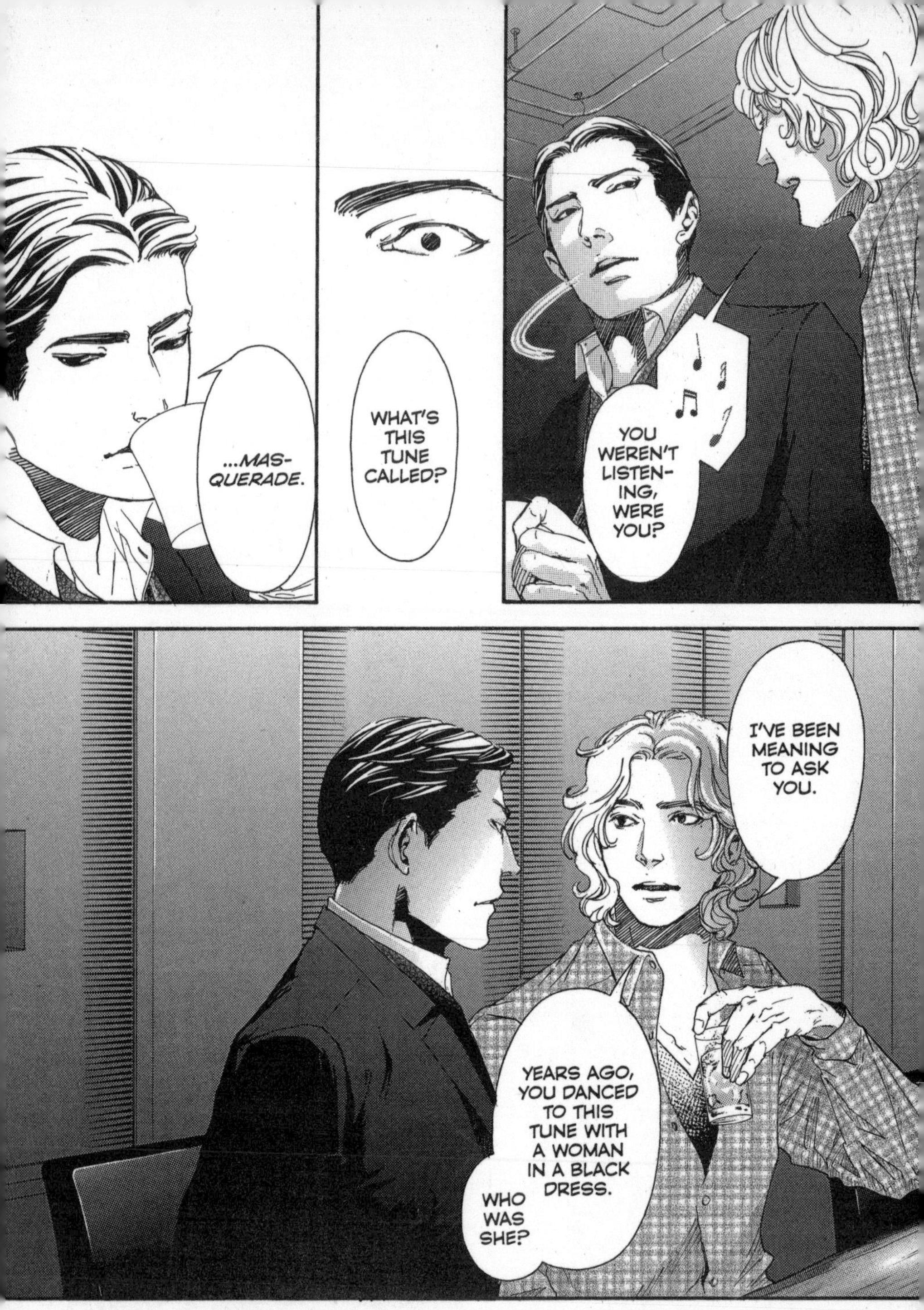
YOU WEREN'T LISTENING, WERE YOU?
WHAT'S THIS TUNE CALLED?
...MASQUERADE.
I'VE BEEN MEANING TO ASK YOU.
YEARS AGO, YOU DANCED TO THIS TUNE WITH A WOMAN IN A BLACK DRESS.
WHO WAS SHE?

END OF CHAPTER 16

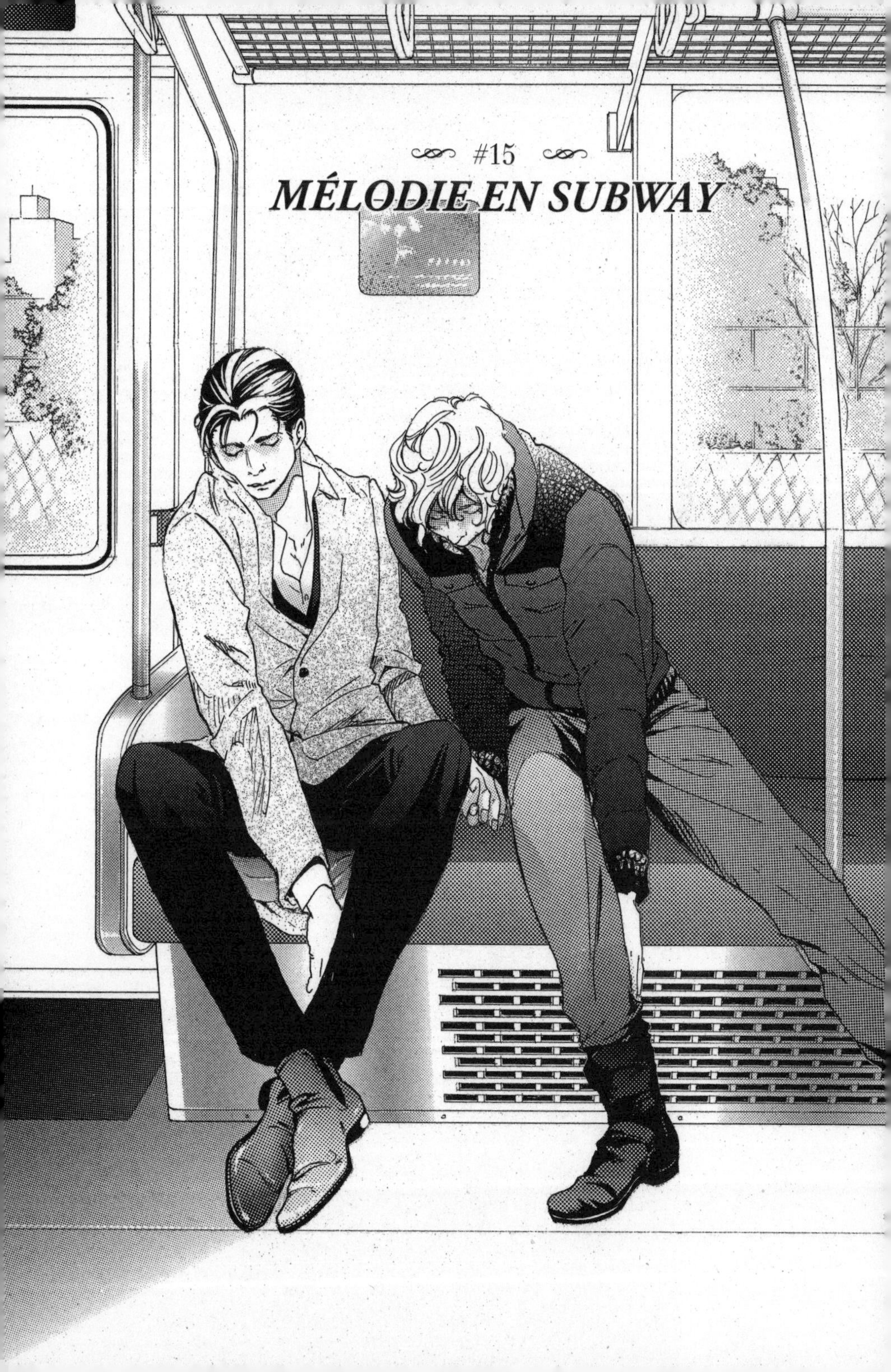
#15
MÉLODIE EN SUBWAY

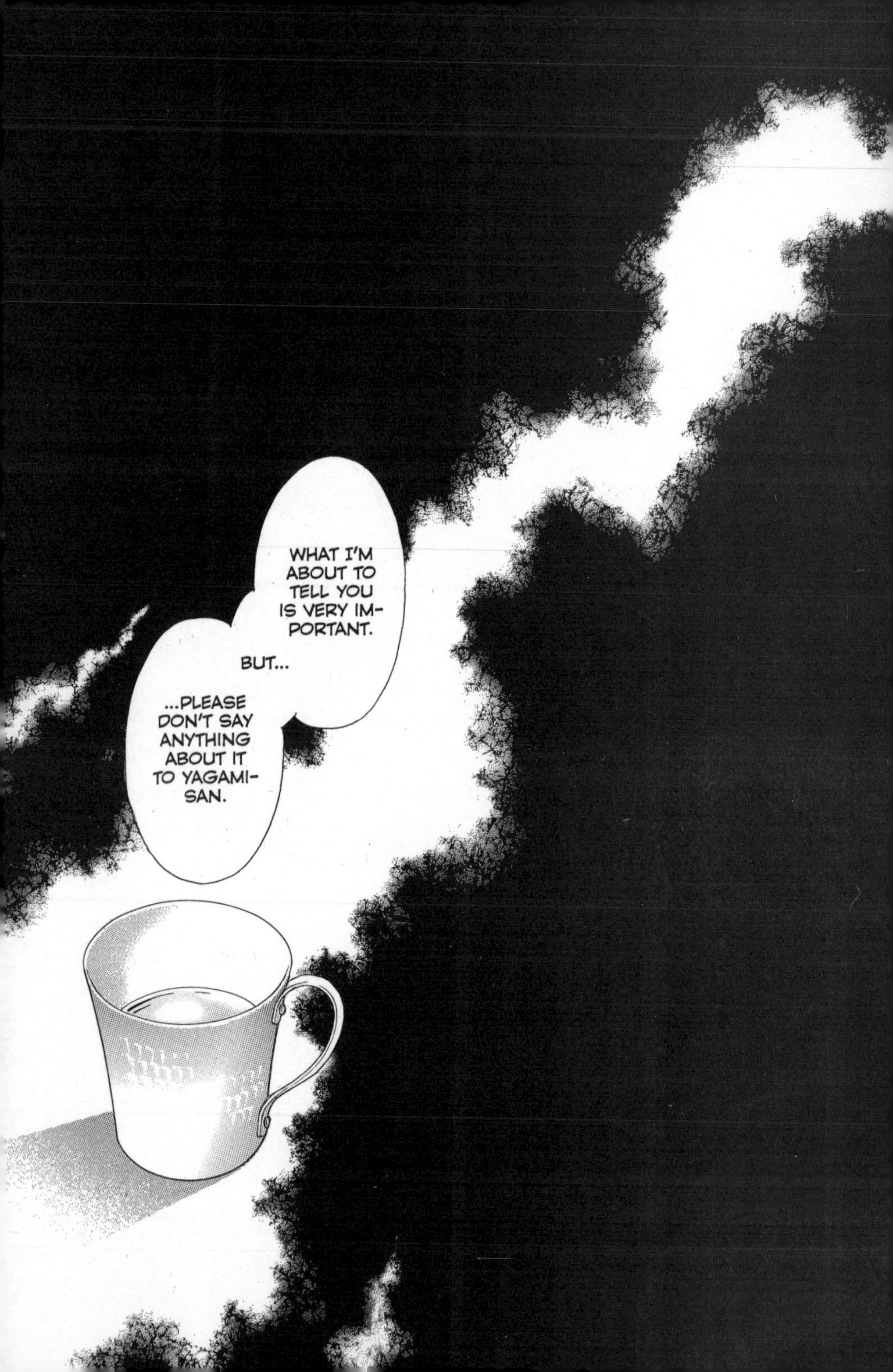
WHAT I'M ABOUT TO TELL YOU IS VERY IMPORTANT.
BUT... ...PLEASE DON'T SAY ANYTHING ABOUT IT TO YAGAMI-SAN.

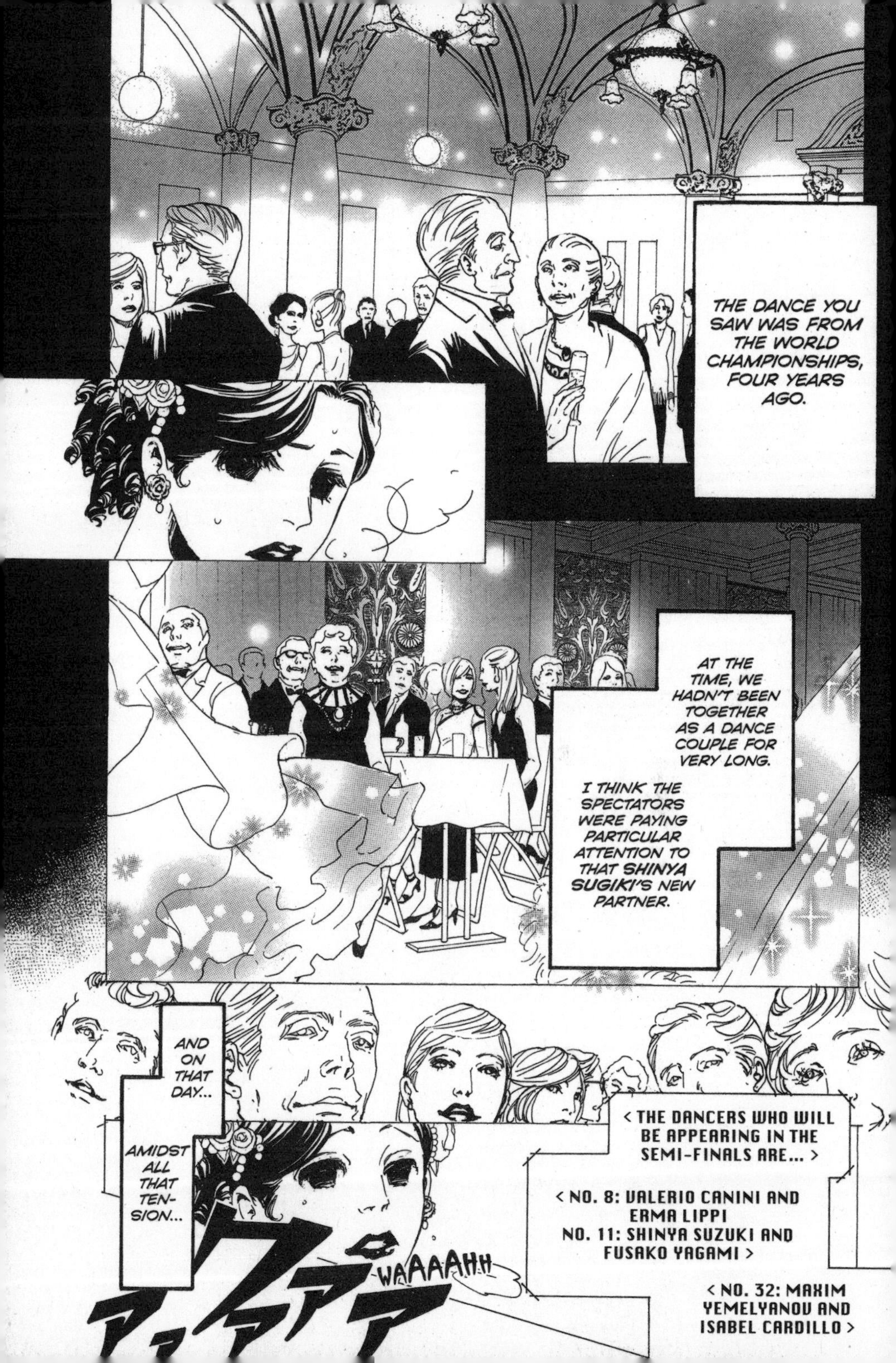
THE DANCE YOU SAW WAS FROM THE WORLD CHAMPIONSHIPS, FOUR YEARS AGO.
AT THE TIME, WE HADN'T BEEN TOGETHER AS A DANCE COUPLE FOR VERY LONG.
I THINK THE SPECTATORS WERE PAYING PARTICULAR ATTENTION TO THAT SHINYA SUGIKI'S NEW PARTNER.
< THE DANCERS WHO WILL BE APPEARING IN THE SEMI-FINALS ARE... >
< NO. 8: VALERIO CANINI AND ERMA LIPPI NO. 11: SHINYA SUZUKI AND FUSAKO YAGAMI >
< NO. 32: MAXIM YEMELYANOV AND ISABEL CARDILLO >
AND ON THAT DAY...
AMIDST ALL THAT TEN-SION...
WAAAAHH

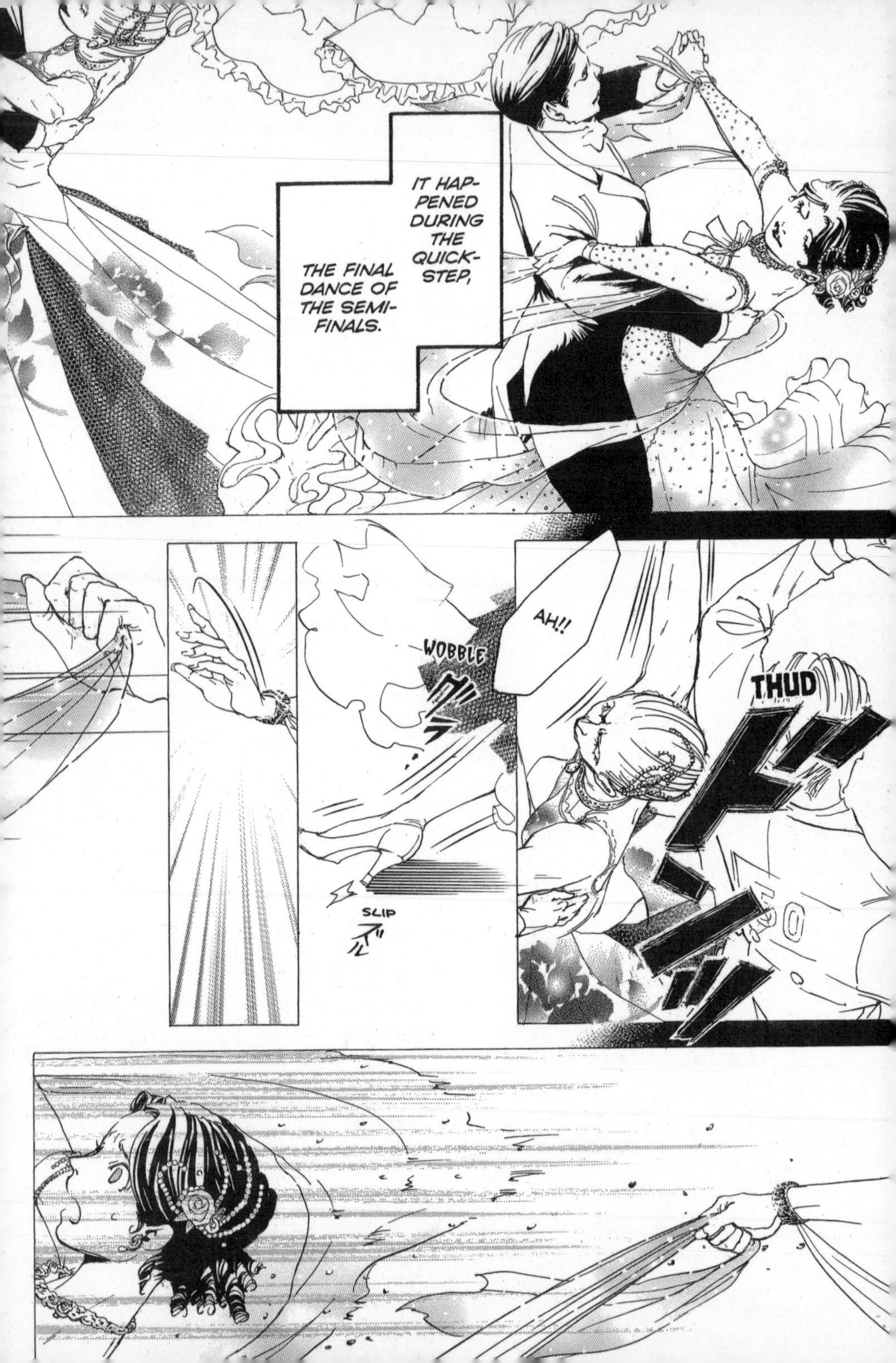
IT HAPPENED DURING THE QUICKSTEP,
THE FINAL DANCE OF THE SEMI-FINALS.
AH!!
THUD
WOBBLE
SLIP

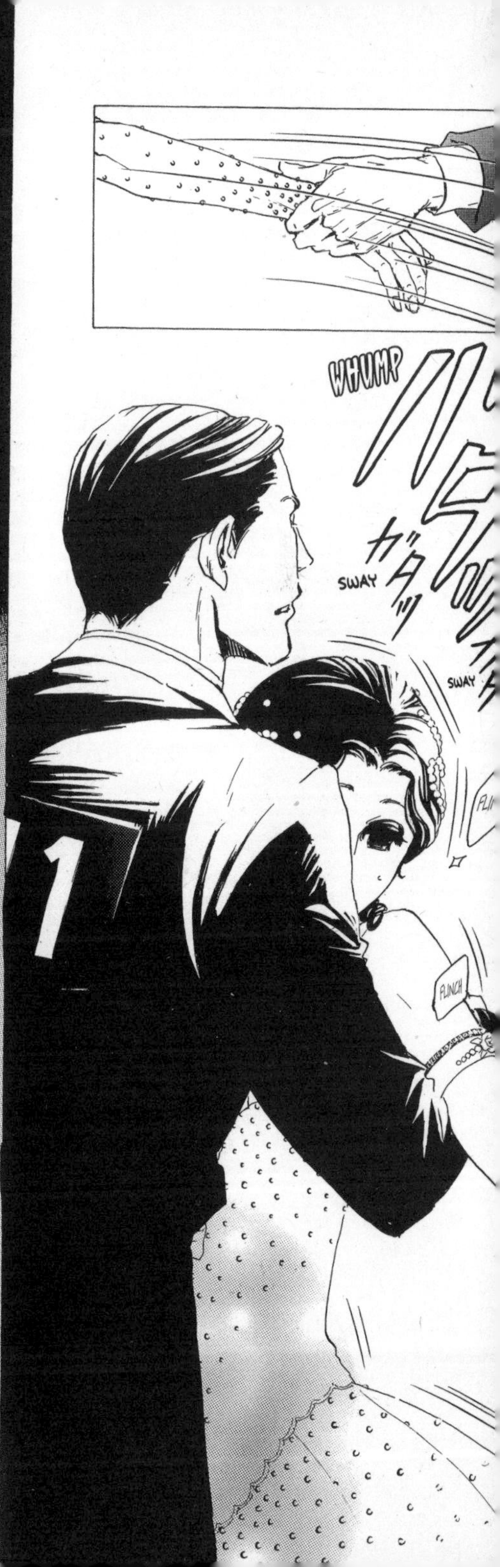
WHUMP
ガタッ
SWAY
SWAY
FLINCH
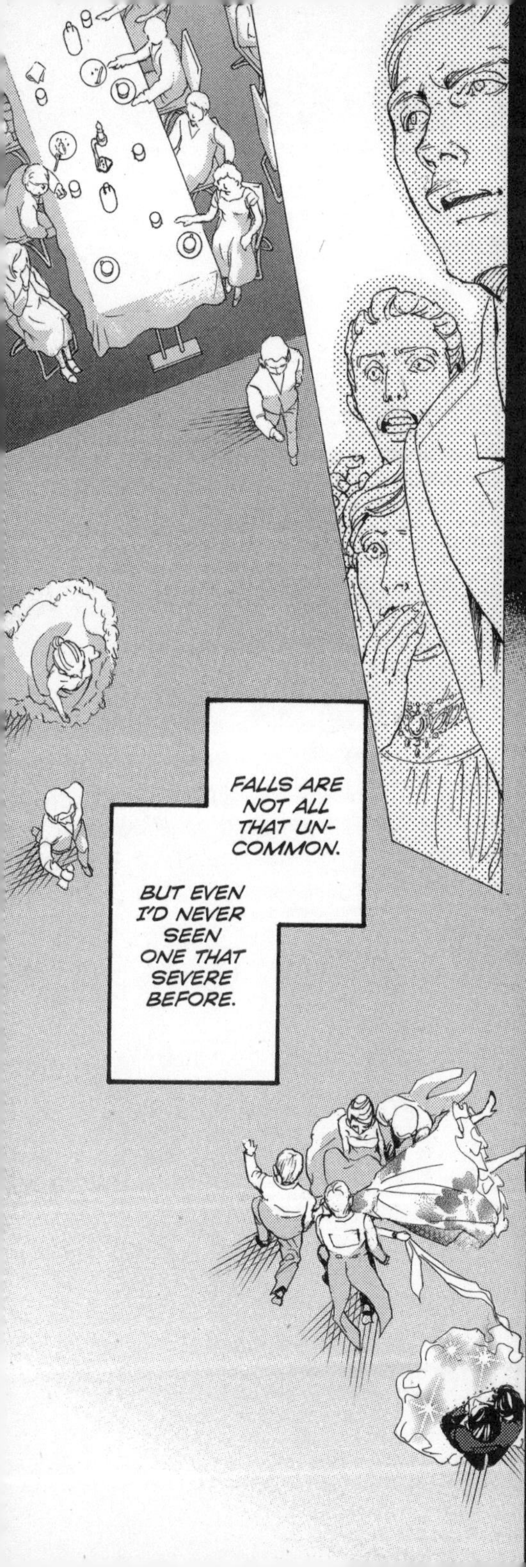
FALLS ARE NOT ALL THAT UN-COMMON.
BUT EVEN I'D NEVER SEEN ONE THAT SEVERE BEFORE.

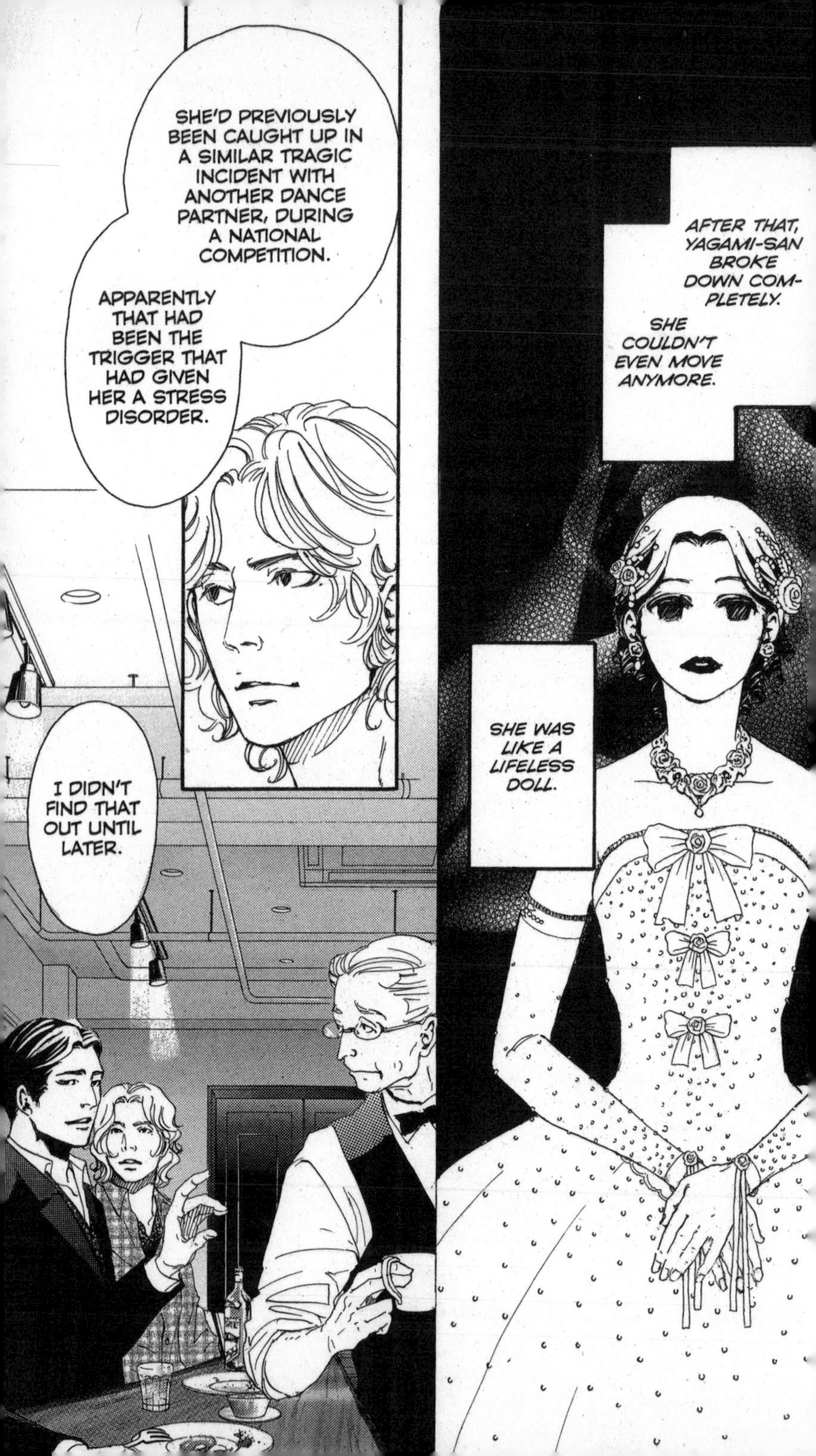

AFTER THAT, YAGAMI-SAN BROKE DOWN COM-PLETELY.
SHE COULDN'T EVEN MOVE ANYMORE.
SHE WAS LIKE A LIFELESS DOLL.
SHE'D PREVIOUSLY BEEN CAUGHT UP IN A SIMILAR TRAGIC INCIDENT WITH ANOTHER DANCE PARTNER, DURING A NATIONAL COMPETITION.
APPARENTLY THAT HAD BEEN THE TRIGGER THAT HAD GIVEN HER A STRESS DISORDER.
I DIDN'T FIND THAT OUT UNTIL LATER.

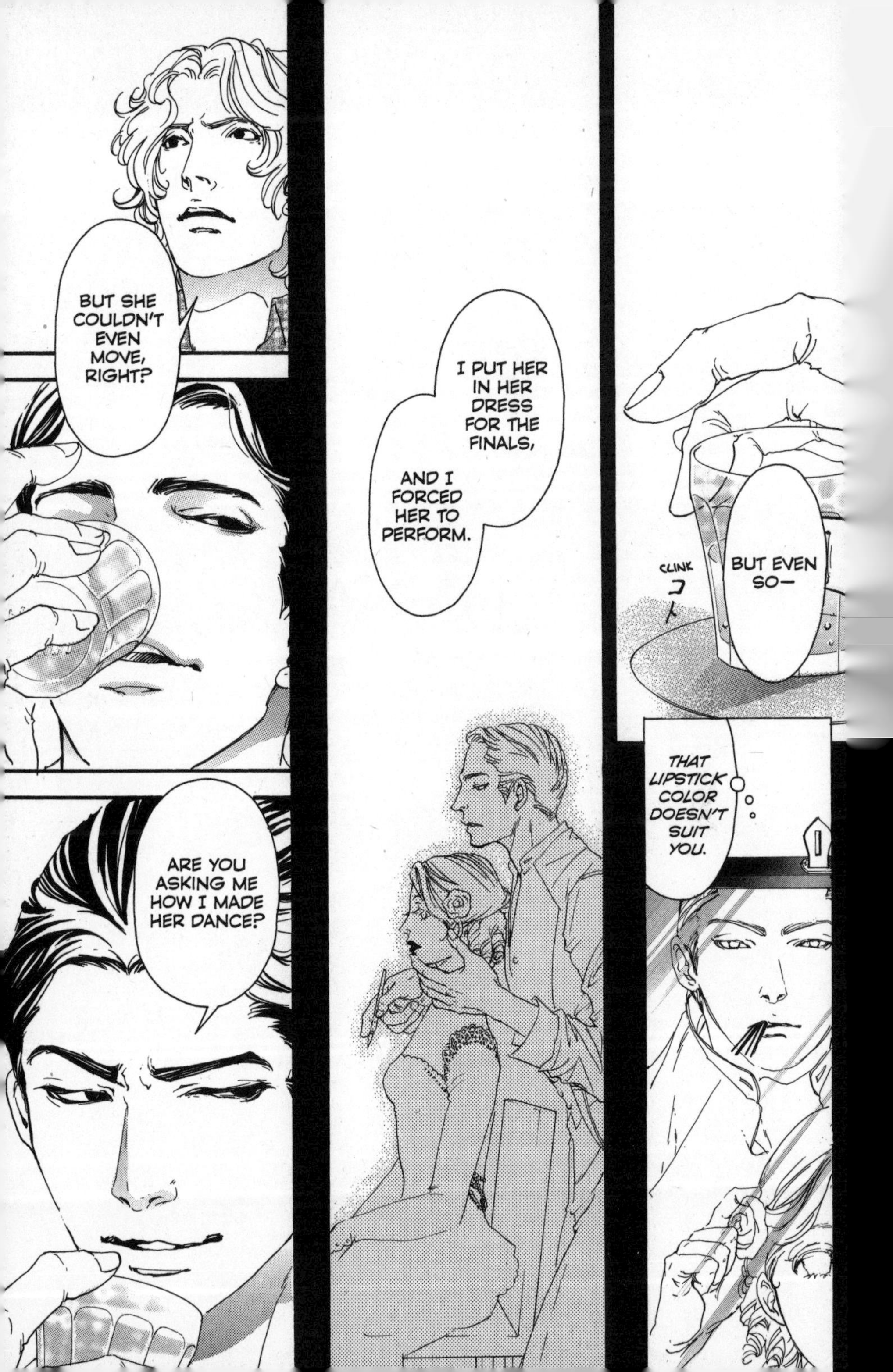
BUT SHE COULDN'T EVEN MOVE, RIGHT?
ARE YOU ASKING ME HOW I MADE HER DANCE?
I PUT HER IN HER DRESS FOR THE FINALS,
AND I FORCED HER TO PERFORM.
BUT EVEN SO—
CLINK
コト
THAT LIPSTICK COLOR DOESN'T SUIT YOU.

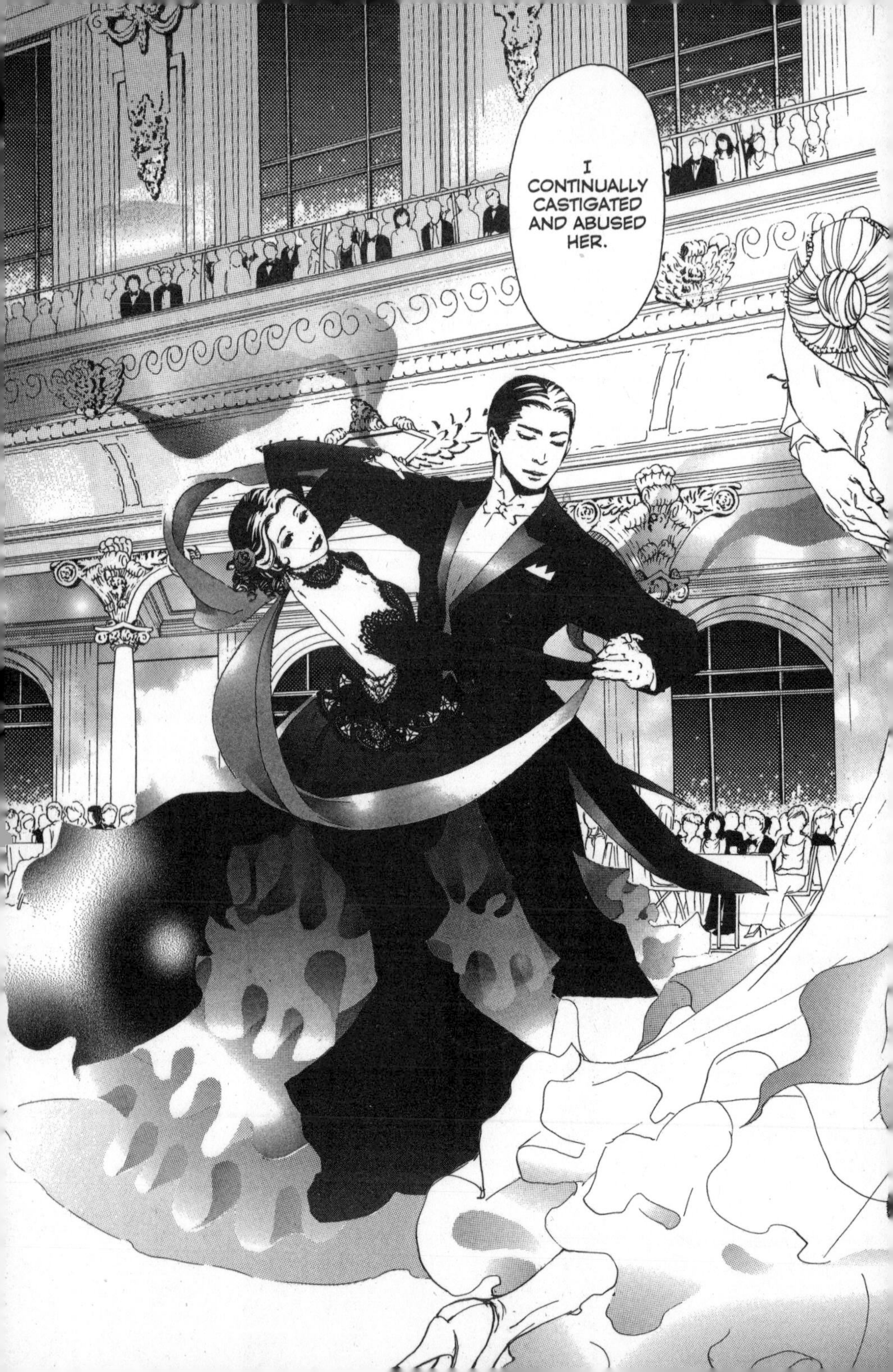
I CONTINUALLY CASTIGATED AND ABUSED HER.

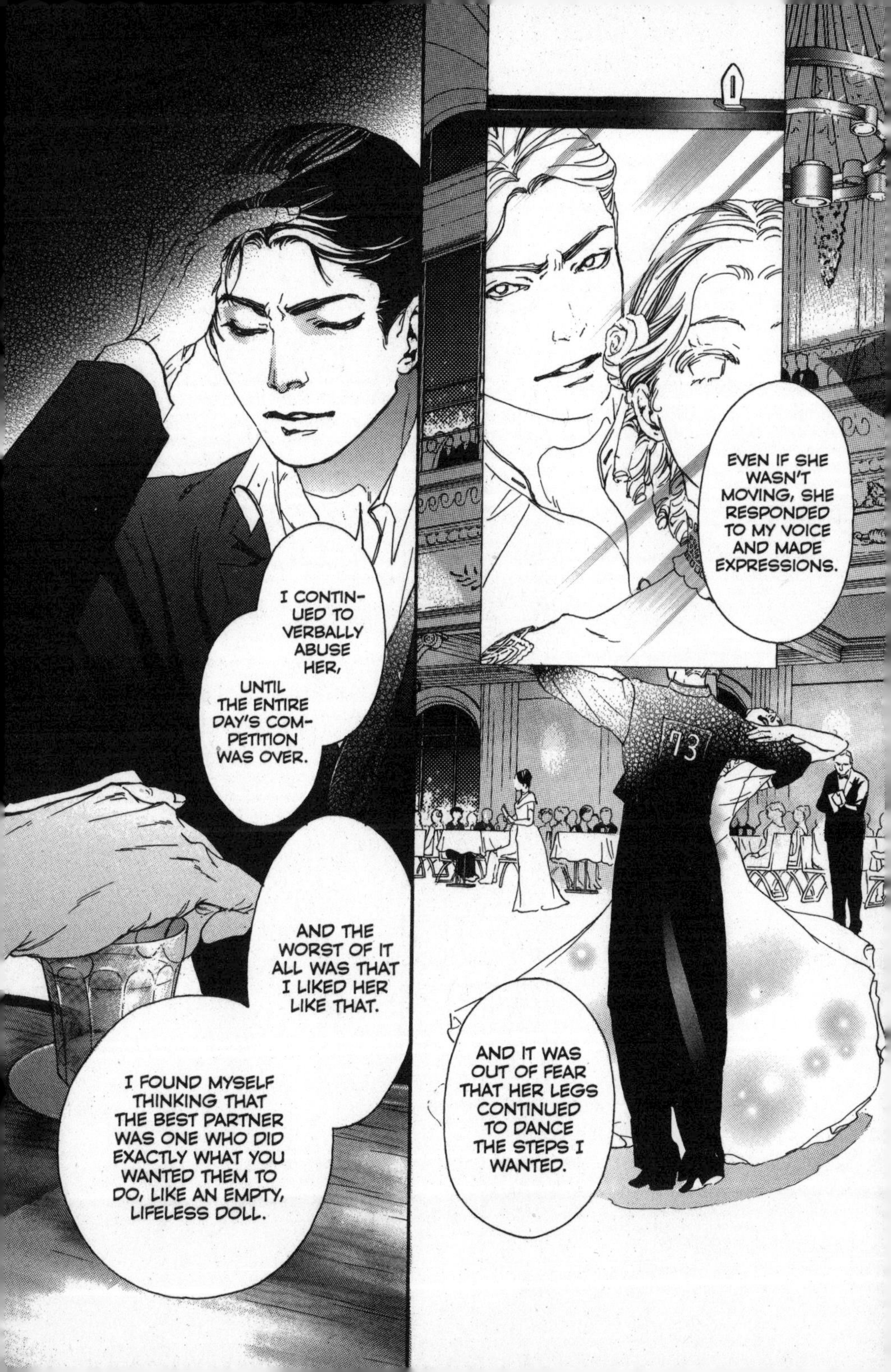
EVEN IF SHE WASN'T MOVING, SHE RESPONDED TO MY VOICE AND MADE EXPRESSIONS.
AND IT WAS OUT OF FEAR THAT HER LEGS CONTINUED TO DANCE THE STEPS I WANTED.
I CONTIN-UED TO VERBALLY ABUSE HER,
UNTIL THE ENTIRE DAY'S COM-PETITION WAS OVER.
AND THE WORST OF IT ALL WAS THAT I LIKED HER LIKE THAT.
I FOUND MYSELF THINKING THAT THE BEST PARTNER WAS ONE WHO DID EXACTLY WHAT YOU WANTED THEM TO DO, LIKE AN EMPTY, LIFELESS DOLL.

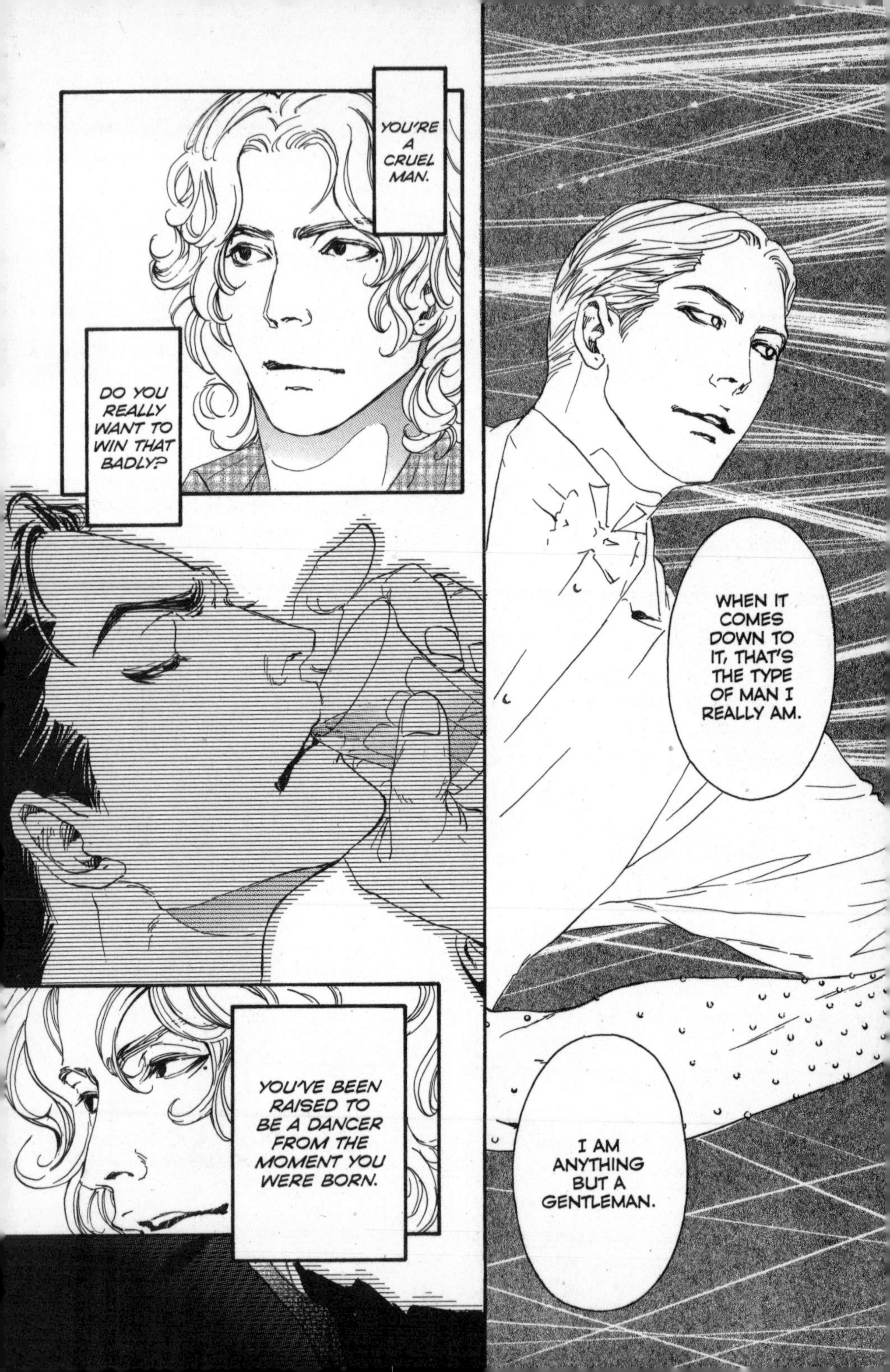
WHEN IT COMES DOWN TO IT, THAT'S THE TYPE OF MAN I REALLY AM.
I AM ANYTHING BUT A GENTLEMAN.
YOU'RE A CRUEL MAN.
DO YOU REALLY WANT TO WIN THAT BADLY?
YOU'VE BEEN RAISED TO BE A DANCER FROM THE MOMENT YOU WERE BORN.

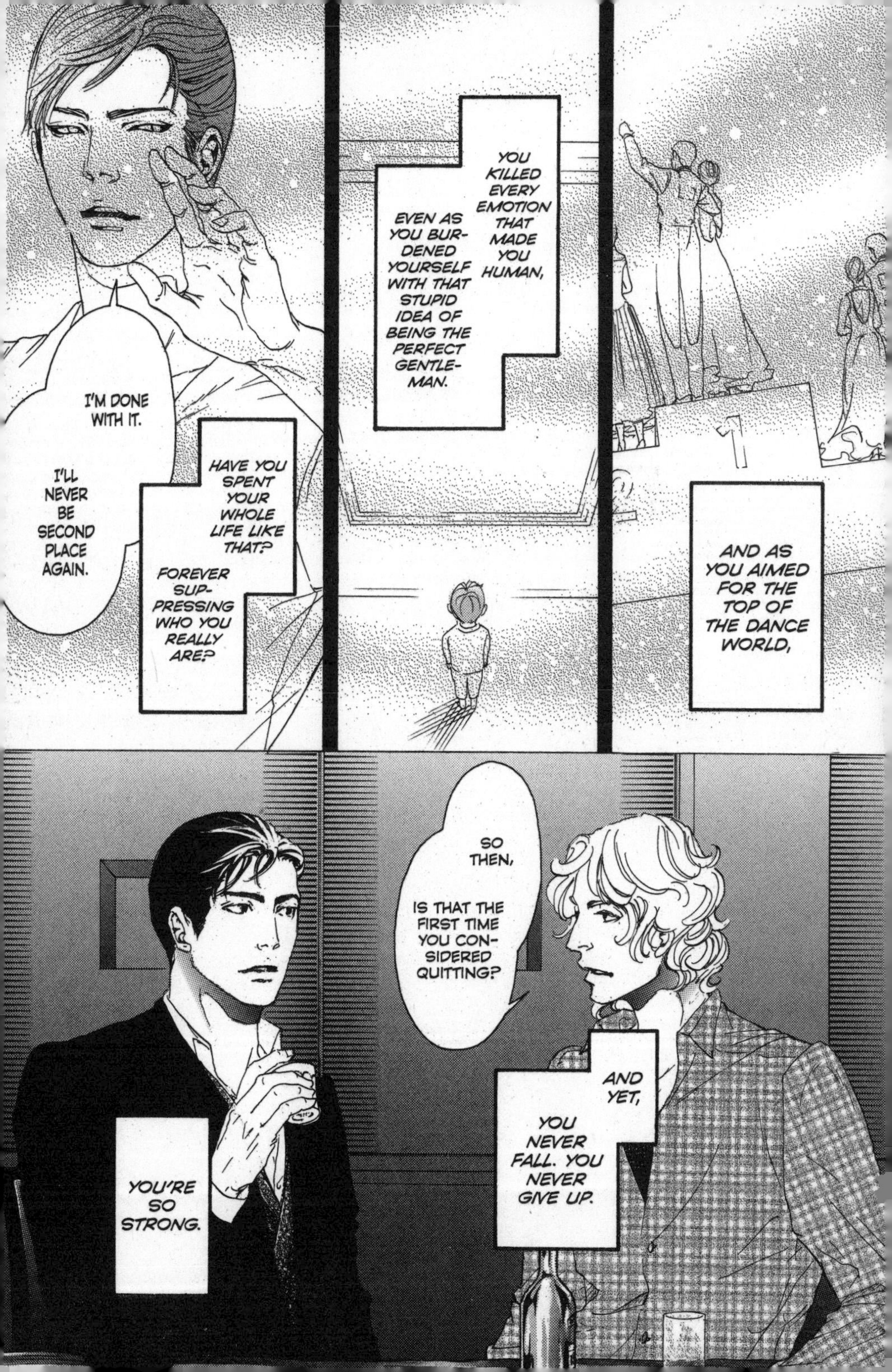
AND AS YOU AIMED FOR THE TOP OF THE DANCE WORLD,
YOU KILLED EVERY EMOTION THAT MADE YOU HUMAN,
EVEN AS YOU BURDENED YOURSELF WITH THAT STUPID IDEA OF BEING THE PERFECT GENTLEMAN.
HAVE YOU SPENT YOUR WHOLE LIFE LIKE THAT?
FOREVER SUPPRESSING WHO YOU REALLY ARE?
I'M DONE WITH IT.
I'LL NEVER BE SECOND PLACE AGAIN.
SO THEN,
IS THAT THE FIRST TIME YOU CONSIDERED QUITTING?
AND YET,
YOU NEVER FALL. YOU NEVER GIVE UP.
YOU'RE SO STRONG.

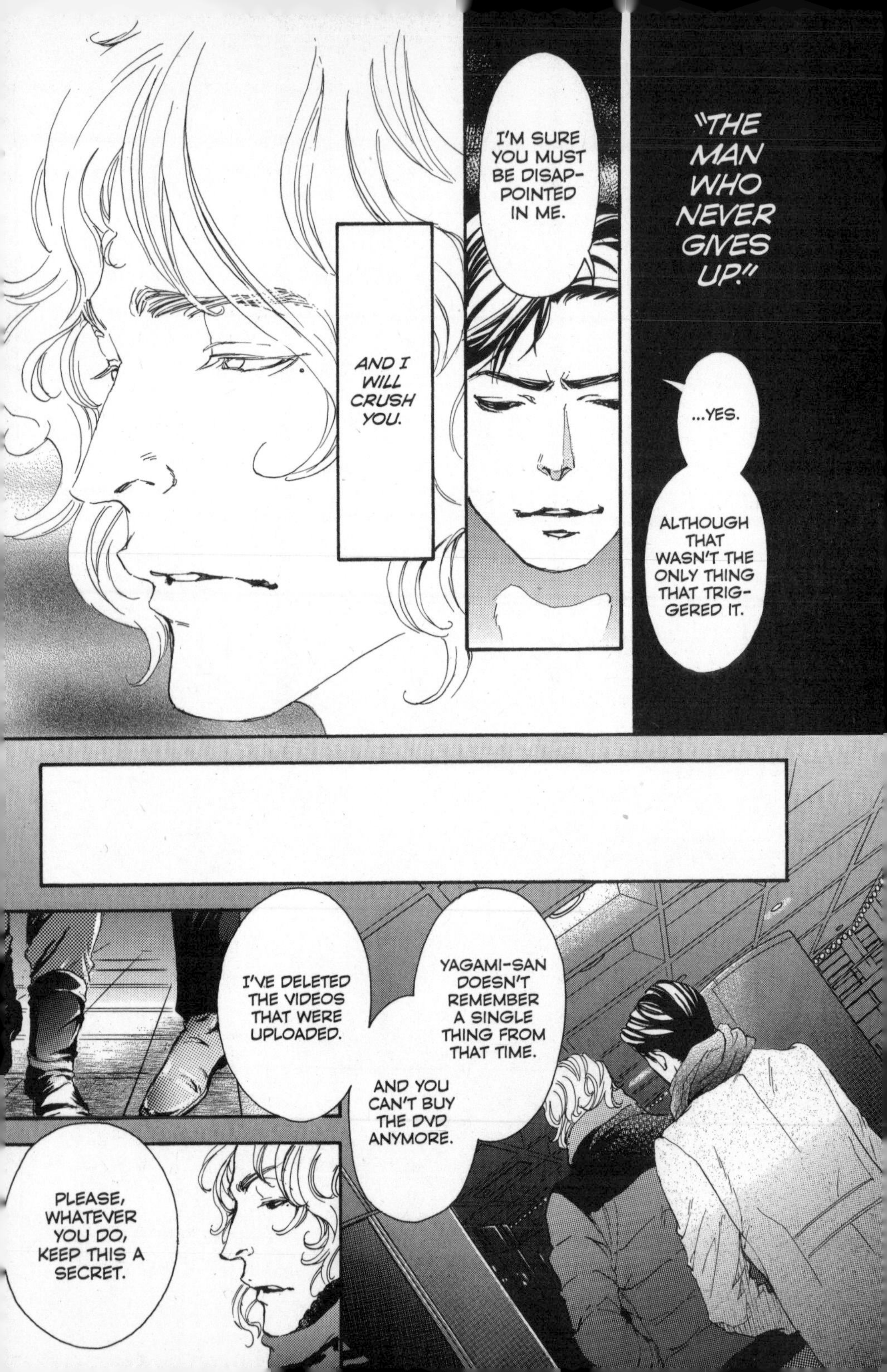
"THE MAN WHO NEVER GIVES UP."
...YES.
ALTHOUGH THAT WASN'T THE ONLY THING THAT TRIGGERED IT.
I'M SURE YOU MUST BE DISAPPOINTED IN ME.
AND I WILL CRUSH YOU.
YAGAMI-SAN DOESN'T REMEMBER A SINGLE THING FROM THAT TIME.
I'VE DELETED THE VIDEOS THAT WERE UPLOADED.
AND YOU CAN'T BUY THE DVD ANYMORE.
PLEASE, WHATEVER YOU DO, KEEP THIS A SECRET.

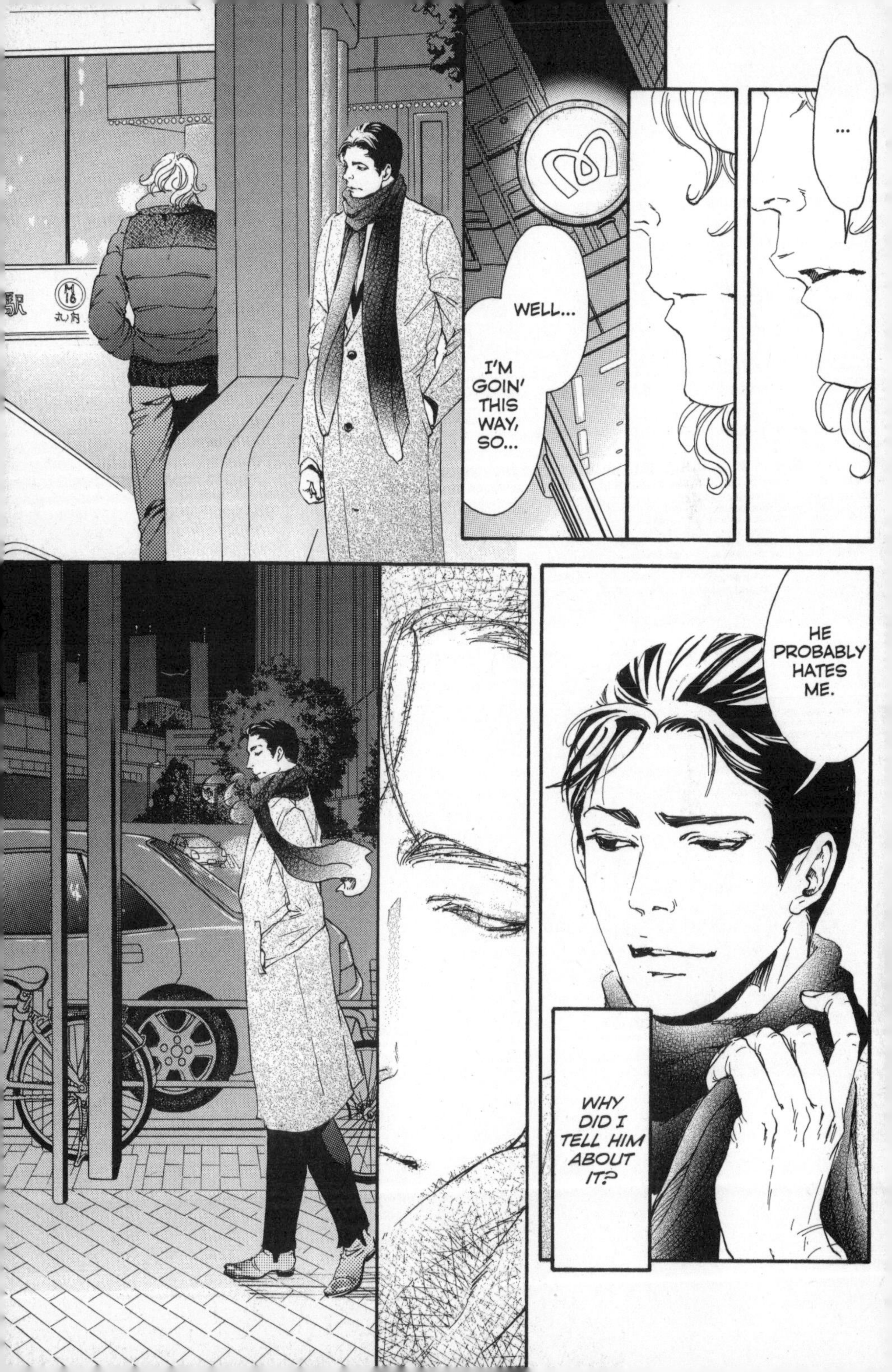
...
WELL...
I'M GOIN' THIS WAY, SO...
HE PROBABLY HATES ME.
WHY DID I TELL HIM ABOUT IT?

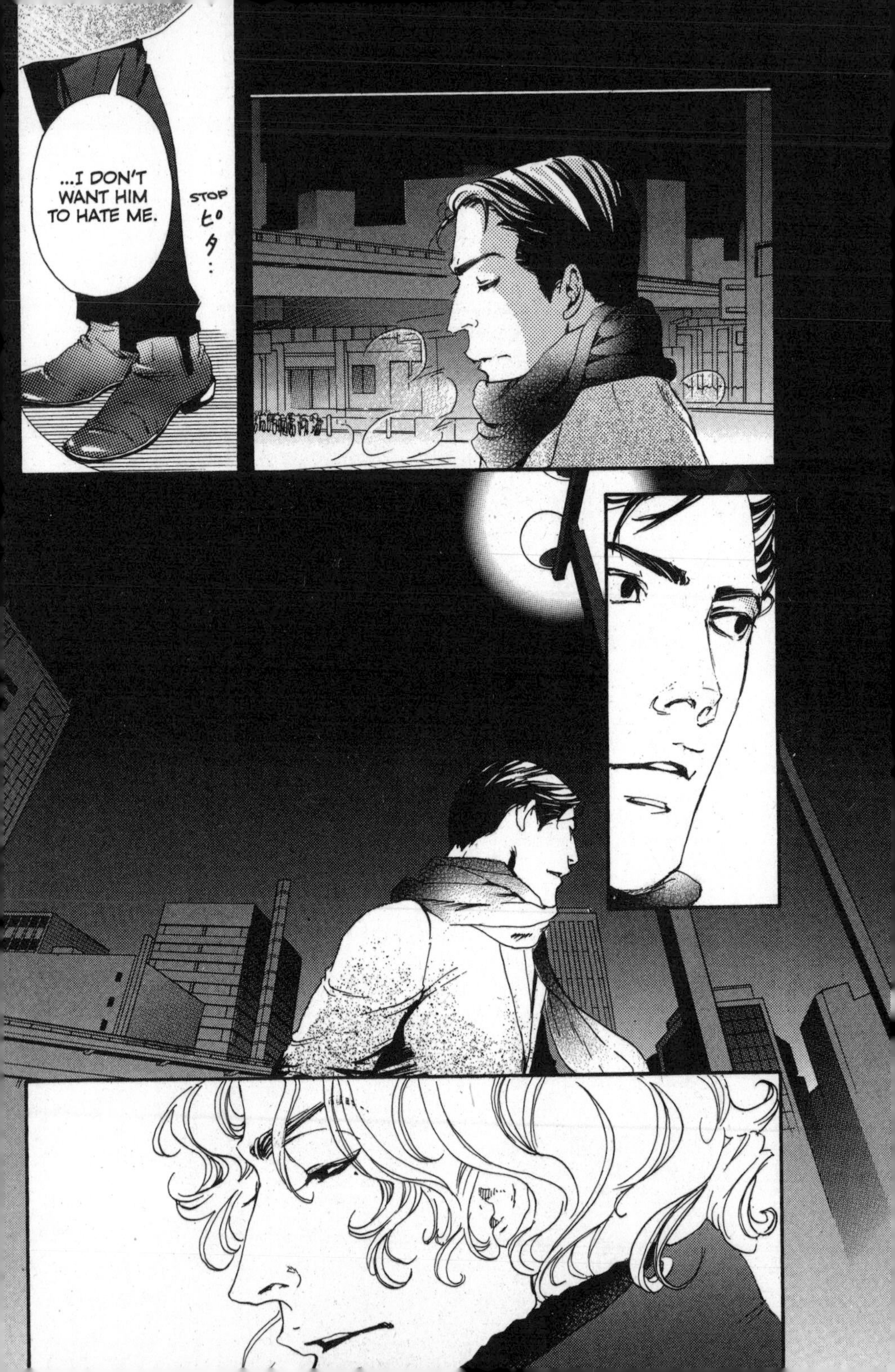
...I DON'T WANT HIM TO HATE ME.
STOP
ピタ…

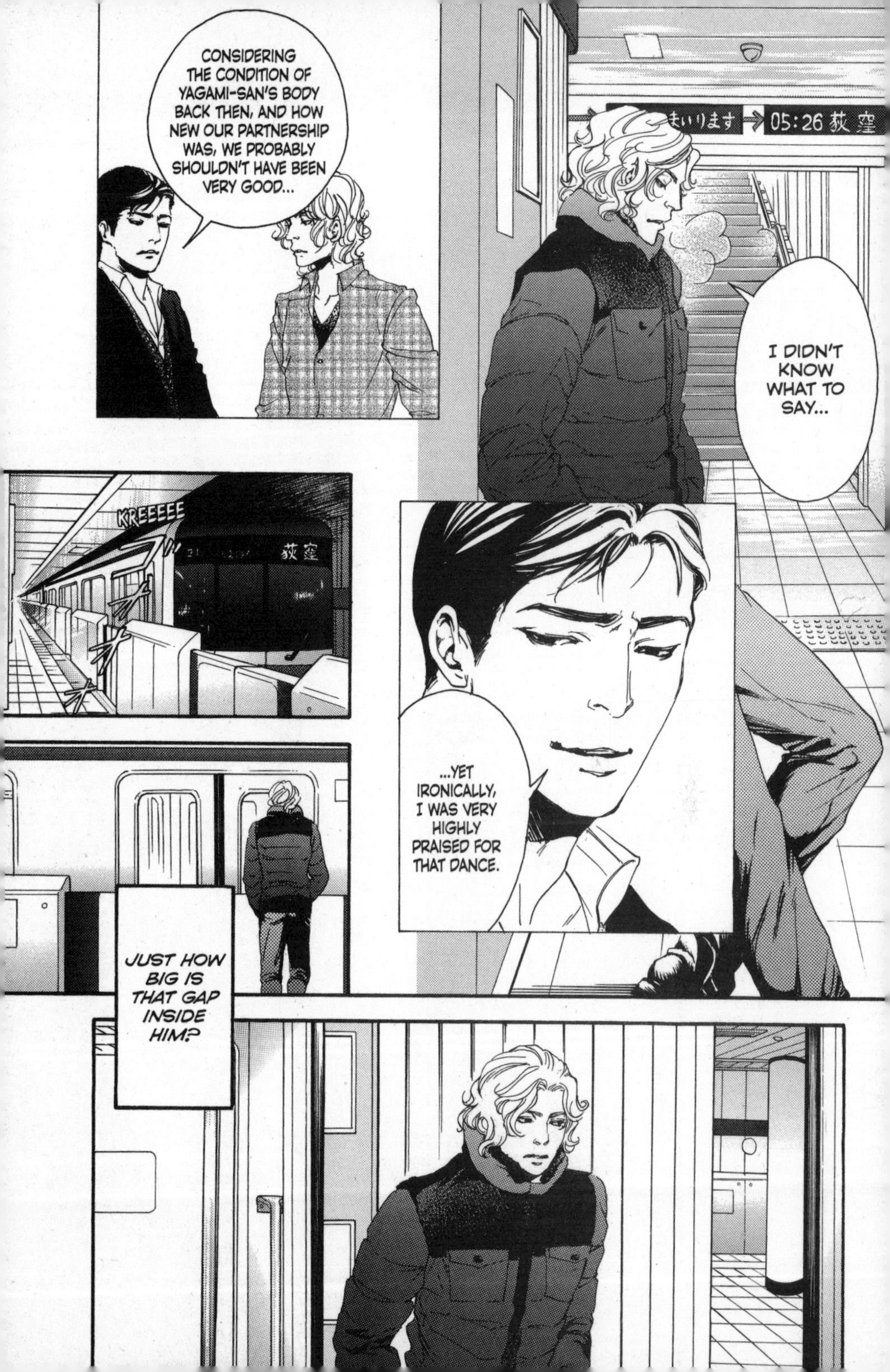
まいります
05:26 荻窪
I DIDN'T KNOW WHAT TO SAY...
CONSIDERING THE CONDITION OF YAGAMI-SAN'S BODY BACK THEN, AND HOW NEW OUR PARTNERSHIP WAS, WE PROBABLY SHOULDN'T HAVE BEEN VERY GOOD...
...YET IRONICALLY, I WAS VERY HIGHLY PRAISED FOR THAT DANCE.
KREEEEE
荻窪
JUST HOW BIG IS THAT GAP INSIDE HIM?

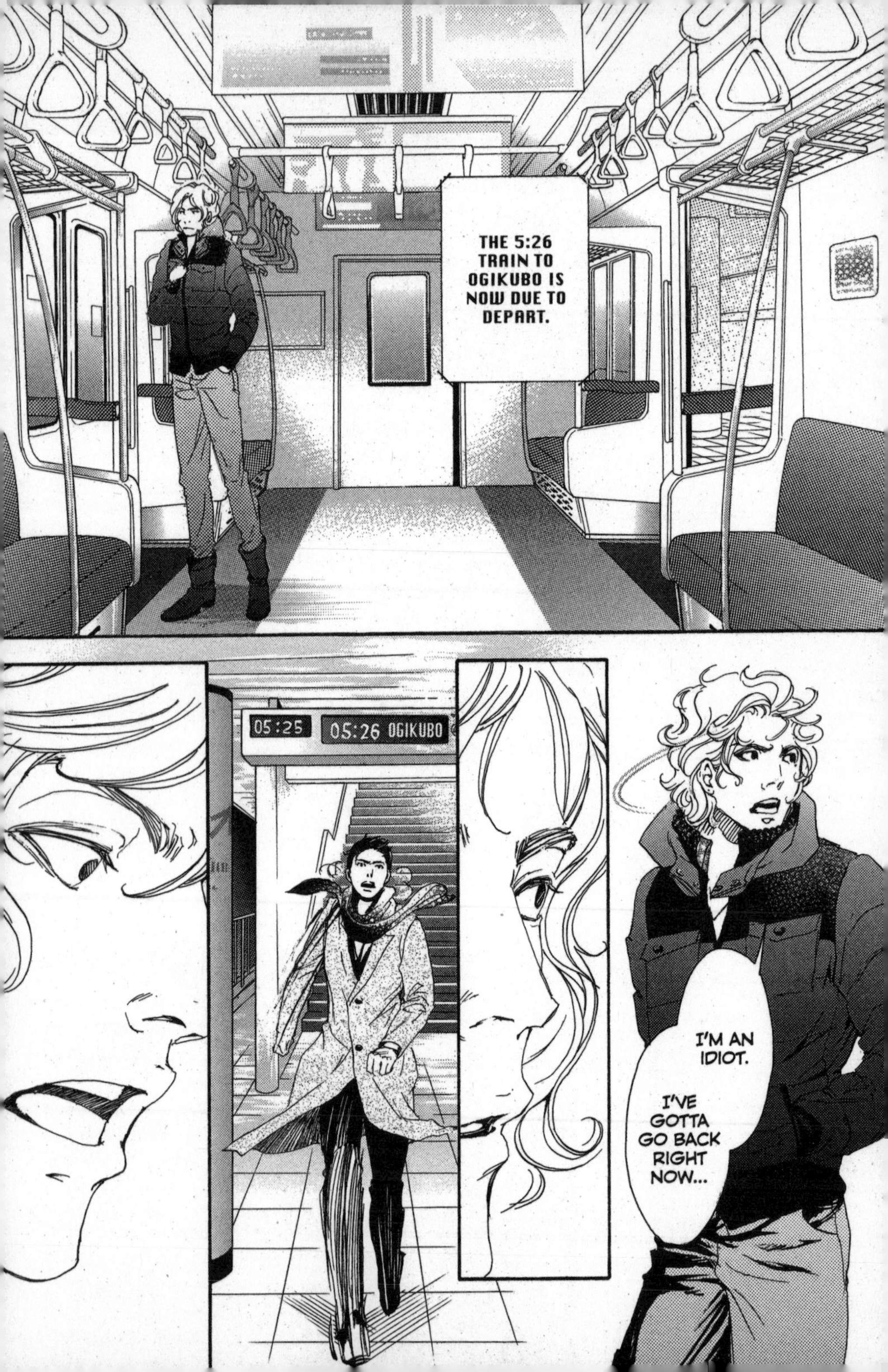
THE 5:26 TRAIN TO OGIKUBO IS NOW DUE TO DEPART.
I'M AN IDIOT.
I'VE GOTTA GO BACK RIGHT NOW...
05:25
05:26 OGIKUBO

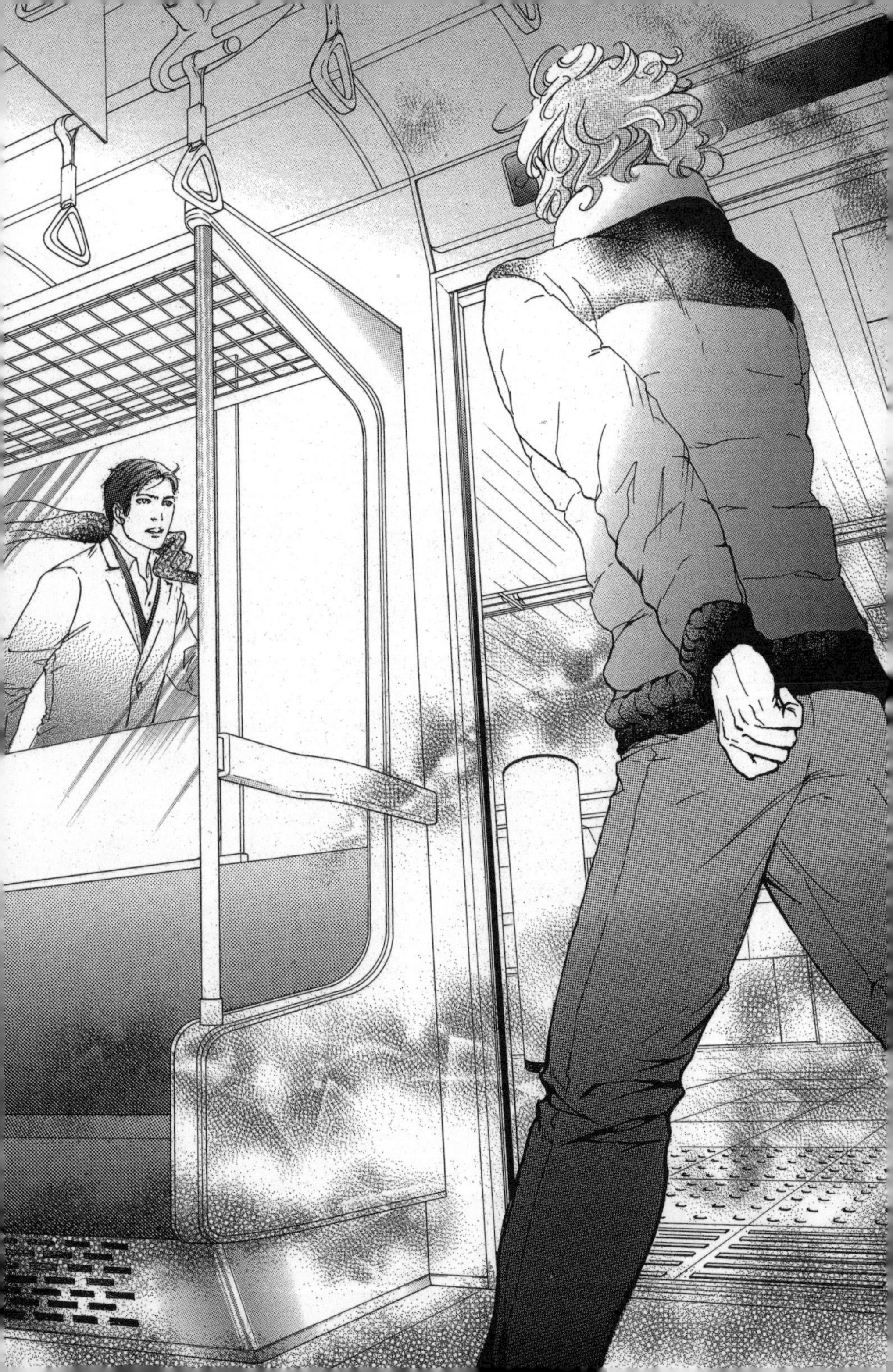

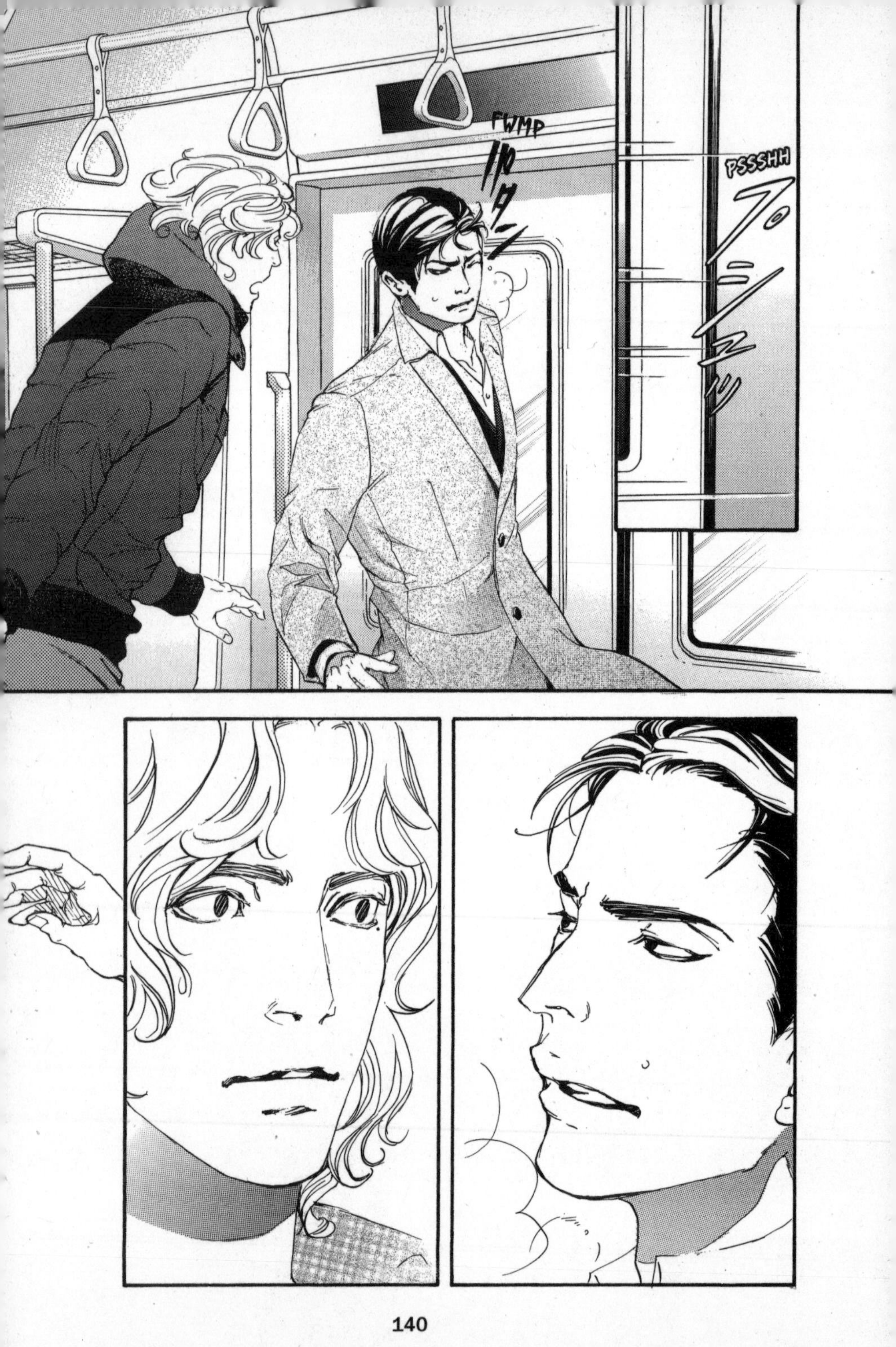
FWMP
PSSSHH

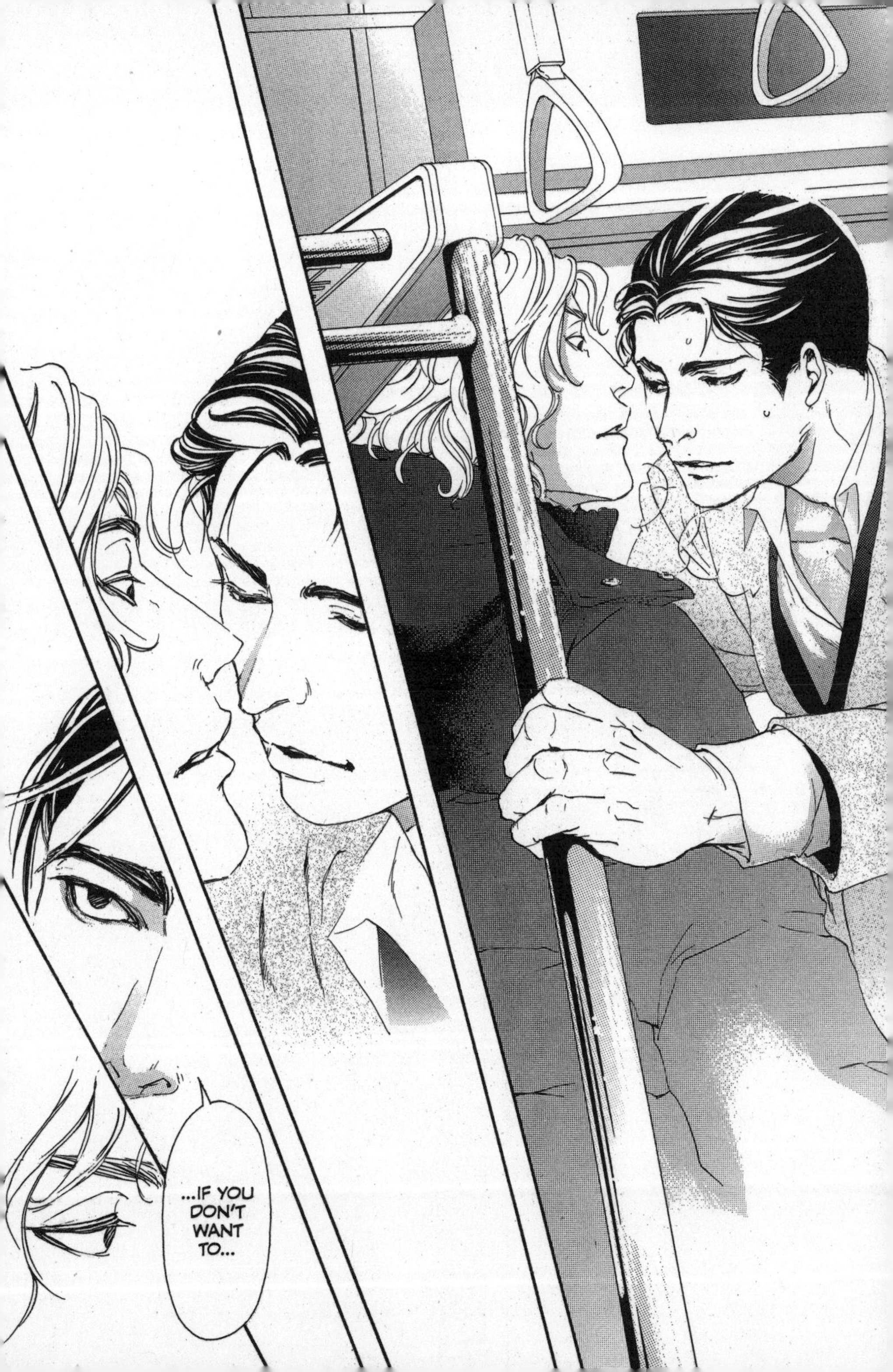
...IF YOU DON'T WANT TO...

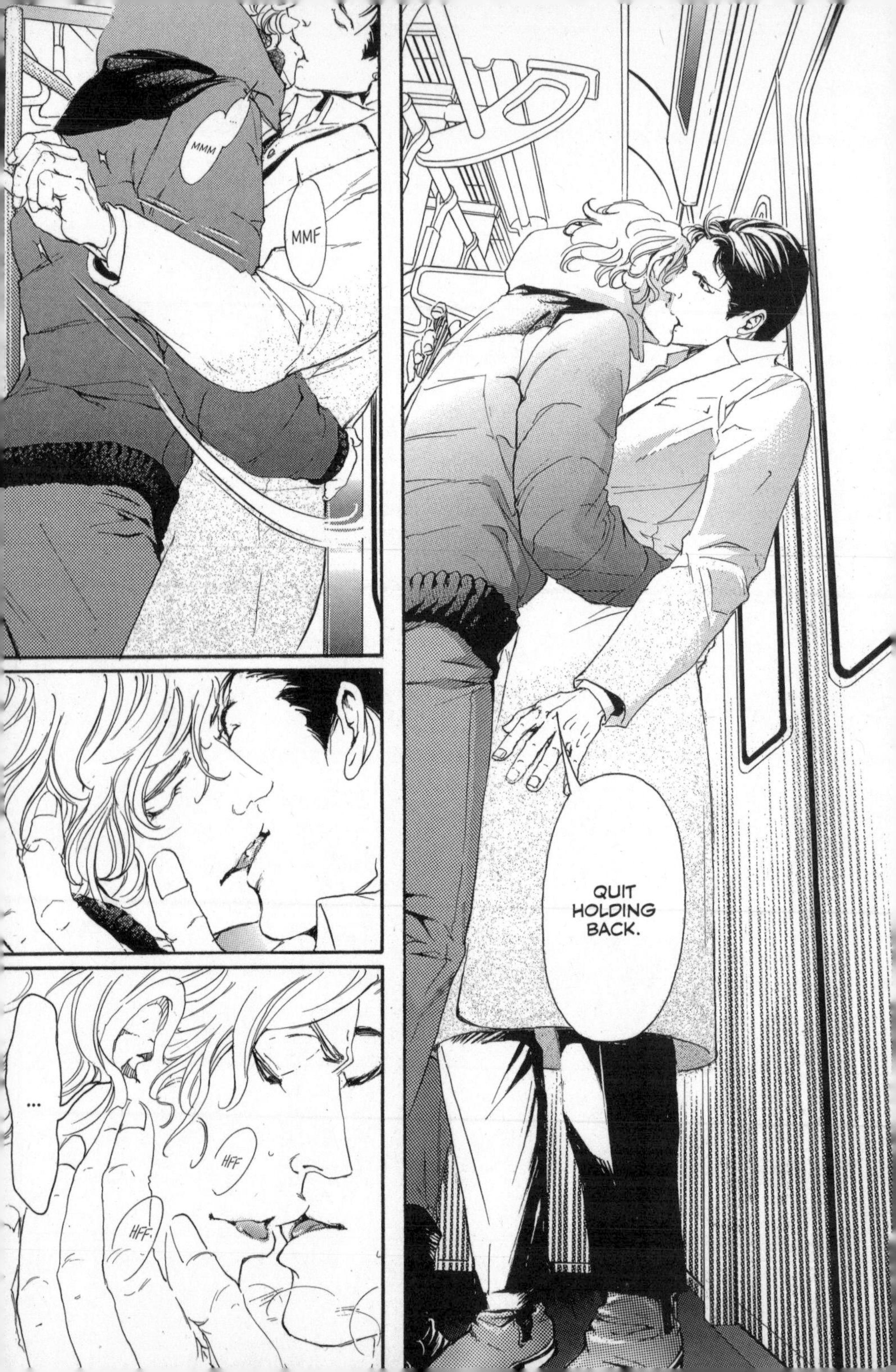
QUIT HOLDING BACK.
...
MMM
MMF
HFF
HFF
...

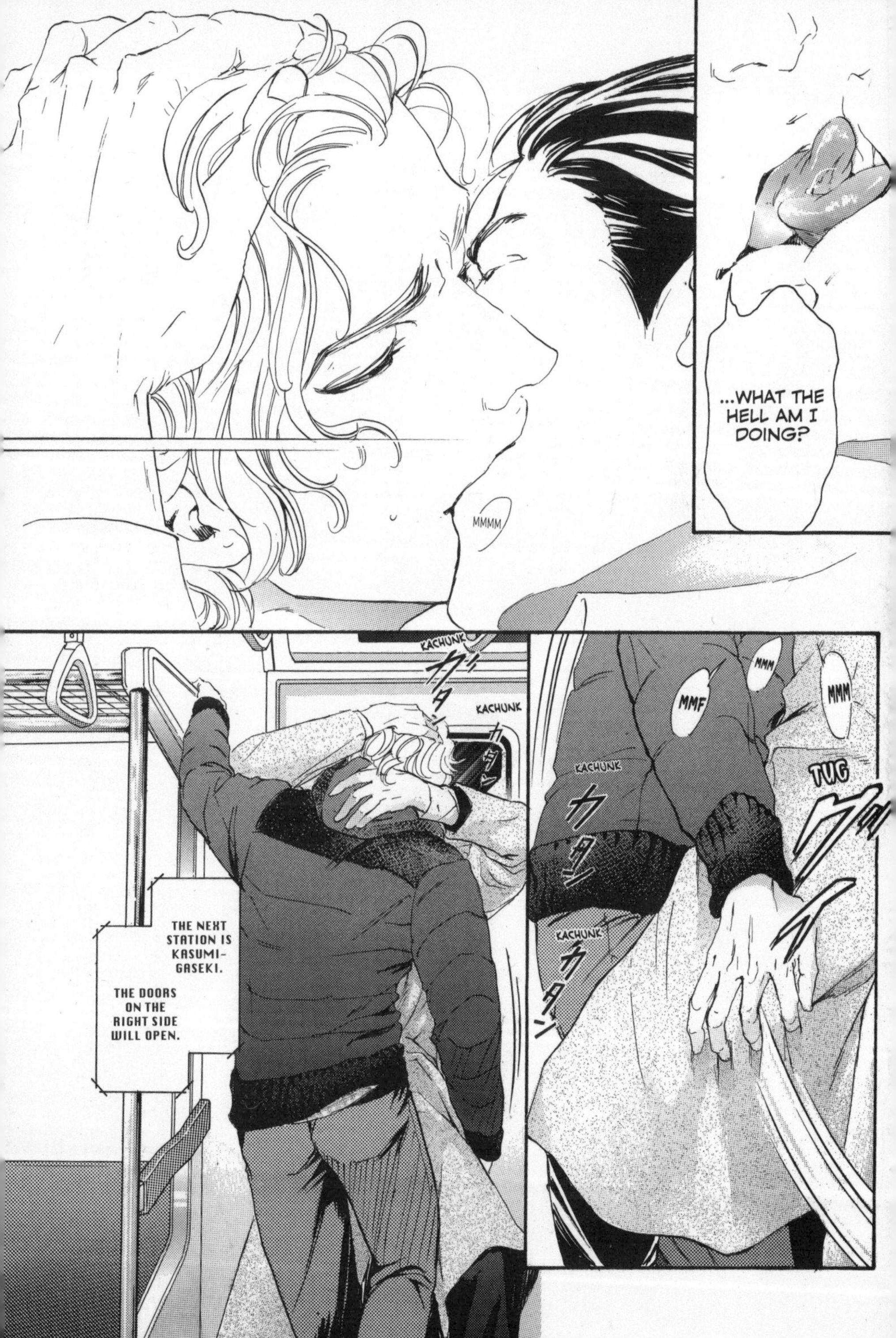

...WHAT THE HELL AM I DOING?
MMMM
MMM
MMM
MMF
TUG
KACHUNK
KACHUNK
KACHUNK
KACHUNK
THE NEXT STATION IS KASUMI-GASEKI.
THE DOORS ON THE RIGHT SIDE WILL OPEN.

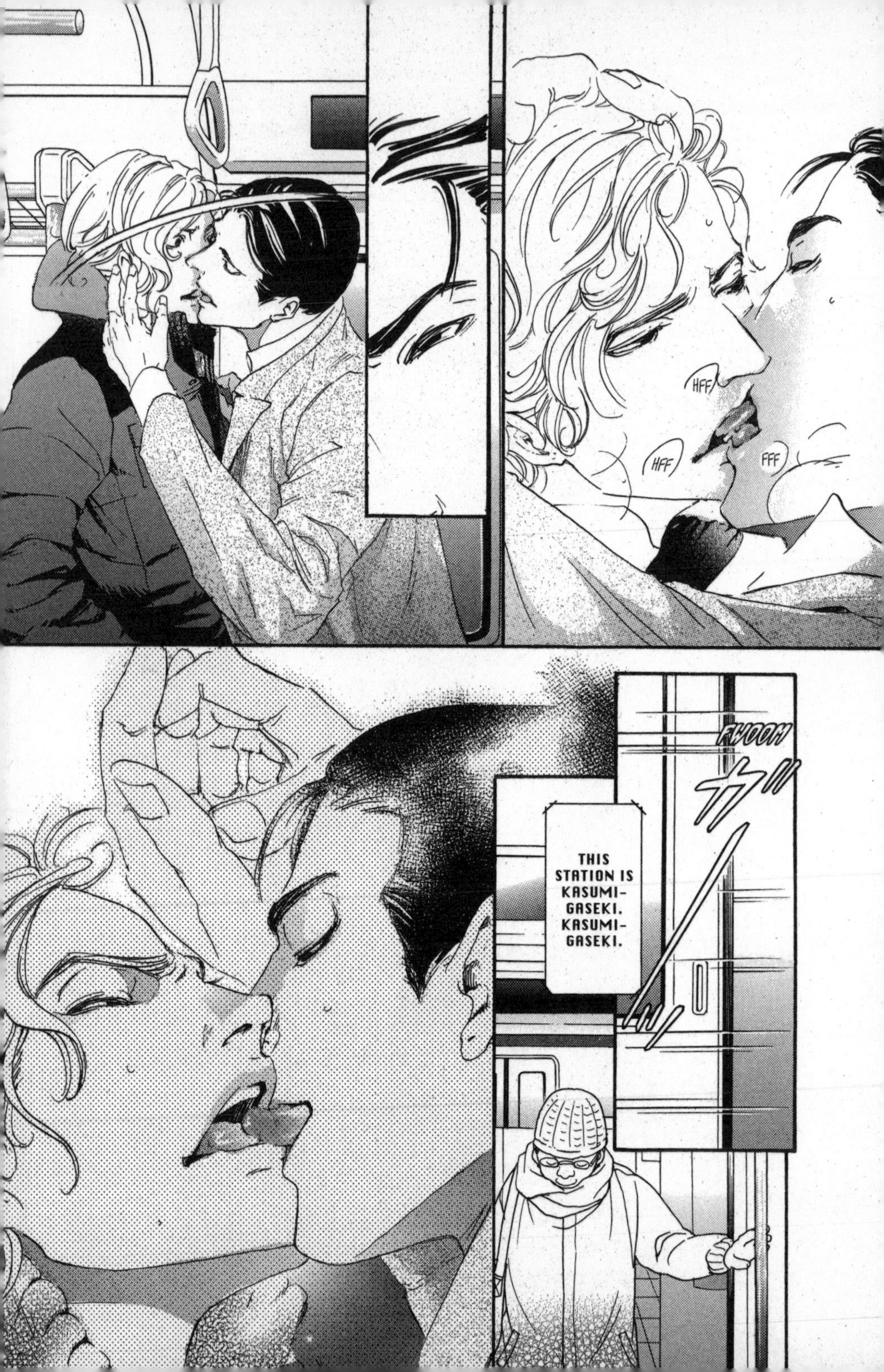
HFF
FFF
HFF
FWOOM
THIS STATION IS KASUMI-GASEKI. KASUMI-GASEKI.

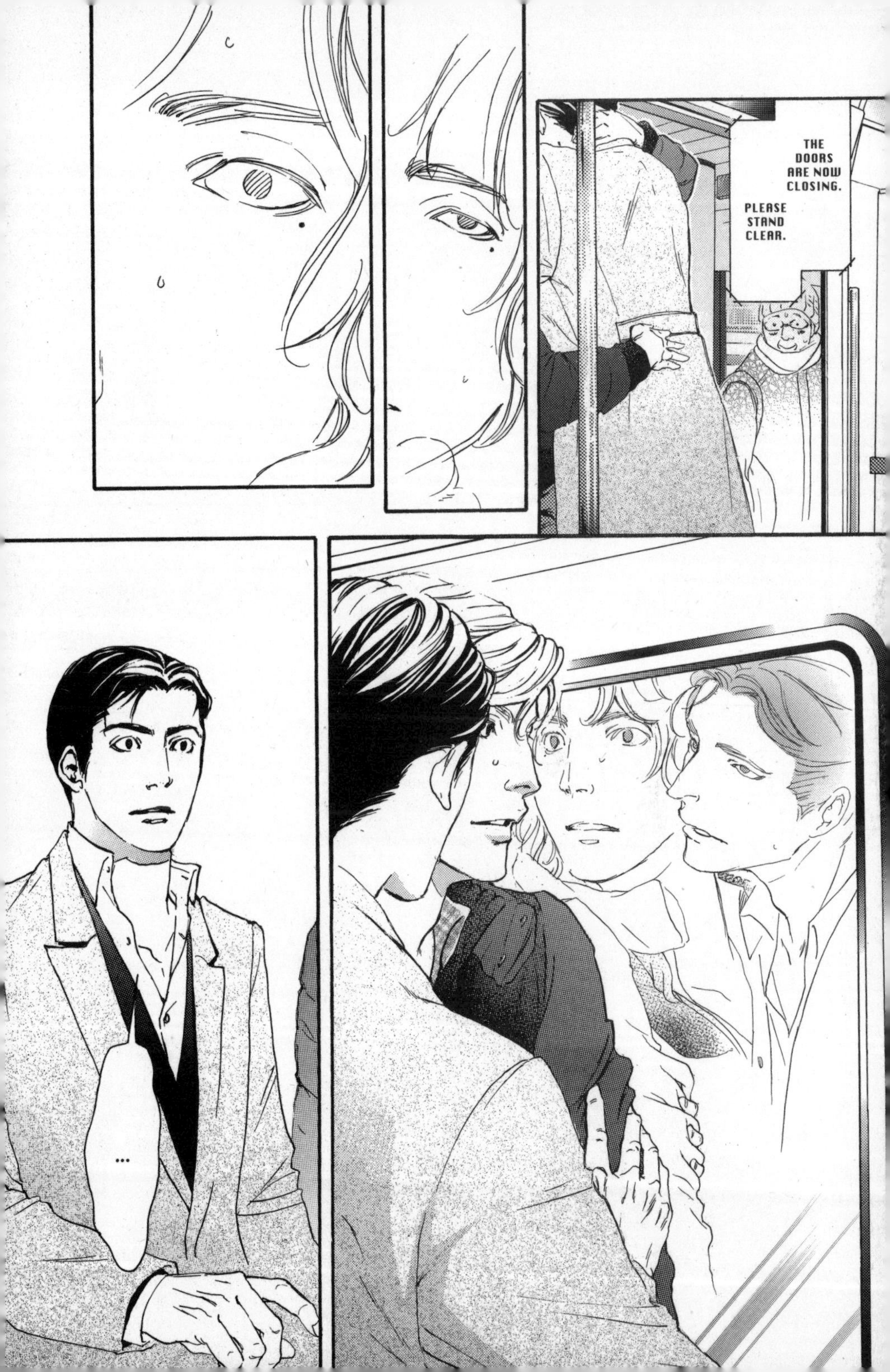
THE DOORS ARE NOW CLOSING.
PLEASE STAND CLEAR.
...

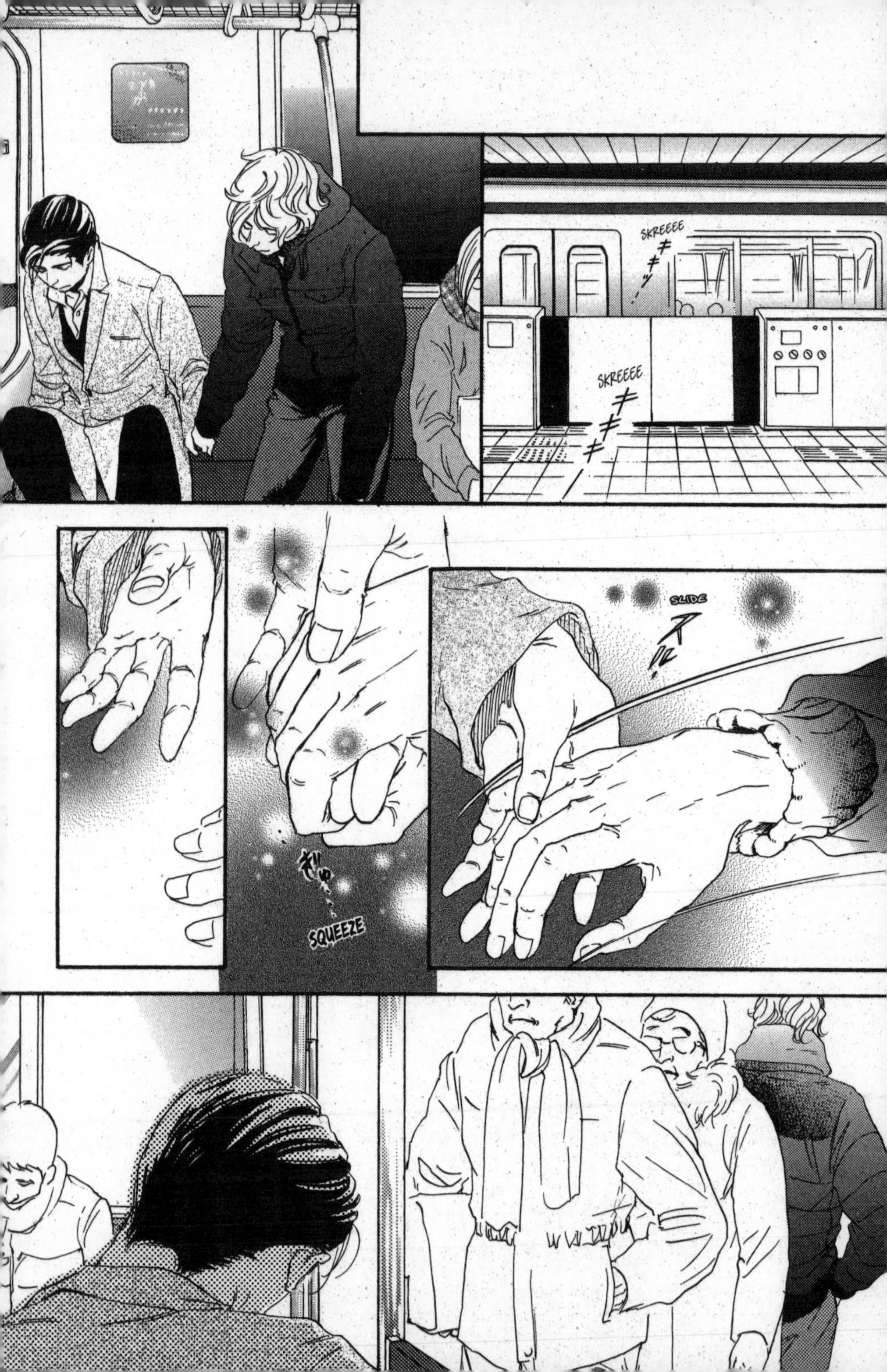
SKREEEE
SKREEEE
SLIDE
SQUEEZE

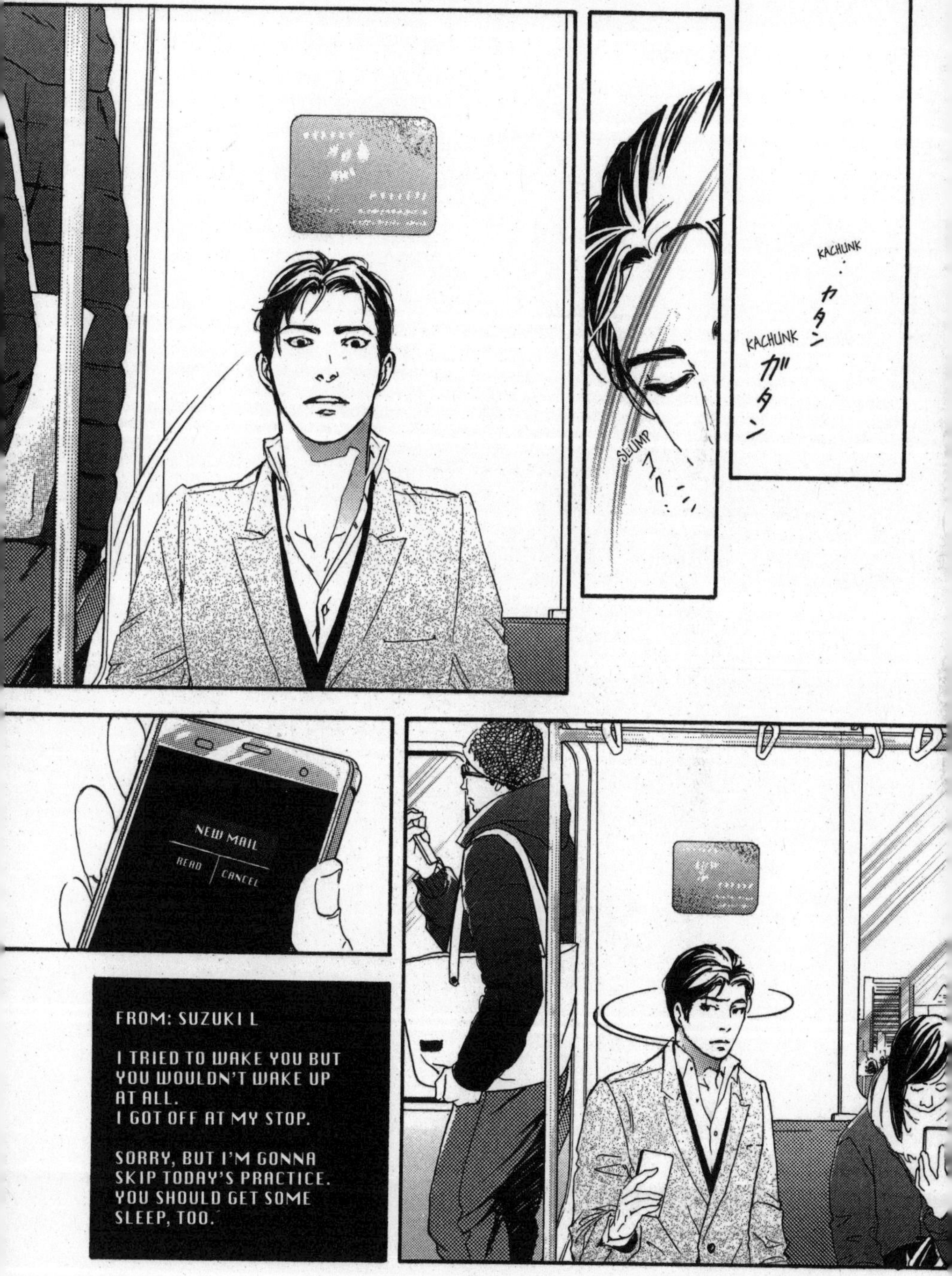
KACHUNK
カタン
KACHUNK
ガタン
SLUMP
NEW MAIL
READ
CANCEL
FROM: SUZUKI L
I TRIED TO WAKE YOU BUT YOU WOULDN'T WAKE UP AT ALL.
I GOT OFF AT MY STOP.
SORRY, BUT I'M GONNA SKIP TODAY'S PRACTICE. YOU SHOULD GET SOME SLEEP, TOO.

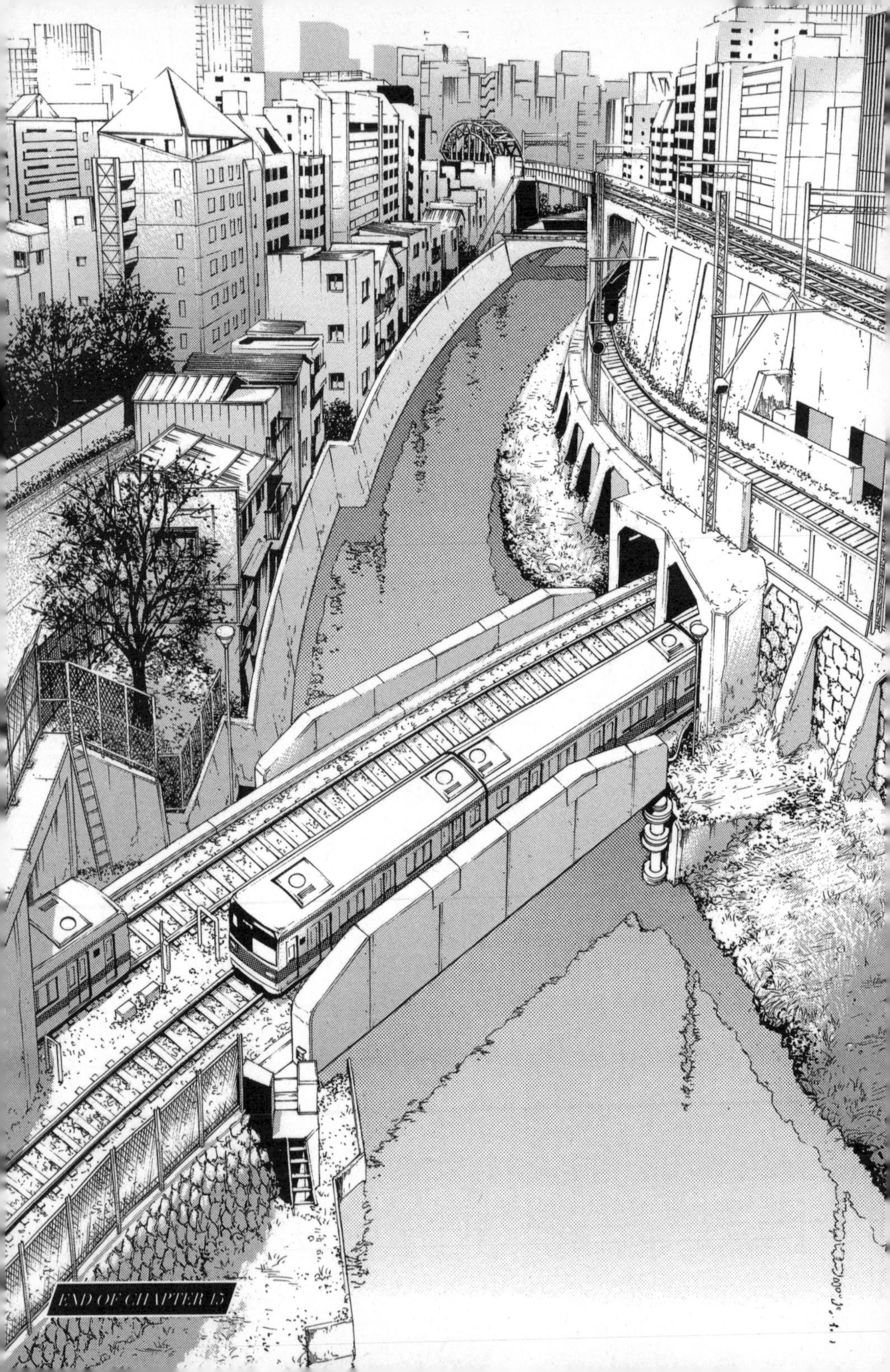
END OF CHAPTER 15

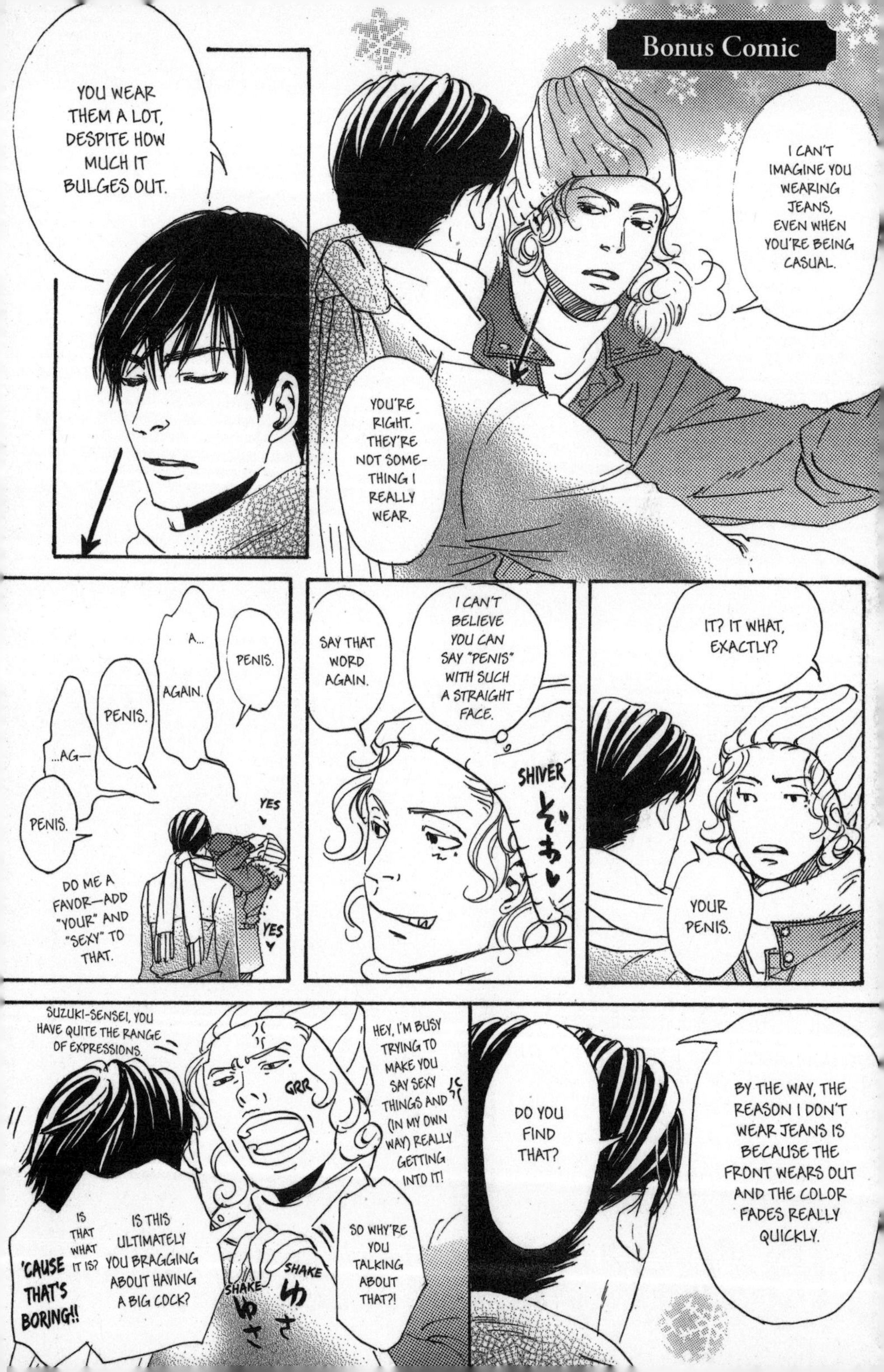
Bonus Comic
I CAN'T IMAGINE YOU WEARING JEANS, EVEN WHEN YOU'RE BEING CASUAL.
YOU'RE RIGHT. THEY'RE NOT SOME-THING I REALLY WEAR.
YOU WEAR THEM A LOT, DESPITE HOW MUCH IT BULGES OUT.
IT? IT WHAT, EXACTLY?
YOUR PENIS.
I CAN'T BELIEVE YOU CAN SAY "PENIS" WITH SUCH A STRAIGHT FACE.
SAY THAT WORD AGAIN.
SHIVER
PENIS.
A... AGAIN.
PENIS.
...AG—
PENIS.
YES
YES
DO ME A FAVOR—ADD "YOUR" AND "SEXY" TO THAT.
BY THE WAY, THE REASON I DON'T WEAR JEANS IS BECAUSE THE FRONT WEARS OUT AND THE COLOR FADES REALLY QUICKLY.
DO YOU FIND THAT?
HEY, I'M BUSY TRYING TO MAKE YOU SAY SEXY THINGS AND (IN MY OWN WAY) REALLY GETTING INTO IT!
SUZUKI-SENSEI, YOU HAVE QUITE THE RANGE OF EXPRESSIONS.
GRR
SO WHY'RE YOU TALKING ABOUT THAT?!
SHAKE
SHAKE
IS THIS ULTIMATELY YOU BRAGGING ABOUT HAVING A BIG COCK?
IS THAT WHAT IT IS?
'CAUSE THAT'S BORING!!

10 DANCE

SPECIAL CHAPTER

TANGO NOTTURNO

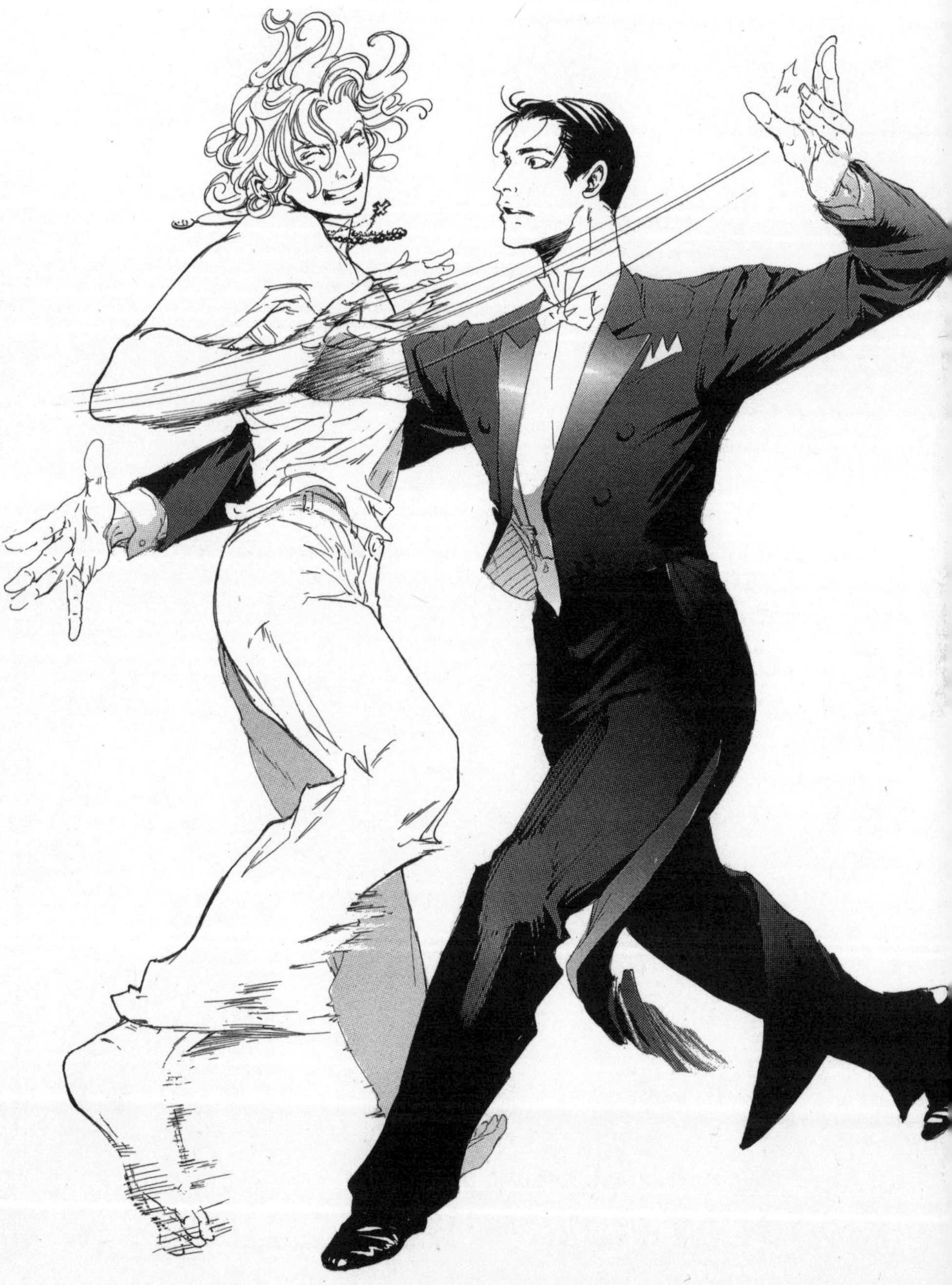

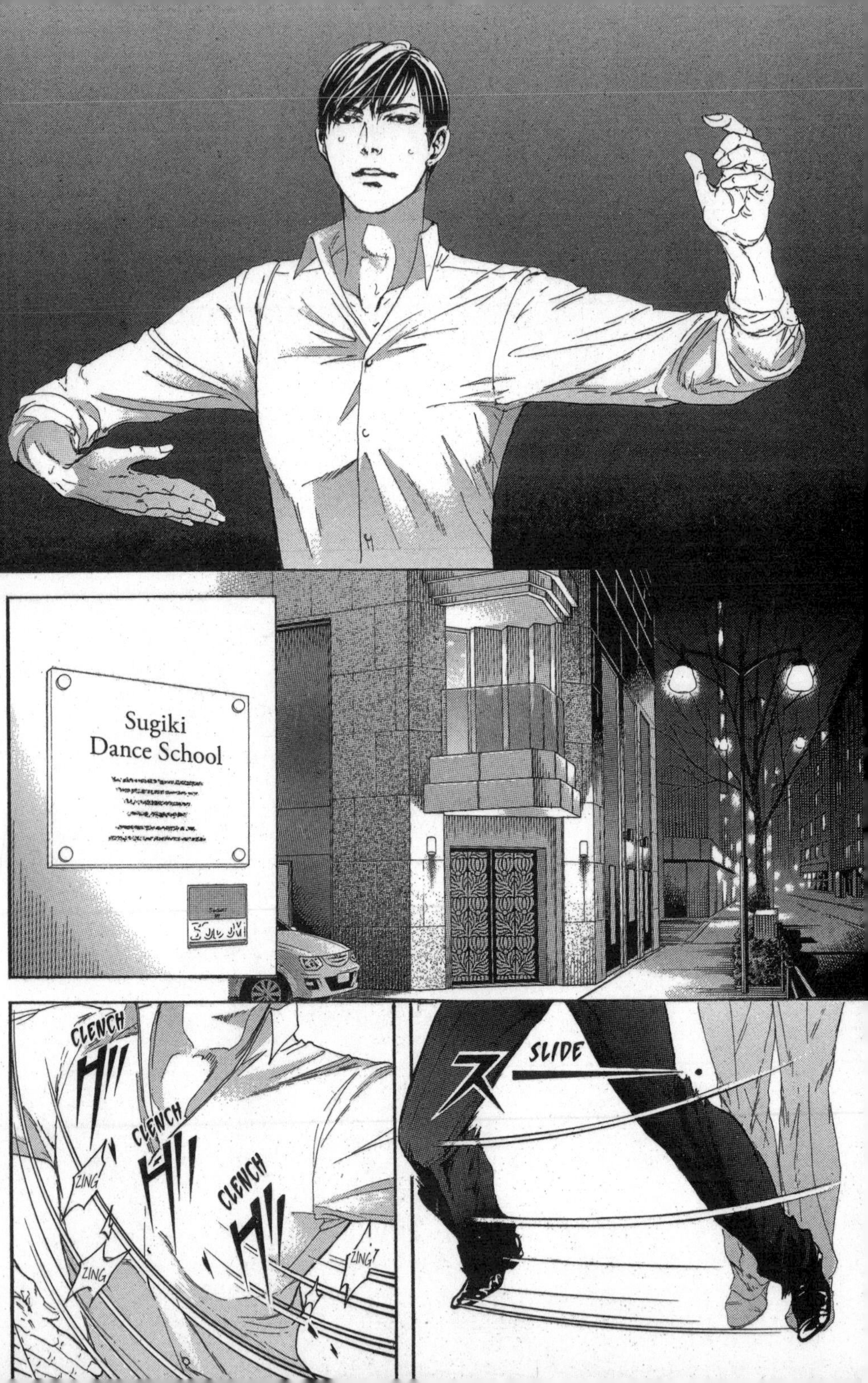
Sugiki
Dance School
ス
SLIDE
CLENCH
CLENCH
CLENCH
ZING
ZING
ZING

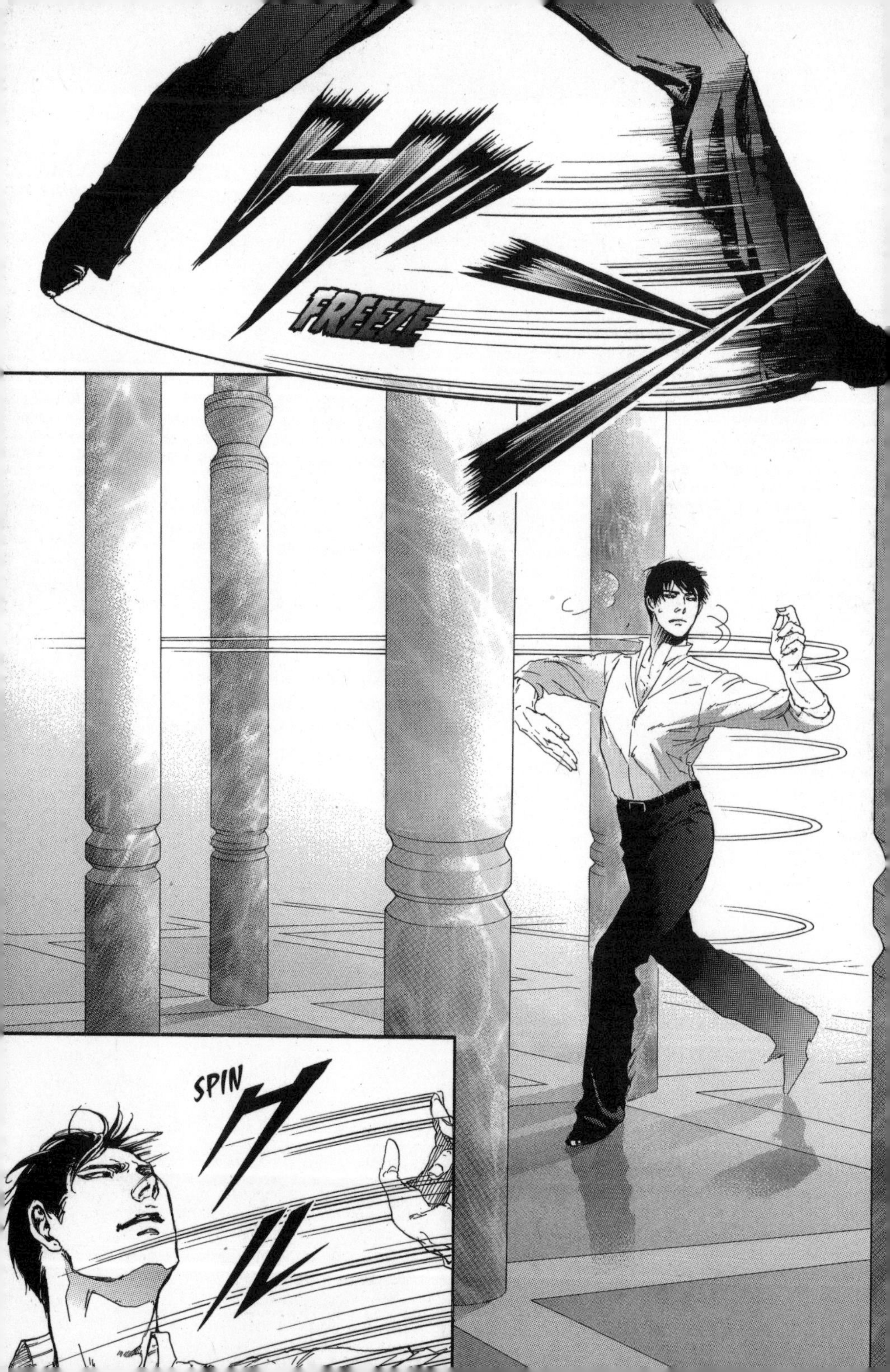
FREEZE
SPIN

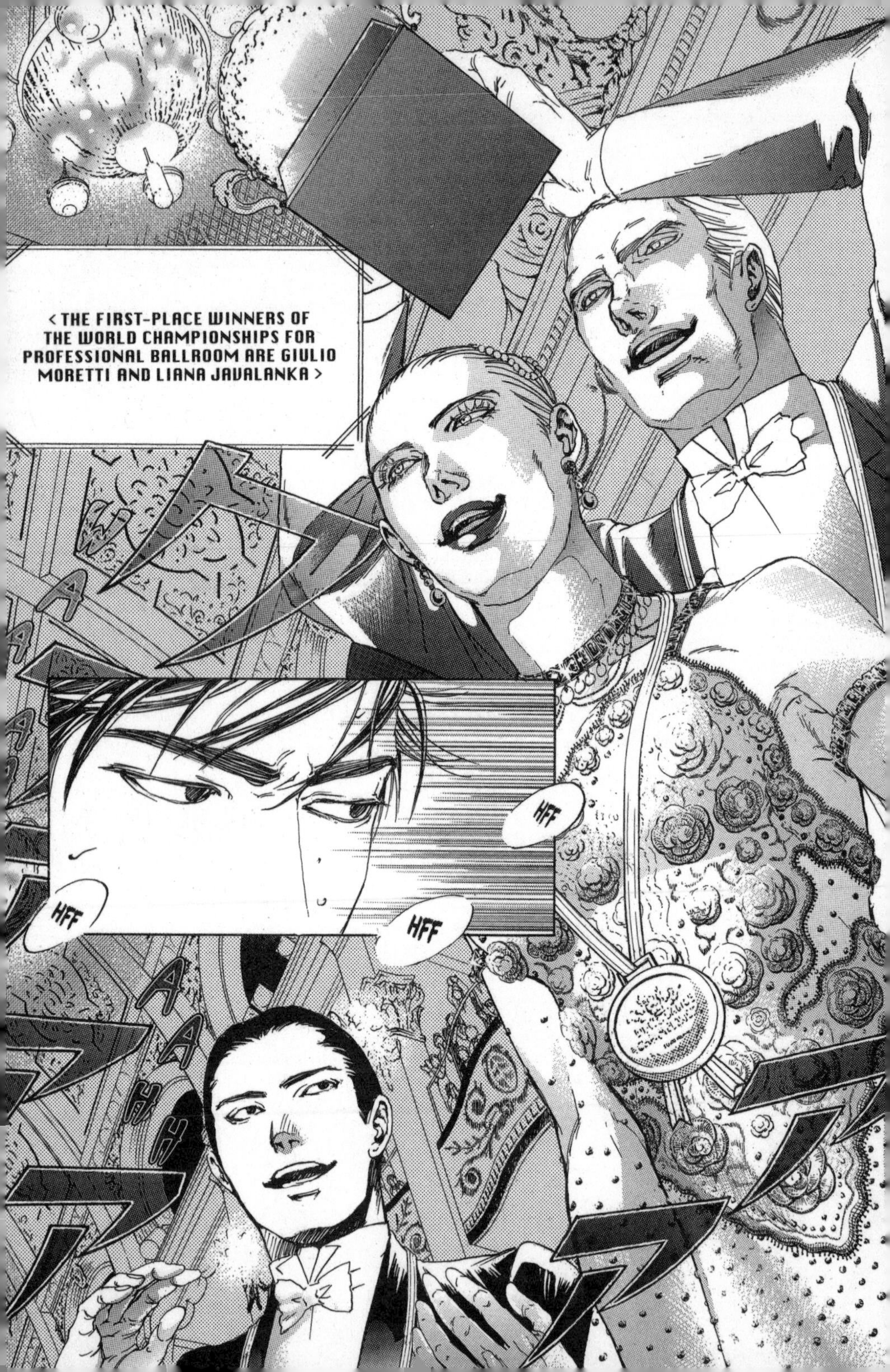
< THE FIRST-PLACE WINNERS OF THE WORLD CHAMPIONSHIPS FOR PROFESSIONAL BALLROOM ARE GIULIO MORETTI AND LIANA JAVALANKA >
HFF
HFF
HFF

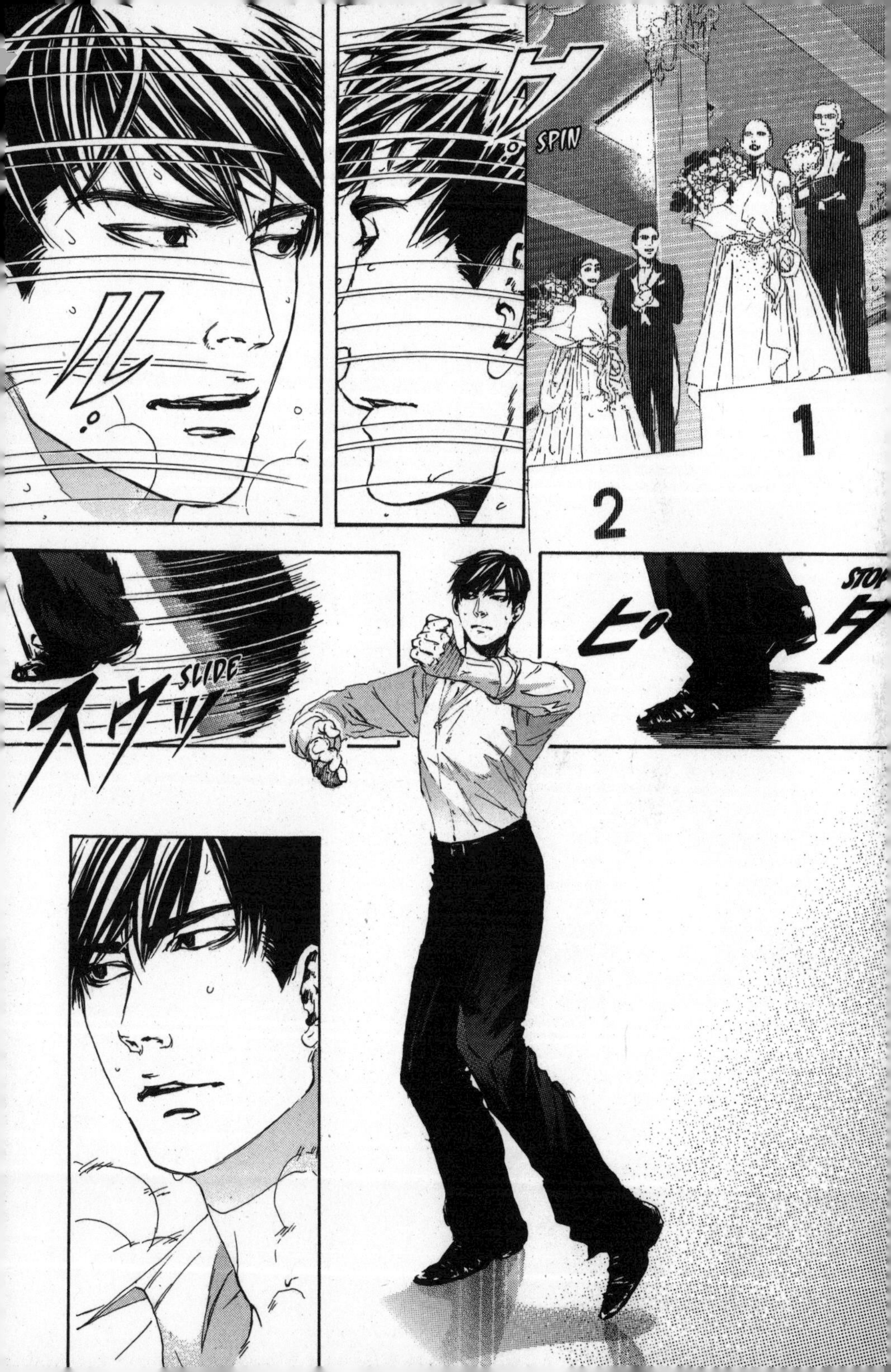

1
2
SPIN
STOP
SLIDE

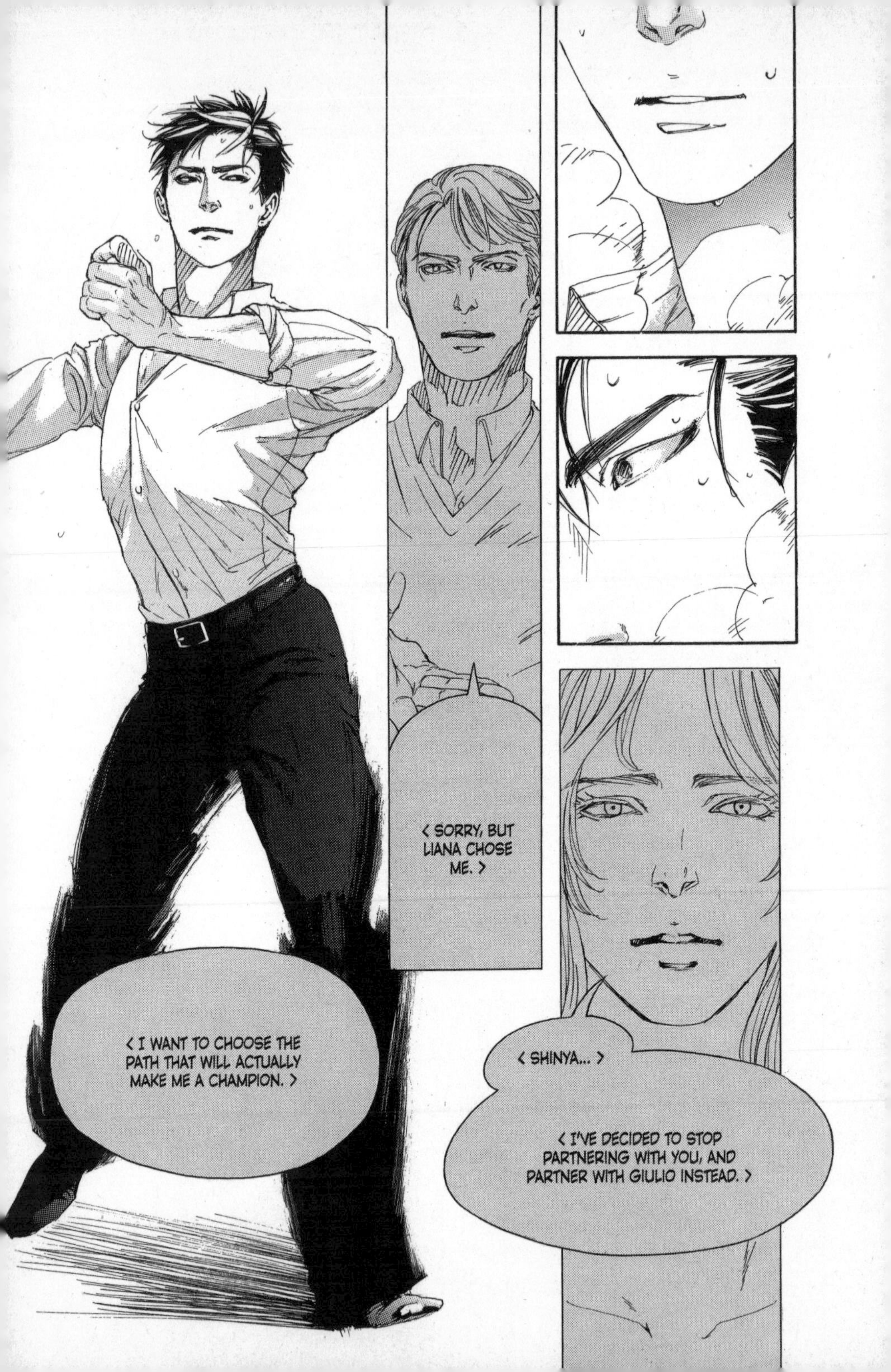
< SHINYA... >
< I'VE DECIDED TO STOP PARTNERING WITH YOU, AND PARTNER WITH GIULIO INSTEAD. >
< SORRY, BUT LIANA CHOSE ME. >
< I WANT TO CHOOSE THE PATH THAT WILL ACTUALLY MAKE ME A CHAMPION. >

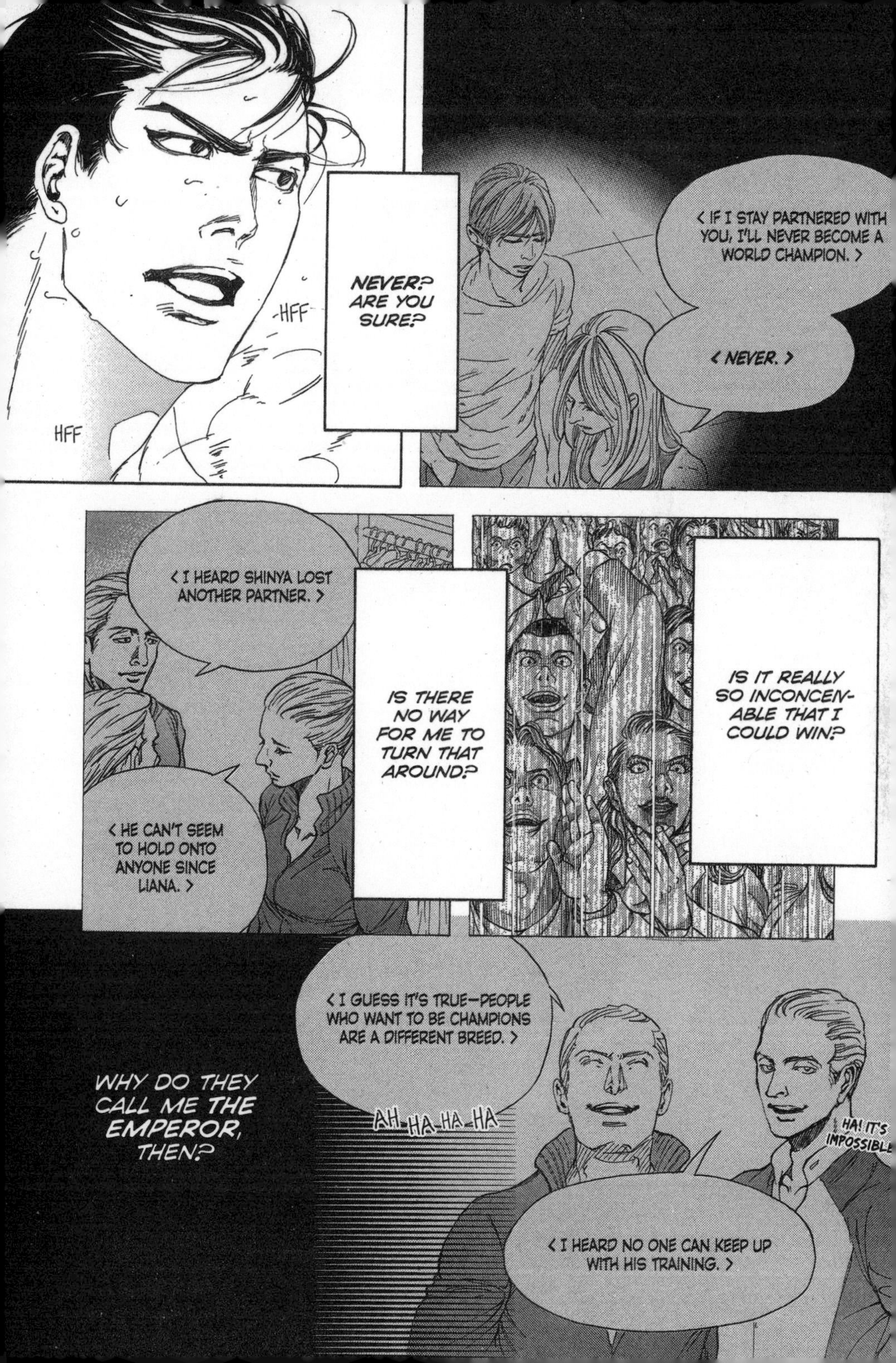
< IF I STAY PARTNERED WITH YOU, I'LL NEVER BECOME A WORLD CHAMPION. >
< NEVER. >
NEVER? ARE YOU SURE?
HFF
HFF
IS IT REALLY SO INCONCEIVABLE THAT I COULD WIN?
IS THERE NO WAY FOR ME TO TURN THAT AROUND?
< I HEARD SHINYA LOST ANOTHER PARTNER. >
< HE CAN'T SEEM TO HOLD ONTO ANYONE SINCE LIANA. >
HA! IT'S IMPOSSIBLE
< I GUESS IT'S TRUE—PEOPLE WHO WANT TO BE CHAMPIONS ARE A DIFFERENT BREED. >
AH HA HA HA
< I HEARD NO ONE CAN KEEP UP WITH HIS TRAINING. >
WHY DO THEY CALL ME THE EMPEROR, THEN?

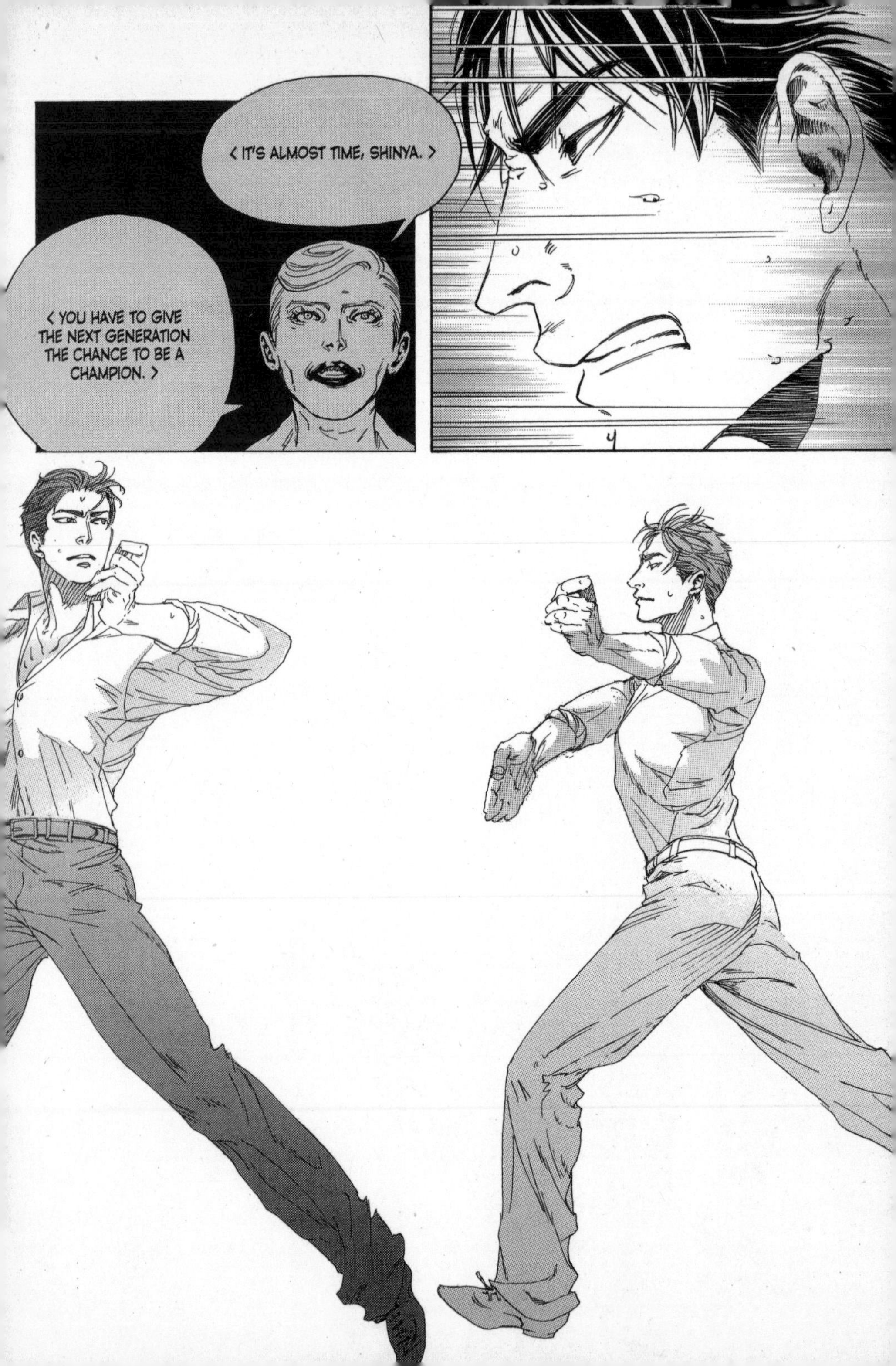
< IT'S ALMOST TIME, SHINYA. >
< YOU HAVE TO GIVE THE NEXT GENERATION THE CHANCE TO BE A CHAMPION. >

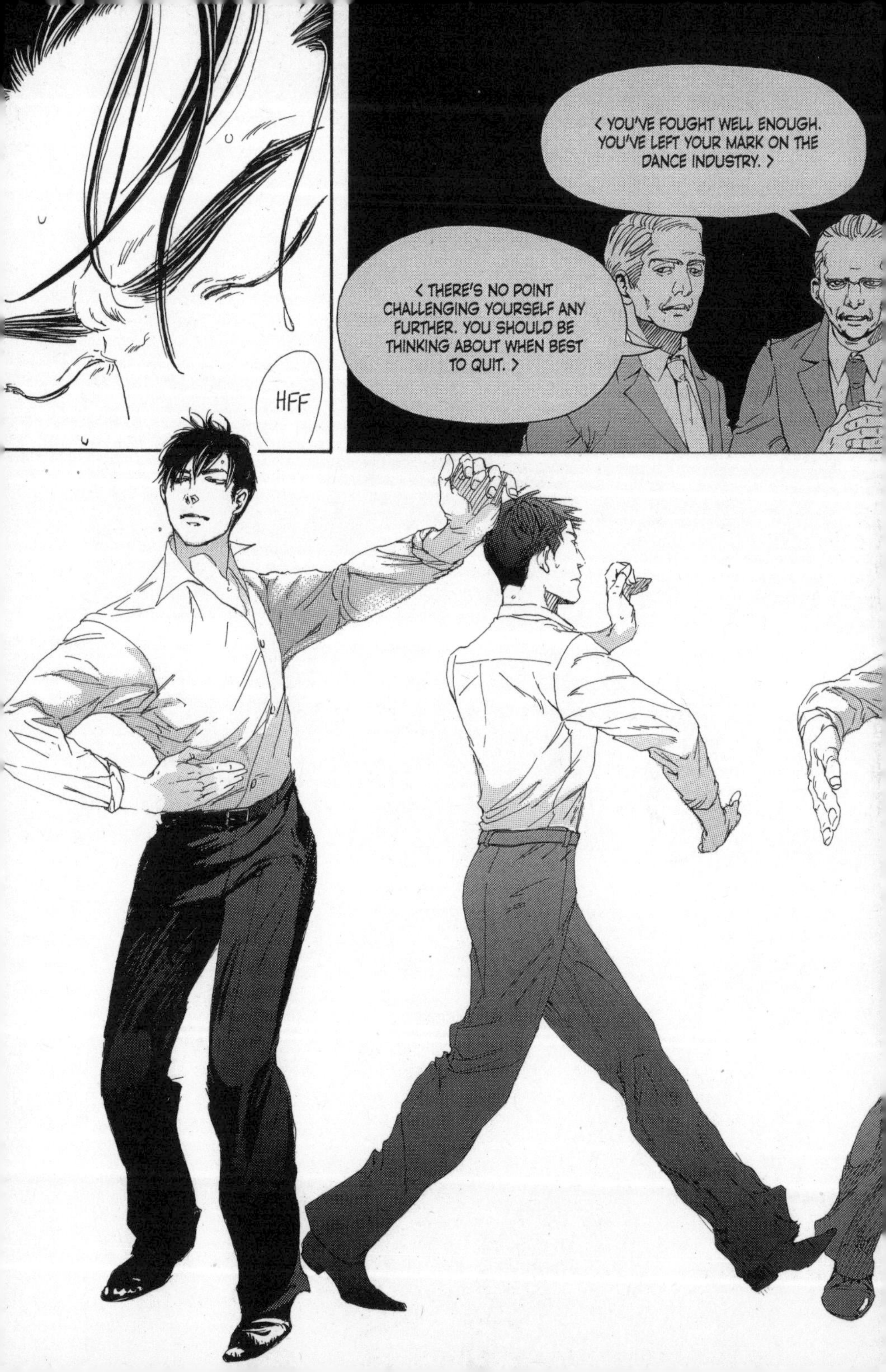
< YOU'VE FOUGHT WELL ENOUGH. YOU'VE LEFT YOUR MARK ON THE DANCE INDUSTRY. >
< THERE'S NO POINT CHALLENGING YOURSELF ANY FURTHER. YOU SHOULD BE THINKING ABOUT WHEN BEST TO QUIT. >
HFF

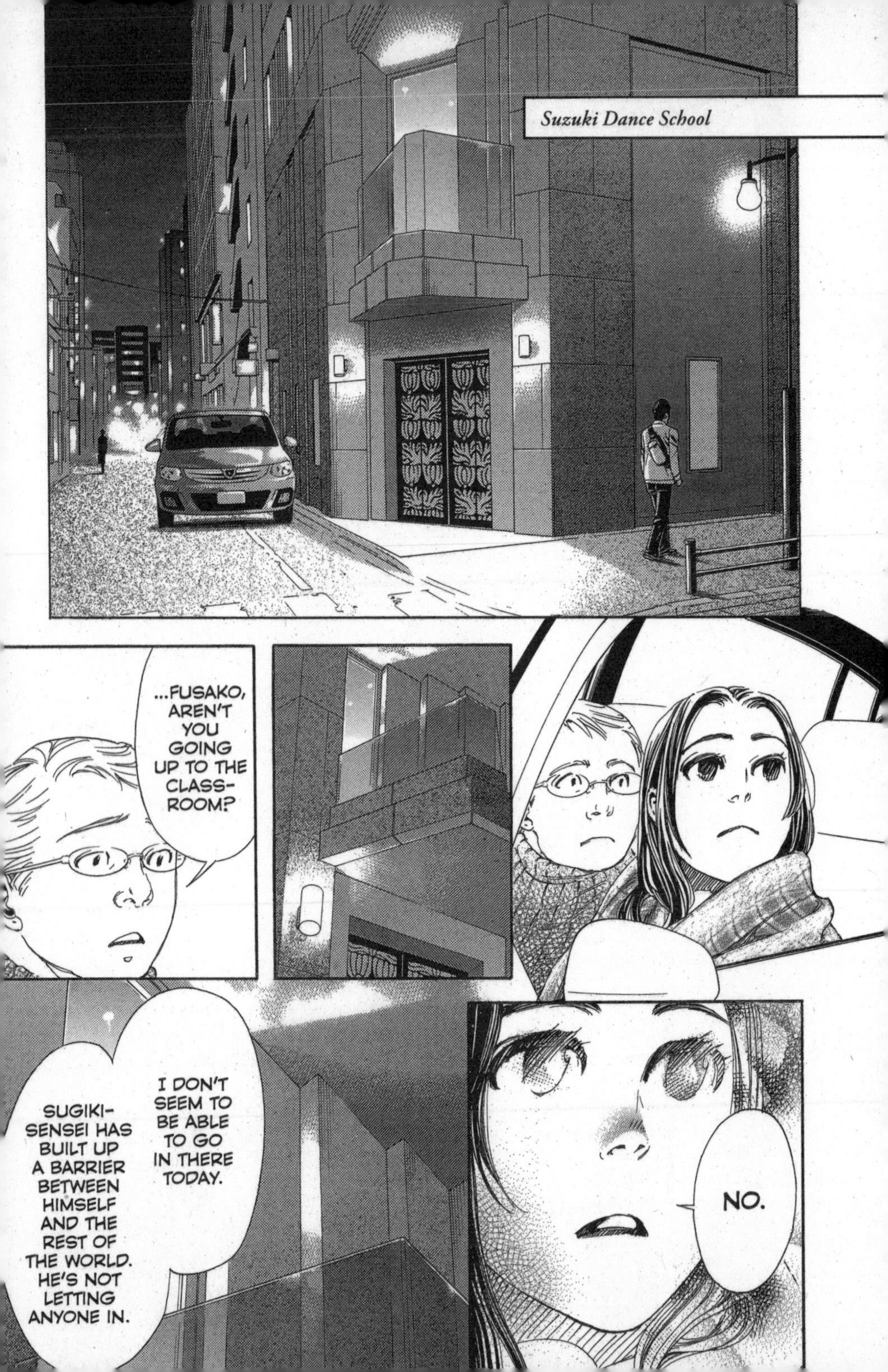
Suzuki Dance School
...FUSAKO, AREN'T YOU GOING UP TO THE CLASS-ROOM?
NO.
I DON'T SEEM TO BE ABLE TO GO IN THERE TODAY.
SUGIKI-SENSEI HAS BUILT UP A BARRIER BETWEEN HIMSELF AND THE REST OF THE WORLD. HE'S NOT LETTING ANYONE IN.

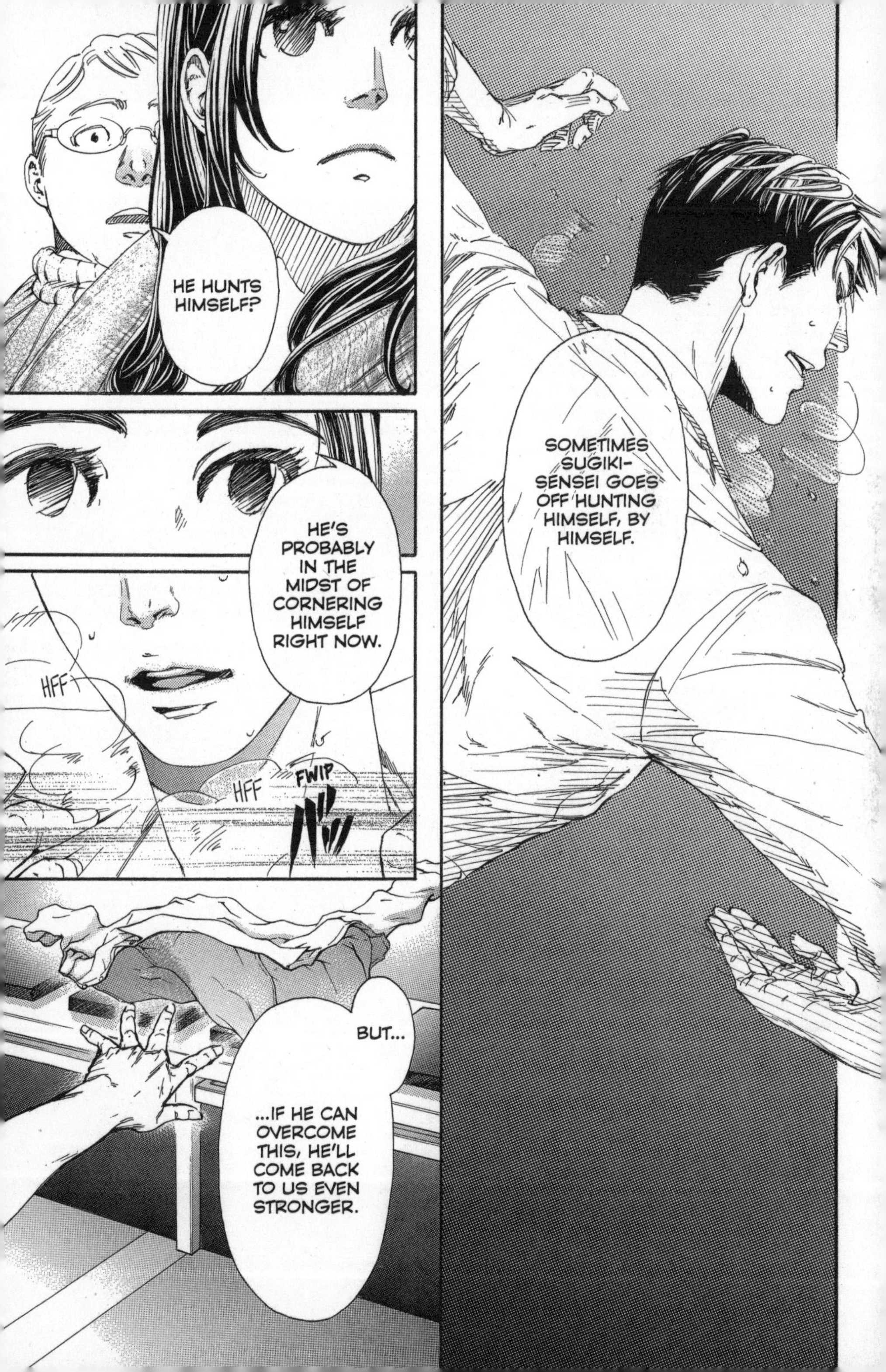
SOMETIMES SUGIKI-SENSEI GOES OFF HUNTING HIMSELF, BY HIMSELF.
HE HUNTS HIMSELF?
HE'S PROBABLY IN THE MIDST OF CORNERING HIMSELF RIGHT NOW.
HFF
HFF
FWIP
バッ
BUT...
...IF HE CAN OVERCOME THIS, HE'LL COME BACK TO US EVEN STRONGER.

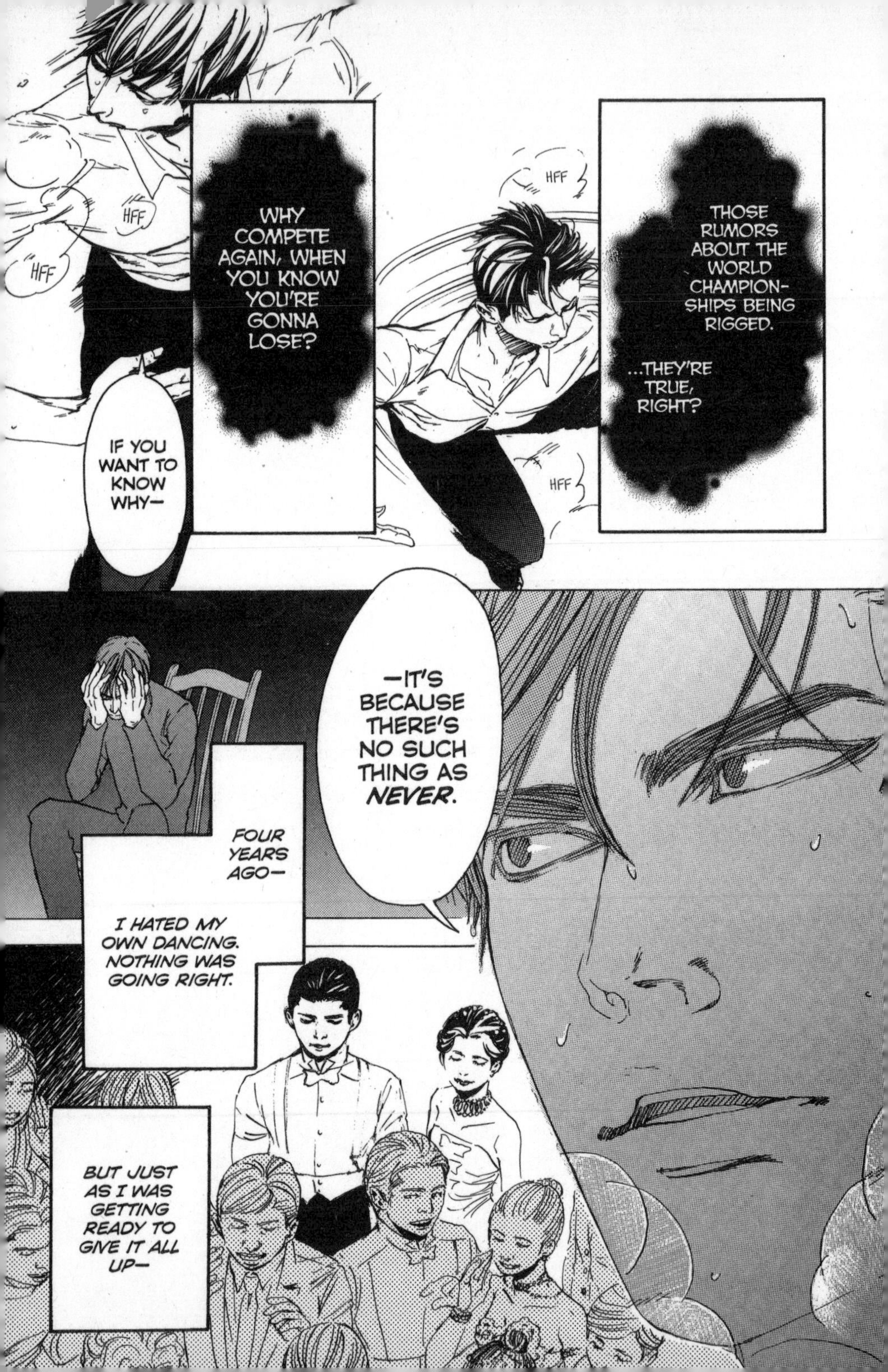
HFF
THOSE RUMORS ABOUT THE WORLD CHAMPION-SHIPS BEING RIGGED.
...THEY'RE TRUE, RIGHT?
HFF
WHY COMPETE AGAIN, WHEN YOU KNOW YOU'RE GONNA LOSE?
HFF
HFF
IF YOU WANT TO KNOW WHY—
—IT'S BECAUSE THERE'S NO SUCH THING AS *NEVER*.
FOUR YEARS AGO—
I HATED MY OWN DANCING. NOTHING WAS GOING RIGHT.
BUT JUST AS I WAS GETTING READY TO GIVE IT ALL UP—

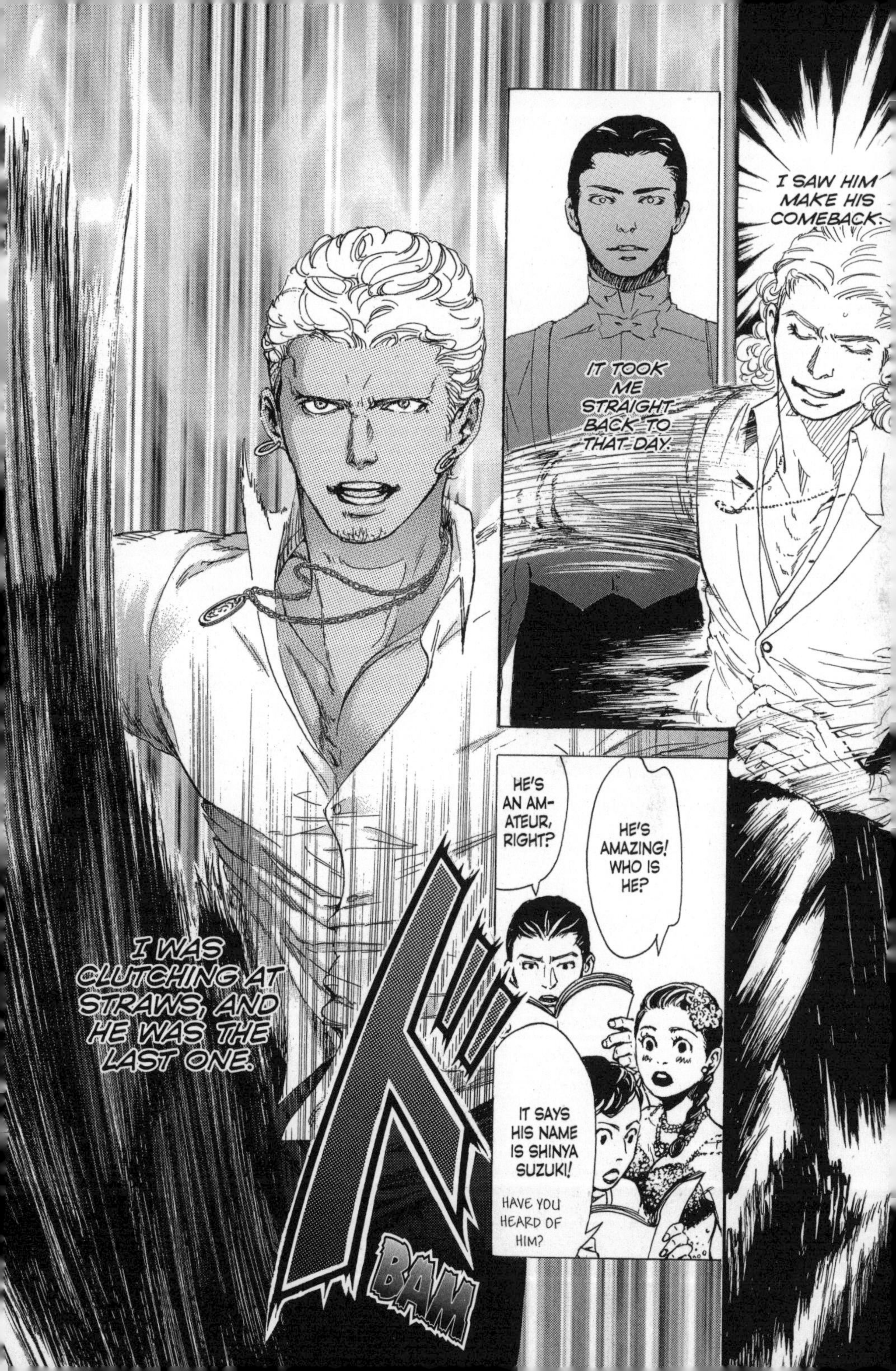
I SAW HIM MAKE HIS COMEBACK.
IT TOOK ME STRAIGHT BACK TO THAT DAY.
HE'S AMAZING! WHO IS HE?
HE'S AN AMATEUR, RIGHT?
IT SAYS HIS NAME IS SHINYA SUZUKI!
HAVE YOU HEARD OF HIM?
I WAS CLUTCHING AT STRAWS, AND HE WAS THE LAST ONE.
BAM

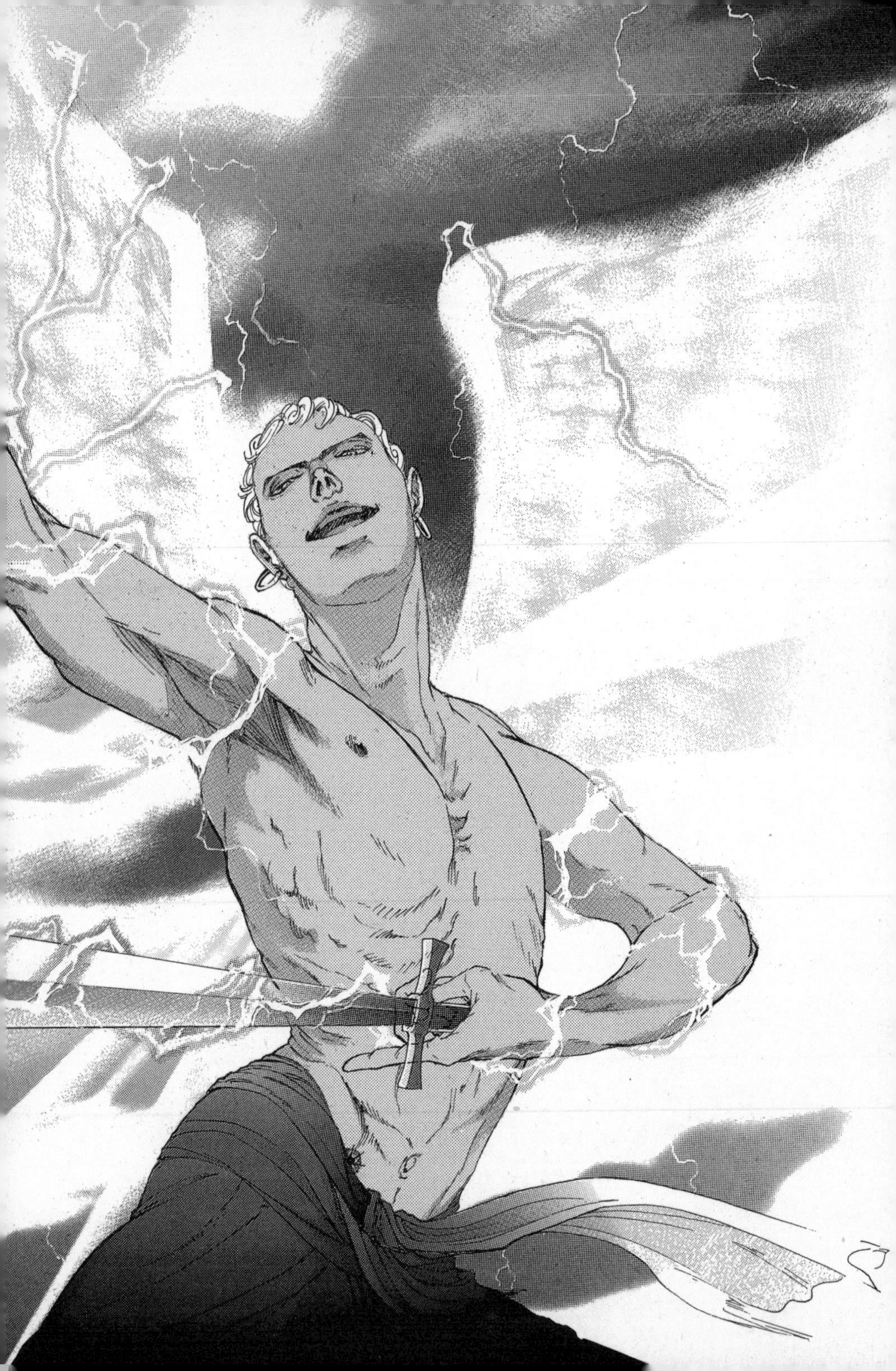

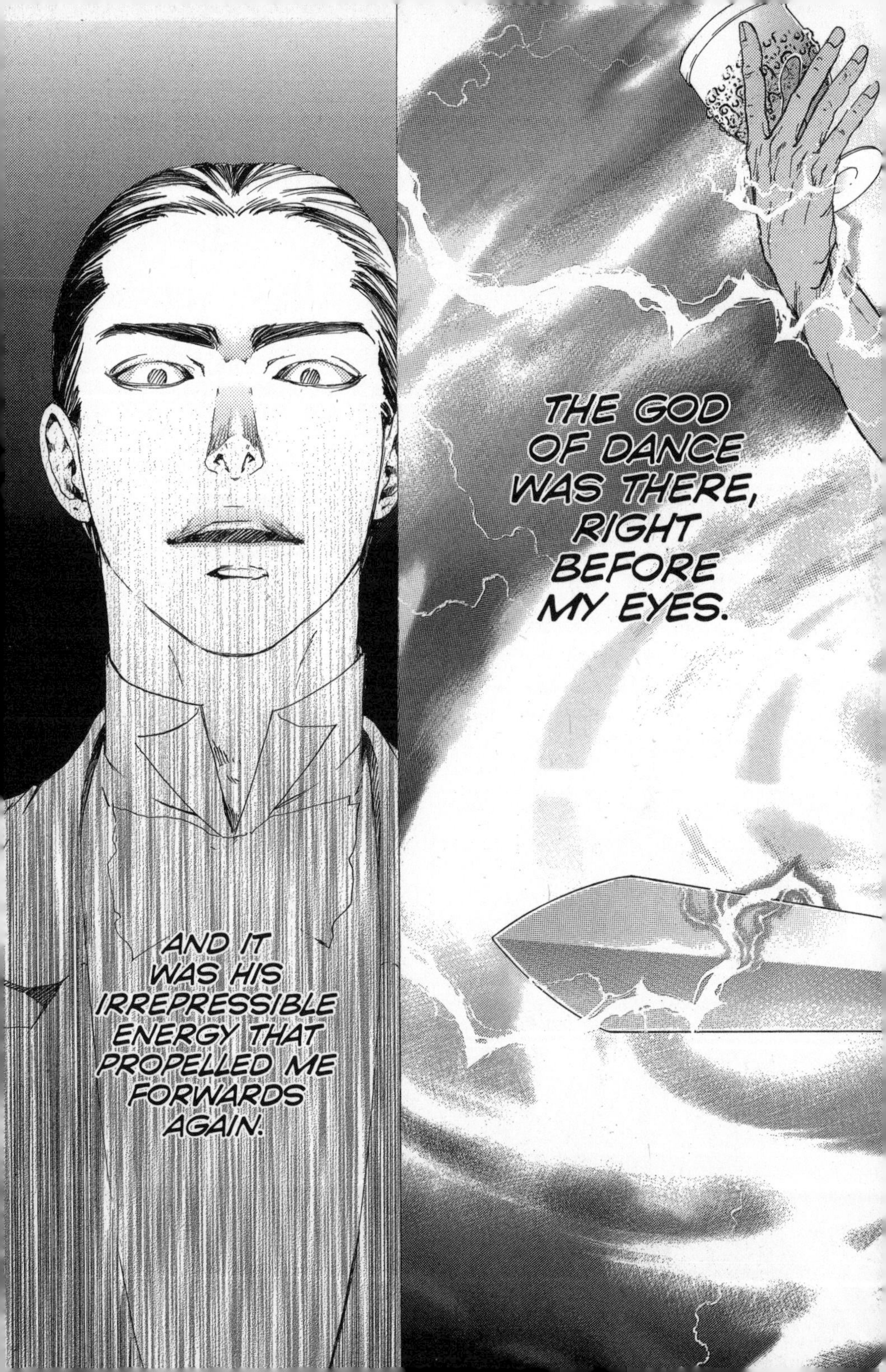
THE GOD OF DANCE WAS THERE, RIGHT BEFORE MY EYES.
AND IT WAS HIS IRREPRESSIBLE ENERGY THAT PROPELLED ME FORWARDS AGAIN.

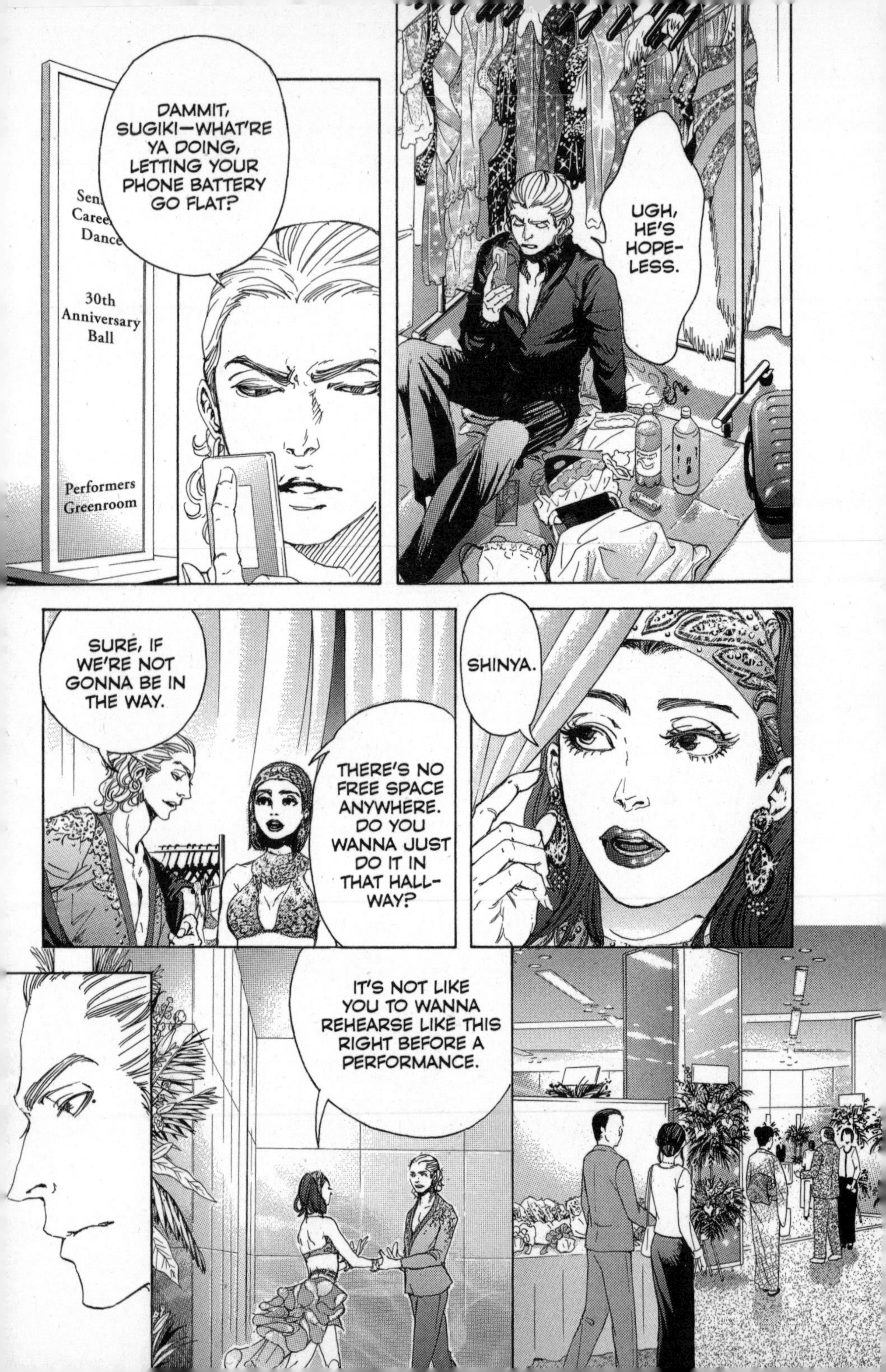
UGH, HE'S HOPE-LESS.
DAMMIT, SUGIKI—WHAT'RE YA DOING, LETTING YOUR PHONE BATTERY GO FLAT?
30th Anniversary Ball
Performers Greenroom
SHINYA.
THERE'S NO FREE SPACE ANYWHERE. DO YOU WANNA JUST DO IT IN THAT HALL-WAY?
SURE, IF WE'RE NOT GONNA BE IN THE WAY.
IT'S NOT LIKE YOU TO WANNA REHEARSE LIKE THIS RIGHT BEFORE A PERFORMANCE.

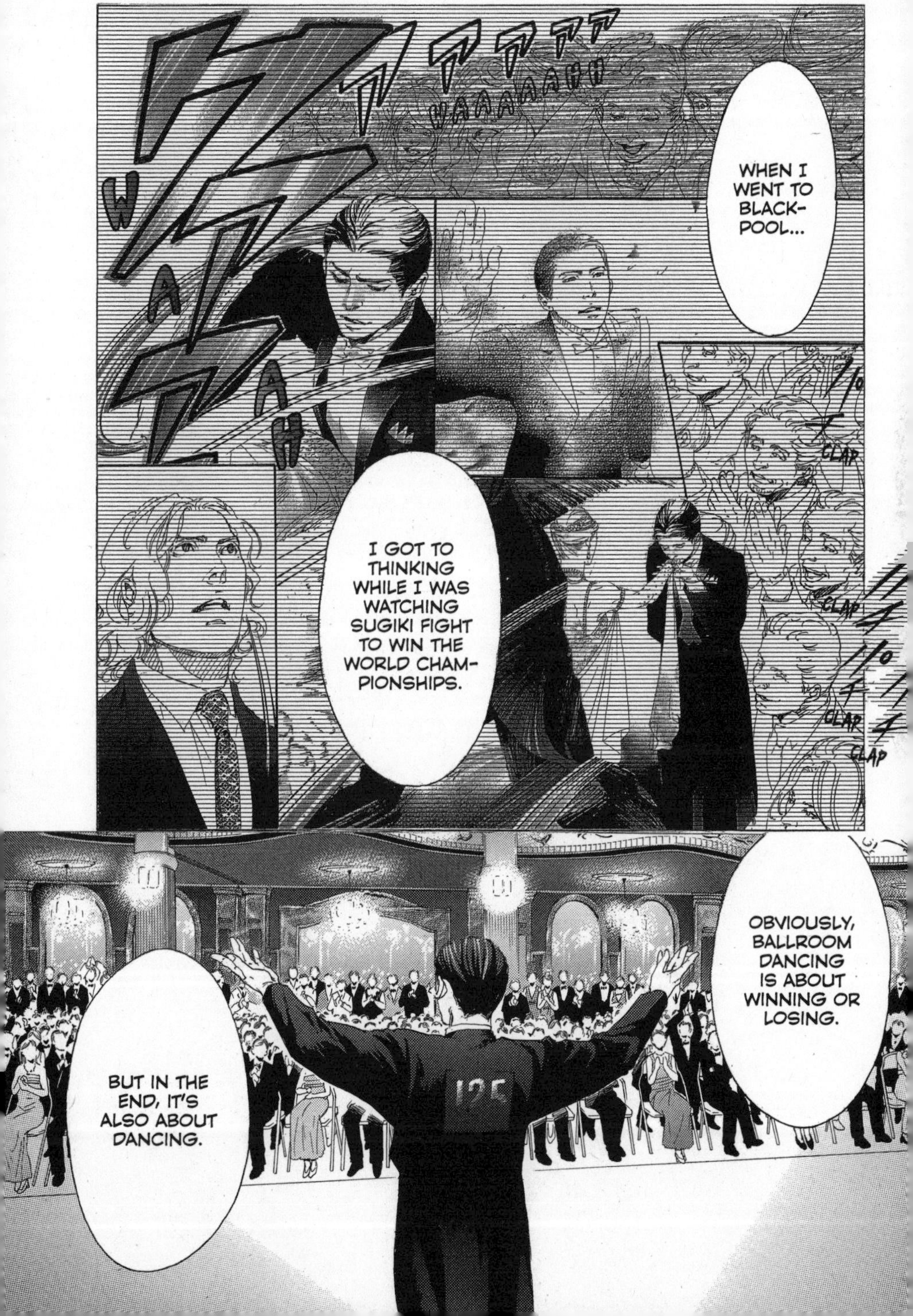

WHEN I WENT TO BLACKPOOL...
CLAP
CLAP
CLAP
CLAP
I GOT TO THINKING WHILE I WAS WATCHING SUGIKI FIGHT TO WIN THE WORLD CHAMPIONSHIPS.
OBVIOUSLY, BALLROOM DANCING IS ABOUT WINNING OR LOSING.
BUT IN THE END, IT'S ALSO ABOUT DANCING.

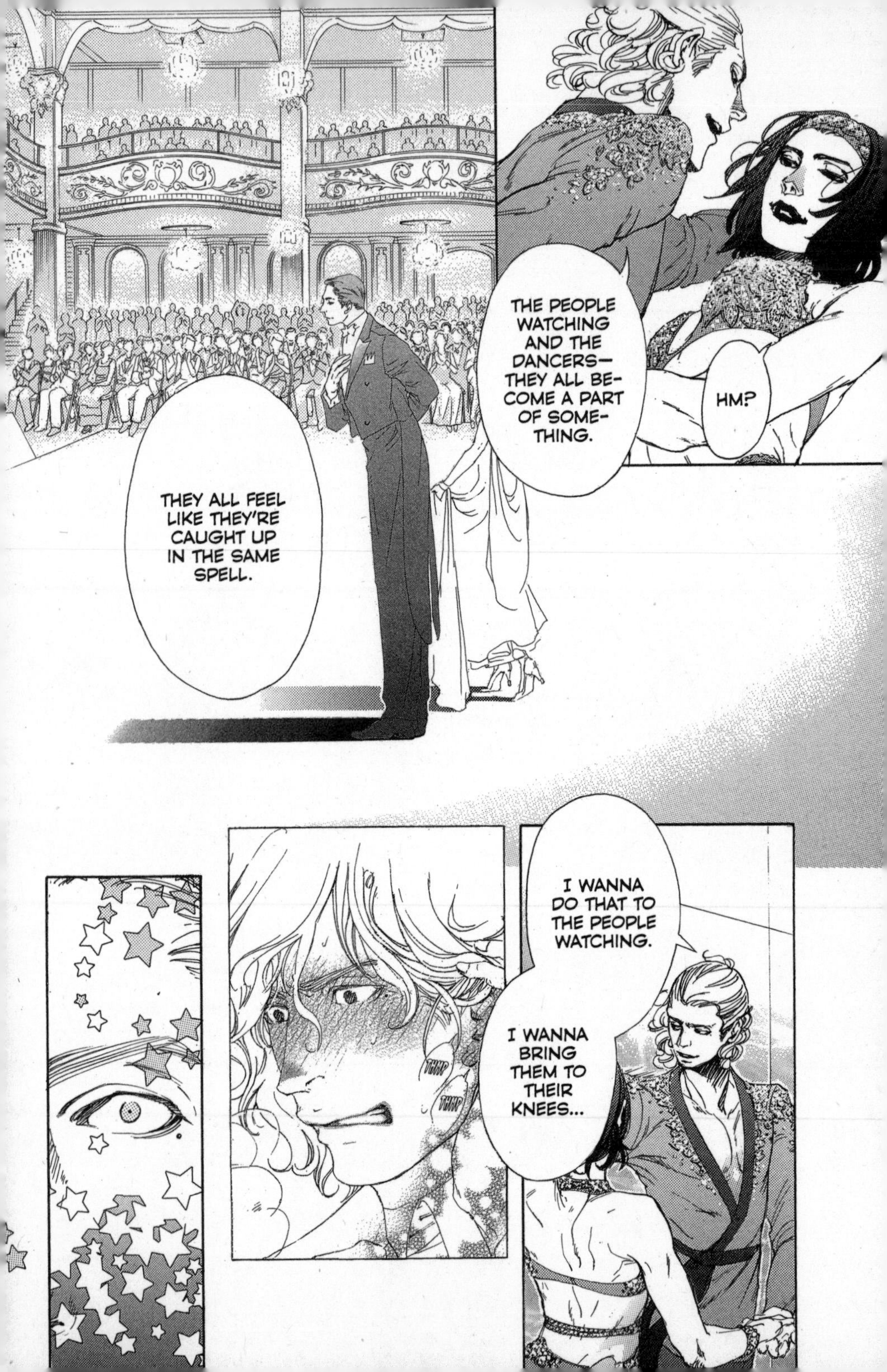
HM?
THE PEOPLE WATCHING AND THE DANCERS— THEY ALL BE-COME A PART OF SOME-THING.
THEY ALL FEEL LIKE THEY'RE CAUGHT UP IN THE SAME SPELL.
I WANNA DO THAT TO THE PEOPLE WATCHING.
I WANNA BRING THEM TO THEIR KNEES...
THMP
THMP

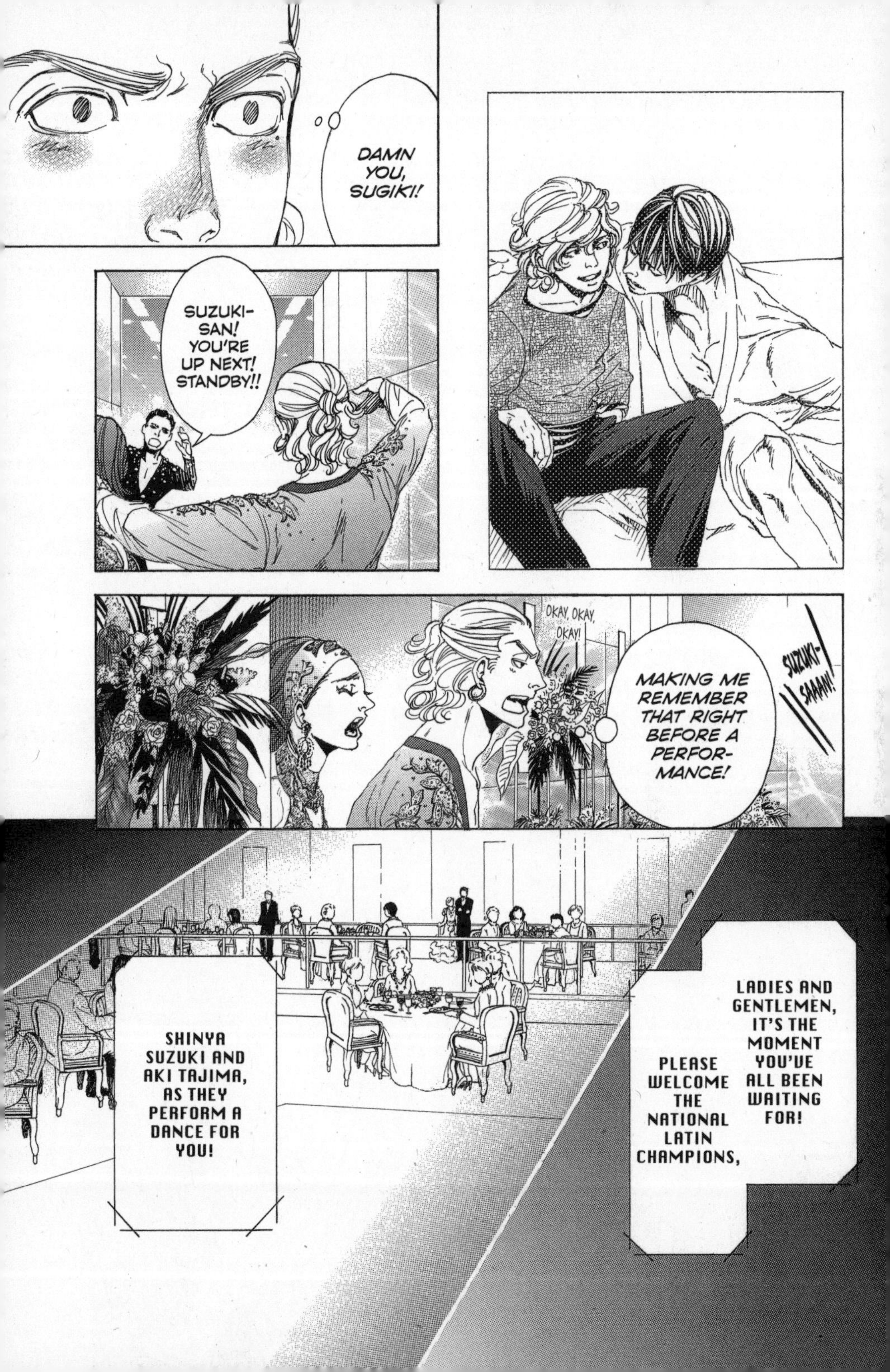
DAMN YOU, SUGIKI!
SUZUKI-SAN! YOU'RE UP NEXT! STANDBY!!
SUZUKI-SAAAN!
MAKING ME REMEMBER THAT RIGHT BEFORE A PERFORMANCE!
OKAY, OKAY, OKAY!
LADIES AND GENTLEMEN, IT'S THE MOMENT YOU'VE ALL BEEN WAITING FOR!
PLEASE WELCOME THE NATIONAL LATIN CHAMPIONS,
SHINYA SUZUKI AND AKI TAJIMA, AS THEY PERFORM A DANCE FOR YOU!

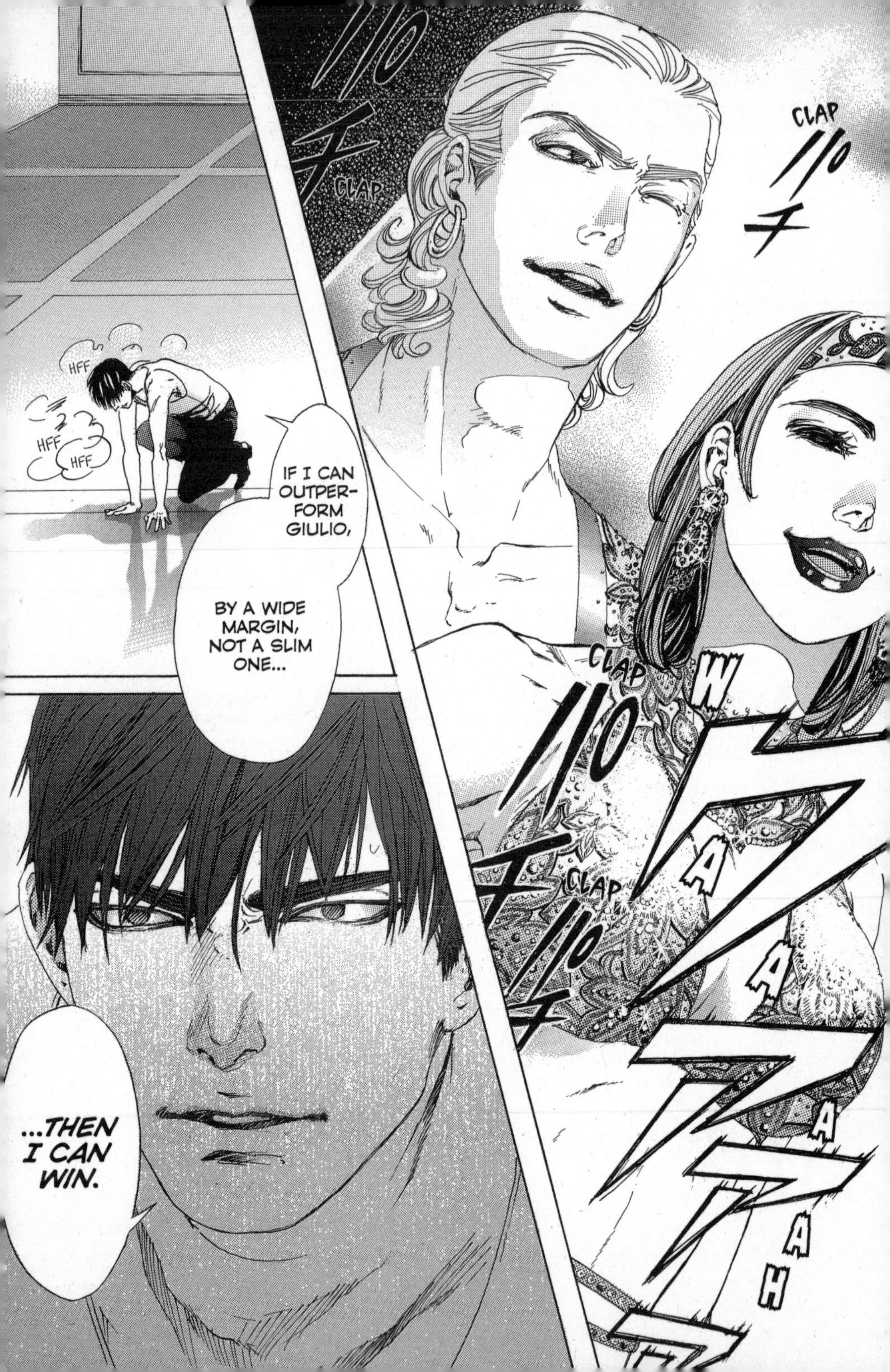
CLAP
CLAP
CLAP
CLAP
WAAAAH
HFF
HFF
HFF
IF I CAN OUTPERFORM GIULIO,
BY A WIDE MARGIN, NOT A SLIM ONE...
...THEN I CAN WIN.

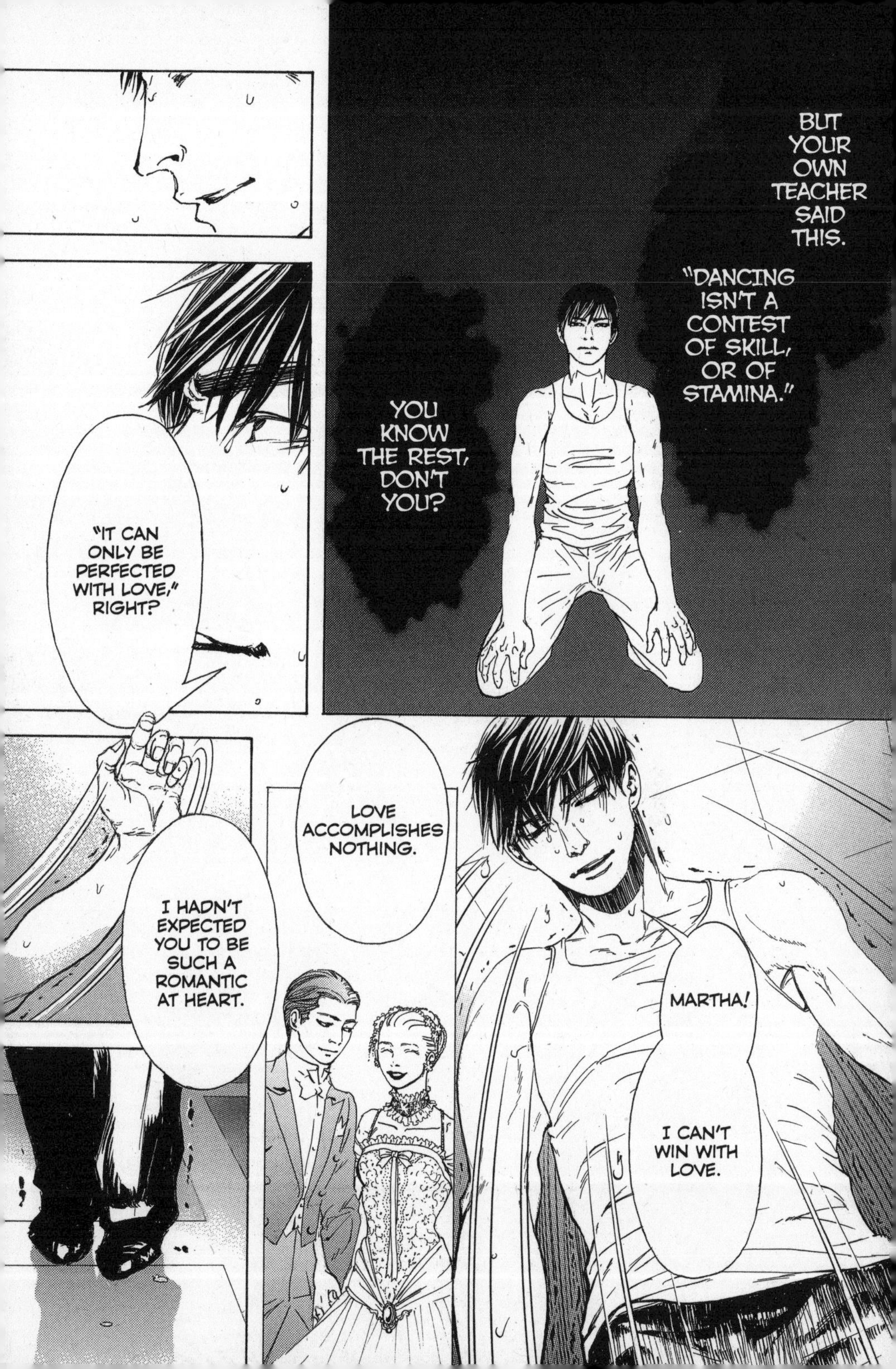
BUT YOUR OWN TEACHER SAID THIS.
"DANCING ISN'T A CONTEST OF SKILL, OR OF STAMINA."
YOU KNOW THE REST, DON'T YOU?
"IT CAN ONLY BE PERFECTED WITH LOVE," RIGHT?
MARTHA!
I CAN'T WIN WITH LOVE.
LOVE ACCOMPLISHES NOTHING.
I HADN'T EXPECTED YOU TO BE SUCH A ROMANTIC AT HEART.

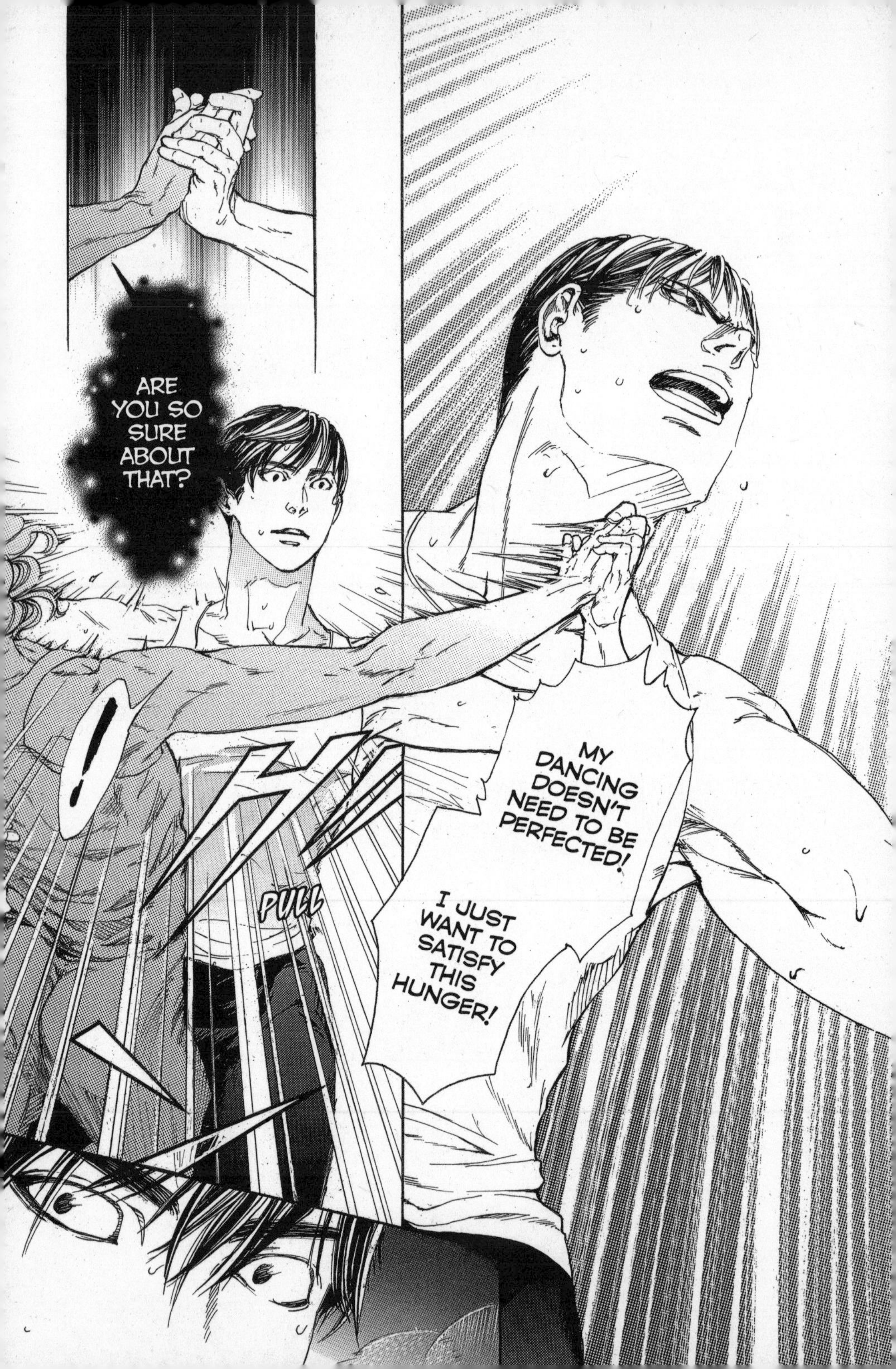

MY DANCING DOESN'T NEED TO BE PERFECTED!
I JUST WANT TO SATISFY THIS HUNGER!
ARE YOU SO SURE ABOUT THAT?
!
PULL

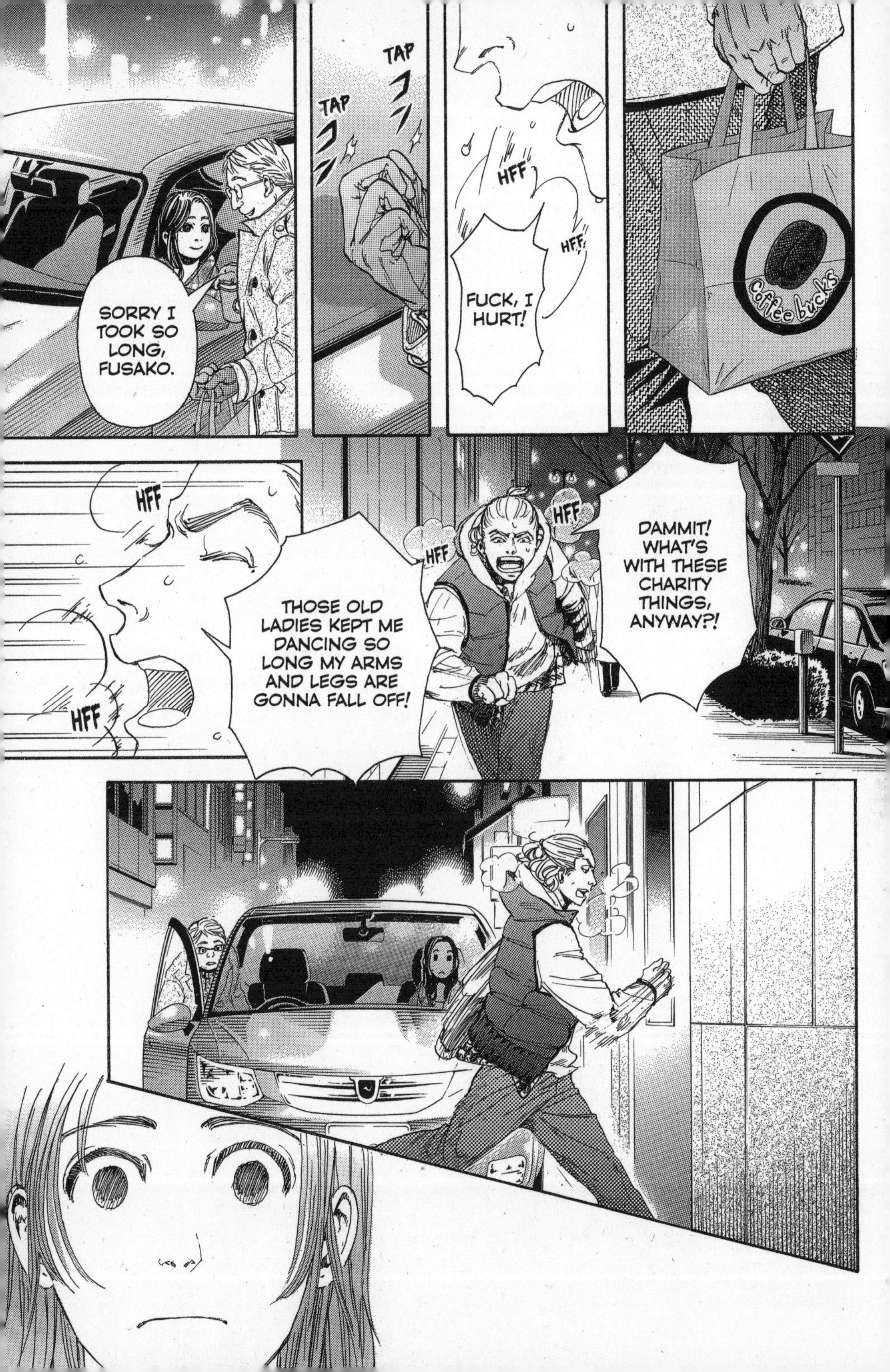
Coffee bucks
HFF
HFF
FUCK, I HURT!
TAP
TAP
SORRY I TOOK SO LONG, FUSAKO.
HFF
HFF
DAMMIT! WHAT'S WITH THESE CHARITY THINGS, ANYWAY?!
HFF
THOSE OLD LADIES KEPT ME DANCING SO LONG MY ARMS AND LEGS ARE GONNA FALL OFF!
HFF

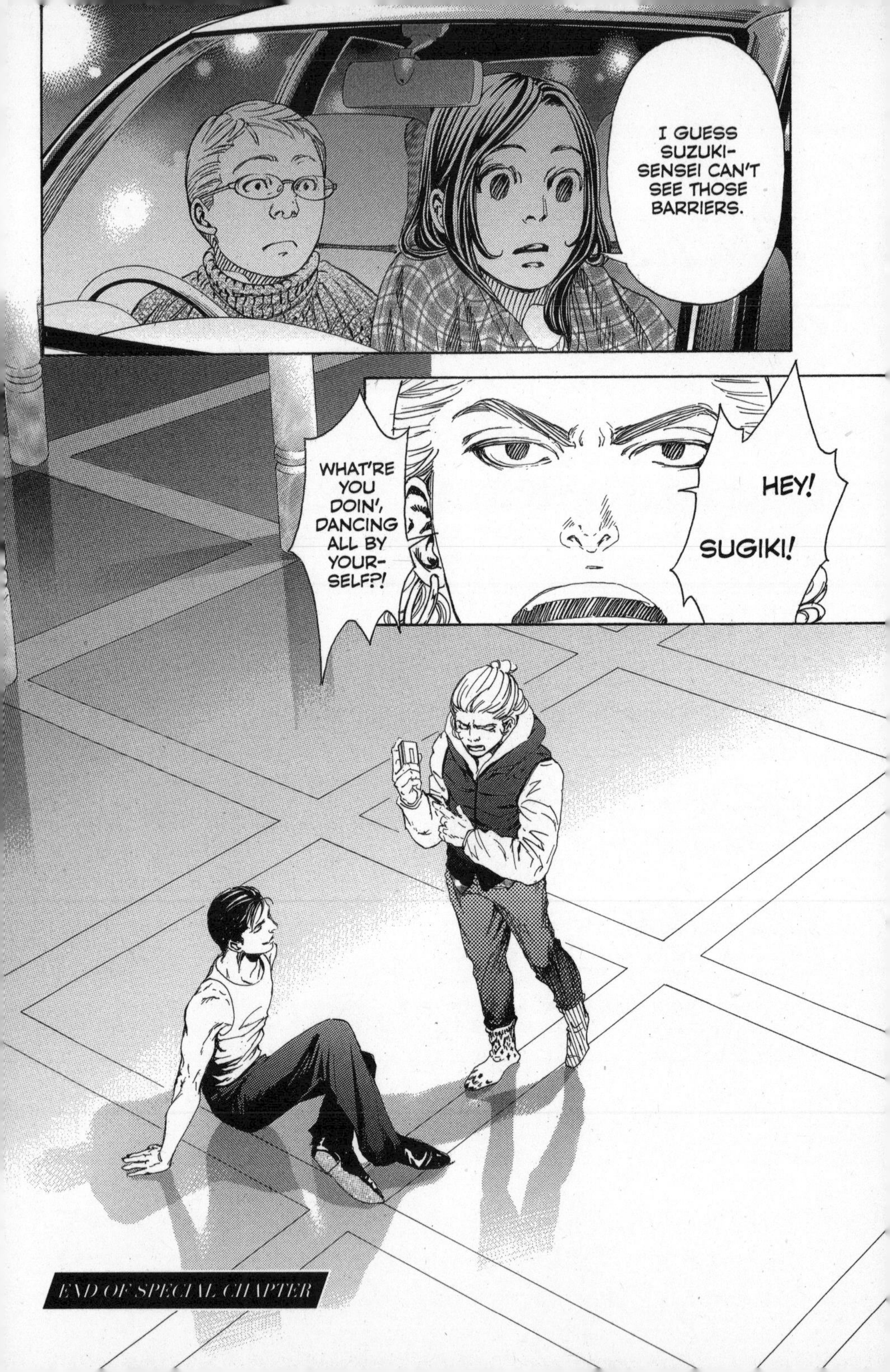
I GUESS SUZUKI-SENSEI CAN'T SEE THOSE BARRIERS.
HEY! SUGIKI!
WHAT'RE YOU DOIN', DANCING ALL BY YOURSELF?!
END OF SPECIAL CHAPTER

Thank you for waiting so long for volume 3!
I think it's even sweeter than volume 2.
I can almost hear the quips already about how "you two are like a lovesick couple who've just started dating." Now, continuing on from volume 2, I'd like to tell you about the songs that inspired the chapter titles, their dance category, and a little about each story.

Chapter 11: I Kiss Your Hand, Monsieur

Originally *I Kiss Your Hand, Madame* / Tango
I really hope you enjoyed reading this chapter, but it took all I had in me to write so many verbally abusive lines. I was given the OK to draw this story by *Takeshobo*, and I was told that N-san helped out, despite not being my editor. Thank you very much, N-san!!

Chapter 12: My Favorite Things

Originally the same name (from *The Sound of Music*) / Waltz
Norman is actually one of my favorite things. I feel like *10 DANCE* has a lot of odd characters, but Norman Owen is one of the oddest. When I took the time to stop and think it over, I realized he's got quite a detailed background. You'll learn about it gradually, so take your time and enjoy him. He's probably both very sadistic and very masochistic.

Chapter 13: You and the Ginza Night and the Music

Originally *You and the Night and the Music* / Quickstep
This is a very cool song and I love it. Lots of different people have done versions of it, so please consider giving it a listen.
...What can I say? These two sure do love each other. I have nothing else to say. They're so satisfied with their normal lives.

Chapter 14: Masquerade

Originally the same name / Viennese Waltz
When this was printed in the magazine, they said this was the Shonentai version... What? It's the Khachaturian version. I don't think there is any song better suited to making you feel insecure. And yes, here it is! I'm relieved that I finally got the reveal the woman in the black dress.

Chapter 15: *Mélodie en Subway*

Originally *Mélodie en sous-sol* (*Underground Melody*) / Foxtrot
Jean Gabin and Alain Delon are both very nice. Scenes of men putting lipstick on women have always made me feel like I'm looking at something taboo, but I wonder why? Oh Suzuki, you said never again, even if hell freezes over, and yet...

Special Chapter: *Tango Notturno*

Originally the same name / Tango
This is a stand-alone story that I was given the OK to draw for *Young Magazine the 3rd*.
I drew it while things were all over the place, so it was full of mistakes. I'm sorry about that. I've fixed it now.

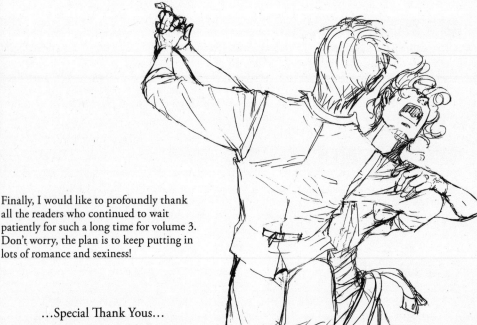

Finally, I would like to profoundly thank all the readers who continued to wait patiently for such a long time for volume 3. Don't worry, the plan is to keep putting in lots of romance and sexiness!

...Special Thank Yous...

Satoko Ariga-sama, Kyoko Omori-sama, Saki Ozaki-sama, Chiaki Ozawa-sama, Yukie Shishido-sama, Akira Suzuki-sama, Yoko Tadano-sama, everyone in the *Young Magazine* Editorial Department, designer Fukumura-sama, Ota-sama, my teacher Inoue, my own U-chan, Yuki Uewaki-sama, Ran Shimoda-sama, Koichi Nishio-sama, Yumi Kojima-sama, the business people, the people at the printing office, the many bookstores, coordinator T-sama, and all my dear readers.

井上佐藤
Inouesatoh

10 DANCE

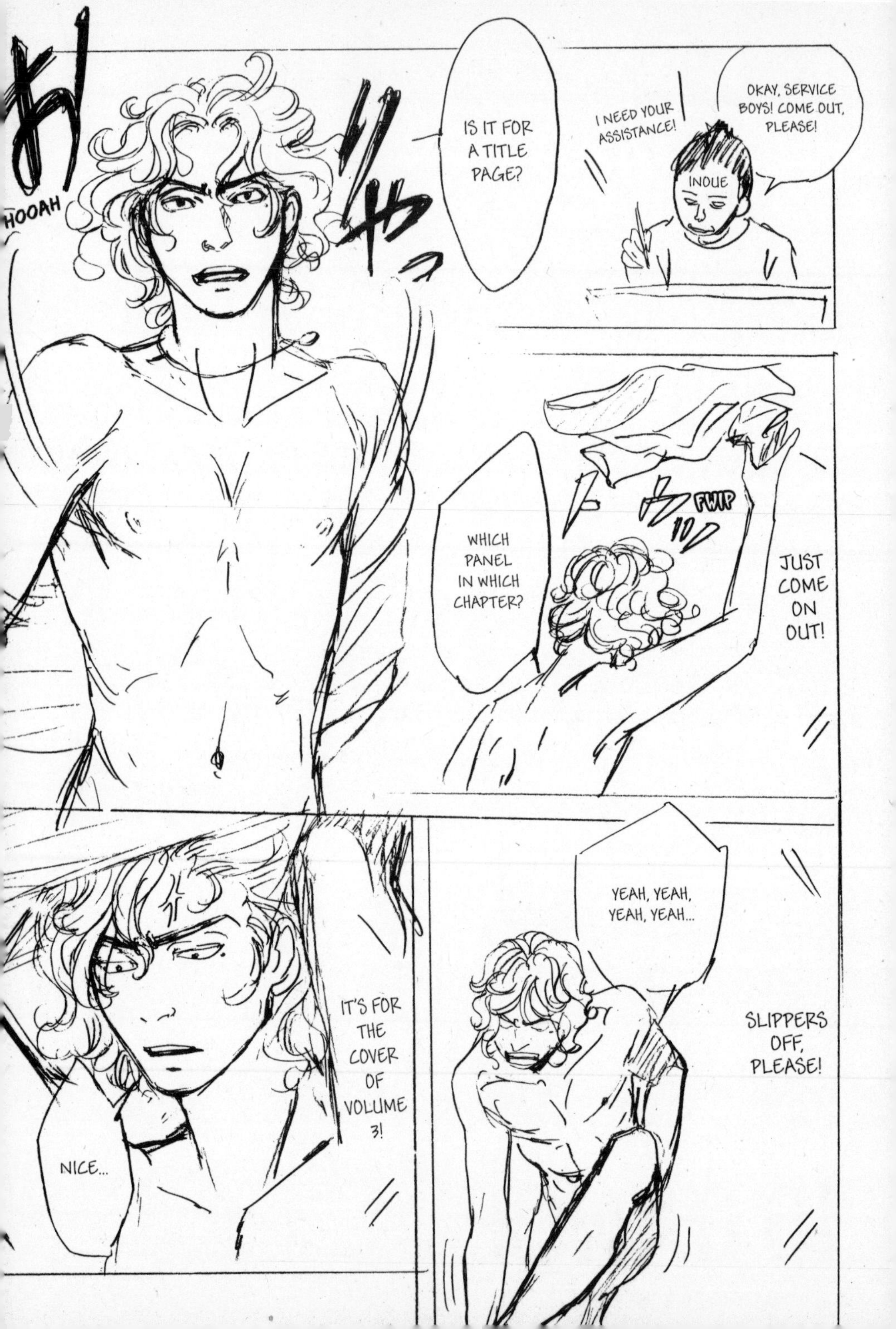
OKAY, SERVICE BOYS! COME OUT, PLEASE!
I NEED YOUR ASSISTANCE!
INOUE
FWIP
JUST COME ON OUT!
WHICH PANEL IN WHICH CHAPTER?
IS IT FOR A TITLE PAGE?
HOOAH
SLIPPERS OFF, PLEASE!
YEAH, YEAH, YEAH, YEAH...
IT'S FOR THE COVER OF VOLUME 3!
NICE...

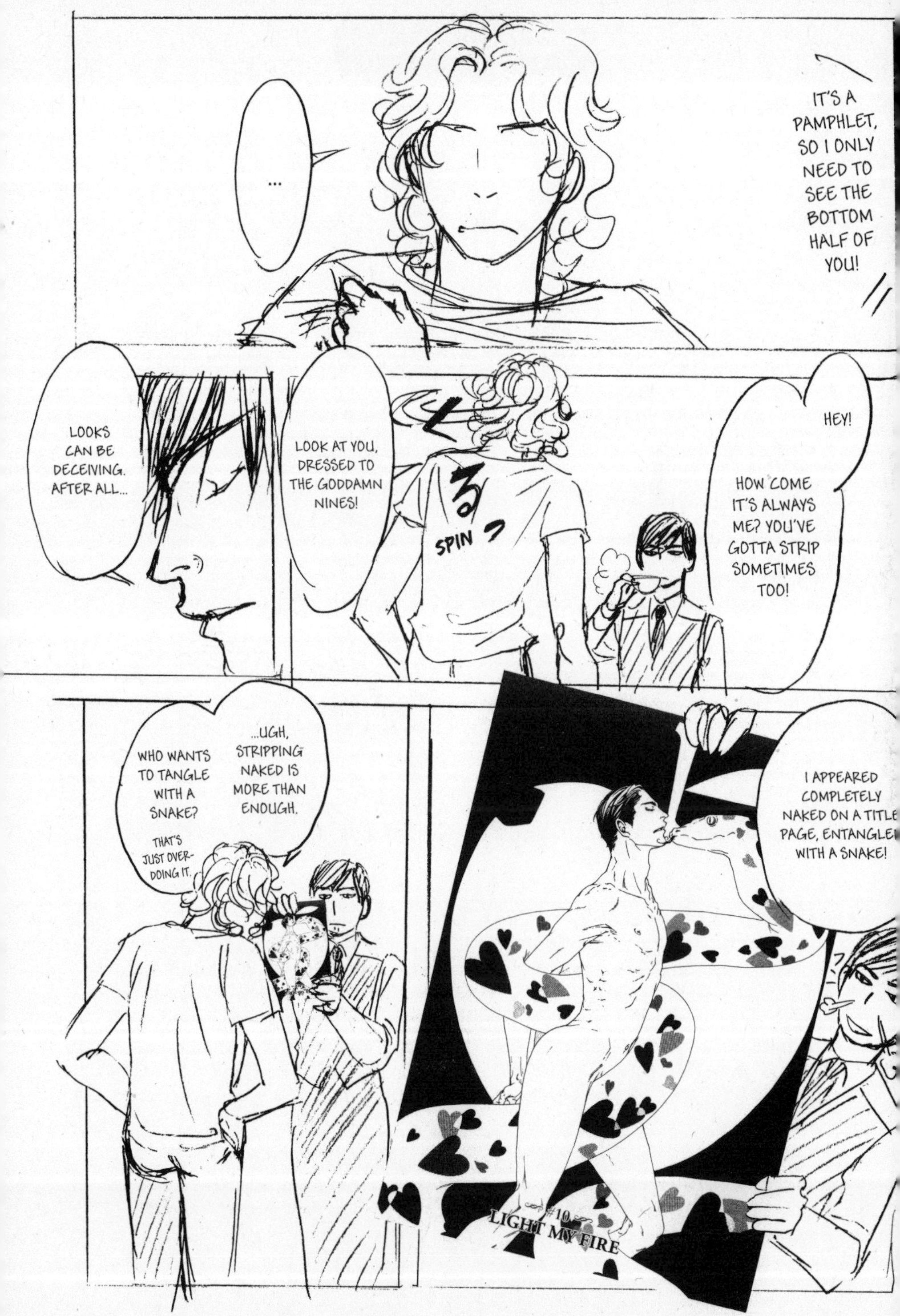
IT'S A PAMPHLET, SO I ONLY NEED TO SEE THE BOTTOM HALF OF YOU!
...
HEY!
HOW COME IT'S ALWAYS ME? YOU'VE GOTTA STRIP SOMETIMES TOO!
LOOK AT YOU, DRESSED TO THE GODDAMN NINES!
くる
る
SPIN
LOOKS CAN BE DECEIVING. AFTER ALL...
I APPEARED COMPLETELY NAKED ON A TITLE PAGE, ENTANGLE WITH A SNAKE!
#10
LIGHT MY FIRE
...UGH, STRIPPING NAKED IS MORE THAN ENOUGH.
WHO WANTS TO TANGLE WITH A SNAKE?
THAT'S JUST OVER-DOING IT.

Mélodie en Subway, page 2

This chapter title is a play on words from the title of the 1963 French movie, *Mélodie en sous-sol*, which means "underground melody" in English. The English title for this movie was *Any Number Can Win*. It starred Jean Gabin and Alain Delon.

Ultimate strength and terror, page 59 & 60

In this conversation, Suzuki uses the word *saikyou* without any *kanji* to specify its meaning. Depending on the *kanji* used, this word has multiple meanings, including 'ultimate strength' and 'ultimate terror.' Suzuki seems to be implying both at once, or leaving it up to Sugiki (and the reader) to decide, both when he asks Sugiki what he was seeking, and when he answers that he was seeking it himself.

Male ballet dancers, page 56

Male ballet dancers wear a special dance belt instead of underwear, which holds their genitals tightly against their body at the front, both to protect them and to minimize bulge and movement. The penis is pointed directly upwards, straight and center, while the back of belt is more like a thong, to eradicate visible panty line and reveal butt muscles. Young Suzuki clearly found this hysterical, while young Sugiki was horrified to have the girls talking about it!

Koji Yakusho, page 62

The taxi driver is referring to the 1996 Japanese film *Shall we Dance?* It starred Koji Yakusho and Tamiyo Kusakari, and ballroom dancing was a central theme.

5-chome, page 62

Japanese addresses are very different from Western addresses. Streets do not have names, but rather cities are divided up into wards, and then districts within the ward, and then divisions, called *cho*. These have subdivisions called *chome* which cover several blocks. The *chome* are then numbered, and the individual blocks within them are given numbers as well, and finally, each building in a block is given a number. So 5-chome refers to an area that covers several blocks of the city somewhere nearby, and the other taxi drivers would know the area he meant.

Congress workshops, page 64

Congresses are multi-day Dancesport festivals that often include performances, workshops, and social dance opportunities.

International Dance Competitions, page 66

The competitions that determine one's world ranking are not quite as clear-cut as Sugiki makes out. In reality, different countries can apply to the *World Dance Council* (WDC) to host a competition in any year that can affect one's world ranking. Although some are held every year, such as the *Blackpool Dance Festival* and the *UK Open*, many others are one-off events, or only held every few years. The number of events that count towards one's world ranking can also change each year, and the locations of some of the biggest events (including the *10 Dance* itself) also change each year. Events that count towards one's world ranking are also assigned different levels (from 1-5), and level 1 events grant much higher scores to winners than level 5 events. The author has clearly simplified things for the sake of the story, as in reality the world of professional dance can be very complicated and confusing!

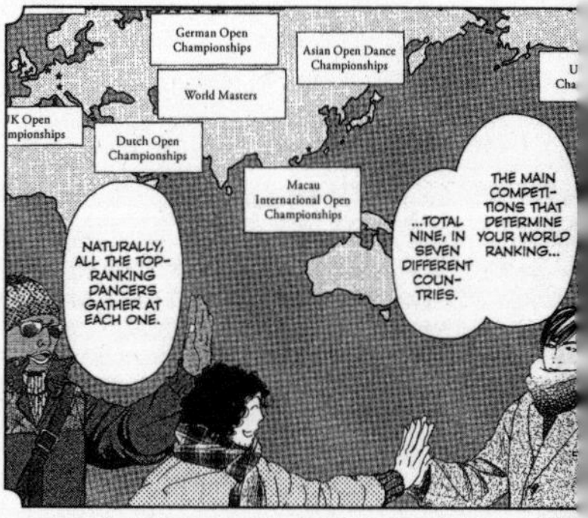
German Open Championships
Asian Open Dance Championships
World Masters
Dutch Open Championships
Macau International Open Championships
THE MAIN COMPETITIONS THAT DETERMINE YOUR WORLD RANKING...
...TOTAL NINE, IN SEVEN DIFFERENT COUNTRIES.
NATURALLY, ALL THE TOP-RANKING DANCERS GATHER AT EACH ONE.

Comiket, page 75

Comiket is a large event held twice a year in Japan for lovers of anime, manga and game culture. It is a celebration of fan culture, and many female artists take part and sell their fan-works at booths. It is held in August and late December (when Sugiki was at the train station) and it is common to see lots of these women lugging huge suitcases through the nearby train stations during this time!

Suzuki's Spanish/English, page 85 & 86

Suzuki is switching back and forth between Spanish and English (Japanese in the original) while speaking to his sisters. The basic meaning of the mixed language sentences is as follows:

> "Don't complain about your turn in the kitchen to me!"
> "Mom decided it?"
> "Seriously, you all need to stop complaining about this to me."
> "Help them out."
> "And that fashion magazine, ask Aki about it."
> "Those matcha-flavored sweets, yes, I'll send them soon."
> "Don't fight about it so much!"
> "I'm going to ask Lisa!"

Shonentai, page 174

Shonentai are a popular idol group in Japan, who first debuted in the mid-1980s with a single that was also called *Masquerade.*

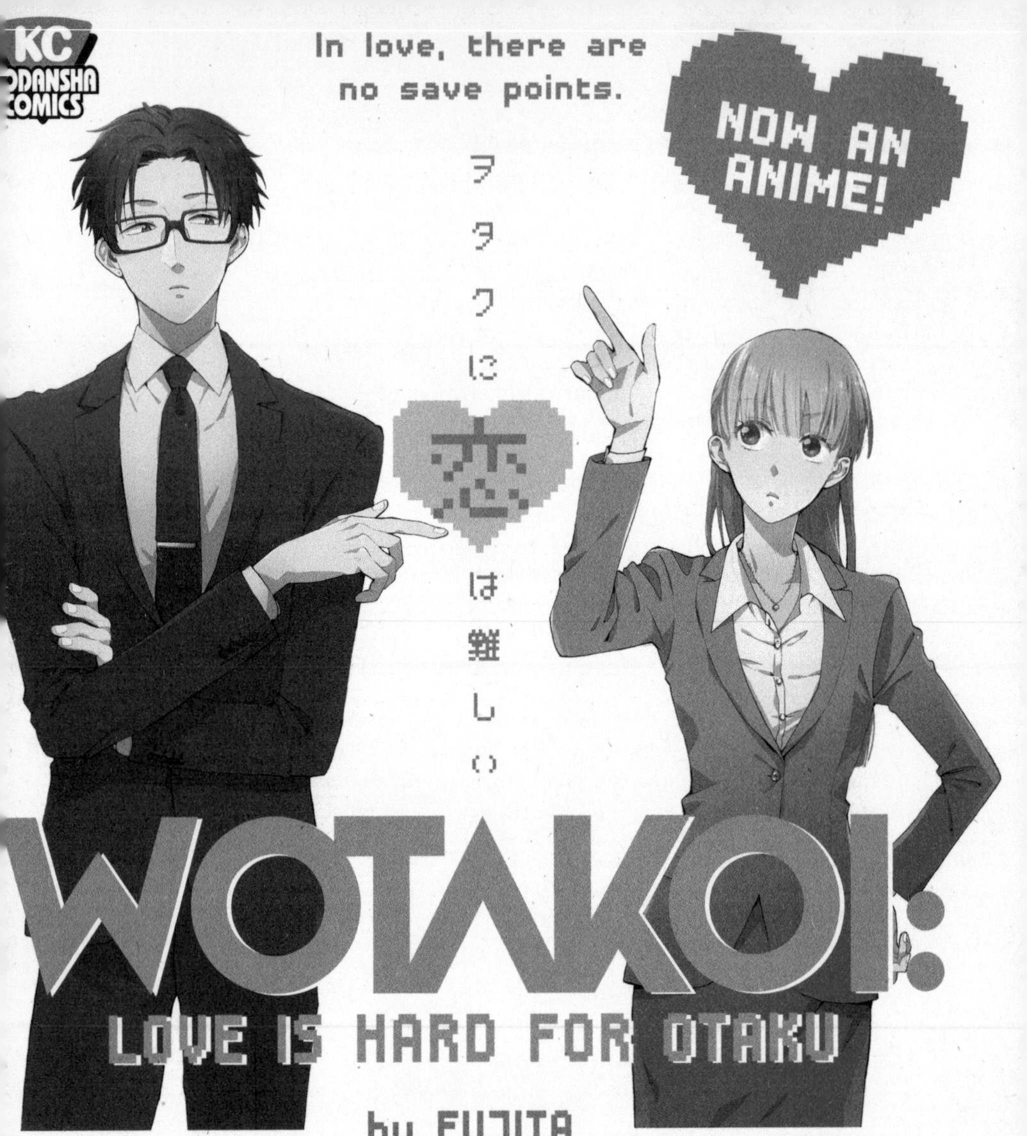
KC KODANSHA COMICS
In love, there are no save points.
NOW AN ANIME!
ヲタクに恋は難しい
WOTAKOI:
LOVE IS HARD FOR OTAKU
by FUJITA

Narumi has had it rough: Every boyfriend she's had dumped her once they found out she was an otaku, so she's gone to great lengths to hide it. At her new job, she bumps into Hirotaka, her childhood friend and fellow otaku. When Hirotaka almost gets her secret outed at work, she comes up with a plan to keep him quiet. But he comes up with a counter-proposal: Why doesn't she just date him instead?

ANIME OUT NOW
FROM SENTAI FILMWORKS!

A BL romance between a good boy who didn't know he was waiting for a hero, and a bad boy who comes to his rescue!

Masahiro Setagawa doesn't believe in heroes but wishes he could: He's found himself in a gang of small-time street bullies, and with no prospects for a real future. But when high school teacher (and scourge of the streets) Kousuke Ohshiba comes to his rescue, he finds he may need to start believing after all... in heroes, and in his budding feelings, too.

Hitorijime My Hero

Memeco Arii

KC
KODANSHA
COMICS

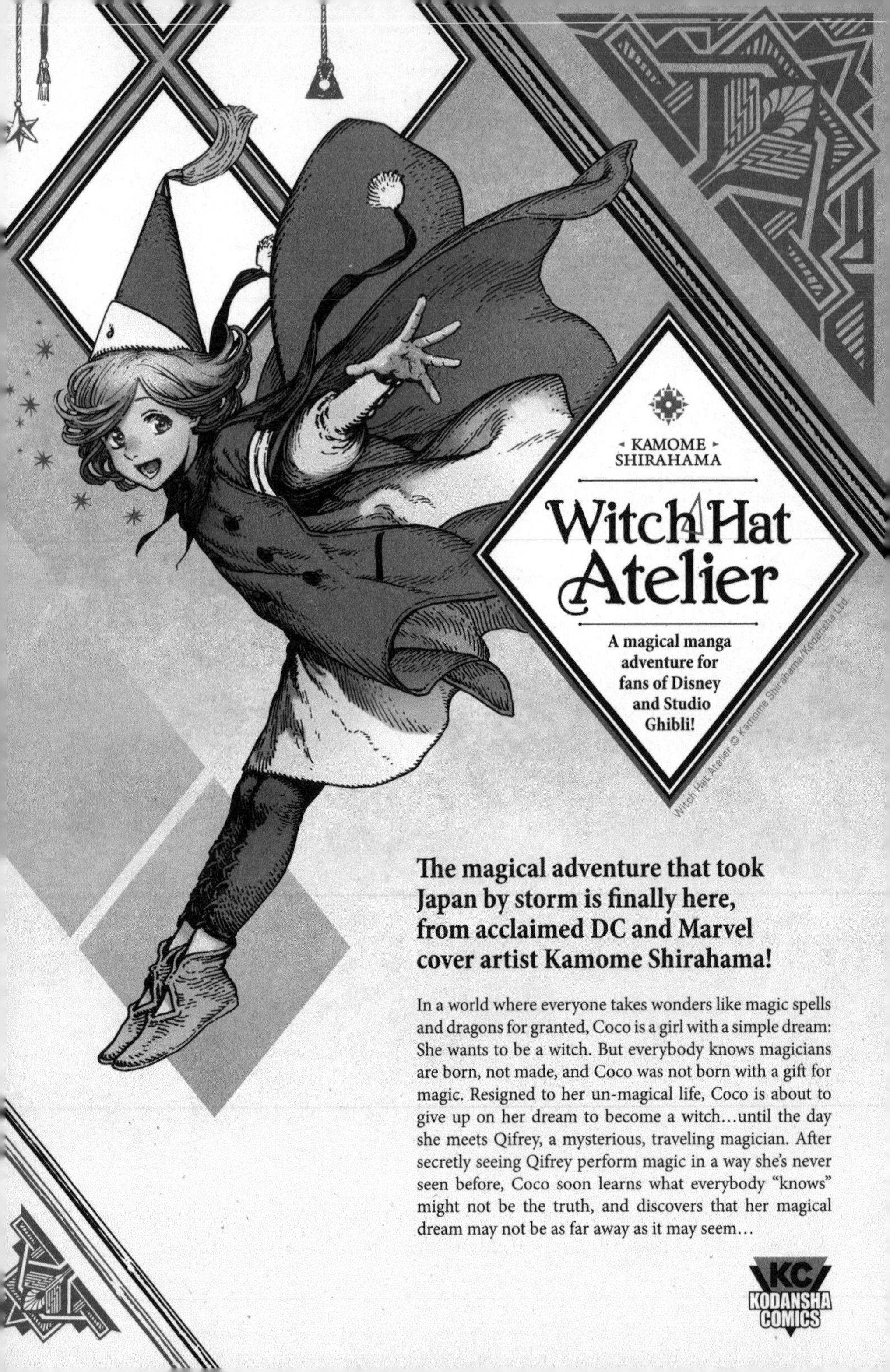

EDENS ZERO
エデンズゼロ

HIRO MASHIMA IS BACK! JOIN THE CREATOR OF *FAIRY TAIL*
AS HE TAKES TO THE STARS FOR ANOTHER THRILLING SAGA!

A high-flying space adventure! All the steadfast friendship
and wild fighting you've been waiting for...IN SPACE!

At Granbell Kingdom, an abandoned amusement park, Shiki has lived his entire
life among machines. But one day, Rebecca and her cat companion Happy appear
at the park's front gates. Little do these newcomers know that this is the first
human contact Granbell has had in a hundred years! As Shiki stumbles his way
into making new friends, his former neighbors stir at an opportunity for a robo-
rebellion... And when his old homeland becomes too dangerous, Shiki must join
Rebecca and Happy on their spaceship and escape into the boundless cosmos.

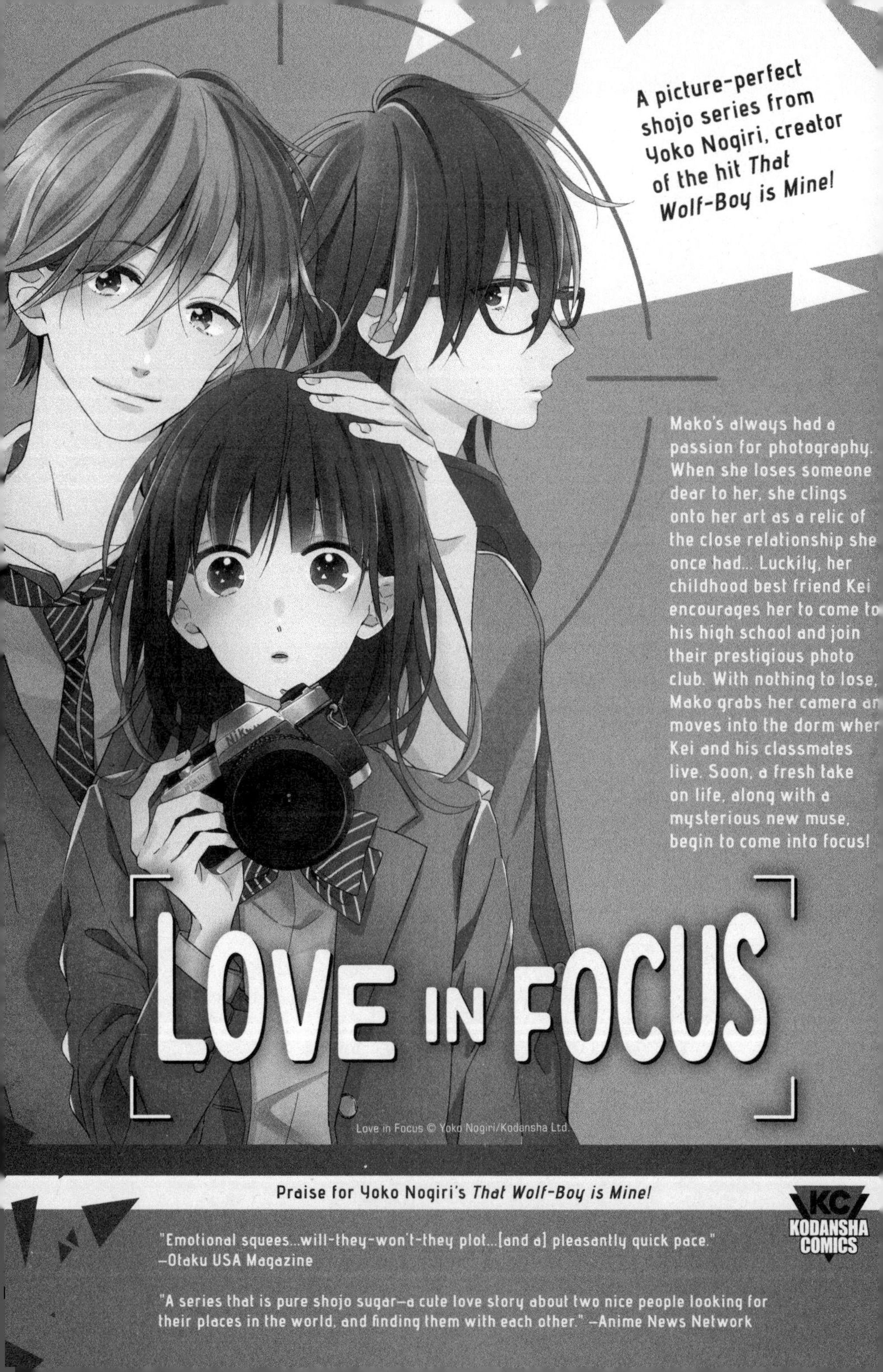
A picture-perfect shojo series from Yoko Nogiri, creator of the hit *That Wolf-Boy is Mine!*
Mako's always had a passion for photography. When she loses someone dear to her, she clings onto her art as a relic of the close relationship she once had... Luckily, her childhood best friend Kei encourages her to come t his high school and join their prestigious photo club. With nothing to lose, Mako grabs her camera an moves into the dorm wher Kei and his classmates live. Soon, a fresh take on life, along with a mysterious new muse, begin to come into focus!
LOVE IN FOCUS
Love in Focus © Yoko Nogiri/Kodansha Ltd.
Praise for Yoko Nogiri's *That Wolf-Boy is Mine!*
KC
KODANSHA COMICS
"Emotional squees...will-they-won't-they plot...[and a] pleasantly quick pace." —Otaku USA Magazine
"A series that is pure shojo sugar—a cute love story about two nice people looking for their places in the world, and finding them with each other." —Anime News Network

Princess Jellyfish

Akiko Higashimura

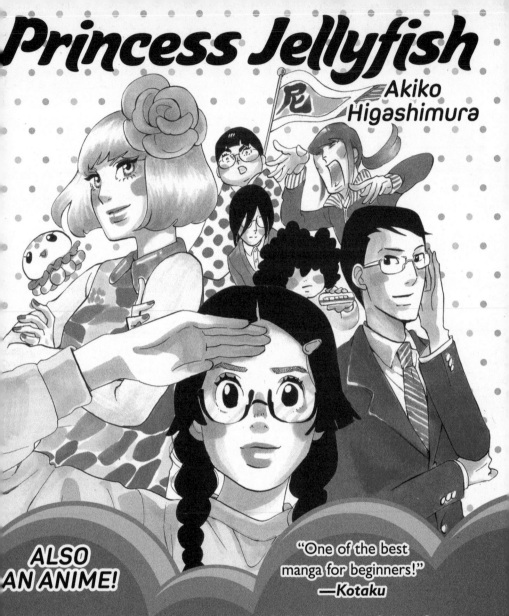

ALSO AN ANIME!

"One of the best manga for beginners!"
—*Kotaku*

Tsukimi Kurashita is fascinated with jellyfish. She's loved them from a young age and has carried that love with her to her new life in the big city of Tokyo. There, she resides in Amamizukan, a safe-haven for geek girls where no boys are allowed. One day, Tsukimi crosses paths with a beautiful and fashionable woman, but there's much more to this woman than her trendy clothes...!

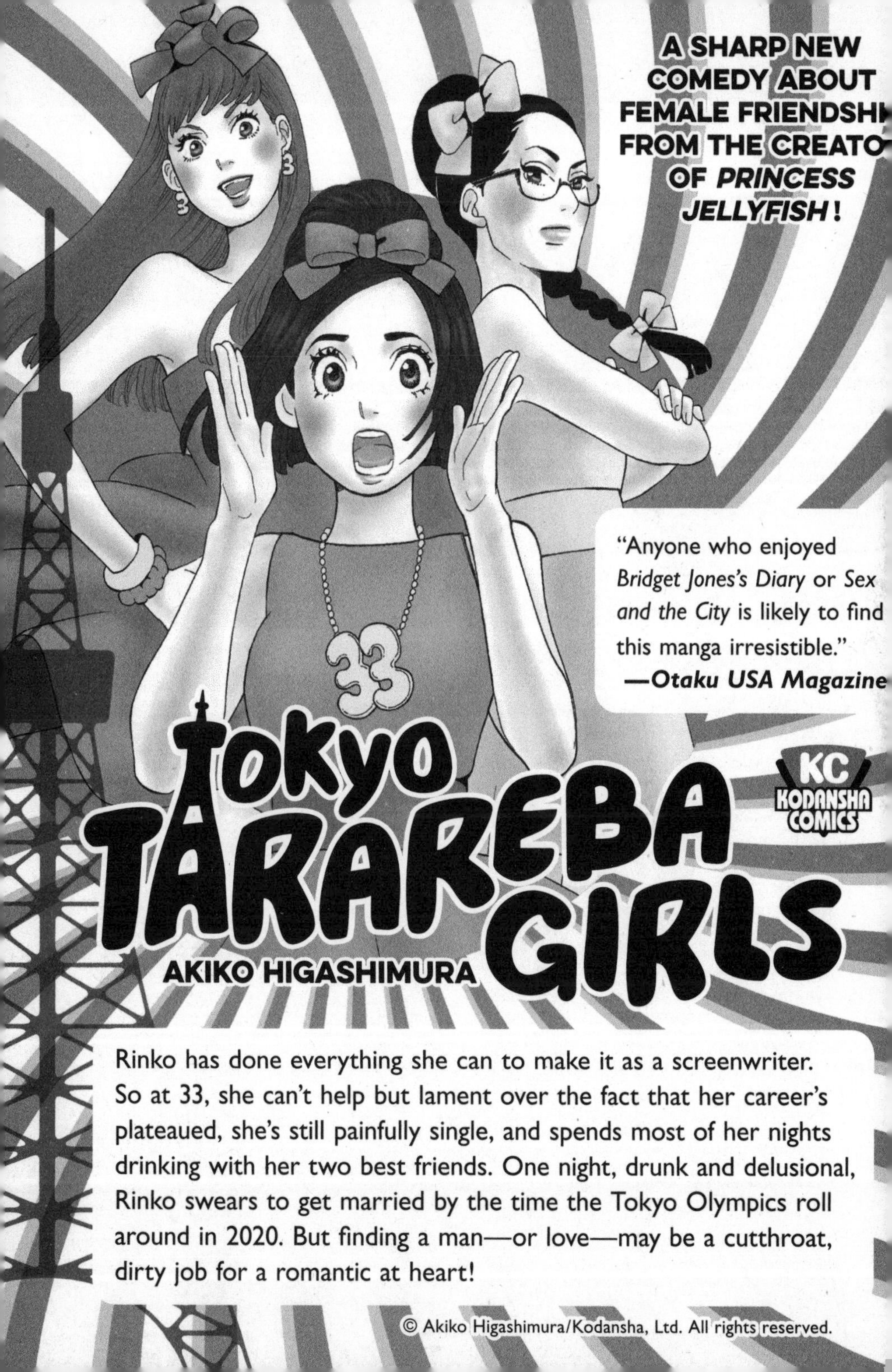
A SHARP NEW COMEDY ABOUT FEMALE FRIENDSHI FROM THE CREATO OF *PRINCESS JELLYFISH*!
"Anyone who enjoyed *Bridget Jones's Diary* or *Sex and the City* is likely to find this manga irresistible."
—*Otaku USA Magazine*
KC KODANSHA COMICS
TOKYO TARAREBA GIRLS
AKIKO HIGASHIMURA
Rinko has done everything she can to make it as a screenwriter. So at 33, she can't help but lament over the fact that her career's plateaued, she's still painfully single, and spends most of her nights drinking with her two best friends. One night, drunk and delusional, Rinko swears to get married by the time the Tokyo Olympics roll around in 2020. But finding a man—or love—may be a cutthroat, dirty job for a romantic at heart!
© Akiko Higashimura/Kodansha, Ltd. All rights reserved.

THE STORY STARTS **HERE!**

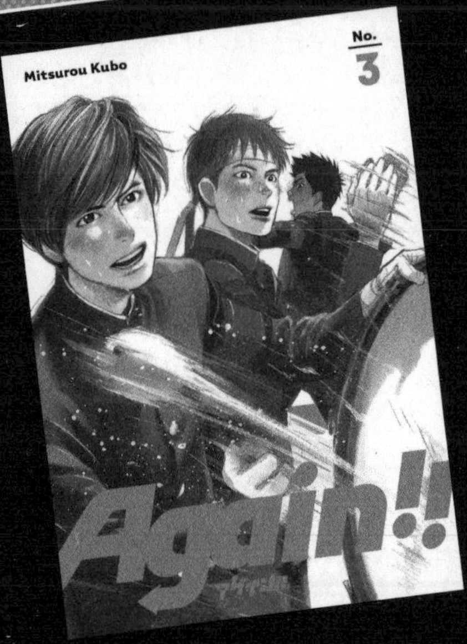
Mitsurou Kubo
No. 3
Again!!

Again!!

アゲイン!!

Kinichiro Imamura isn't a bad guy, really, but on the first day of high school his narrow eyes and bleached blonde hair made him look so shifty that his classmates assumed the worst. Three years later, without any friends or fond memories, he isn't exactly feeling bittersweet about graduation. But after an accidental fall down a flight of stairs, Kinichiro wakes up three years in the past... on the first day of high school! School's starting again—but it's gonna be different this time around!

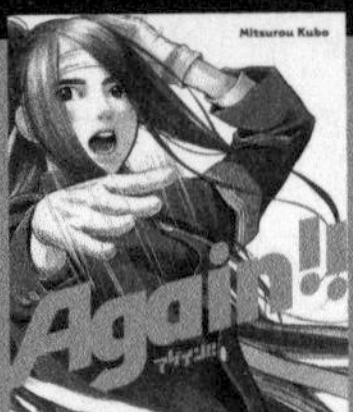
Mitsurou Kubo
Again!!
No. 1

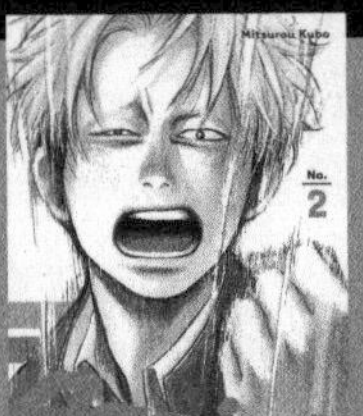
Mitsurou Kubo
No. 2
Again!!

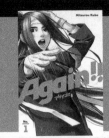

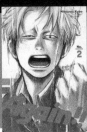

Vol. 1-3 now available in **PRINT** and **DIGITAL**!
Vol. 4 coming August 2018!

Find out **MORE** by visiting:
kodanshacomics.com/MitsurouKubo

ABOUT MITSUROU KUBO

Mitsurou Kubo is a manga artist born in Nagasaki prefecture. Her series *3.3.7 Byoshi!!* (2001-2003), *Tokkyu!!* (2004-2008), and *Again!!* (2011-2014) were published in *Weekly Shonen Magazine*, and *Moteki* (2008-2010) was published in the seinen comics magazine *Evening*. After the publication of *Again!!* concluded, she met Sayo Yamamoto, director of the global smash-hit anime ***Yuri!!! on ICE***. Working with Yamamoto, Kubo contributed the original concept, original character designs, and initial script for ***Yuri!!! on ICE***. *Again!!* is her first manga to be published in English.

KC KODANSHA COMICS

Kodansha COMICS

"I'm pleasantly surprised to find modern shojo using cross-dressing as a dramatic device to deliver social commentary... Recommended."

-Otaku USA Magazine

The prince in his dark days

By Hico Yamanaka

A drunkard for a father, a household of poverty... For 17-year-old Atsuko, misfortune is all she knows and believes in. Until one day, a chance encounter with Itaru–the wealthy heir of a huge corporation–changes everything. The two look identical, uncannily so. When Itaru curiously goes missing, Atsuko is roped into being his stand-in. There, in his shoes, Atsuko must parade like a prince in a palace. She encounters many new experiences, but at what cost...?

A Kodansha Comics Trade Paperback Original.

Published in the United States by Kodansha Comics, an imprint of Kodansha USA Publishing, LLC, New York.

Publication rights for this English edition arranged through Kodansha Ltd., Tokyo.

First published in Japan in 2017 by Kodansha Ltd., Tokyo.

ISBN 978-1-63236-767-9

Printed in the United States of America.

www.kodanshacomics.com

9 8 7 6 5 4 3 2 1

Translation: Karhys
Lettering: Brndn Blakeslee
Editing: Lauren Scanlan
Kodansha Comics Edition Cover Design: Phil Balsman